Clinical Treatment and Research in Child Psychopathology

CHILD BEHAVIOR AND DEVELOPMENT
Series Editor: **Dennis P. Cantwell, M.D.**

Clinical Treatment and Research in Child Psychopathology

A.J. Finch, Jr., Ph.D.
Virginia Treatment Center for Children
Virginia Commonwealth University
Richmond, Virginia

and

Philip C. Kendall, Ph. D.
University of Minnesota
Minneapolis, Minnesota

SP MEDICAL & SCIENTIFIC BOOKS
a division of Spectrum Publications, Inc.
New York • London

SPECTRUM PUBLICATIONS, INC.
175-20 Wexford Terrace, Jamaica, New York 11432

Library of Congress Cataloging in Publication Data
Main entry under title:

Treatment and research in child psychopathology.

Includes index.
1. Mentally ill children—Research. 2. Child psychotherapy. I. Finch, A.J., 1944-
RJ499.T83   618.9'28'91   78-5246
ISBN 0-89335-041-9

To my family—Kaye, Paul and Alison (AJF)
To my parents—Stella and Charles (PCK)

Contributors

WILLIAM T. CHANCE, Ph.D.
Department of Pharmacology
Medical College of Virginia
Richmond, Virginia

AUSTIN M. DESLAURIERS, Ph.D.
Center for Austic and Schizophrenic
    Children
Devereaux Foundation
Devon, Pennsylvania

DANIEL M. DOLEYS, Ph. D.
Center for Developmental and Learning
    Disorders
University of Alabama in Birmingham
Birmingham, Alabama

A.J. FINCH, Jr., Ph.D.
Virginia Treatment Center for Children
Richmond, Virginia

REX FOREHAND, Ph.D.
Department of Psychology
University of Georgia
Athens, Georgia

JEANETTE HAWKINS-SEARCY, Ph.D.
Orange-Person-Chatham Mental Health
    Center
Pittsboro, North Carolina

THOMAS HOBBS, M.A.
Western Mental Health Center
Birmingham, Alabama

MICHAEL HOLT, Ph.D.
Western Mental Health Center
Birmingham, Alabama

J. WALTER JACOBS, Ph.D.
J.S. Tarwater Developmental Center
Wetumpka, Alabama

MARY JEANNE KALMANN, Ph.D.
Department of Pharmacology
Medical College of Virginia
Richmond, Virginia

PHILIP C. KENDALL, Ph.D.
Department of Psychology
University of Minnesota
Minneapolis, Minnesota

MARK H. LEWIS, M.A.
Department of Psychology
George Peabody College for Teachers
Nashville, Tennessee

THOMAS H. OLLENDICK, Ph.D.
Department of Psychology
Indiana State University
Terre Haute, Indiana

STEVE PEED, Ph.D.
Department of Psychiatry
Medical College of Virginia
Richmond, Virginia

JOHN A. ROSECRANS, Ph.D.
Department of Pharmacology
Medical College of Virginia
Richmond, Virginia

SAMUEL A. SAXON, P.D.
Center for Developmental and Learning
Disorders
Birmingham, Alabama

J. DANIEL SEARCY, Ph.D.
Johnston County Mental Health Center
Smithfield, North Carolina

RULPH F. WAGNER, Ph.D.
Department of Psychology
Valdosta State College
Valdosta, Georgia

EDITOR'S PREFACE

This volume is one of a series on Child Behavior and Development. The volumes in this series are designed to present up-to-date research data in the areas of clinical psychopathology and abnormal development in childhood.

The editors of the current volume quite rightly point out that researchers in the field of child psychopathology and providers of treatment for disturbed children do not have to be separate individuals, although this is most often true in today's real world. Most of the research in childhood psychopathology is done in university settings by people who do not provide direct service. Conversely, those who have the most clinical experience, and probably have the most access to raw clinical data in the field of childhood psychopathology, do not have the time, inclination, support, or all of these to conduct independent research. The editors state that one of their goals is to reflect what they call "the scientist practitioner models in the delivery of mental health services". Their comittment to this model is based upon their belief that it is the model most likely to maximize not only advancement of knowledge in the field but to improve the efficacy of our treatment modalities.

The series editor agrees whole heartedly with this model, particularly as it applies to graduates of child psychiatry fellowship programs. Child psychiatrists are in short supply in the United States, there being only slightly more than 1,000 board-certified child psychiatrists now practicing. The bulk of these are in private practice and have little academic contact. That academic contact tends to be of a teaching nature, on a voluntary basis, at a variety of different types of institutions. In many child psychiatry programs throughout the United States, these voluntary faculty members or full time faculty members, who are primarily clinicians, serve as role models for the graduates of that program.

The end product of a fellowship training program in child psychiatry could, theoretically, be any one of three types of individuals: a pure artist, a pure scientist, or a scientifically minded artist. The pure artist would be the pure practitioner of his art. The best of these individuals would be able to use his clinical skills to apply currently recognized solutions to currently recognized clinical situations. The pure scientist, on the other hand, would probably not acquire or use clinical skills and in his pursuit of ultimate truth might not be prepared to take action on data which he recognizes as inadequate. As such, although a solid scientist, he may be a danger to his patients despite his ability to think scientifically. The third type, the scientifically minded artist (or the scientist practitioner), as described by the editors of this volume, should be the sought after end product of any fellowship training program in child psychiatry. For that matter he probably should be the most acceptable end product of any training program geared to turn our specialists in delivery of mental health services to children.

The scientifically minded artist will think scientifically but will acquire and use his clinical skills effectively. He will accept the fact that at the same time he is searching for the ultimate truth in his investigative work, he must frequently take action on inadequate data in his therapeutic work. The scientist-artist must acquire in his training years the dual personality necessary to reconcile the rather contradictory approaches of the clinician and of the scientist. As a clinician he must be a pragmatist, he must treat children and their families using information that he knows as a scientist is based on incomplete and inadequate data. To be effective as a clinician he must be able to deliver this treatment with therapeutic enthusiasm. On the other hand, as a scientist, he cannot accept enthusiastic therapeutic claims without evidence. And he must develop the capacity for critical evaluation of data and for making controlled observations in a clinical context. Most importantly, he must be able to critically evaluate new knowledge as it appears in psychiatric and psychological literature. Finally, this scientist-artist must integrate what he learns in his clinical practice so that one contributes to the other.

If such scientist-artists or scientist practitioners are to be graduates of training programs geared to turn out deliverers of mental health services to children, research training and an appreciation of research as it applies to clinical psychopathology must be an important and integrated part of any training program. Volumes such as these will make good source books for such training programs whatever the primary discipline.

Dennis P. Cantwell, M.D.
Los Angeles, California
Dec. 1978

Preface

At one time the main interest in psychological research with children focused on developmental trends and learning processes with normals while the rather sparse child clinical literature contained primarily case material or diagnostic testing studies. Only within the last decade has research into child psychopathology begun to focus on the implications for treatment and not until 1973 was there a psychological journal (*Journal of Abnormal Child Psychology*) devoted exclusively to research and treatment of behavioral pathology in childhood and adolescence. A recognition of the growing amount of research activity in child psychopathology and of the increased social concern for "problem children" was the main impetus for the founding of this journal and similarly stimulated our interest in editing this book.

The present book was designed to meet two objectives: (1) to provide contemporary examples of the interplay of research and treatment across a variety of topics in child psychopathology and (2) to reflect a commitment to the scientist–practitioner model for the delivery of mental health services.

Our motivation for providing examples of the interplay of research and treatment stems from a desire to elicit modeling in others working in the area. Researchers and providers of treatment do not have to be separate. Although this may sound presumptuous, it accurately reflects our belief in the need for both increased rigorous basic research and treatment research in a coexisting fashion within child psychopathology. By providing representative programs we are hoping that others will be better able to design similar programs within their particular area of interest in child psychopathology.

Preface

A commitment to the scientist–practitioner model for the delivery of mental health services is based upon our belief that this is the model most likely to maximize advancement of knowledge and, thus, improve the effectiveness of treatment. Traditionally, clinical psychologists have been trained as both scientist and practitioner. However, while this model has been adopted as the ideal to which most graduate programs strive, the fact is that program emphasis at most universities widely miss the mark. In the cases where a favorable balance is struck, it is often within the group of faculty members rather than any individual member. That is, some professors are practicing clinicians—they supervise practicums, attend staff conferences, and see clients, but spend limited time in research. On the other hand, other professors engage themselves in research team meetings, reading and writing journal articles, supervising thesis and dissertations and find little time for clients. Nevertheless, when the group is organized and heads are counted, the scientist–practitioner model appears in effect. Unfortunately, the ideal is not reached within the individual and it is the individual with whom most graduate students identify and subsequently model their professional behavior. We feel that attaining the scientist–practitioner goal is not impossible and hope that this collection of chapters will reflect its possibility.

In line with the need for an increase in treatment research within child psychopathology and in line with our commitment to the dual professional role, the present book includes two sections. The first section contains six chapters which include summaries of research areas related to child psychopathology with a special concern for treatment implications. The second section, a series of eight chapters, is devoted to treatment procedures which, for the most part, are of a data-based tradition. All contributions to this text are original papers prepared especially for this purpose.

Specifically, Chapter One provides an overview of research methods including strategies for research and for sequencing of the research methods. The second chapter examines children's responses to experiences of success and failure and accentuates both adaptive and maladaptive outcomes. In the third chapter an often overused yet psychologically vague clinical construct—anxiety—is examined. The emphasis here after 4 years of research, is on the difficulty in the measurement of anxiety in children. Chapter Four discusses the literature on locus of control and its implications for child personality. Research into hyperactivity is discussed in Chapter Five, and Chapter Six concludes the first section by discussing a 5-year sequence of studies investigating impulsivity. A research-based treatment procedure, which has been developed to modify impulsivity is presented.

The second section of the book contains an up-to-date and relevant selection of empirically oriented treatment approaches. The first chapter of the treatment section delineates a program for training parents to be modifiers of the noncompliant behavior of their children. Encopresis and enuresis are given separate yet coordinated consideration in the following two chapters with emphasis placed on lasting treatment effects. Chapter Ten contains an overview of learning disabilities, including theory, behavioral characteristics, diagnosis, treatment, and problems in the area. Chapter Eleven presents an empirical approach to the treatment of autistic children from an ego-psychology theoretical orientation, while Chapters Twelve and Thirteen reflect behavioral treatment approaches with retardate and delinquent populations, respectively. Finally, the benefits and problems of drug treatment with children are discussed in Chapter Fourteen.

Many people have added to our knowledge of children and have been responsible for our continued interest in the area. Four who stand out are H. C. Rickard, Michael Dinoff, Austin M. DesLauriers, and Philip C. Eichner. To these we say: "Thanks." A special thanks goes to L. E. Montgomery, John R. Morgan, M. Sue Kendall, and Garry L. Edwards for their comments on the preparation of this book. Finally, to Ms. Shirley Truman, who typed and retyped only to be asked to type again, we extend our gratitude.

Contents

Clinical Treatment and Research in Child Psychopathology

Part I

Research in Child Psychopathology

Chapter One

Strategies for Research in Child Psychopathology*

PHILIP C. KENDALL and A. J. FINCH, JR.

Research in child psychopathology is an area very much in need of increased attention since both the actual number of studies and their depth have been less than optimal. Several reasons probably account for these shortcomings. One is that, compared to adulthood, childhood is a relatively brief period of life which often elicits the feeling "why bother, the child will grow out of it." Another limiting factor is that few children come to the attention of mental health workers until after they have encountered school problems for several years.

Probably the most important factor contributing to the limited research in child psychopathology, however, is a lack of commitment to research by mental health professionals working with children. Although lip-service is given to the importance of scientific investigations, such verbalization is generally nonproductive. Moreover, many professionals in the area of child treatment are either untrained or undertrained in the methods of scientific inquiry. Rarely do child psychiatrists receive more than a passing mention of how to design a research project. Similarly,

*The preparation of this material was supported by a National Institute of Mental Health Fellowship (#1 F31 MH05270-01) awarded to Philip C. Kendall.

psychiatric social workers and psychiatric nurses usually receive little more than mention of the fact that research exists. Clinical psychologists traditionally have viewed themselves as the research experts in the mental health field since they generally hold a research degree (Ph.D.). Unfortunately, many clinical psychologists are not vitally interested in research. Clinical psychology is an area with which most people become involved because of their interest in working with troubled individuals, and even if their initial interests were research oriented, they find that most of their experimental, research, and design courses involve the study of rats, college sophomores, and yields of corn. One of the authors still vividly remembers wondering during a difficult statistics exam what the yield of corn A as opposed to corn B when fertilizer 1 vs. fertilizer 2 was employed had to do with his interest in disturbed children. Many a potential researcher's interest may have been lost in the midst of such pondering. Yet, even if interest in research is not extinguished by some apparently unrelated material, it is frequently difficult for the potential researcher to generalize from the nonclinical material to real world clinical data. As a result, those interested in research often must learn the needed skills on their own.

The purpose of the present chapter is to present an introduction to research strategies in child psychopathology that might serve as a stimulus to elicit additional interest in the area. In addition, these strategies are developed into a sequence for programmatic research. Rather than writing a cookbook, we have attempted to prepare an outline of some effective research strategies and to show how they have been productive in a clinical setting.

RESEARCH METHODS

A general organization of the methods of research in the social and behavioral sciences results in the following categorization: (1) experimental studies; (2) correlational studies; (3) naturalistic observations; and (4) case studies. Each of these methods has advantages and disadvantages and each provides a different kind of information. Experimental studies refer to the manipulation of variables and the subsequent evaluation of the effects of the manipulation on scores on a dependent variable (variable on which change is being measured). As a part of the experimental method the researcher plans to control the unwanted effects of variables which are not being manipulated and evaluated. The laboratory setting is usually selected to allow for the maximum control procedures.

Correlational analyses involve neither manipulation of an independent variable nor the assessment of effects. In contrast to the experimental approach, a correlational study provides information in the form of the covariation of measures, that is, an analysis of the way in which two measures relate to each other.

Naturalistic observation is a method which asserts that the laboratory is not the real world, that contrived experiments produce contrived results, and that accurate analysis of real behavior requires that the behavior be observed under natural conditions. While the natural quality cannot be argued, the lack of control associated with such observation can be a drawback.

Lastly, the case-study method involves an intensive examination of an individual subject. Accurate data on the target behaviors are tracked over time, and an analysis of the changes in behavior are made as a function of imposed conditions.

In accord with our intent to provide a strategic introduction to research in child psychopathology rather than a text on the research methods, each of the above methods will be discussed in an overview fashion. Many other authors have written detailed material on the procedures for research, statistical analysis, and experimental design (e.g., Winer, 1971; Ray, 1962; Edwards, 1960). Here, each of the methods will be introduced as strategies for investigation followed by the proposed use of all of these methods within a sequence of research studies.

Experimental Strategies

The experimental methods are the *sine qua non* of psychology as a science. They are the methods which provide the most sophisticated outcome information, since they yield probability statements regarding cause and effect. Since a complete discussion of the experimental methods is beyond the scope of this chapter, only the most important issues within this method for use in examining child psychopathology and treatment will be considered. Two types of experimental strategies will be described—direct clinical manipulation and manipulation by selection.

The major feature of the experimental method is that the variables of interest to the researcher are manipulated (varied) in order to evaluate the effects of that manipulation upon the dependent variable (scores obtained). For example, variable A is manipulated—high level of A and low level of A—and the effects of the levels of A are examined in terms of the resulting variation in the dependent score (e.g., variable B). Such manipulation and its resulting effects allow for causal statements concerning the variables A and B.

The most beneficial use of the experimental method in child psychopathology is when a variable is *clinically* manipulated. Clinical manipulation is achieved when the levels of the independent variable are determined by the experimental clinician who arranges for the appearance of different quantities or values (levels) of the variable. For example, the researcher interested in persistence behavior (dependent variable) in children could experimentally examine the effects of task difficulty (independent variable) on persistence. Two groups (for the present discussion they are matched subjects) are separately and individually exposed to two tasks which are time consuming to complete but which differ meaningfully on their level of difficulty. The experimenter can clinically manipulate the amount of task difficulty by adjusting clinical situations, the actual task objects, or the instructions. The researcher is asking the question: Does such a manipulation of task difficulty affect the persistence of the subjects?

In contrast to the direct clinical manipulation where the clinician adjusts the levels of the independent variable, manipulating levels of a variable by *selection* does not provide the control of the levels. Manipulation by selection is a procedure, usually related to subject characteristics, in which distinct subject groups are chosen for comparison. For example, if one were interested in the persistence behavior of normal and non-normal children, the experimenter would not clinically manipulate levels of normality. Rather, subjects would be selected from predetermined normal and non-normal groups. With manipulation by selection (e.g., normal and non-normal children), the unwanted variation of other variables can enter and confound the research. That is, the two groups may differ in important ways that might go undetected by the researcher. This is a drawback of the method that can be mitigated by matching subjects on known relevant characteristics.

In general, the experimental method is the method of choice for researchers in child psychopathology and treatment. The use of manipulated levels of the independent variable and the cause–effect statements that can be made from the results are strong points. An additional value of the experimental method as well as a requirement of it is the control of all variables other than the experimental variables.

In the study of child personality, psychopathology, and treatment, manipulation (experimental) studies are vital if etiological or therapy data are to be properly evaluated on a large scale. Experimentation allows for the application of the most advanced statistical analyses and subsequently the most sophisticated outcome information. Nevertheless, there are situations when, for various reasons, one does not want to manipulate the levels of a certain variable (e.g., ethics), and still other situations where the variable cannot be manipulated (e.g., birth disorders). In such situations the manipulation of the independent variable is best done by selection. Both methods of manipulation have their place in research with children. In order to clarify the application of the experimental strategies, an example from both child personality and treatment will be discussed.

Child Personality

The psychology of the child which considered the child as a "small adult" has been almost entirely abandoned and replaced by the point of view that children are learning agents that develop into adult personalities as the result of their history of both positive and negative experiences. Unfortunately, research into child personality has suffered from an adult-like "pure-trait" approach which assumes that a personality disposition is likely to emerge across most situations. Recent conceptualizations, however, have advanced our understanding by adopting a behavioral perspective in which environmental contingency manipulations are considered. Applying both the clinical manipulation and manipulation by selection strategies to the investigation of child personality could produce a study like the following:

Independent variables.

Clinical manipulation—a situational manipulation to produce a high stress or a low stress condition (e.g., ego-involving task instructions versus nonego-involving ones on a task requiring performance)

Manipulation by selection—a subject manipulation to identify high anxious and low anxious subjects. Selection based upon ratings, test scores, or the rate of a particular behavior.

Dependent variables.

The dependent measures (physiological—galvanic skin response, heart-rate; self report—level of anxiety during the task) would be measured at an initial resting period and again during the manipulation.

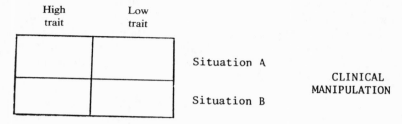

Fig. 1. An experiment for child-personality research including both clinical manipulation and manipulation by selection.

The experiment in Fig. 1 is designed to investigate the anxiety reactions of subjects in two situations. When the initial resting level of anxiety is subtracted from the level of anxiety measured during the task, a score which indicates the individual's anxiety reaction is obtained. This score is then analyzed. The use of the direct manipulation variable allows an assessment of the effects of the situation on the occurrence of anxiety in subjects in general. The selection of subjects on the basis of their trait scores (high or low anxiety) allows an evaluation of different subject types. A significant main effect for trait in the absence of other significant outcomes would suggest that regardless of the situation the personality disposition is related to observed differences. On the other hand, a significant main effect for situations would support the importance of the environmental context (and not client traits) in understanding behavior. In addition, the use of both manipulation procedures allows for an examination of the interaction of subject characteristics and situations. The proposed use of multiple dependent measures allows for analysis of the consistency of the effects across these measures as well as the effects on each measure.

Child Treatment

One could argue that global theories of psychotherapy which contend that all clients can benefit from a unidimensional treatment approach do not appear to fit the data. Indeed, why should a clinician expect one therapy to work for all types of psychopathology? Continuing this line of argument, one could hypothesize that the various pathologies are selectively susceptible to modification with strategies conducted according to different treatment theories. If this is so, careful research should determine which treatments are effective for which child psychopathologies.

An application of the previously described clinical and selection manipulations to the examination of treatment effectiveness could produce a study like the following:

Independent variables.

Clinical manipulation—a treatment manipulation which varies the type of treatment

Manipulation by selection—a subject manipulation to isolate subjects who are at different levels on the target behavior

Repeated measurement—the assessment of target behavior at pretreatment, posttreatment, and follow-up (a within-subjects comparison)

The experiment in Fig. 2 is a $2 \times 2 \times 3$ design planned to examine the differential effectiveness of a reinforcement vs. a response-cost procedure on the target behaviors of impulsive and reflective children. The effectiveness is examined across the repeated measurements: pretreatment, posttreatment, and follow-up. The use of the direct clinical manipulation of the contingencies allows for an assessment of the effects of these different conditions, while the selection of two types of children allows the investigator to determine if the contingencies effect both types of children similarly. The question is: Do the different groups respond differently under the two conditions? As in the personality example,

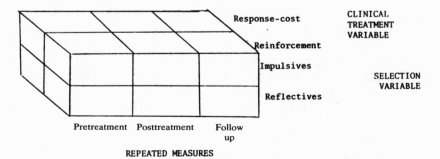

Fig. 2. An experiment for child-treatment research including both clinical manipulation and manipulation by selection.

examining the interaction of persons and conditions (selected and clinically manipulated variables) and the use of multiple dependent measures are important. In research involving treatment, another vital procedure is the repeated assessment of treatment effects, which can provide valuable information regarding the durability of change.

Perhaps the area of greatest research activity should be an examination of differential treatment effectiveness for distinct groups of children. Thus, both clinical manipulation and manipulation by selection strategies are important tools in clinical research involving the experimental method.*

Correlational Strategies

The clinical researcher invariably discovers that certain variables are "off limits" and that he/she† must avoid both direct and selective manipulation. Due to the ethical principles guiding our work with children, the breadth of vulnerable variables increases, and justifiably so. Correlational strategies are sometimes used as a next-best substitute when manipulation of variables is not possible, but researchers often find correlations to be a method of choice. It is to this topic, the purposeful use of correlation strategies in child-clinical research, that we now turn.

A correlation represents the degree of interrelatedness of two variables. In either a positive or negative direction, a high correlation enables one to make some reasonably probable predictions about a child's score on one variable from his score on the other. Low correlations suggest the lack of a relationship and thus provide limited predictive ability.

When a researcher embarks on a correlational investigation, the explicit purpose may be to examine whether or not a relationship exists, to assess the degree of a given relationship, or, for practical purposes, to evaluate the reliability of the measures being used (e.g., inter-observer reliability, test–retest reliability). No matter what the purpose for calculating correlation coefficients, the procedure requires obtaining pairs of scores or observations.

Use of correlational approaches does not allow the researcher to

---

*The interested reader is referred to Kiesler (1971) for an advanced discussion of psychotherapy research designs.

†Rather than burden the entire chapter with the clumsy phrase "he/she, his/her", the authors have sought reading ease by using the male pronoun.

determine the effects or probable causes of observed changes that take place. Strategically, while correlational analyses can be useful as exploratory techniques or as an economical pilot investigation, they are more valuable for (1) the intensive examination of the dependent measures being used and (2) providing ancillary information from an experimental investigation. At this point we shall explore these two main strategies of correlational inquiry.

Intensive Examination of Dependent Measures

The use of correlational analyses to examine an array of dependent variables can vary in complexity from the simple correlation of two dependent measures to the extensive factor analysis of a matrix of measures (or test items).

Simple Correlation. The simplest correlational technique is to determine the degree of relationship among the dependent measures by calculating a correlation coefficient for each pair of measures. The value of the measure can be partially assessed by examining its relative importance in accounting for portions of the variability in the behavior that is being examined. A very high correlation between measures would suggest that, along with their obvious lack of independence, perhaps both measures need not have been taken since they are apparently measuring the same thing. The question then is: Does the addition of the second measure improve prediction? Does it account for a meaningful portion of additional variability? Calculation of the appropriate correlation can aid the researcher in seeking answers to these questions.

Factor Analysis. On the complex end of the analysis-of-dependent-measures continuum is the factor analytic procedure. Factor analysis is probably most useful as an analysis of dependent measures. Factor analytic investigations can seek to examine items within a single test (inventory) or to isolate dimensions of independently gathered dependent measures (e.g., self-report, rating scales, physiological measures).

The factor analytic method utilizes as its data the intercorrelations of a number of variables presented in matrix form. One may attempt to make sense of a small matrix of correlations by "eyeballing" a consistency, viz., a cluster of variables. One may infer that these variables (cluster) are measuring the same dimension of behavior or that there exists a hypothetical variable (the cluster of variables) which is composed of all the variables that correlate highly. The contribution of each variable is equivalent to its correlation with the hypothetical variable. Eyeballing another correlation matrix may reveal that each variable is relatively independent of the others. In such a case there would be no hypothetical variable which "organizes" several of the variables in the matrix. Unfortunately, "eyeballing" is extremely limited in that the researcher cannot be certain of his estimates nor can he eyeball the contribution of each variable to the factor. In addition, eyeballing is neither objective nor scientific. Fortunately, factor analysis provides the advanced methodology for examining correlation matrices, identifying those variables which contribute to hypothetical clusters, and indicating the degree of their contribution.

Following the identification of relevant factors within a single test or within a domain of variables, a score for each factor can be computed from the items or variables that compose each factor. Thus, a score can be calculated for each factor separately. These factor-specific scores are distinct from the overall score obtained from the entire test. Following the scoring of the specific factors as well as overall scoring, analyses to determine the significance of the outcome can use both overall and factor-specific dependent measures. The use of such factor-specific analyses have been useful in:*

1. Constructing new tests (or inventories) to measure each separate factor
2. Generating separate hypotheses
   a. to enhance the prediction of the effects of special manipulations
   b. to advance the specificity of group comparison
3. Improving the precision of relationships
4. Examining qualitative differences in the construct purportedly measured by an inventory by analyzing different subject groups separately
5. Develop theoretical issues

It has not been our present purpose to explain the mathematical procedures of factor analysis nor to attempt even a brief discussion of all the factor analytic issues. However, the following brief description of the stages of a factor analysis (without mathematical formulae) and the mention of a relevant issue (subjectivity) should increase the reader's basic understanding of the technique and encourage its use in research. Our brief tangential excursion into "the land of more than three dimensions" is justified by its contribution to the strategic use of factor analysis.

---

*Sources for supportive material include (1) Levenson, 1973; (2a) Finch *et al.*, 1976a; (2b) Kendall *et al.*, 1976a; (3) Abramowitz, 1973; (4) Finch *et al.*, 1976a; (5) Kendall *et al.* (unpublished manuscript).

Factor Analytic Stages and Subjectivity. The standard stages of a factor analytic investigation involve: (1) the selection of variables; (2) computing the correlation matrix; (3) extracting unrotated factors; (4) rotating the factors; and (5) interpreting the rotated factor matrix (Comrey, 1973).

The first two stages of a factor analysis should be familiar to most readers since all areas of psychological inquiry have the freedom of variable selection and since the correlation matrix is commonly used by researchers. Although real world constraints on variable selection such as ethics and parsimony do exist, factor analysis does not remove these constraints nor provide additional ones. In factor analysis, as within the computation of any correlation matrix where alternatives do exist, the decision as to the type of correlation coefficient that should be calculated is data-based and nonsubjective.

The subjective aspects of factor analysis are more apparent in the next three computing stages. In all cases, however, the experienced and knowledgeable researcher can minimize subjectivity. Properly used, canned computer programs can aid the researcher in this direction, as can a careful consideration of other issues—the type of data, the expectation of dependent or independent factors, and the method for estimating communalities.*

The process of factor extraction has several procedures which can be followed, and each procedure has advantages and disadvantages (see Gorsuch, 1974). In the majority of child psychopathology research, however, extracted factors which are unrotated are of little meaning. In this regard, and in light of the similarities of the outcomes of the various extraction procedures, our brief discussion will turn to factor rotation.

The expected dependency of the factors should be included in the determination of the rotation procedure. Factor rotation can be (1) orthogonal or (2) oblique. Orthogonal factors are at right angles to each other and are, as you would expect, not correlated with each other and are thus independent. It is possible to have more than three orthogonal factors—despite the absence of a human capability to perceive such! Oblique factor solutions provide factors which are not at right angles and which are correlated to some degree.

The last stage of a factor analysis involves factor interpretation. Basically, a factor is interpreted by examining the variables (e.g., items, tests) that meaningfully contribute to it. The contributing variables will,

---

*In every correlation matrix all variables are correlated with each other. Only half of the matrix is presented in that the remaining half is identical. The diagonal of the matrix (the variables correlation with itself) is empty since self-correlations are not computed. For the conducting of a factor analysis these communalities must be estimated.

ideally, suggest an inclusive label for the factor. The actual label which is chosen should represent the most subjective aspect of the procedure. Regardless of the choice, however, the label is based on the variables which hierarchically contribute to the factor (factor loadings). As a partial control for potential label misinterpretation, the researcher should present the loadings and, thus, allow the reader to "work through" the conceptualization of the label.

The factor analytic procedures can apparently be viewed as differentially sensitive to the "subjectivity" criticism. We do not argue that a degree of arbitrariness destroys the analysis nor do we denounce its involvement. Rather, it should be self-evident that a familiarity with factor analysis, its procedures, stages, and areas of subjectivity, should be beneficial in its strategic use.

Ancillary Information

Another use of correlational methods that should be noted concerns the *purposeful* computation of correlation coefficients as an adjunct to the main purpose of the research and as a potential source of hypotheses. As an example we return to the study designed to illustrate the use of both clinical and selection-type manipulations in child-clinical treatment research (evaluating reinforcement and response-cost for impulsive and reflective children). The reader will recall that a $2 \times 2 \times 3$ design with 3 repeated measures was suggested. An analysis of variance would be an appropriate statistical evaluation technique and should be calculated. Let us assume that response-cost but not reinforcement produced a significant improvement for impulsive but not for reflective children. The implication is indeed meaningful—impulsives are more responsive to response-cost than to reinforcement. Additional information would be valuable: is the degree of impulsivity directly related to the effectiveness of response-cost? If such a relationship exists, it would have treatment implications. Do the measures of the effectiveness of response-cost correlate with the number of response-cost occurrences? If so, then the more the response-cost incidences the greater the effectiveness of the procedure. Such correlational information, gathered in an ancillary fashion, is a source of both potentially useful data and hypotheses for future examination.

The above is but one example of the utility of ancillary correlational analyses. The strategy is indeed a viable one. Moreover, it is practical, economical, and productive.

Strategies for Naturalistic Observation

The third research method we are considering is naturalistic observation. Although therapists have always been concerned with behavior change, it is only recently that systematic, quantifiable methods for observing naturally occurring behavior have been developed. The ability to track the target behavior *in vivo* from pre- to posttreatment, and during treatment, maximizes the accuracy of the outcome evaluation.

Using a portion of the outline provided by Wright (1960) we will consider five methods of acquiring observational information. These are: (1) diary description; (2) target description; (3) time sampling; (4) event sampling; and (5) trait rating.

The first, the diary description, employs the technique of having an observer record behavioral episodes on a day-to-day basis. The entries are usually the events which catch the attention of the observer or which are of special consequence to the subject. If this diary keeper is the client, many problems such as faking, forgetting, and inaccuracy will occur. If someone else keeps the record, that person must maintain constant contact with the subject. Regardless of who is keeping the diary, this method leaves room for observer bias, unreliable recording, unwarranted interpretation, and subsequently inefficient data evaluation.

The second method of observation, target description, is the planned observing and recording of a behavior sequence under chosen conditions. The target is either the behavior of a specific child or a specific behavior of a group of children. The target is observed and the description is in narrative style. The field observer in this case records everything that is related to the targeted child or behavior. These records are much more detailed than the diary data. In fact, such records contain everything the observer can see pertaining to the target and allows the target to remain within the context in which it occurred. The limitations of target description are its time-consuming nature and its requirement of excessive manpower.

The third method is time sampling. The time sampling procedure fixes the observer's attention upon specific aspects of behavior and is done within precise and short time intervals. Prior to any actual time sampling of behavior, codes are established to gather precise information about targeted behavior and to allow for an efficient quantitative evaluation. The reliability of the coders is demonstrated prior to actual observation, and the length and spacing of the coding intervals are also predetermined. In both instances, however, the actual codes and/or the code intervals can be developed for the specific behaviors and conditions of each study rather than relying on a standard set of codes.

Time sampling has several advantages: (1) observer reliability is maximized; (2) it allows for systematic control of what is to be observed; (3) it is easily applied to single-subject research designs; and (4) it is an attempt to standardize observation.

The disadvantage of time sampling is that behavior is recorded in frequencies and, thus, the record of the actual behavioral event misses some of its qualitative value. The price of economy is the loss of comprehensiveness. In order to improve the time sampling technique, records may be kept of antecedent and consequent conditions as well as of the sampled behavior.

The fourth method we are considering is event sampling. The principle here is that in order to record a sufficient amount of data on a low frequency behavior the examiner should sample events rather than time. Time sampling might select only a few intervals in which a target behavior occurs, whereas event sampling requires recording of each target event. One of the disadvantages of event sampling is that while the procedure does adapt well to low frequency behaviors, it tends to break up the continuity of time by its selective sampling. In addition, event sampling overlooks many behaviors which might otherwise have been coded.

Fifth, we have trait ratings. In this procedure the observer (teacher, nurse, parent) watches the target subject over a period of time and then rates the subject on a series of traits. One weakness of this approach is that ratings are completed long after the observations were made and observer bias can enter. Another drawback is that the actual frequency of behavior is sacrificed for a more global description.

We have now considered five approaches to the naturalistic observation and recording of behavior. Next we will discuss several general issues which are relevant to all methods of observing natural behavior, as they can affect the accuracy and usefulness of observation. They include the effect of the coder's presence, the effect of the setting on the sample, demand characteristics and experimental bias, instrumentation, and unobtrusive measures.

Let us assume that the clinician has targeted a behavior, outlined a method for the actual coding, defined the codes, achieved reliable coders, and is ready to begin. The next question is: What effect will the presence of the coder have on the behavior? In order to minimize any possible effect, the coders are introduced into the setting earlier than actual recording is to begin. Thus, the client or the family is allowed to habituate to the coder's presence.

The setting in which the codes are recorded is also of concern since it can influence the results of the observational tracking. If the behavior occurs in more than one setting, it should be recorded in several settings. In addition to information about total frequency and the conditions that elicit the behavior, the discrepancies in the rate of the target behavior across different settings may prove to be of diagnostic value.

When one considers the coders themselves, additional problems arise. These problems are best described by the phrase "experimenter bias." Coders who are aware of the treatments and who are involved in the project can bias the recording of behavior, either intentionally or unintentionally (see O'Leary and Kent, 1973). Such bias can be reduced by keeping coders naive to as much of the treatment program and/or research design as possible.

Another approach used to insure accuracy in the observation and recording of behavior is the implementation of "brass nob" mechanical instruments. Examples of such aides include electronic counters, time-lapse cameras, and radio transmitters. The use of instrumentation fits well within the use of unobtrusive measures (see Webb *et al.*, 1966). In this regard we can consider (1) erosion measures, (2) accretion measures, and (3) archives. Erosion methods involve, for example, observing how much wear a floor covering receives as a count of public traffic around a certain locale. Accretion measures are indicative of behavior in that the behavior leaves a residual (e.g., a measure of anxiety might be the number of cigarette butts left in an ash tray). Archives, used by many sociologists, are exemplified by marriage records, birth and death records, hospital files, etc. Using these nonreactive methods can produce a wealth of valuable, unobtrusively observed information.

We have considered several approaches to acquiring observational data and made several suggestions to reduce bias in such data. These strategies, carefully applied, are extremely valuable to the practicing clinician as well as the researcher, since observation is where treatment *and* science begin.

Case Study Strategies

When a researcher examines a case study via one of the single-subject strategies (see Hersen and Barlow, 1976), the comparison is between the performances of the same subject during periods of time in which he was differentially treated rather than between the performance of two or more groups which received differential treatment. Therefore, the single-subject receives all the effects of the manipulated independent variable at various times. The investigator should be aware that there are limitations to such an application of the treatments. Comparing two treatments, if one is not reversible, is essentially impossible. For example, examining the effects of a surgical procedure vs. a nonsurgical one is not a possibility with a single-subject since once the surgery is performed there is no undoing it. Also, if one is interested in confirming or disconfirming hypotheses about behavior in general, the single-subject strategies would be insufficient, whereas group studies would be appropriate.

Nevertheless, the use of a single-subject strategy to evaluate an individual case is a valuable source of hypotheses for later investigation (Kendall and Nay, 1978). Evidence for the "source of hypotheses" function of single case studies is apparent in the historically vital case of "little Albert" (Watson and Rayner, 1920). More recent, and specifically related to the source of hypotheses derived from case studies, is an evaluation of impulse control (Kendall and Finch, 1976) which provided not only evidence of an apparently successful treatment but also several noteworthy hypotheses for later investigation.

Single-Subject Design Strategies

The use of single-subject strategies is clearly an advance over the case studies which were fraught with biased observation and lacking in accurate measurement. By controlling observation techniques and acquiring reliable measurement the single-subject strategy has been raised to the level of semi-scientific information presented in a more rigorous fashion than was usual for case studies.

The presentation of single case data usually conforms to a time series functional analysis. Essentially, an accurate record of the frequency of occurrences of the behavior(s) in question is plotted along a time dimension (see Fig. 3). In order to designate the imposed conditions (the levels of the manipulation) the letters A, B, C, and D have been used. Generally, A denotes a no-treatment phase, while B, C, or D stand for successive treatments.

The use of a no-treatment phase prior to the imposing of treatment conditions provides the case study analyst with baseline information. Baseline data is the pretreatment measurement of the naturally occurring frequency of the behavior. The baseline information is very important since in its absence there is nothing with which to compare the effects of the treatment. Without baseline data, the changes in behavior, both desirable and undesirable, could be due to any one of an array of uncontrolled factors. Although the inclusion of baseline data does not

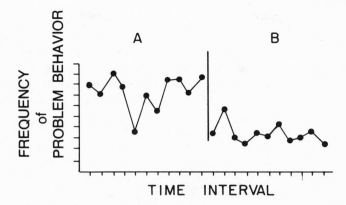

Fig. 3. An illustration of behavioral frequency plotted along a time dimension with an imposed condition (B).

prevent the interference of uncontrolled factors, when baseline data is properly gathered (see methods of naturalistic observation) the case study analyst has an assessment of the magnitude of the problems, a description of the trend of the problem behavior(s), and a rate of behavior that allows for noting a change in the behavior during the treatment condition.

In order to provide the most useful baseline information, several recommendations should be followed. First, the behavior to be recorded should be operationally defined. This means defining the behavior as precisely as possible in concrete, observable terms. Second, the actual recorders of the behavior should be reliable. This means that coders must learn the codes, practice them, and achieve a high level of reliability for each code. Third, the setting for the coding should not be restrictive. For example, a setting should not be selected which might foster or prevent the behavior. Finally, baseline data should be gathered for a sufficient amount of time to provide a representative data base. This requires many observations across time and until the rate appears to be relatively stable. While one can make recommendations which will be valuable for the recording of baseline data, one cannot specify the exact length of a given baseline. The judgement as to when to terminate the collection of baseline data is the therapist's, and subsequent therapeutic considerations enter into the .decision. Clearly, low-rate behavior will demand a more extended baseline period in order to gather meaningful data than would a high-rate behavior.

Once baseline data have been gathered and the treatment is about to be imposed, the A phase of the single-subject strategy is complete. Next comes the installation of treatment—the B phase—while accurate recording of behavior continues. When a change in the behavioral rate is apparent at the point of treatment installation, the treatment is considered to be responsible for the alteration of the behavior. For example, if results are similar to those presented in Fig. 3, the B condition can be said to be primarily responsible for the decrease in the rate of problem behavior. The immediacy of the observed change supports the efficacy of the B treatment condition.

Reversal. Case study analysts have at times employed a reversal strategy to evaluate treatment in an A–B time series. This procedure attempts to bring about a return to baseline by removing treatment and reinstating the previous condition. Evaluation of a favorable nature for the effectiveness of the treatment would require that the positive change due to treatment "wash out" when treatment is removed. That is, the reversal (return to A phase) would demonstrate that the treatment was the agent of change because when it was removed the treatment effects disappeared.

There are several problems associated with the reversal procedure. The most obvious is the issue of the power of the treatment. If the treatment powerfully establishes a new behavioral repertoire, then the withdrawal of the treatment may not result in a change in rate. Here the desired long lasting quality of the treatment is directly pitted against the attempt to demonstrate control by a reversal. It is the therapist's responsibility to evaluate carefully the results of reversals in treatment conditions. In addition, another dilemma of the reversal is that such conditions allow the client to retrieve the undesirable behavior. Moreover, whether the conditions of the first baseline (A) can be matched during the second baseline is doubtful. Even if preexperimental baseline conditions appear to have been reproduced, there is still the question of whether or not the client perceives it as similar. That is, a client's perception of the second baseline can be markedly altered by carry-over or contrast effects from previous conditions (Kendall *et al.*, 1975).

Reversal with Replication. The reversal with replication strategy requires that the A–B portion of the time series be repeated. A–B–A–B. The control of the target behavior by the treatment (B) condition is evident when a dramatic change in the desired direction occurs at each change in treatment (see Fig. 4). That is, the high rate of an undesirable behavior such as verbal aggression is reduced during the treatment phase, returns to its previous undesirable level when treatment is removed (return to baseline), and is again suppressed by the last treatment phase. The replication of the A–B change in behavior adds further credence to the findings that the treatment affected the target behavior.

Several problems of the reversal with replication strategy are

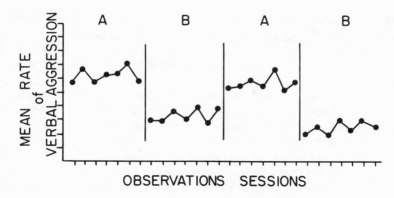

Fig. 4. An illustration of an A–B–A–B strategy.

noteworthy. First, it is subject to sequence effects, which are the unwanted effects due to order and contrast. Essentially the A–B–A–B strategy is subject to criticism due to the possibility that the change was due to the order of the treatment conditions (treatment having occurred first). Additionally, the second A and B conditions can be meaningfully different from the first A and B conditions due to the contrasting of the treatment/no-treatment sequence. Such sequence effects hinder interpretation of the efficacy of the treatment condition.

An even more important criticism of the A–B–A–B strategy presents itself when the rate of behavior, following the return to baseline, fails to reflect the change in conditions. Is this due to the generalizing of the treatment to no-treatment conditions, which would be a therapeutically favorable event, *or* is it due to a lack of experimental control where the treatment conditions are not having an effect? Such an unresolvable dilemma makes the A–B–A–B of somewhat limited utility.

Lastly, practical real-world limitations also hinder the use of the reversal-with-replication strategy. Here, the feelings of the subject(s) and staff are of concern. If subjects are kept blind as to the nature of the experiment, as is necessary to pinpoint active ingredients of treatment and to get unconfounded results, then the apparently confusing alternation in the subject's environment can foster mistrust and suspicion. Similarly, unit staff must tolerate the misbehavior during no-treatment phases.

When proven treatment strategies are available, it is difficult to justify the use of a reversal design since withholding of treatment is unethical. At our present state of knowledge, however, reversal designs may have some utility. Fortunately, our knowledge of more sophisticated single-subject strategies allows the case-study analyst to improve his examination of the individual as well as avoid the ethical and practical problems of the reversal strategy. One of the better alternatives is the multiple baseline design.

Multiple Baseline. The multiple baseline strategy is useful to demonstrate that behavior change is due to the intervention and not some extraneous life event. This is done by simultaneously recording baseline data on several behaviors (or in several settings), and applying treatment to only one of the behaviors (in one of the settings) and not the other(s). The remaining baselines serve as controls to assure that the treatment condition and not extraneous events caused the observed change. The untreated baseline represents what the course of untreated behavior looks like (see Fig. 5). As can be seen in Fig. 5, the baseline frequency of off-task classroom behavior was relatively high. The success of the treatment procedure is evident in the systematic change (reductions) following the installation of treatment. The observation that the change occurred with no apparent change in other baselines is evidence for

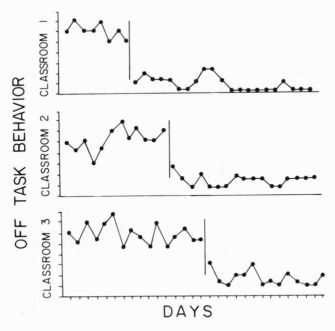

Fig. 5. An illustration of a multiple baseline strategy across classrooms.

treatment effectiveness. The reliability of the treatment procedure is indicated by the repeated change which occurs with treatment across the three behaviors. Also, the strength of the treatment is seen in the immediacy of the reduction of the target behaviors and in the lasting effects.

In adopting the multiple baseline strategy several recommendations should be followed. The first, which is also related to other single-subject strategies, requires that care be taken not to implement treatment following an extreme data point. The number of baselines is important, and several baselines (at least three) should be used. Lastly, care should be taken to insure that the behaviors are independent. The selection of independent behaviors is important to insure that the treatment does not produce changes in behavior(s) in addition to the one behavior to which treatment is applied (see Kazdin and Kopel, 1975).

The single-subject strategies discussed thus far are not exhaustive of the possibilities. Rather, they represent the most widely used single case designs. In using these procedures or in the critical examination of such research, there are criteria for evaluation. The next section will provide a brief discussion of such criteria and a consideration of some of the potential sources of invalidity in single case studies.

Criteria for Evaluation

When one is examining the incidence of behaviors across a time series plot, the usual attempt is to demonstrate treatment effectiveness due to imposed conditions. The following general criteria apply to all single case designs:

1. Examine baseline data carefully for any apparent pretreatment trends. If the occurrence of the behavior was on the decline before treatment, then the effects of treatment are only superimposed on the downward trend and cannot be isolated. Therefore, baselines should reflect relative stability in the behavior.
2. Provide data from numerous observations. This is necessary to evaluate the possibility of previous trends, and it is also vital for evaluation of the scope of the data. The data points on the plot of rate and time periods should represent these numerous observations and not averages of large blocks of time. Although no rule for the number of observations is being offered, it is generally suggested that numerous observations be made and presented. The greater the number of observations, the more representative is the analysis.

3. For a complete evaluation of the treatment condition, evidence of generalization (Kendall, in press) and follow-up should be presented. The length and completeness of the data presentation determine the extensiveness of the analysis of treatment effects that can be made.

Potential Sources of Invalidity

It is assumed within the strategies of single-subject treatment evaluation that when the observed change in behavior occurs concurrently with the imposition of the treatment, the treatment produced the effect on behavior. This assumption can be invalid due to several interfering sources. Only some of these are discussed here, and the reader is directed to Campbell and Stanley (1963) for further elaboration. Those to be discussed are as follows:

1. *Simultaneous occurrence of specific events.* This potential source of invalidity is in regard to real life occurrences which happen at the same time as treatment intervention. For example, self-depreciating statements made by a depressed young man may decrease when treatment begins and may be attributed to therapist intervention. However, a phone call from a former girl friend, which occurred simultaneously with the initiation of treatment, might well have been the source of behavior change rather than anything the therapist did.
2. *Passage of time.* Another potential invalidity is that the seemingly apparent success of treatment was due purely to the passage of time. For example, a reduction in inappropriate verbal behavior an adolescent female could be due to maturation and not to the treatment conditions. In work with children this is a most important concern.
3. *Recording instruments.* When one assumes that the desired behavior change was due to the treatment, one also assumes that the recording instruments were not altered in any way and that they remained highly reliable. Here, changes in the calibration of mechanical measuring instruments or changes in the reliability of human behavioral coders can be a source of invalidity.
4. *Regression.* When a subject's behavior is being monitored and recorded it is usually because the behavior occurs at an undesirable rate—too high or too low—since clients are usually selected to seek treatment due to these extremes. Mathematically, extreme

scores tend to regress toward the mean; that is, they become less extreme. Thus, regression of the rate of behavior can be a source of invalidity in research.

These and other potential sources of invalidity can influence the evaluation of treatment effectiveness, and the single case analyst should carefully examine his procedures in the light of known factors that can confound his results.

PROGRAMS OF RESEARCH: SEQUENCING

Now that we have described some utilitarian methods of research and discussed their use in child-clinical problems, let us look at some of the issues that more specifically involve the implementation of research programs.

Although individual studies can produce useful knowledge, it is the planned research program that will make the most valuable contribution to the problems of child psychopathology. Such a research program will involve a series of studies designed to answer related questions, with one study generating hypotheses as well as immediately useful findings, and each study building on the one before. Let us look at how this process can be set in motion.

To begin with, the investigator should be trained in both clinical and research skills if the questions asked (and answered, hopefully) are to have specific relevance to clinical issues. This requires training in the scientist–professional tradition. Too often the researcher operates in relative isolation in the laboratory, and his findings have little application for the practicing clinician. The clinician with research skills, however, knows the problems he faces daily and can expect that his research efforts will provide solutions for some of them. Initially, the clinical researcher may find himself interested in a certain problem behavior (e.g., encopresis) or the behaviors of a particular problem group (e.g., delinquents). Many questions and issues attract the clinician's interest in regard to the problem he selects, and so many topics exist that selection and focus can be difficult. Once he has narrowed his focus, the clinician must then establish a sequence of his research in order to have maximum impact on the problem chosen. The role of impulsivity in childhood psychopathology, a topic of interest to the present authors (see Chapter Six), is illustrative of the proposed method of sequencing investigations, and reference to Chapter Six may provide clarity and cohesiveness for the reader.

The final choice of the topic for a research program may be based on the personal interests of the investigators, some relevant issues within the practitioners' routines, the stimulating work of other researchers, or the general *Zeitgeist* of the field. In any case, the research program should begin with the researchers entering the actual environment in which the target behaviors occur. Go to the classroom, the home, or the ward or unit. Spend time globally observing and accurately recording the naturally occurring frequencies of the behavior of interest. Notice antecedents and consequences of the behavior, and discuss the treatments being used. In this initial stage, naturalistic observation without intervention is the method of choice. The course of events within the naturalistic observation should include operationally defining the target behavior, establishing codes and coder reliabilities, acquiring behavioral ratings, coding from various settings, calculating frequency and rating scale data, and drawing some general conclusions. The intensive study of a sampled child in a case study might provide a valuable source of hypotheses at this time.

In order to expand the knowledge at hand in regard to the target behavior, the next step might be several correlational studies. Here it is suggested that measures which have an established literature and which are relevant to the behavior in question be utilized. Essentially, once the behavior has been isolated and operationalized, its relative covariation with other measures should be examined. In addition, the internal structure of the measures as they are used with the particular research population should be evaluated via factor analytic procedures. In general, such correlational analyses aid in the understanding of the relative dependence or independence of the behavior under investigation.

Having begun a research program based on naturalistic observation and results of correlational studies, the investigators should find themselves well prepared to conduct experiments that will produce meaningful results. With the data base already gathered, other issues will be clear—the appropriate choice of independent variables (and levels of each independent variable), the reliability of the dependent measures, and the isolation of relevant variables to be controlled. It is the purpose of the preceding endeavors, of course, to best approximate such an ideal.

The experiments to be conducted at this point fit the "effects of" description. That is, meaningful levels of independent variables need to be examined to assess their effects. At this stage, individual independent variables that are most relevant should be examined separately rather than as large treatment packages (e.g., behavior therapy vs. insight therapy). After conducting a satisfactory series of such experiments the investigators are aware of the effects of someone doing precisely this or that, imposing certain conditions, or establishing varying contingencies.

Factorial experiments and repeated measures designs are recommended here. The examination of the effects of direct manipulation should be done with an additional selection (subject) manipulation. Thus, the potential outcome which reveals that certain conditions produce the desired effects on certain types of subjects may be identified.

Application of the acquired knowledge about the effects of various manipulations could then be examined as a treatment package. Here, the results of previous studies will have provided the data as to the effectiveness of various therapist behaviors. Perhaps another intensive case study using a single-subject strategy would fit here, where the intent would be to evaluate the "therapeutic" treatment effects. Various single-case strategies were discussed earlier and are available to the therapist (see Hersen and Barlow, 1976; Kendall and Nay, 1978), and using single-case methods can aid in isolating and evaluating therapeutic effects.

Experimental group studies of treatment effectiveness are appropriate at this stage of the research program. Use of both clinically direct manipulations and manipulations by selection in a factorial design are recommended. As an example, assume that the utility of a problem solving training approach to improve prosocial behavior of a group of delinquent males is to be evaluated. Forty subjects are randomly assigned to groups (treatment and attention control) and to the occasions for treatment. Repeated measures of several dependent variables are carefully monitored, and the outcome is statistically evaluated via the appropriate analysis of variance. Thus, the efficacy of the treatment is evaluated by a group experiment. The inclusion of a subject variable, such as "type of juvenile offense," and the division of subjects into status–nonstatus offender types would produce additional information. Nonetheless, the single group evaluation of the treatment procedure allows the researcher to make statements about the generality of the findings and is a necessity to establish general principles.

Of ancillary interest to the group comparison experimental method, and yet quite important, is the change over time of the dependent measures for each separate subject. Knowledge of individual changes can be a valuable source of hypotheses as well as important data in and of itself. What is being suggested is that the 20 treated subjects be functionally analyzed on an individual basis by examining the consistency of change over time across each of the subjects.

The proposed sequencing of methods implies that the researching clinician is skilled in the variety of methods. Correspondingly, the present authors argue against the unnecessary separation of "correlationists," "experimentalists," or "case-study analysts." No one method can answer all questions, whereas a variety of methods in a systematic sequence and for a variety of reasons can maximize research resources and result in a more rapid advancement of scientific knowledge than traditional separatist approaches.

RESEARCH ISSUES IN CHILD PSYCHOPATHOLOGY

A number of issues related to research in child psychopathology are important to us. In this regard, several strategies concerning these issues are meaningful. Before the present chapter draws to a close, we shall briefly discuss five such issues: choice of research setting; role of theory; use of paraprofessionals; research blocks; and research focus.

Choice of Research Setting

The mental health researcher who is working within a mental health setting has several advantages over one in an academic setting, and vice-versa. Essentially, the clinician who functions in a hospital, school system, or campus clinic has a population of troubled individuals on which the research can be conducted. The applied nature of the research takes precedence since the setting, in most cases, wants to know the answer to a question, and correspondingly the results are generally of practical rather than of theoretical importance. In contrast, the academic clinician has high quality manpower to conduct exquisitely designed theses and dissertations. Theory guides the formulation of research questions, and potential long range importance is the yield. The clinical researcher can profit from an affiliation with a clinical setting, and the setting can benefit from the research outcomes. Fostering these affiliations has an as yet unfulfilled status.

An additional advantage of the affiliations with clinical settings revolves around multiple disciplines. The psychologist can often find himself/herself in a position where his research and clinical skills go uncommunicated to members of other disciplines. Similarly, the work of researchers from other disciplines involved in mental health go unread by the psychologist. Upon the critical examination of research by a member of another discipline, the applied or practical question can arise—so what? How can I use this finding? While the research clinician should not be disheartened, this real world question and the resulting efforts to answer it are indeed beneficial. Working within a clinical setting can allow for intelligent cross-discipline communication.

In another sense, conducting research in the clinical setting can be achieved by an alteration of the present job descriptions for clinical psychologists. Too often the clinician is forced into one of two slots—academic or practitioner. If academics is selected, research is required and some less-than-necessary studies are conducted. If a clinic setting is chosen, research is an extra and the case load often prohibits such extravagances. Yet the clinician was trained as both a researcher and a practicing clinician. Making job descriptions that are half clinical and half research would be to create a job designed for the scientist–practitioner. Clearly, the availability of such positions would strengthen such a training emphasis.

Role of Theory

When the clinician becomes interested and involved in a research problem, his "theoretical" viewpoint will provide direction. Unfortunately, theory can become a set of blinders that force observation to comform to it, restrict potentially valuable treatments, and isolate only certain variables as relevant. Theory can be beneficial if held in perspective and altered as new findings emerge. Rigid theoretical adherence can serve only to hinder rather than guide research. In making observations, the behaviors being observed should not be violated by theory. Similarly, choosing variables for investigation should be determined in part by theory and to a greater degree by the issues which concern the researcher's problem. Theory should be considered, but the results of the research should lead the program of study.

Use of Paraprofessionals

A great deal of the child's day (in class or on a ward or unit) is spent with people other than the professional clinician. Within the treatment institution (e.g., family, school, hospital ward) the line staff are increasingly becoming a vital part of treatment, as evidenced by the increasing reports of institutions adapting some type of token (operant) approach (Kazdin and Bootzin, 1972). The use of paraprofessional staff relieves the overburdened professional staff from some management duties and similarly allows the professional to research a larger client population.

Researchers and treatment providers in the field of child psychopathology would benefit from an efficient use of paraprofessional help. The administration of certain experimental conditions, rating scales, and questionnaires are only some of the possible roles for paraprofessionals. In addition, paraprofessionals can be valuable contributors when they serve as unobtrusive coders of behavior, distributors of tokens, keepers of the data, and in some cases, supervisors of other paraprofessional helpers.

Research Blocks

One problem frequently faced by research-clinicians is the availability of a limited number of subjects. For example, 40 in-patients might be hospitalized for an average of 6 months. When this is the case, a total of only 80 subjects would be available for research participation during any given year. If several studies employing the same measures are conducted, subjects would become bored and, more importantly, experimentally sophisticated.

One method of dealing with this problem is through the development of research programs in two or more areas or blocks. The present authors maintain research blocks in the areas of anxiety and impulsiveness. These separate areas permit conducting twice as many investigations with unsophisticated subjects as would otherwise be possible. Requiring experimentally unsophisticated subjects becomes a major concern when any form of treatment is involved since repeated evaluations become necessary.

In selecting areas for the formation of research blocks, certain guidelines should be followed. First, the researchers should select areas which are of equal or near equal personal interest since a proportionate investment of time and effort will be required if they are to be meaningfully developed. Second, each area should be applicable to the population available for investigation. Little is gained by research blocks when a separate population has to be found for each block. Finally, care should be taken to insure that the research areas are in fact independent. This might be accomplished by an initial correlational study to determine the relationship between the measures used in each of the research areas. Thus, through the development of research blocks, the research–clinician can maintain experimentally unsophisticated subjects while continuing to make research progress.

Research Focus

The concluding issue within child psychopathology research that we will consider is the importance of research focus. A failure to develop focus, with careful identification and limitation of the measures to be obtained, probably has been the major cause of the failure to complete many applied research projects. What is being suggested is that, at least in the developing stages of the research program, a limit be set on the number of measures obtained in a given investigation.

Experience has dictated that only one or two new independent or dependent variables be included in any one study. Such an approach helps to insure that researchers have clearly formulated their hypotheses and planned their analyses before data collection begins. The clarity of one's thinking is greatly improved when the number of data entries is within reason.

As one continues to sequence studies and a research program matures, the number of variables investigated in any one study may be increased. Here, the researcher is more familiar with previous research and has developed a conceptualization of the area. However, even in advanced studies within a particular research block, it is better to make portions of the study a replication and introduce only one or two new variables at a time. It is simply too difficult to interpret findings when four or five new variables, about which the researcher knows a limited amount, are introduced simultaneously. The process becomes aversive, and the individual is likely to procrastinate excessively. On the other hand, adopting a strategy or method to one's clinical research efforts requires pacing and, at times, restraint, but such containment keeps the multitude of loose ends within reasonable scope. The methodological research approach that focuses on a target problem is the integral portion of the successful development of clinical research programs.

SUMMARY

In this chapter we have discussed a variety of research methods and strategies for their application to child psychopathology. Each method was described and particular attention was directed toward the advantages and disadvantages of each. In addition, we have urged for the development of research programs using the suggested procedures for the sequencing of studies. Lastly, several related research issues were considered.

REFERENCES

Abramowitz, S. I. (1973). Internal–external control and social–political activism: a test of the dimensionality of Rotter's internal–external scale. *Journal of Consulting and Clinical Psychology* 40:196–201.

Campbell, D. T., and Stanley, J. C. (1963). Experimental and quasi-experimental designs for research and teaching. In N. L. Gage, ed., *Handbook of Research on Teaching.* Chicago: Rand McNally.

Comrey, A. L. (1973). *A first Course in Factor Analysis.* New York: Academic Press.

Edwards, A. L. (1960). *Experimental Designs in Psychological Research* (revised edition). New York: Holt, Rinehart and Winston, Inc.

Finch, A. J., Jr., Anderson, R., and Kendall, P. C. (1976a). Anxiety and digit span performance in emotionally disturbed children. *Journal of Consulting and Clinical Psychology* 44:874.

——, Kendall, P. C., and Montgomery, L. E. (1976b). Qualitative difference in the experience of state-trait anxiety in emotionally disturbed and normal children. *Journal of Personality Assessment* 40:522–531.

Gorsuch, R. L. (1974). *Factor Analysis.* Philadelphia: W. B. Saunders Company.

Hersen, M., and Barlow, D. H. (1976). *Single Case Experimental Designs.* New York: Pergamon.

Kazdin, A. E., and Bootzin, R. R. (1972). The token economy: an evaluative review. *Journal of Applied Behavioral Analysis* 5:343–372.

——, and Kopel, S. A. (1975). On resolving ambiguities of the multiple-baseline design: problems and recommendations. *Behavior Therapy* 6:601–608.

Kendall, P. C. Assessing generalization and the single-subject strategy (in press). *Behavior Therapy.*

——, and Finch, A. J., Jr. (1976). A cognitive-behavioral treatment for impulse control: A case study. *Journal of Consulting and Clinical Psychology* 44:852–857.

——, and Nay, W. R. (1978). Treatment evaluation strategies. In W. R. Nay, *Multimethod Clinical Assessment.* New York: Gardner Press–John Wiley & Sons.

——, Nay, W. R., and Jeffers, J. (1975). Timeout duration and contrast effects: A systematic evaluation of a successive treatments design. *Behavior Therapy* 6:609–615.

——, Finch, A. J., Jr., and Mahoney, J. (1976a). Factor specific differences in locus of control for emotionally disturbed and normal children. *Journal of Personality Assessment* 40:42–45.

——, Finch, A. J., Jr., Mikulka, P. J., and Colson, W. (unpublished manuscript). *Multidimensional assertive behavior: Conceptualization and empirical support.* Richmond, Virginia Commonwealth University.

Kiesler, D. J. (1971). Experimental designs in psychotherapy research. In A. E. Bergin and S. J. Garfield, eds., *Handbook of Psychotherapy and Behavior Change.* New York: Wiley.

Levenson, H. (1973). Multidimensional locus of control in psychiatric patients. *Journal of Consulting and Clinical Psychology* 41:397–404.

O'Leary, K. D., and Kent, R. N. (1973). Behavior modification for social action: research tactics and problems. In L. A. Hamerlynck, P. O. Davidson, and L. E. Acker, eds., *Behavior Therapy: Methodology, Concepts and Procedure.* pp. 69–96. Champaign, Ill.: Research Press.

Ray, W. S. (1962). *Statistics in Psychological Research.* New York: The Macmillan Company.

Watson, J. B., and Rayner, R. (1920). Conditioned emotional reactions. *Journal of Experimental Psychology* 3:1–12.

Webb, E. J., Campbell, D. T., Schwartz, R. D., and Sechrest, L. (1966). *Unobtrusive Measures: Nonreactive Research in the Social Sciences.* Chicago: Rand McNally.

Winer, B. (1971). *Statistical Principles in Experimental Design.* New York: McGraw-Hill.

Wright, H. F. (1960). Observational child study. In P. Mussen, ed., *Handbook of Research Methods in Child Development.* New York: Wiley.

Chapter Two

Success and Failure Implications for Child Psychopathology

THOMAS H. OLLENDICK

Mental health professionals have long been concerned about the effects of success and failure on the young child's development and adjustment. It is evident that young children are confronted by many difficult and seemingly insurmountable situations that are not easily nor readily resolved and that cannot always be met with success. The child's reaction following failure in these situations is related not only to his emotional adjustment and development but also to his ability to learn and to profit by experience (Keister, 1943; Keister and Updegraff, 1937; Zunich, 1964). Responding appropriately in situations involving failure or great difficulty is valued.

The purpose of this chapter is to trace the evolution of the effects of success and failure on personal development and adjustment, to review briefly a representative group of studies concerning success and failure from a social learning framework, and to explore the implications of the effects of success and failure on the development, treatment, and prevention of child psychopathology.

BACKGROUND

Since the early 1900's, when Freud (1917) asserted that failure and its resulting frustration was one of the primary causative factors underlying neurosis, mental health professionals have placed heavy emphasis on failure and frustration in the development of emerging maladaptive behavior. Freud stated: "... people fall ill in consequence of a 'frustration' ... in all cases of neurosis investigated the factor of frustration was demonstrable. You will no doubt have understood that this statement was not intended to reveal the whole secret of the aetiology of the neuroses, but that it merely emphasized an important and indispensable condition" (Freud, 1917, p. 353). It might be added that although Freud placed heavy emphasis on the effects of failure and frustration as causative of neurosis, he also acknowledged the importance of such effects in healthy personality development. His emphasis was, however, on the maladaptive effects. Similarly, Rosenzweig (1938) classified the maladaptive reactions that result from failure and frustration: extrapunitive, intrapunitive, and impunitive. The child who displays an extrapunitive reaction directs his anger and frustration onto some external person or thing while the child who exhibits an intrapunitive reaction attributes the blame to himself. The child who employs an impunitive reaction tends to avoid blame, conceal his anger, or in some other way deny the frustrating aspects of the situation. As with Freud, Rosenzweig emphasized the maladaptive nature of failure and frustration. Other early theorists tended to do likewise. Dollard, Doob, Miller, Mowrer, and Sears (1939) proposed that frustration following a failure experience resulted in aggression. Aggressive behavior as a result of frustration is observed in simple animal learning experiments. Experimenters who have trained animals to run in a straight runway and then have withheld reward during a period of extinction have noted that the animals exhibit aggressive and destructive behavior toward the runway and other pieces of the apparatus. The behavior of children is not too different. When subjected to frustration and failure, certain children are observed biting, hitting, kicking, and exhibiting other acting-out aggressive behaviors.

Still another early theory concerned with a specific maladaptive response pattern to frustration was proposed by Barker, Dembo, and Lewin (1943). These theorists proposed that frustration leads to behavior that indicates the occurrence of regression. These investigators subjected children of preschool age to "quite severe frustration." The children were first rated in terms of the maturity of their play in a small group with some toys of average appeal. They were then allowed to enter another area in which more interesting toys were present (newer toys). After a period of exposure to the more desirable toys, the children were removed from that area and separated from it by a wire screen. The constructiveness of play with the original toys was then rated again. Most of the children became disorganized, showed disturbances in their play, and became apathetic and generally restless. The rated maturity of constructiveness of play with the original toys following frustration was significantly lower when compared to the earlier ratings. Regression is also quite evident outside the laboratory setting. Childish attitudes and responses are frequent when failure experiences reach a certain intensity. Pouting, complaining, and reverting to earlier modes of behavior are typical responses to such experiences. Another clinically maladaptive reaction resulting from frustration and failure is response fixation (Maier, 1956). Maier contended that when an organism is sufficiently frustrated, problem-solving capacities are lost and instead a rigid or stereotyped pattern of responding is adopted. Maier stated that a frustrated person's behavior is aimless and without a goal. Outside the laboratory, fixative behaviors are manifested in compulsive actions, repetitious behaviors, and superstitions.

A still more recent theory concerned with the maladaptive response patterns of frustration and failure is that of Selye (1956). So far we have dealt primarily with specific maladaptive responses in well-defined situations. But the human condition also contains situations in which stress is both drastic and prolonged. For example, exposure to serious illness, prolonged failure experiences, and sickness of a parent are all conditions which place a child under severe strain. Selye has studied situations involving prolonged stress and strain. He has subjected various laboratory animals to many kinds of stress, including exposure to cold and the injection of poisons. What invariably happens is that certain physiological reactions occur which allow the organism to adjust to its situation. However, this recovery is only temporary, for after several weeks of this intensive stress the animal dies of exhaustion. Selye has termed this sequence of events the *general adaptation syndrome*: initial alarm at stress, recovery or resistance, and, at last, exhaustion and death. In addition to his findings involving prolonged stress, Seyle found that if during the period of prolonged stress an organism is exposed to another stressful situation, the animal quickly dies. It appears that in attempting to adapt to the original stress, the animal becomes helpless against a second form of stress. Certainly the effects of frustration and failure are drastically implicated in this system.

In these early theoretical views of failure and frustration, emphasis was placed on the negative aspects of these experiences. McCandless (1967) cautioned against this typical connotation of failure and frustration as "bad." He suggested that failure and frustration are neither "good" nor "bad," they simply exist. What early theorists probably meant by "failure is bad" was that frequent and prolonged failure experiences are damaging to personal development and adjustment. More moderate experiences might be facilitative.

Unlike the early formulations, recent approaches to failure and frustration have not focused on specific reaction patterns analogous to clinically maladaptive behavior. Rather, more emphasis has been placed on delineating the motivational and response-directing properties of failure and frustration. These new emphases allow for adaptive as well as maladaptive reactions. Representative of these contemporary approaches are Amsel's (1958) frustrative-nonreward theory and Ferster and Skinner's (1957) schedules of reinforcement, especially partial-reinforcement schedules. While it is not within the scope of this paper to critically review these positions, the implications are clear. The frustrative-nonreward theory (see Endsley, 1967, for a review of this theory with children) predicts that failure to receive an expected reward is frustrating and that the arousal of a frustrative reaction invigorates or motivates subsequent behavior. In nonreward frustration, learning occurs in the presence of both failure and success. Under partial reinforcement, learning occurs under similar conditions. Since learning occurs in the presence of such frustration-produced cues (some responses reinforced, others not), when extinction trials are begun the child is already familiar with failure (nonreward) and its frustrating consequences. It seems that this unpleasant but educating experience enables the child to endure greater failure and more frustration in the extinction stage (Deese and Hulse, 1967). The continuously successful child, on the other hand, has never experienced frustration associated with a failure response and his behavior rapidly extinguishes.

Other representative approaches concerned with the motivating effects of failure are Atkinson's (1953) achievement motivation theory and White's (1959) competence motivation theory. Achievement motivation theory predicts differential effects of success and failure depending upon the general level of need for achievement in the individual. Atkinson postulated three variables in determining behavior potential. Tendency to perform a certain behavior is directly related to motive × incentive × expectancy. Motive refers to a general disposition to strive for success (Ms) when confronted with a subjective probability of success (Ps) for the task in question, and the incentive value (Is) of the task is assumed to equal $1 - Ps$. Incentive value is defined in this fashion so as to capture the idea that more shame is experienced when failing at an easy task than when failing at a difficult task, and that more pride is experienced when succeeding at a difficult task than when succeeding at an easy task. Because incentive and subjective probability of success are reciprocally related, the maximum absolute value for incentive $\times$ probability occurs when $Ps = 0.50$. In that condition $Ps \times Is = 0.25$; for any other value of Ps the product of incentive $\times$ probability must be below that numerical value. In Atkinson's model, need for achievement is viewed as motive (Ms), and experimentally manipulated success and failure is viewed as subjective expectancy (Ps). Success or failure on a task may change its attractiveness because subjective probability of success for the task is thereby altered. Thus, if a low need for achievement individual came into a situation expecting failure (low Ps) but was to succeed on the task, Ps should increase and move toward 0.50. Also, if a high need for achievement individual came into a situation expecting success (high Ps), but was to fail on the task, Ps for the task should decrease and move closer to 0.50. On the other hand, success on the task by the high need for achievement person should widen the gap between Ps for the task and the 0.50 value. Failure on the task by the low need for achievement person would have a similar effect. Atkinson would maintain that with experimental failure for success-oriented individuals their performance would increase and that with experimental success for low success-oriented individuals their performance would increase. This is so since optimal behavior is obtained when the Ps value is near 0.50. On the other hand, he would predict that with experimental success for high success-oriented individuals and with experimental failure for low success-oriented individuals performance would decrease. This is so since the Ps values for these groups are further away from the Ps value of 0.50. In reviewing research emanating from achievement motivation theory, Weiner (1967) concluded that while failure experiences dampen the performance of children low in achievement motivation the performance of those high in achievement motivation is enhanced. In discussing a similar theory regarding competence motivation, Hunt (1969, p. 39) stated: "... persistent or courageous competence motivation probably derives from experiences of success intermixed with an increasing proportion of failures and from success won only at the expense of prolonged effort." Thus, achievement motivation, competence motivation, frustrative-nonreward, and partial schedules of reinforcement all assign a motivating or invigorating force to failure experiences. Failure, as McCandless (1967) suggested, is neither "good" nor "bad."

SOCIAL LEARNING APPROACH

Social learning theory (Rotter, 1954; Rotter *et al.*, 1972) is one theory by which an attempt can be made to integrate the varied effects of success and failure experiences and to explore their implications for child psychopathology in a systematic fashion. Rotter states that "the unit of investigation for the study of personality is the interaction of the individual and his meaningful environment" (1954, p. 85) and that this interaction, "as described by personality constructs, has a directional aspect" (1954, p. 97). Such a statement stresses the importance of goal directed behavior in a specific situation or environment. Goal directed behavior is inferred from the reinforcing qualities of the goal; people strive to attain or to avoid certain aspects of their environment. Finally, Rotter postulates that "the occurrence of a behavior of a person is determined not only by the nature or importance of goals or reinforcements but also by the person's anticipation or expectancy that these goals will occur" (1954, p. 102). To determine what behavior will occur, the psychological situation, the reinforcement value of the goal to be achieved for that behavior, and the expectancy of attaining that reinforcement must all be considered. The major working formula states that the potential for a behavior to occur in a specific situation is a function of the reinforcement to occur following that behavior. Put in general form, the potential for a certain behavior is highest when both reinforcement value and expectancy are high. Expectancy is considered to be a function of situational expectancy (developed as a function of the success and failure experiences in the specific situation) and generalized expectancy (developed from successes and failures in other situations and generalized to the present one) (Rotter, 1954, pp. 165–168). In novel situations, generalized expectancy is more important since the person has no gauge of the specifics required; he relies on generalized expectancies derived from other experiences. Once experience is obtained, the importance of generalized expectancy diminishes and specific expectancies for that situation assume primary importance. In recent advances of social-learning theory, Rotter, Chance, and Phares (1972) have suggested that a set of problem solving generalized expectancies be included in the derivation of overall expectancy level. Locus of control (Lefcourt, 1976; Phares, 1976; Rotter, 1966, 1975, see also Chapter four) is postulated as one such problem-solving generalized expectancy. Other constructs such as achievement motivation and competence motivation appear to be related as well. The magnitude of generalized expectancy is determined by a past history of success and failure experiences in similar situations.

Phares states: "Successful past experience with a given behavior will lead one to expect that it will work in the future. Failure will decrease the individual expectancy that the behavior will achieve a given goal. Expectancies for the outcomes of behaviors are learned, and they depend upon the degree of success or failure that they have enjoyed in the past" (1976, p. 13). As with generalized expectancies, situational expectancies are learned but accrued within a given situation.

The implications of social learning theory for the effects of success and failure on child psychopathology are evident. A history of success or failure affects the development of both generalized expectancies for goal attainment and specific problem-solving generalized expectancies such as locus of control. Further, success or failure, in a specific situation determines situational expectancies for that situation. Response to success and failure, thus, is determined by the interaction of the generalized expectancies (for goal attainment and problem solving), and the specific, situational expectancies. The psychological situation and the reinforcement value are also important determiners of response to success and failure but their roles have been less researched (Phares, 1957, 1971), especially with children. The remainder of this paper considers the effects of expectations of success and failure on behavior, acknowledging that prediction of behavior potential would be considerably more accurate were the effects of the psychological situation and reinforcement value also systematically included.

Expectancy of success and failure exerts a powerful role on the child's motivation to attempt a variety of tasks and can be observed in children as early as 2 years of age (Mussen et al., 1974). That young children are capable of conceptualizing success and failure experiences (Bialer, 1961) and attributing them to their own actions versus others is attested to by a plethora of early childhood locus of control scales (Battle and Rotter, 1963; Crandall et al., 1965; Mischel et al., 1974; Nowicki and Duke, 1974; Stephens and Delys, 1973). Such scales are reported to reliably and validly assess the child's awareness and attribution of responsibility for behavior (for further discussion see Chapter Four).

That generalized expectancies (accrued from a history of success and failure experiences) and situational expectancies (accrued from success and failure experiences in a specific situation) affect performance is illustrated by a series of studies conducted by Stevenson and Zigler and their colleagues. Utilizing a discrimination learning task, Stevenson and Zigler (1958) reported that retarded children performed poorer than nonretarded children of the same mental age. They reasoned that the greater failure experiences of retarded children caused them to have relatively low generalized expectancies of success and a greater willingness to settle for low levels of goal attainment. These authors also experimentally induced success and failure experiences in a group of normal children through a series of pretraining tasks characterized by either continuous success (100%) or partial success (33%). Those experiencing more success (leading to a heightened situational expectancy for success) performed at a higher level, being less willing to settle for a low level of success. Using this same task, Gruen and Zigler (1968) found that lower class and retarded children (both characterized by low generalized expectancies for success) were willing to settle for lower levels of success than were middle class children of comparable mental age. The findings for retarded children replicated those of Stevenson and Zigler (1958) while the findings for social class replicated earlier results of Odum (1967). Gruen and Zigler (1968) also experimentally induced success and failure in their lower class, middle class, and in retarded children through pretraining tasks of a high degree of success (90%) or low degree of success (10%). These manipulations did not alter the subsequent performance of the lower class and retarded children but did alter that of the middle class children. These findings were interpreted to mean that, unlike the middle class children, the lower class and retarded children have such entrenched attitudes and expectancies that short term experimental manipulations of success and failure have little effect on their performance. Findings for the middle class children were consonant with those of Stevenson and Zigler (1958)—success in the situation led to a heightened situational expectancy while failure led to a diminished expectancy. Ollendick and Gruen (1971) found that middle class underachievers in school settings were willing to settle for a lower level of success than were their counterparts of similar mental age who were performing up to expectation. In fact, the performance of academic underachievers was similar to those of the lower class and retarded children of Gruen and Zigler (1968). Similar findings were reported by Kier and Zigler (1975). Postulating that intense success and failure experiences would alter the situational expectancies of retarded children, Ollendick, Balla, and Zigler (1971) experimentally induced continuous success or continuous failure in retarded children. Success or failure was administered over three consecutive days and across three different experimental tasks. Children in the success condition were profusely praised and told "That's good" or "You really know how to do this." Children in the failure condition were highly criticized. They received nonverbal criticism in the form of frowns and head shakes during the tasks and verbal statements such as "You're not very good at this" and "You aren't getting any right." Indeed, when the experiences were sufficiently intense, success experiences raised situational expectancy while failure experiences lowered it. The performance of the success-engendered group approached that of middle class children observed in other studies while the failure-induced group's performance was lowered below that previously observed on this task. Finally, utilizing this same discrimination learning task, Gruen, Ottinger, and Ollendick (1975) examined the performance of retarded children routinely experiencing quite differing degrees of success in school. One group of retarded children had been enrolled in special education classes where an effort had been made to provide the children with a high number of successful learning experiences. This was achieved by reducing the difficulty of schoolwork and by giving profuse praise for their learning efforts. A second group of retarded children remained in the regular classroom, had failed at least one grade, and experienced much more failure. A group of nonretarded children of the same mental age was also included for comparative purposes. Results supported the social learning hypothesis: retarded children remaining in the regular classroom evidenced lower levels of expectancy of success than did either the retarded children in the special classroom or the normal children of the same mental age who did not differ in their levels of expectancy of success. Additionally, internal locus of control as measured by the Bialer (1961) scale was predictive of a high expectancy of success on this task. In summary, the history of success and failure experiences (generalized expectancy) and interpolated success and failure experiences (situational expectancy) affect performance on this task in line with the predictions of social learning theory.

Cromwell (1963) has summarized studies that have also demonstrated the utility of social learning theory in predicting the response to success and failure of retarded and nonretarded children on a variety of other tasks. It was hypothesized by Heber (1957, cited in Cromwell) that when predominant success experience occurs the retarded child would make greater initial gains in performance than the intellectually normal child. It was expected that the retarded child, possessing a low generalized expectancy, would be more affected by the novel success experience and increase his expectancy of success in that situation. The intellectually normal child, possessing a relatively higher generalized expectancy, would be expecting success and consequently, be less affected by the success experience. As predicted, the increment from initial to final performance on a simple reaction-time task for the retarded group, under the success condition, was greater than the increment for the intellectually normal group. Conversely, under failure conditions, Gardner (1958, cited in Cromwell) predicted that the absolute magnitude of change would be greater for normal children than retarded ones and that the normal children would more often increase in performance after the failure. Gardner assumed that the magnitude of failure was a function of the discrepancy between generalized expectancy and the actual failure outcome. This meant that if a generalized expectancy for success was high, the magnitude of failure experienced was high. If generalized expectancy was low, the failure was of less magnitude. Gardner also assumed that the normal children possessed a type of problem-solving generalized expectancy characterized by "If I try harder, I might succeed." The retarded child, due to limited ability and a history of failure, more likely possessed a problem-solving generalized expectancy of "I'll fail anyway." As expected, the normal group showed a greater absolute magnitude of change on a card sorting task than did the retarded group after failure, even though both groups tended to increase their performance following failure. Additionally, more normal children than retarded children increased their performance following failure, supporting the second part of Gardner's hypothesis. The implications of these two studies are relatively straightforward. Success experiences are more likely to enhance the subsequent performance of children low in generalized expectancy while failure experiences are more likely to enhance the performance of children high in generalized expectancy. It should be recalled that at least two conditions are necessary for these effects to be observed: (1) the child must be capable of conceptualizing the success or failure experience (Bialer, 1961), and (2) the success or failure experience must be of sufficient intensity (Ollendick et al., 1971). These findings and predictions from social learning theory are notably similar to those ascribed to achievement motivation theory (Atkinson, 1953) and competence motivation theory (White, 1959).

Two final studies will be examined to illustrate the utility of social learning theory in understanding the effects of success and failure experience. Ollendick (1974) employed the social learning construct of a generalized expectancy of success to predict persistence behavior. In this study, normal children assessed to be either high or low in generalized expectancy of success (as assessed by locus of control and achievement) were administered an extremely difficult but soluble task. What happens to a child who expects success and to a child who expects failure when faced with difficulty and probable failure? Social learning theory predicts that the generalized expectancy interacts with the situational expectancy to determine the degree of persistence. The child with the high generalized expectancy of success should persist in the face of failure for a longer time than the child with a low generalized expectancy for success.

Indeed, such results were found. In fact, the high expectancy of success child persisted nearly twice as long as the low expectancy of success child. Finally, Ollendick (1976) investigated the persistence behavior of normal children varying in levels of expectancy of success following induced success and failure. Eighty children were divided into either high or low generalized expectancy of success groups and then randomly assigned to one of four success–failure conditions: 100% success–0% failure; 67% success–33% failure; 33% success–67% failure; and 0% success–100% failure. Specific expectancies for success or failure were experimentally induced on three tasks preceding the criterion persistence task. Instructions for the tasks stressed excellence of performance, personal satisfaction in effort, and that successful performance would be rewarded (a dime for each of three tasks). Children in success conditions were allowed to succeed at the designated tasks and told "That's good ... You got that one ... You are really good at this and you deserve the dime since you tried so hard and did so well." Children in the failure conditions were interrupted prior to successful task completion and told "Time is up on that one ... You didn't get it right ... You aren't very good at this and you don't deserve the dime for your performance ... You must try harder after this." Results revealed significant effects for the success–failure manipulations and for the interaction of generalized expectancy and the success–failure manipulations. A trend of significance was noted for the effect of high versus low generalized expectancy. For the high expectancy group, the failure conditions (33% success–67% failure, and 0% success–100% failure) produced significantly greater persistence behavior than did the success conditions (67% success–33% failure, 100% success–0% failure). Further analysis revealed the 33% success–67% failure condition to produce significantly greater persistence than the other three conditions. On the other hand, for the low expectancy group, the success conditions (100% success–0% failure, 67% success–33% failure) produced significantly greater persistence behavior than did the failure conditions (33% success–67% failure, 0% success–100% failure). Further analysis revealed the 67% success–33% failure condition to produce significantly greater persistence than the other three conditions. Results of these two studies are consistent and supportive of previously cited findings. High expectancy of success children persist longer, endure the frustrating consequences of failure, and in fact, become more motivated following such failure experience. Low expectancy of success children, on the other hand, persist less, become agitated with the frustrating consequences of failure, and become less motivated and resigned to failure in the face of difficulty.

IMPLICATIONS FOR CHILD PSYCHOPATHOLOGY

The findings regarding the utility of social learning theory in understanding the effects of success and failure experiences are consistent. Across a range of tasks and across a variety of children the results indicate that situational success and failure experiences differentially affect children depending upon their level of generalized expectancy for success or failure. Further, in that these generalized expectancies are determined by histories of success or failure experiences as suggested by Phares (1976), the role of such events in the young child's development and adjustment takes on increasing importance.

The implications of this brief review of the effects of success and failure experiences for child psychopathology are intriguing. Is success good or bad? Is failure good or bad? As McCandless (1967) has suggested, viewing these experiences in such connotative terms is delimiting. Early theorists assigned a clinically maladaptive role to failure and frustration experiences; contemporary theorists have assigned a motivating or invigorating role. The present review suggests a combination. The effects of these experiences are dependent upon the child and his prior history of success and failure experiences. Generalized expectancies of success, determined largely by the child's psychosocial history, interact with situational success and failure experiences to determine subsequent performance.

At the onset, it was stated that mental health professionals have maintained an enduring concern over the child's typical response to frustration and failure. It was further noted that such reactions were related not only to a child's emotional development and adjustment but also to his ability to profit from experience. Clearly, modern day living is replete with a variety of failure and frustrating experiences. How might we best prepare a child for these experiences so that he might avoid the debilitating effects of either unrealistically high or low expectancies of success which result in childhood adjustment problems? The overall model which is proposed is a variant of an "immunity to disease" model. Within this model, heightened tolerance to stress is viewed as developing through progressively greater exposure to frustrating events associated with failure experiences. Tolerance is fostered by allowing the child to experience small amounts of failure, in doses which can be assimilated without undue negative reaction. This, of course, would be dependent upon the conceptual maturity of the child and would progress along the lines indicated by Hunt (1969) for competence motivation and would employ partial schedules of reinforcement. The child would meet with more success initially and then be gradually introduced to failure experiences. In fact, as early as 1937, Keister and Updegraff suggested a similar method of training to ameliorate a child's unhealthy reaction to failure. They state "The tasks should be graded in difficulty so that the child experiences success in the earlier ones and gradually works up to problems which are difficult for him. The later tasks must be of such difficulty that the child does not succeed immediately but is forced to persevere, to continue to try if he is to attain success. The child must be able to see progress and previous success" (1937, p. 245).

The optimal amount of success and failure to be experienced is an empirical question and awaits additional research. The theoretical views presented by Hunt (1969) and Weiner (1967) and the empirical research of Ollendick (1976) represent initial attempts to explore such parameters for children already possessing fixed histories of success and failure experiences. Research on young children not yet possessing clear histories of success and failure is lacking. Due to ethical reasons, it may be that such investigations examine animal behavior to establish such parameters. Certainly the work of Denenberg (1964) is suggestive. He has established that mild forms of noxious stimulation during the infancy of animals results in less exaggerated emotional reactions during stress in adulthood. Might not the same be true for children?

While the foregoing is somewhat speculative, certain facts remain. Success and failure experiences are of importance to the developing child and result in different levels of expectancies. Such expectancies affect performance and help determine responses to new success and failure experiences. The implications of these experiences for the development, treatment, and perhaps, prevention of child psychopathology, are intriguing.

REFERENCES

Amsel, A. (1958). The role of frustrative nonreward in noncontinuous reward situations. *Psychological Bulletin* 55:102–119.

Atkinson, J. W. (1953). The achievement motive and recall of interrupted and completed tasks. *Journal of Experimental Psychology* 46:381–390.

Barker, R. G., Dembo, T., and Lewin, K. (1943). Frustration and regression: an experiment with young children. In R. G. Barker, J. S. Kounin, and H. F. Wright, eds., *Child Behavior and Development*. New York: McGraw-Hill.

Battle, I., and Rotter, J. B. (1963). Children's feelings of personal control as related to social class and ethnic group. *Journal of Personality* 31:482–490.

Bialer, I. (1961). Conceptualization of success and failure in mentally retarded and normal children. *Journal of Personality* 29:303–320.

Crandall, V. C., Katkovsky, W., and Crandall, V. J. (1965). Children's belief in their own control of reinforcements in intellectual–academic achievement situations. *Child Development* 36:91–109.

Cromwell, R. (1963). A social learning approach to mental retardation. In N. R. Ellis, ed., *Handbook of Mental Deficiency*. New York: McGraw-Hill. pp. 41–91.

Deese, J., and Hulse, S. (1967). *The psychology of learning*. New York: McGraw-Hill.

Denenberg, V. A. (1964). Critical periods, stimulus input, and emotional reactivity: a theory of infantile stimulation. *Psychological Review* 71:235–351.

Dollard, J., Doob, L. W., Miller, N. E., Mowrer, O. H., and Sears, R. R. (1939). *Frustration and aggression*. New Haven: Yale University Press.

Endsley, R. C. (1967). Determinants of frustration and its motivational consequences in young children. In W. W. Hartup and N. L. Smothergill, eds., *The young child*. Washington, D.C.: National Association for the Education of Young Children.

Ferster, C. G., and Skinner, B. F. (1957). *Schedules of reinforcement*. New York: Appleton-Century-Crofts.

Freud, S. (1917). *Introduction to psychoanalysis*. New York: Washington Square Press.

Gardner, W. I. (1958). Reactions of intellectually normal and retarded boys after experimentally induced failure. Unpublished doctoral dissertation, George Peabody College for Teachers.

Gruen, G. E., and Zigler, E. (1968). Expectancy of success and the probability learning of middle-class, lower-class, and retarded children. *Journal of Abnormal Psychology* 73:343–352.

——, Ottinger, D. R., and Ollendick, T. H. (1975). Probability learning in retarded children with differing histories of success and failure in school. *American Journal of Mental Deficiency* 79:417–423.

Heber, R. F. (1957). Expectancy and expectancy changes in normal and mentally retarded boys. Unpublished doctoral dissertation, George Peabody College for Teachers. Nashville, Tenn.

Hunt, J. McV. (1969). The impact and limitations of the giant of developmental psychology. In D. Elkind and J. H. Flavell, eds., *Studies in Cognitive Development*. New York: Oxford University Press.

Keister, M. E. (1943). The behavior of young children in failure. In R. G. Barker, J. S. Kounin, and H. E. Wright, eds., *Child Behavior and Development*. New York: McGraw-Hill.

——, and Updegraff, R. (1937). A study of children's reactions to failure and an experimental attempt to modify them. *Child Development* 8:241–248.

Kier, R. J., and Zigler, E. (1975). Success expectancies and the probability learning of children of low and middle socioeconomic class. Unpublished manuscript, New Haven: Yale University.

Lefcourt, H. M. (1976) *Locus of Control: Current Trends in Theory and Research*. Hillsdale, New Jersey: Lawrence Erlbaum Associates.

Maier, N. R. F. (1956). Frustration theory: restatement and extension. *Psychological Review* 63:370–388.

McCandless, B. R. (1967). *Children: Behavior and Development*. New York: Holt, Rinehart, and Winston.

Mischel, W., Zeiss, R., and Zeiss, A. (1974). Internal-external control and persistence: validation and implications of the Stanford Preschool internal–external scale. *Journal of Personality and Social Psychology* 29:265–278.

Mussen, P. H., Conger J. J., and Kagan, J. (1974). *Child Development and Personality*. New York: Harper & Row.

Nowicki, S., and Duke, M. P. (1974). A preschool and primary internal-external control scale. *Developmental Psychology* 10:874–880.

Odum, R. D. (1967). Problem-solving strategies as a function of age and socioeconomic level. *Child Development* 38:747–752.

Ollendick, T. H. (1974). Level of *n* achievement and persistence behavior in children. *Developmental Psychology* 10:457.

—— (1976). Success and Failure Experiences. Unpublished manuscript, Indiana State University. Terre Haute, Indiana.

——, Balla, D., and Zigler, E. (1971). Expectancy of success and the probability learning performance of retarded children. *Journal of Abnormal Psychology* 77:275–281.

——, and Gruen, G. E. (1971). Level of *n* achievement and probability learning in children. *Developmental Psychology* 4:486.

Phares, E. J. (1957). Expectancy changes in skill and chance situations. *Journal of Abnormal and Social Psychology* 54:339–342.

—— (1971). Internal-external control and the reduction of reinforcement value after failure. *Journal of Consulting and Clinical Psychology* 37:386–390.

—— (1976). *Locus of Control: A Personality Determinant of Behavior*. Morristown, New Jersey: General Learning Press.

Rosenzweig, S. (1938). A general outline of frustration. *Character and Personality* 1:151–160.

Rotter, J. B. (1954). *Social Learning and Clinical Psychology*. Englewood Cliffs, New Jersey: Prentice-Hall.

—— (1966). Generalized expectancies for internal versus external control of reinforcement. *Psychological Monographs* 80: (1, whole No. 609).

——, Chance, J. E., and Phares, E. J. (1972). *Applications of a Social Learning Theory of Personality*. New York: Holt, Rinehart, & Winston.

—— (1975). Some problems and misconceptions related to the construct of internal versus external control of reinforcement. *Journal of Consulting and Clinical Psychology* 43:56–67.

Selye, H. (1956). *The Stress of Life*. New York: McGraw-Hill Book Company.

Stephens, M. W., and Delys, P. (1973). A locus of control measure for preschool children. *Developmental Psychology* 9:55–65.

Stevenson, H. W., and Zigler, E. (1958). Probability learning in children. *Journal of Experimental Psychology* 56:185–192.

Weiner, B. (1967). Implications of the current theory of achievement motivation for research and performance in the classroom. *Psychology in the Schools* 4:165–172.

White, R. W. (1959). Motivation reconsidered: the concept of competence. *Psychological Review* 66:297–333.

Zunich, M. (1964). Children's reactions to failure. *Journal of Genetic Psychology* 104:19–24.

Chapter Three

The Measurement of Anxiety in Children: Research Findings and Methodological Problems

A. J. FINCH, JR. and PHILIP C. KENDALL

Many adults view childhood as a carefree time in which the child is engaged in endless play and pretend activities without any responsibility or worry. However, those professionals who come in contact with the casualties of this period know that all is not as it might initially appear. Children have many of the same anxieties, worries, doubts, and fears as do adults, although these feelings may be manifest in different ways. Whereas adults are frequently able to label what it is that is bothering them and are therefore in a better position to deal with their problems, children generally lack the verbal skills and self-awareness necessary to identify and label areas of concern. Consequently much of their behavior is difficult to understand and we must infer more than is frequently necessary with adults.

From a research point of view, children are both a welcome relief and a nightmare. Children generally enjoy the attention of adults and consequently enjoy participating in research projects. On the other hand, standardized instructions are almost impossible if one is to insure that each child understands what is expected. Furthermore, children are in a stage of constant change which makes it necessary to move quickly if we are to learn about how they are rather than about how they were.

The present chapter deals with children and the anxiety they experience. As its title reflects, we will focus on both our empirical findings and on the problems we have experienced in our attempts to learn about this emotion in children. Before our work began and at some point in the future we would and possibly will see things differently. However, at this point in time we must include a focus on our problems. Our 4-year program of research into anxiety in children will be reviewed and our "insights" discussed, but our "problems" will be detailed since they have emerged as our unexpected leading characters. Despite this unexpected fact, we feel we know much more than we did and have faith that our persistence will continue to provide us with additional information in this area.

HISTORICAL BACKGROUND

Although the word "anxiety" is of relative recent usage, the general feeling of uneasiness and dread associated with the emotion has been discussed for centuries. McReynolds (1975) states that although man has probably always experienced anxiety, the development of the *concept* of anxiety did not emerge until the classical Greek era. Similarly, although the concept of anxiety has existed for years, it was not until the late nineteenth and early twentieth century that role of anxiety in emotional disturbance began to be emphasized. Even then the early mention of anxiety in humans was primarily in clinical usage and it was not until the 1950's that research with humans began to focus on the problem of anxiety. One of the main reasons for this was a lack of objective measurement instruments, and it was not until Taylor's (1953) Manifest Anxiety Scale was introduced that the body of research with anxiety began to develop. Later, the Children's Manifest Anxiety Scale (CMAS) was introduced by Castaneda, McCandless, and Palermo (1956) and research into the nature and effects of anxiety on children began. Gradually a number of anxiety scales for children were developed.

RESEARCH PROGRAM

We became interested in anxiety in children through our clinical work with emotionally disturbed youngsters. It became evident to us that we talked about our children being "anxious," "nervous," and/or "tense" without data to support the use of these terms or an adequate understanding of what the terms meant. Since we were attempting to establish an empirical and scientific base for our treatment and research with children, we began our search for useful measurement instruments for the assessment of anxiety in children.

Reliability

After examining several available anxiety scales for children we selected the Children's Manifest Anxiety Scale (CMAS) developed by Castaneda, McCandless, and Palermo (1956) as having the most potential to meet our needs. Its reliability was well established with normal children but there was limited information available with emotionally disturbed children. Since we felt that it would be necessary to demonstrate reliability with this population before we could employ the CMAS with any degree of confidence, our first study (Finch et al., 1974b) was designed. Thirty emotionally disturbed youngsters in residential treatment were individually administered the CMAS at the beginning and end of a 3-month period. An individual administration was felt to be necessary since many of our children had academic problems which would interfere with their responses. This procedure has been employed in all of our research with emotionally disturbed subjects. For the anxiety and for the Lie-scale of the CMAS the correlation between the two administrations was good and the mean values did not differ significantly, thus, suggesting that the CMAS was a reliable measure with this population.

Approximately half-way through our reliability study with the CMAS, the State-Trait Anxiety Inventory for Children (STAIC) was introduced by Spielberger (1973). This inventory was developed as a research tool for the study of anxiety in elementary school children. In addition the STAIC contained a 20-item scale (A-Trait) designed to measure the relatively stable predisposition to experience anxiety states as well as a 20-item scale (A-State) designed to measure the momentary variations in anxiety. Reliability and validity data with normal children were good (see Spielberger, 1973).

Since we felt that the conceptualization of anxiety as having an A-State and A-Trait component was a useful one, it was decided to add it to our research program. Since data were not available with emotionally disturbed children our first study with the STAIC was an investigation of its reliability. Again 30 emotionally disturbed children were tested at the beginning and end of a 3-month period. The obtained reliabilities were lower than those obtained by Spielberger (1973) with normal children. In addition, the test–retest reliability of the A-State was higher than that for the A-Trait which also was in disagreement with the relationship found with normals. Measures of internal consistency were good. It was suggested that emotionally disturbed children probably maintain relatively high levels of A-State anxiety which would account for the high test–retest reliability of the A-State scale. In other words, since emotionally disturbed children are more likely to be experiencing elevated anxiety at any given moment, one would expect their scores to be consistently elevated on the A-State and, thus, the high test–retest reliability of that portion of the STAIC.

Validity

After these preliminary studies we were reasonably pleased with the reliability of the CMAS and to a lesser extent the STAIC. Our attention was directed at the problem of validity. How was the validity of these scales to be determined? At that point we felt that a demonstration of the ability of the CMAS and STAIC to differentiate between emotionally disturbed and normal children would provide us with an indication of their validity since as a group the disturbed children would be expected to be more anxious. Montgomery and Finch (1974) administered the CMAS and the STAIC to 60 emotionally disturbed children and 60 normals who were matched on mental age. It was found that the disturbed group obtained significantly higher scores on both the A-State and A-Trait portions of the STAIC and on the anxiety portion of the CMAS while the normal group obtained a higher L-scale score (this is an 11 item scale similar to the L-scale on the MMPI).

Further along this line, it was thought to be useful to determine the utility of these scales to correctly differentiate the emotionally disturbed youngster from the normal one by establishing cut-off scores for the CMAS, A-State, and A-Trait scales. In addition, a combined STAIC score also was employed. These scores resulted in Montgomery and Finch (1974) being able to identify correctly 62% of the disturbed group with the CMAS, 65% with the A-State, 63% with the A-Trait, and 65% with the combined STAIC score. Misclassifications of 33%, 29%, 37%, and 35%, respectively, were obtained with normals. Despite the degree of overlap of scores of the two groups, the authors interpreted their results as demonstrating the validity of the CMAS and STAIC since one would not expect every emotionally disturbed child to be more anxious than every normal child because anxiety is only one of a number of variables which may contribute to a child being labeled emotionally disturbed.

The results of the Montgomery and Finch (1974) study supported the validity of the CMAS and STAIC in general, but the validity of the STAIC A-State and A-Trait scales in particular are dependent also on the ability of the A-State to reflect momentary changes in anxiety while the A-Trait remains relatively constant. Sitarz (Note 1), in thinking about how to assess such validity, reasoned that psychological testing should serve as a sufficient stressor to produce increases in state anxiety but that it should not affect A-Trait and therefore provide a test of the validity of the A-State and A-Trait scales. She reasoned further that the degree of structure of the test and whether or not the examiner was present would result in differing degrees of state anxiety change. Employing 30 emotionally disturbed youngsters she found that under all conditions A-State remained constant while A-Trait increased during an unstructured test with the examiner present. Her results were in marked contrast to those obtained by Newmark, Wheeler, Newmark, and Stabler (1975) who found with a group of normal children increases in A-State anxiety in response to psychological testing but no change in A-Trait. Sitarz (Note 1) concluded that the emotionally disturbed children may have had difficulty conceptualizing anxiety in the manner required by the STAIC. More specifically, the STAIC instructions require distinguishing between feelings *now* (A-State) and feelings *in general* (A-Trait). Another consideration was that the emotionally disturbed children might differ from normals in their experiencing of anxiety.

Since some question was raised about the ability of the STAIC A-State scale to reflect changes in momentary anxiety while the A-Trait remained constant with emotionally disturbed children, Finch, Kendall, Montgomery, and Morris (1975) further investigated the sensitivity of these scales, in this case to changes in anxiety associated with a failure experience. They assigned 36 emotionally disturbed children to either a failure group, a failure plus ego-involving instructions group, or a test–retest control group. Finch *et al.* (1975) hypothesized that increases in A-State anxiety would be associated with both the failure and the failure plus ego-involving instructions experiences but not with the test–retest group. In addition it was expected that A-Trait would be expected to remain constant for all groups according to State-Trait theory (see Spielberger, 1972). The children's task was a series of anagrams ranging from very difficult to impossible. This task resulted in a significant increase in *both* A-State and A-Trait anxiety for *all* three groups with the most increase associated with the failure plus ego-involving instructions, followed by the failure condition, and finally by the control group. While these results were entirely unexpected, two possible explanations for the observed outcome were considered. First, it is possible that emotionally disturbed children were unable to discriminate between state and trait anxiety because their feeling at any given moment (A-State) superceded their previous history of feelings (A-Trait) resulting in both state and trait anxiety being vulnerable to situational stress. This explanation is at least partially consistent with drive theory (Spielberger, 1966), since the disturbed children are more anxious and since drive theory suggests that under high drive fine discriminations are more difficult.

The second possible explanation offered by Finch *et al.* (1975) was that traits, including A-Trait anxiety, are not firmly established in emotionally disturbed children. A number of studies have reported differences between disturbed populations and normal ones on developmental tasks and it may be that the personality development of this group is more fluid and less static than would be expected in normal development.

Noting the inconsistencies in the results obtained in the studies noted above, Finch, Kendall, Dannenburg, and Morgan (in press) investigated the effects of task difficulty with a group of 30 disturbed youngsters divided into older and younger groups. They found that with the older group A-State anxiety increased following the more difficult task while A-Trait remained unchanged. These results supported State-Trait theory (Spielberger, 1966) and tended to support the results of Spielberger (1973) and Newmark *et al.* (1975) and to be in disagreement with those of Sitarz (Note 1) and Finch *et al.* (1975). The inconsistency in the results of the present study with emotionally disturbed children and those of the Sitarz and the Finch *et al.* studies is confusing since, although none of the subjects were the same, subjects were from the same institution. There is no readily available explanation for these results and we find ourselves at an initial loss for words. One possible partial explanation that we are presently investigating is related to a difference in instructions. In the Spielberger (1973) and Finch *et al.* (in press) studies subjects were instructed to respond on the second A-State as they believed they would feel during an examination and as they felt during the task, respectively, with the A-Trait given under standard instructions. In the Sitarz (Note 1) and Finch *et al.* (1975) studies, the A-State was administered immediately after the respective tasks under standard instructions (i.e., how you feel right now) with the A-Trait also being administered under standard conditions. The exact nature of the instructions in the Newmark *et al.* (1975) study are not known. Whether or not this subtle difference in instructions is responsible for such divergent results is unknown but is presently being explored.

An additional series of studies will be discussed in this section primarily because of their relevance to our concern with the *validity* of the STAIC. In these studies Moore (Note 2) questioned the ability of emotionally disturbed children to make the discriminations required on the three point A-State and A-Trait scales (i.e., hardly ever, sometimes, often). To evaluate this contention a *True–False* form of the STAIC was developed (i.e., the same items requiring only a true or false response) and three separate studies were designed.

The first was a reliability study identical in design to the Finch, Montgomery, and Deardorff (1974b) study except that the modified true–false STAIC was employed. Thirty emotionally disturbed children were individually administered tests at the beginning and end of a 3-month period. Test–retest reliability was lower for the A-State than the A-Trait portion of the true–false STAIC. Although this finding is similar to the results obtained with normal children it is dissimilar to the findings with emotionally disturbed children using the unmodified STAIC.

The second portion of Moore's (Note 2) thesis dealt with the validity of the true–false STAIC and was modeled after the Montgomery and Finch (1974) study. She administered the true–false STAIC to 40 emotionally disturbed and 40 normal children. Neither A-State nor A-Trait scores were found to be different for the two groups. Unfortunately, this portion of her thesis contained several unavoidable problems such as the normal children generally being from a lower socioeconomic background and containing considerably more Black subjects than did the emotionally disturbed group. These problems were the result of one school district being unwilling to allow us to administer the tests to their students and our being unable to find another school system which more closely met her needs in the short period of time available for the completion of this project. The initial conclusion that the modified STAIC cannot discriminate normal from emotionally disturbed children must be tempered since the meaning of the results of this portion of the study was complicated by uncontrolled variables.

In the third portion of her thesis Moore (Note 2) attempted to determine the sensitivity to change of the true–false A-State scale while investigating whether or not the A-Trait portion of this modified form would remain constant. She employed a procedure exactly like the one employed by Finch *et al.* (1975). Thirty emotionally disturbed youngsters were assigned to one of three groups; a failure plus ego-involving instructions group, a failure only group, or a test–retest control group. The results indicated no increase in A-State anxiety for any of the groups and that the groups reported less anxiety on the A-Trait scale for the second administration. Moore attributed the decrease in anxiety on A-Trait to the subject's increased familiarity with her on the second testing session.

Originally we had hoped that the true–false form of the STAIC would provide us with some understanding of the inconsistent results we obtained with the standard form. Unfortunately this was not the case and we terminated this study with more inconsistent data. However, some useful information was obtained since we came to believe that the results we had previously obtained were not due to the format of the test itself. Thus, we were left with at least two possible hypotheses: that A-State and A-Trait anxiety are qualitatively different in emotionally disturbed and normal children or that some procedural differences are responsible.

Correlates of Anxiety in Children

The next portion of the research program to be discussed deals with our efforts to attempt to understand the emotion of anxiety by exploring the relationship between anxiety, behavior, and other constructs. The studies in this section represent a mixture of interests and reflect the diversity of our research team.

In the first study Deardorff, Finch, and Royal (1974) predicted that children who bit their fingernails would self-report more anxiety than children who did not. They administered the CMAS to 90 seventh and eighth grade normal children and then examined their nails to determine if they had been bitten. They did not find any difference between anxiety levels in children with bitten nails and those with unbitten ones. Interestingly, the incidents of bitten nails in this group of children was well below previous research (see Pierce, 1972). Deardorff *et al.* (1974) suggest that other factors than anxiety should be considered as contributing to nailbiting.

Finch and Nelson (1974a) examined the relationship between anxiety and locus of conflict with emotionally disturbed children. Locus of conflict (Armentrout, 1971) describes the type of behavior manifestation which is responsible for a youngster being called emotionally disturbed. In internalization of conflict, the conflict is between the individual's impulses and their inhibitions. Consequently, behaviors are rigidly controlled and the child experiences subjective discomfort. In externalization of conflict, the conflict is between the child's actions and the reactions they bring about in others. Behavioral manifestations are freely discharged into the surrounding environment and society suffers. Quay (1972), in factor analytic research, had suggested that anxiety should be more closely associated with internalization of conflict.

To test this relationship Finch and Nelson (1974a) individually administered the CMAS to 50 children and then had their special education teachers complete behavioral ratings which indicate locus of conflict. No significant relationship between either internalization or externalization of conflict and anxiety was found. These authors suggested that with extremely anxious populations, such as emotionally disturbed children, the relationship might not have been found because of the decreased variance in the measures. Despite the absence of a relationship being found between anxiety and locus of conflict some interesting differences between males and females were found. Boys were rated as exhibiting more internalization of conflict, more externalization of conflict, and more maladjustment than were girls. However, girls reported experiencing significantly more subjective anxiety on both the CMAS and the A-Trait portion of the STAIC. Finch and Nelson (1974a) suggested that this finding may provide some indication as to why more boys are referred for psychiatric treatment. That is, the behavior manifestation of disturbances in boys are more obvious and pervasive despite the fact that emotionally disturbed girls experience more anxiety.

To investigate the relationship between locus of conflict and anxiety in a different population Nelson, Kendall, Finch, Kendall, and Nelson (1974) individually administered the STAIC and CMAS to 54 delinquents in state training centers and obtained ratings on locus of conflict from their classroom teachers. Once again neither CMAS nor A-Trait anxiety were related significantly to either internalization or externalization of conflict. However, A-State anxiety was related significantly to internalization of conflict with this delinquent population. It was suggested by Nelson et al. (1974) that, with delinquents, internalization of conflict is more related to fluctuating situational anxiety than to stable individual difference.

Here too, as was the case with emotionally disturbed children, boys were rated as exhibiting more internalization and externalization of conflict as well as more maladjustment than girls. Likewise the delinquent girls reported significantly more subjective anxiety than did the boys. Again relatively high scores were obtained on all measures.

To further extend the body of research on the relationship between locus of conflict and anxiety, Nelson, Finch, Kendall, and Gordon (in press) administered the STAIC and CMAS to 63 public school children and obtained locus of conflict ratings from their teachers. With this population it was found that both internalization and externalization of conflict as well as the total maladjustment index were correlated with CMAS anxiety but not with A-Trait anxiety. The total maladjustment index correlated significantly with A-State anxiety. Unlike the results with emotionally disturbed and delinquent groups, there was not a difference in either the anxiety scores or locus of conflict ratings between normal boys and girls.

Given the results of the three studies investigating the relationship between anxiety and locus of conflict it would appear that with high anxious groups (emotionally disturbed and delinquent) there is not a relationship between trait anxiety (CMAS and A-Trait) and either internalization or externalization of conflict. However, with normal children both CMAS and A-Trait anxiety are related to all measures. We believe that any relationship between anxiety and locus of conflict is eroded when disturbed subjects are employed.

In discussing proxemics (the spacing that humans and animals maintain between themselves and others) several investigators have attributed a large role to anxiety in the determination of space needs (McBride et al., 1965; Newman and Pollack, 1973; Tolor, 1968). High anxious individuals would be expected to require more space between others and themselves than would low anxious ones. To test this hypothesis Kendall, Deardorff, Finch and Graham (1976) administered the STAIC to 20 emotionally disturbed boys and 20 normal boys and then obtained measures of personal space requirements. Emotionally disturbed boys were found to require significantly more space than were normal boys but subjects high on anxiety did not require more space than those low on anxiety. Kendall et al. (1976a) concluded that while emotionally disturbed boys do appear to require more space than normals, anxiety does not appear to be responsible for that difference and the contributions of other factors need to be explored.

One area which is frequently mentioned as being related to anxiety is locus of control. Locus of control refers to whether the individual perceives both positive and negative event outcomes to be the result of his behavior (internal locus of control) or the result of luck, chance, fate, or other individuals (external locus of control) (see Chapter Four in this book). The reader should note that locus of conflict and locus of control are different concepts! The locus of control research results with adults suggested that individuals who saw their behavior as being under control of external factors were more likely to experience increased anxiety. In order to investigate this relationship with emotionally disturbed children, Finch and Nelson (1974b) individually administered two measures of locus of control and the CMAS and STAIC to 50 emotionally disturbed children in residential treatment. Anxiety as measured by the CMAS was significantly related to both locus of control measures but neither the A-State nor the A-Trait portions of the STAIC were associated with an external locus of control. These authors interpreted their results as suggesting that a feeling of not being in control of what happens to oneself is related to feelings of anxiety as measured by the CMAS. They suggest that the CMAS and the STAIC may be measuring different types of anxiety and that this might account for the different results obtained with the two scales.

In the final study to be discussed in this section Lira, White, and Finch (1977) investigated the relationship between the STAIC and the Profile of Mooa States (POMS) developed by McNair, Lorr, and Droppleman (1971). The POMS was designed to provide a quickly administered efficient method of assessing transient affective states and measures six identifiable affective states: (1) tension-anxiety, which is defined by adjectives describing elevations in musculoskeletal tension; (2) anger-hostility, which reflects moods of anger, irritation, and antipathy toward other persons; (3) depression-dejection, which indicates a mood of depression with concomitant feelings of personal inadequacy; (4) vigor-activity, which reflects a mood characterized by ebullience, vigorousness and high energy; (5) fatigue-inertia, which represents a mood characterized by weariness, inertia, and low energy level; (6) confusion-bewilderment, which represents a mood of bewilderment and muddle-headedness. Also a Total Mood Disturbance score is obtained.

The STAIC and the POMS were administered to a group of 41 behavior-problem adolescents in a state facility for delinquents. Results indicated a significant correlation between A-State anxiety of the STAIC and the anger-hostility and the vigor-activity portions, as well as the Total Mood Disturbance score of the POMS. A-Trait anxiety correlated significantly with the depression-dejection, the confusion-bewilderment, the tension-anxiety factors as well as the Total Mood Disturbance of the POMS.

It would have been expected that the POMS measures would have correlated with the A-State portion of the STAIC since the POMS was designed as a measure of transient affective states. However, Lira *et al.* (in press) noted that the POMS is designed to measure mood states over the last *week* while the STAIC A-State asks the subject to respond how he/she feels at *this very moment*. They continue by stating that the POMS instructions are qualitatively discrepant from those of the STAIC and therefore may reflect more enduring effective responses than the A-State. By A-Trait criteria these affective responses would appear to reach trait proportions.

In this section various correlates of anxiety have been examined. As the reader is probably now aware, there were no overwhelming consistencies in the data. Our findings contain useful information, yet the problematic nature of assessing anxiety in children via the self-report method stands out. In summary, we have reported that: whether or not a child bites his fingernails is not related to his level of anxiety as measured by the CMAS; whether an emotionally disturbed child acts out his conflicts or internalizes them is not related to his anxiety level as measured by the CMAS or the A-State and A-Trait portions of the STAIC; with delinquents, internalization of conflict is associated with the A-State portion of the STAIC but not with the A-Trait or CMAS; with normals anxiety as measured by the CMAS was related to both internalization and externalization of conflict as well as the total maladjustment index while the A-State was related only to the total maladjustment index and A-Trait was not related to any of the ratings; personal space requirements of emotionally disturbed and normals were not related to anxiety although emotionally disturbed boys required more space; an external locus of control was related to anxiety as measured by the CMAS; and with delinquents the A-State portion of the STAIC was related to both the anger-hostility and the vigor-activity factors of the POMS as well as the Total Mood Disturbance score while the A-Trait portion of the STAIC was related to the depression–dejection, the confusion–bewilderment, and the tension–anxiety factors, as well as the Total Mood Disturbance score.

We are puzzled by the lack of any consistency among these results. This may simply reflect the difficulty in studying self-report measures obtained from subjects who are perhaps unskilled at the task of self-analysis and who are at times unmotivated. Or, our results may simply reflect the degree of complexity of anxiety in children.

Factor Analytic Investigations

Since a number of investigators (Cattell and Scheier, 1961; Endler, 1975; Kendall *et al.*, 1976b) had suggested that trait anxiety is not a unitary construct, Finch, Kendall, and Montgomery (1974a) felt that the exact nature of this multidimensionality in children should be examined through factor analysis. The responses of 125 emotionally disturbed and

120 normal children to the CMAS where factor analysis using an oblique rotation since correlated factors were expected. Three anxiety factors and two Lie factors were obtained. Factor I was called *anxiety: worry and oversensitivity* and was composed of six items from the anxiety portion of the CMAS which were related to excessive worry (i.e., "I worry most of the time."; "I worry when I go to bed.") and the tendency to allow one's feelings to be hurt with the slightest provocation (i.e., "My feelings get hurt easily."; "My feelings get hurt easily when I am scolded."). Factor II was called *Lie: social impeccability* and was composed of six items from the Lie portion of the CMAS which were related to those perfect characteristics (i.e., "I am always nice to everyone."; "I am always good.") which at best are only closely approximated by even the "best behaved" child. Factor III was called *anxiety: physiological* and was composed of five items from the anxiety portion of the CMAS that were related to difficulties with physiological processes (i.e., "I have trouble swallowing."; "I often feel sick at my stomach."). Factor IV was called *anxiety: concentration* and was composed of four items from the anxiety portion which were related to distractibility and uncertainty (i.e., "It is hard for me to keep my mind on my school work."; "It is hard for me to keep my mind on anything."). The final factor was labeled *Lie: over self-control* and was represented in three items from the lie portion of the CMAS which reflected an ability to maintain unexpected self-control (i.e., "I never get angry."; "I never say things I shouldn't.").

Following the identification of these factors, Finch, Kendall, and Montgomery (1974a) noticed that the three anxiety factors which were obtained appeared to correspond to those manifestations of anxiety which are encountered in clinical practice and therefore probably reflected a valid distinction. They concluded by hypothesizing that more accurate predictions could be made as to the behavioral manifestations exhibited by children who score high on these specific factors than using the unidimensional overall score. In a later section of this chapter we will return to this point and examine its validity.

After having contrasted the findings of Sitarz (Note 1) and Finch *et al.* (1975), that A-Trait may vary as a function of stress with emotionally disturbed children, with those of Newmark *et al.* (1975) and Spielberger (1973) who reported only A-State changes with normal children, Finch, Kendall, and Montgomery (1976b) raised the question as to what extent one is entitled to interpret scores on a particular inventory as indicating the same construct when different populations are involved. They hypothesized that a *qualitative* difference in anxiety may exist between normal and emotionally disturbed children as well as the quantitative difference reported by Montgomery and Finch (1974). To test this hypothesis Finch *et al.* (1976b) compared the factor structure of the STAIC from a group of emotionally disturbed children to that obtained with a group of normal children of the same mental age. With the emotionally disturbed group, four factors were obtained with two of the factors being composed entirely of A-State items and two composed entirely of A-Trait items. The two A-State factors were composed of either the positive (i.e., "I feel very pleasant."; "I feel very good.") or negative (i.e., "I feel very worried."; "I feel very upset.") descriptors of the A-State scale and accounted for significantly more of the variance than did the two A-Trait factors. The A-Trait factors were composed of items dealing with worry and with indecisiveness, rumination, and other obsessive characteristics, respectively.

For the normal group, six factors were found with four factors being composed of A-State items and two composed of A-Trait items. One of the A-State factors contained 9 of the 10 positive description items while the other three A-State factors were each composed of three of the negative descriptor items. The two A-Trait factors were composed of either items dealing with being upset and obsessiveness (i.e., "I get upset at home."; "I have trouble making up my mind.") or items dealing with having sweaty hands or insomnia (i.e., "My hands get sweaty."; "It's hard for me to fall asleep at night."). There was no difference in the normal group in the amount of variance accounted for by A-State and A-Trait factors.

The interpretation of these results supported the state–trait distinction since in both analysis items from the A-State and A-Trait scales loaded on different factors. In addition the authors emphasized the importance of considering the subject population when evaluating research findings with anxiety since it would appear that qualitative as well as quantitative differences between emotionally disturbed and normal children exist. Finally, they concluded that traits, at least A-Trait, do not appear to be as firmly established in emotionally disturbed as in normal children since A-State accounted for significantly more variance than did A-Trait with the disturbed group.

A comparison of the factor analysis of the CMAS and STAIC would be expected to indicate certain similarities. Since the CMAS is generally regarded as a trait measure of anxiety, there should be much in common between this measure and the A-Trait factors. The items of the two A-Trait factors with both the disturbed and normal population are similar to many of the items on the CMAS. However, it is evident that the CMAS represents a more multidimensional measure than does the A-Trait since it contains many more items relating to physiological manifestations of anxiety as well as more items dealing with the interfering effects of anxiety on concentration. One area in which we believe the A-Trait portion of the STAIC might be improved is by the addition of items in these two areas.

Higher Mental Processes and Anxiety in Emotionally Disturbed Children

The studies to be discussed in this section deal with the relationship between anxiety and higher mental processes. We use the terms "higher mental processes" rather loosely and realize that other descriptions could be of similar usefulness. However, we prefer to conceptualize the studies in this section as interrelated because each task involved some form of higher mental process.

The relationship between achievement and anxiety in emotionally disturbed children was investigated in three separate studies by Montgomery, Finch, and Kendall (Note 3). In the first study they individually administered the STAIC and standard achievement tests to a group of 41 emotionally disturbed children in two separate sessions without knowledge of the test result on the other measure. They predicted, based on previous research with normal children, that a negative relationship between anxiety and achievement would be found. However, neither A-State nor A-Trait were significantly related to academic achievement.

In their second study the CMAS and standard achievement tests were administered to 37 emotionally disturbed children again without knowledge of their performance on the other measure. They found a significant negative relationship between the anxiety portion of the CMAS and achievement. This finding was as predicted and yet it was in contradiction to their first study where the STAIC was employed as the measure of anxiety.

In their third study they hypothesized that the emotionally disturbed children may have had difficulty making the discriminations required by the STAIC and that the true–false format of the CMAS might have been easier for them. At this time Moore (Note 2) had finished the reliability portion of her thesis and we decided to employ it to determine if, with its true–false format, A-State and A-Trait would be more related to achievement in emotionally disturbed children. Forty-five children were tested in the same manner as in the two previous studies. Again there was not a relationship between either A-State or A-Trait anxiety and achievement.

It was apparent that some difference must exist between the nature of anxiety as measured by the CMAS and the STAIC which would account for the obtained differences. The authors further concluded that one must be aware of the importance of noting what measure of anxiety is employed when discussing anxiety research with children.

Short-term memory as measured by digit span performance is frequently felt to be impaired by the anxiety of psychological testing, and previous research with adults suggests that A-State anxiety is more important than A-Trait anxiety (Hodges and Spielberger, 1969). However, Finch, Anderson, and Kendall (1976a) hypothesized that if the *anxiety: concentration* factor derived by the factor analysis of the CMAS was valid, it would be logical that an inverse relationship would exist between scores on this factor and the scores on the digit span performance, regardless of the relationship between the total CMAS anxiety score and the scores on the other two anxiety factors. They individually administered the CMAS and a standardized digit span task to 38 emotionally disturbed children. Subjects were divided at the median of the total CMAS anxiety scores and at the median on each of the CMAS factors. It was predicted that there would be no difference on digit span performance between those subjects high and low on the total CMAS anxiety score or those high and low on the *anxiety: worry and oversensitivity* and the *anxiety: physiological* factors. However, it was predicted that subjects high on *anxiety: concentration* would perform more poorly than those with low scores. The outcome of this study was as predicted and it was considered to be support for the validity of the *anxiety: concentration* factor. Correspondingly, since only one dimension of trait anxiety was related to digit span performance, this study supported the need to assess trait anxiety in a multidimensional fashion.

In order to investigate the relationship between anxiety and visual–motor development, Finch, Kendall, and Spiro (Note 4) individually administered the CMAS and the Bender Visual–Motor Gestalt Test (Bender, 1938) to a group of emotionally disturbed children. The CMAS was scored for the three anxiety factors and for the total anxiety and lie portions of the scale. The Bender was scored for developmental level and emotional indicators according to Koppitz (1964). The authors found no significant relationships between anxiety, as indicated by the CMAS anxiety score or the *anxiety: worry and oversensitivity* factor of the CMAS, and either the developmental or emotional scoring of the Bender. However, the *anxiety: physiological* and *anxiety: concentration* factor scores were both highly correlated with the Bender emotional indicators—the correlation between the *anxiety: concentration* factor and the Bender emotional score was 0.81! This finding suggests that the relationship between the *anxiety:*

physiological and *anxiety: concentration* factor scores and the Bender emotional indicators may display some general physiological manifestations of anxiety which would interfere with the ability to concentrate and also be reflected on the Bender emotional indicators such as excessive motor activity or impulsiveness.

The studies discussed in this section have dealt with the relationship between anxiety and various higher mental processes. We have found that whether anxiety is related to academic achievement depends on which measure of anxiety is being employed since the CMAS anxiety scale was inversely related to achievement but neither the modified or unmodified A-State or A-Trait portions of the STAIC were related. Likewise, short-term memory as measured by digit span performance was not related to the CMAS anxiety score but was related to the *anxiety: concentration* factor of the CMAS with subjects scoring high on this factor exhibiting significantly lower digit span scores than those obtaining lower scores. Finally visual–motor performance as measured by the Bender Visual–Motor Gestalt Test was found to correspond to some types of anxiety. Although neither the CMAS anxiety scale nor the *anxiety: worry and oversensitivity* factor score were related to either Bender developmental scores or emotional indicators, both *anxiety: concentration* and *anxiety: physiological* were correlated significantly with the emotional indicators.

We believe some of the most interesting research on anxiety in children will eventually emerge from the effects of anxiety on higher mental processes. Presently we are attempting to expand our work in short-term memory and in the learning process itself to increase our understanding of the effects of anxiety in these areas. Certainly, the problems related to measurement are not to be ignored. Perhaps the use of multidimensional trait assessment or some "indicant" of anxiety other than self-report will be productive.

Psychophysiological Measures

Considering the problems and inconsistencies we have encountered in the measurement of anxiety by self-report, it should come as no surprise that we have attempted to utilize other measures of anxiety. Fortunately we were able to purchase some psychophysiological equipment and include it in our research. However, anyone familiar with equipment of this type will appreciate the many equipment problems and failures which have prohibited us from completing but one study to date. At times we have had subjects actively participating in an experimental session despite the fact that they were supposedly "dead" since their heart rate, respiration rate, and Galvanic Skin Responses GSR change were all zeros on our print-outs. Only our desire to achieve accurate scientific measurement and the results of our first study prohibit us from "pulling the plug" on it entirely.

In our first study Finch, Kendall, and Garrison (Note 5) investigated the effects of the sex of the examiner, type of examining task, and failure with ego-involving instructions on anxiety in emotionally disturbed children. Anxiety was measured by the STAIC (A-State and A-Trait), heart rate, respiration rate, and GSR with both number of peaks and magnitude of peaks being recorded on the GSR. Twenty-one emotionally disturbed boys were individually administered the STAIC in one session and then were brought to the testing room for another session. The electrodes were connected and after a brief period in which the subject was allowed to habituate to the equipment, subjects were administered either a difficult block design task or a difficult word puzzle under ego-involving instructions by either a male or female examiner with both sex of examiner and type of task being counterbalanced. After a brief period of time the subjects were stopped and their performance "graded." Since none of the subjects were able to complete the tasks, subjects were thought to have viewed the task as a failure experience. Immediately after the "grading," subjects were asked to complete the STAIC.

Finch, Kendall, and Garrison (Note 5) found significantly more anxiety associated with female examiners on *all* measures. In other words, more A-State and A-Trait anxiety were found with females; more heart beats per minute were found with females; more respirations per minute were found with females; and more GSR spikes and greater GSR magnitudes were found with female examiners. Finding this much consistency in a study of anxiety with emotionally disturbed children was more than we could have hoped for based on our previous findings. In addition we found an increase in heart rate and GSR magnitude associated with the block design task but not with the anagram task. Indeed, the anxiety provoking aspects of a female examiner for male children should be noted.

Finch *et al.* (Note 5) remark that their results indicate the potential usefulness of multiple measures of anxiety in research with children. However, they stress that when inconsistencies are found, as was the case with the task variable in their study, the researcher remains unable to explain his results meaningfully. Certainly multiple measures, including physiological measures, appear to offer some possibilities but they also seem to create new problems for the researcher.

CONCLUSIONS

What have we learned from all of these studies dealing with anxiety in children? We wish we were able to draw dramatic conclusions from an extensive list of definite findings. As the reader is well aware by now we are not able to do this. On the other hand, we do believe we have unearthed some issues and gained some understanding. We believe that while anxiety, as measured by the CMAS and STAIC, is a reliable construct which results in a very similar score on separate administrations, we are somewhat more concerned about the validity of the measures. Both the CMAS and STAIC would appear to be useful in differentiating high anxious groups from normal groups. However, whether or not a high or low score obtained by an individual indicates that a particular child belongs in one group or another cannot be determined with the degree of accuracy we would like.

Of even greater concern to us is the validity of the A-State and A-Trait scales of the STAIC with emotionally disturbed children. We have failed to obtain changes in the A-State when they would have been expected and we have found changes when changes should not have occurred. Likewise the A-Trait has been found to be subject to momentary change. This is entirely inconsistent with state–trait theory (Spielberger, 1966).

We have some concern about whether some demand characteristics in instructions might not be responsible for some of the results obtained. If a minor variation in instructions can make the difference between obtaining results which are predicted as opposed to results which are unexpected, it would appear that we are much too premature in our understanding to be making highly sophisticated predictions.

We are also somewhat concerned about the validity of the state–trait distinction in emotionally disturbed children. The evidence for the validity of this dichotomy with adults would appear to be overwhelming (Spielberger, 1972; Kendall et al., 1976b). However, whether children should be viewed as having strongly established traits is another issue. The evidence for traits with normal children is somewhat supportive, but the data with emotionally disturbed youngsters is contraindicative. Our factor analytic findings would suggest that state and trait anxiety exists within both groups but also suggests that it is qualitatively different. Speculating for a moment, it may be that the factors which contribute to a child being called emotionally disturbed may delay the development of personality traits. We strongly believe that additional research into the disruption of personality development in children who are called emotionally disturbed should be of high priority.

The relationship of anxiety to behaviors and other constructs also would appear to be greatly influenced by population differences. In our opinion there would not seem to be good reason to expect results obtained with one population to generalize to a different one. What this says about the state of personality research in general and anxiety research in particular, we are not sure. What it indicates to us is that our efforts to understand and predict behavior in children are going to have to be more cautious and more specific than we would have previously thought.

Another concern about the state–trait distinction has to do with the nature of trait anxiety. It is our understanding that in Spielberger's State–Trait Theory (Spielberger, 1972) trait anxiety is primarily a unidimensional concept with fear of evaluation being the main determinant. Whether Spielberger considers this to be the only facet or simply the most important one is not clear to us. On the other hand, Endler and his colleagues (1975) have suggested that trait anxiety is multidimensional and the nature of the situation interacts with the person's trait anxiety in that general class of stimuli. We believe that trait anxiety in children is probably multidimensional and this may account for many of our divergent findings. However, despite both our belief and some empirical evidence to substantiate the multidimensional nature of trait anxiety in children we recognize that there is not enough evidence to make any conclusive statements.

Whether or not anxiety has an affect on learning would appear to be both task- and measure-specific. We hope to have some more conclusive evidence in this area in the near future but presently we do not. The relationship between anxiety and higher mental processes (other than short-term memory as measured by digit span and visual–motor performance) needs to be explored. The mental processes we have explored indicate a correspondence to the *anxiety: concentration* dimension of the CMAS. We have been somewhat surprised by the degree of accuracy with which predictions can be made based on scores on this factor—especially since it contains so few items (Finch *et al.*, Note 4). It is our contention that since few items are involved and our predictions have been so accurate, this type of anxiety in children is probably very important.

Although physiological measures of anxiety add precision and a sense of accuracy, they present many new and difficult problems which will need to be dealt with before we can be sure that their addition is worth the cost and effort involved. Similarly when the results are inconsistent, we are left without knowing which criterion of anxiety to believe.

Presently we are tempted to move into the treatment and management of anxiety in emotionally disturbed children. We recognize that our problems with measurement are not resolved and we will continue to attempt to deal with these. However, our original interest in treatment has been suppressed for several years while we have attempted to resolve measurement issues and we have decided to move ahead into treatment while continuing our other work. Despite our problems in measurement we continue to find the area of anxiety in children to be interesting and rewarding.

ACKNOWLEDGMENT

The writing of this material and portions of the actual research were supported by the Small Grants Program of the School of Medicine of Virginia Commonwealth University awarded to the first author and by the National Institute of Mental Health Predoctoral Research Fellowship (#1 F31 MH05270-01) awarded to the second author.

The authors wish to thank the staff of the Virginia Treatment Center for Children for their cooperation during the inconvenience and extra work that these projects created. Our special thanks goes to Ms. Shirley Truman who typed this chapter and most of the studies reported in it without complaining.

REFERENCE NOTES

1. Sitarz, A. M. (1974). *Effects of Psychological Testing on State–Trait Anxiety in Emotionally Disturbed Children.* Unpublished master's thesis, Virginia Commonwealth University. Richmond, Virginia.
2. Moore, J. H. (1976). *The State-Trait Inventory for Children: Reliability and Validity of a Modified Form with Emotionally Disturbed Children.* Unpublished master's thesis, Virginia Commonwealth University. Richmond, Virginia.
3. Montgomery, L. E., Finch, A. J., Jr., and Kendall, P. C. (1976). *Anxiety and achievement in emotionally disturbed children.* Paper presented at the meeting of the Southeastern Psychological Association, March, New Orleans.
4. Finch, A. J., Jr., Kendall, P. C., and Spiro, M. (submitted for publication). *Anxiety, cognitive style and visual-motor performance in emotionally disturbed children.*
5. ——, Kendall, P. C., and Garrison, S. R. (submitted for publication). *Effects of examiner sex and nature of task on failure induced anxiety in emotionally disturbed boys.*

REFERENCES

Armentrout, J. (1971). Parental child-rearing attitudes and pre-adolescents' problem behaviors. *Journal of Consulting and Clinical Psychology* 37:278–285.
Bender, L. A. (1938). *A Visual motor Gestalt test and its clinical use.* New York: American Orthopsychiatric Association Research Monograph, No. 3.

Castaneda, A., McCandless, B. R., and Palermo, D. S. (1956). The children's form of the manifest anxiety scale. *Child Development* 27:317–326.

Cattell, R. B., and Scheier, I. H. (1961). *The Meaning and Measurement of Neuroticism and Anxiety*. New York: Roland Press.

Deardorff, P. A., Finch, A. J., Jr., and Royal, L. R. (1974). Manifest anxiety and nailbiting. *Journal of Clinical Psychology* 30:378.

Endler, N. S. (1975). A person-situation interaction model of anxiety. In C. D. Spielberger and I. G. Sarason, eds., *Stress and Anxiety*. Vol. 1. Washington, D.C.: Hemisphere Publishing Corp.

——, Hunt, Jr. McV., and Rosenstein, A. J. (1962). An S-R Inventory of anxiousness. *Psychological Monographs* 76, No. 17 (Whole No. 536):1–33.

Finch, A. J., Jr., and Nelson, W. M., III. (1974a). Anxiety and locus of conflict in emotionally disturbed children. *Journal of Abnormal Child Psychology* 2:33–37.

——, and Nelson, W. M., III. (1974b). Locus of control and anxiety in emotionally disturbed children. *Psychological Reports* 35:469–470.

——, Kendall, P. C., and Montgomery, L. E. (1974c). Multi-dimensionality of anxiety in children: factor structure of the Children's Manifest Anxiety Scale. *Journal of Abnormal Child Psychology* 2:331–336.

——, Montgomery, L. E., and Deardorff, P. A. (1974d). Children's Manifest Anxiety Scale: reliability with emotionally disturbed children. *Psychological Reports* 34:658.

——, Montgomery, L. E., and Deardorff, P. A. (1974e). Reliability of state-trait anxiety with emotionally disturbed children. *Journal of Abnormal Child Psychology* 2:67–69.

——, Kendall, P. C., Montgomery, L. E., and Morris, J. (1975) Effects of two types of failure on anxiety in emotionally disturbed children. *Journal of Abnormal Psychology* 84:583–585.

——, Anderson, J., and Kendall, P. C. (1976a). Anxiety and digit span performance in emotionally disturbed children. *Journal of Consulting and Clinical Psychology* 44:874.

——, Kendall, P. C., and Montgomery, L. E. (1976b). Qualitative difference in the experience of state-trait anxiety in emotionally disturbed and normal children. *Journal of Personality Assessment* 40:522–530.

——, Kendall, P. C., Dannenburg, M., and Morgan, J. R. (in press). Effects of task difficulty on state-trait anxiety in emotionally disturbed children. *Journal of Genetic Psychology*.

Hodges, W. F., and Spielberger, C. D. (1969). Digit span: an indicant of trait or state anxiety? *Journal of Consulting and Clinical Psychology* 33:430–434.

Kendall, P. C., Deardorff, P. A., Finch, A. J., Jr., and Graham, L. (1976a). Proxemics, locus of control, anxiety and type of movement in emotionally disturbed children. *Journal of Abnormal Child Psychology* 4:9–16.

——, Finch, A. J., Jr., Auerbach, S. M., Hooke, J. F., and Mikulka, P. J. (1976b). The State-Trait Anxiety Inventory: a systematic evaluation. *Journal of Consulting and Clinical Psychology* 44:406–412.

Koppitz, E. M. (1964). *The Bender Gestalt Test for young children*. New York: Grune & Stratton, Inc.

Lira, F. T., White, M. J., and Finch, A. J., Jr. (1977). Anxiety and mood states in delinquent adolescents. *Journal of Personality Assessment* 41:532–536.

McBride, G., King, M. G., and James, S. W. (1965). Social proxemity effects of galvanic skin responses in adult humans. *Journal of Psychology* 61:153–157.

McNair, D. M., Lorr, M., and Droppleman, L. F. (1971). *Manual for the Profile of Mood States*. San Diego: Educational and Industrial Testing Service.

McReynolds, P. (1975). Changing conceptions of anxiety: a historical review and a proposed integration. In I. G. Sarason and C. D. Spielberger, eds., *Stress and Anxiety* Vol. 2, Washington, D.C.: Hemisphere Publishing Corp.

Montgomery, L. E., and Finch, A. J., Jr. (1974). Validity of two measures of anxiety in children. *Journal of Abnormal Child Psychology* 2:293–298.

Nelson, W. M., III, Finch, A. J., Jr., Kendall, P. C., and Gordon, R. H. (1977). Anxiety and locus of conflict in normal children. *Psychological Reports* 41:375–378.

——, Kendall, P. C., Finch, A. J., Jr., Kendall, M. S., and Nelson, S. B. (1974). Anxiety and locus of conflict in delinquents. *Journal of Abnormal Child Psychology* 2:275–279.

Newman, P. C., and Pollack, D. (1973). Proxemics in deviant adolescents. *Journal of Consulting and Clinical Psychology* 40:6–8.

Newmark, C. S., Wheeler, D., Newmark, L., and Stabler, B. (1975). Test-induced anxiety with children. *Journal of Personality Assessment* 39:409–413.

Pierce, C. M. (1972). Nail-biting and thumb-sucking. In A. M. Freeman, and H. L. Kaplan, eds., *The Child*, (Vol. 1) New York: Atheneum.

Quay, H. C. (1972). Patterns of aggression, withdrawal and immaturity. In H. C. Quay and J. S. Werry, eds., *Psychopathological disorder of childhood*. New York: Wiley.

Spielberger, C. D. (1966). Theory and research on anxiety. In C. D. Spielberger, ed., *Anxiety and Behavior*. New York: Academic Press.

——, (1972). Anxiety as an emotional state (ch. 2). In C. D. Spielberger, ed., *Anxiety: current trends in theory and research*. Vol. 1, New York: Academic Press.

——, (1973). *Preliminary manual for the State-Trait Anxiety Inventory for Children ("How I Feel Questionnaire")*. Palo Alto, Calif.: Consulting Psychologists Press.

Taylor, J. A. (1953). A personality scale of manifest anxiety. *Journal of Abnormal and Social Psychology* 48:285–290.

Tolor, A. (1968). Psychological disturbance in disturbed and normal children. *Psychological Reports* 23:659–701.

Chapter Four

Locus of Control Research and Its Implications for Child Personality

J. DANIEL SEARCY and JEANETTE HAWKINS-SEARCY

INTRODUCTION

The concept of internal–external (I–E) control has received much attention in various fields of psychology in the past decade. Research with regard to I–E control indicates that an individual's belief that his actions are the cause of reinforcements he receives is a powerful determinant of behavior. The locus of control concept is characterized as distributing individuals according to the degree to which they accept personal responsibility for what happens to them. Persons characterized as having external locus of control tend to perceive what happens to them as contingent on forces beyond their personal control. Persons characterized as having internal locus of control tend to perceive reinforcements as being a consequence of their own actions. In social learning theory (Rotter, 1954), the locus of control concept is considered to describe a generalized expectancy, operating across a large number of situations, which related to whether or not the individual believes he possesses or lacks power over what happens to him. Rotter (1954) emphasizes that locus of control refers to the individual's belief in his ability to control his reinforcements.

Studies in the area of I–E have demonstrated that internal control (IC) is related to active efforts to interact with and influence the environment (Lefcourt, 1966). Furthermore, IC has been shown to be a determinant of academic achievement and to be related to intelligence (Rotter, 1966). The ill and disabled, the prisoner, the juvenile delinquent, and the culturally deprived have been groups identified as probably possessing a weak belief in IC (Coven, 1970). These findings suggest that IC is of fundamental importance in the degree to which one deals effectively with his environment.

Theoretical rationale for the locus of control construct is derived from Rotter's (1954) social learning theory. In conceptualizing a theory of behavior, social learning theory employs four basic concepts: (1) behavior potential, (2) expectancy of reinforcement, (3) reinforcement value, and (4) the psychological situation.

The concept of behavior is broad in Rotter's theory and includes both overt and covert behaviors. In any situation, a number of behavioral alternatives are available. "Behavior potential," i.e., the likelihood of any one of these behaviors occurring, represents the calculated potentiality, based on its relation to reinforcements, of the occurrence of a specific behavior from these alternatives.

Expectancy is defined as ". . . a subjective probability or contingency held by the individual that any specific reinforcement or group of reinforcements will occur in any given situation or situations (Rotter *et al.*, 1972). Expectancies are determined from one's reinforcement history as well as generalized from other related behavior–reinforcement sequences. According to social learning theory, a reinforcement is an event which changes the potentiality for occurrence of a specific behavior. The establishment of behavior–reinforcement associations occurs through the pairing of these events so that, with learning, expectancies are increased and the events will be paired in the future. In this context, a reinforcement acts to strengthen expectancy so that a particular behavior or event will be followed by that reinforcement in the future. Also, just as behavior extinguishes in the absence of reinforcement, expectancies reduce or extinguish if reinforcement fails to occur once the expectancy is built up. Thus, it is the interaction of expectancy and reinforcement, rather than reinforcement alone, that affects behavior potential.

"Value of reinforcement" refers to a subjective preference for one or more of the available reinforcements over the others. Preferences are acquired through learning and generally show consistency within a culture but are influenced also by the context in which they occur. Value of reinforcement interacts with expectancies to affect behavior potential. If one has no expectation of meeting a goal or acquiring a reinforcement, he is not likely to expend effort in that direction regardless of how attractive the goal may be. Or, one may have every expectation that he can acquire a reinforcement, but make no effort to attain it due to its lack of value to him.

The "psychological situation" refers to the entire context, including the individual's psychological state and interpretations, in which an event occurs. Psychological situations determine both expectancies and reinforcement value and consequently effect behavior potential.

According to Rotter's scheme of behavior, man is a conceptual being who makes order out of his environment by categorizing its components. He formulates classes on the basis of similarities and builds expectancies regarding these classes. Categorization is an extremely complex process that encompasses all situational determinants and results in classes and subclasses of people, events, reinforcements, social situations and so on, practically *ad infinitum*. Experience with one member of a class can be generalized to its other members. These generalized expectancies are considered largely accountable for one's attitudes.

According to Rotter (1966) an infant gradually learns through experiences to differentiate casual relationships between events. When he does not perceive the event and his behavior to be casually related, he does not build expectancies regarding the event's reoccurrence. Neither does its nonoccurrence reduce expectancies when casual relationships are not seen. Therefore, one's perceptions of the casual relationships between events represents an additional factor affecting the building or diminishing of expectancies.

Logically, individuals should differ in the degree to which they view reinforcement as casually related to their own actions. Depending on their reinforcement history, people's expectations vary along a continuum, with some persons more internally oriented than others. Furthermore, such beliefs should affect behavioral choices over a wide variety of situations. However, situational factors also must be considered. A person's belief that a particular behavior will lend to a particular reinforcement involves both his generalized expectancy and his expectancies regarding the specific characteristics of the situation. When the latter are highly structured they tend to contribute more weight. Generalized expectancies are more likely to play a major role in behavior when the situation permits varying interpretation of cues.

According to social learning theory, generalized expectancies are influential in determining the outcome in a new situation. For example, when the child enters his first foreign language class, his expectancies for success are largely generalized from previous academic experiences. However, the same individuals' expectancies for success in studying a second foreign language continue to be influenced by his general academic history but are more finely tempered by his specific experiences with the first language. Expectancies, then, are altered by experiences. As behavior is a function of expectancies of reinforcement and reinforcement value, it follows that changes in behavior can be accomplished by changes in expectancy.

Two general variables are hypothesized as affecting the degree of expectancy changes. The first involves whether or not the event itself is expected. If it is unexpected, its occurrence has greater effect than if it is expected, provided it results in recategorization of the situation. In illustration, a child who has consistently struck out when playing baseball may change his expectancy regarding his batting potential when he suddenly hits a home run. However, the way in which the event is perceived is critical. If it is regarded as random or situation-specific, it will not be recategorized, but if cues suggest that the situation itself has changed, recategorization is more likely to occur. Returning to the baseball illustration, one might suppose that the batter, in retrospect, recognized that his execution of a critical follow-through technique, heretofore unmastered, had led to his batting success. He might then assume he could accomplish the same execution in future trials, and recategorize his view of his batting potential accordingly.

The second variable affecting size of expectancy change involves the number of previous experiences one has had in a specific situation. Repeated experiences in a given situation lend consistency to the cues present and strengthen their meaning. Additional repetitions result in diminishing changes in expectance. Thus, there will be little change in expectancy even if such a situation terminates in a different outcome. The exception occurs if situational cues allow recategorization. The interrelatedness of these two variables clearly requires that any attempt to change expectancies which has been built on repeated experiences must employ a manipulation that elicits recategorization of situational cues.

The area of locus of control has been widely researched. To date, in excess of one thousand studies have been published utilizing locus of control as either a dependent or independent variable. The purpose of this chapter will be to discuss the ever expanding locus of control research with children and the derived implications in regards to child psychology. The remainder of the chapter will be divided into the following sections: (1) the development and use of various locus of control measures specifically designed for children; (2) research regarding the relationship between locus of control and various personality and situational factors, (3) research concerning the modification and derived implications of locus of control.

MEASUREMENT OF LOCUS OF CONTROL IN CHILDREN

A Likert-type scale, developed by Phares (1957) on *a priori* grounds, was the first instrument used to measure locus of control. This scale consisted of 26 statements, half stating external attitudes and half stating internal attitudes. Although crude, it offered promise because the subject's responses and behavior related in the manner predicted by theory and previous experimentation. James' (Note 1) revision retained Phares' format and his most successful items plus filler items. James also found low but significant correlations between the scale and behavior in task situations. Liverant, Rotter, and Seeman (Rotter, 1966) undertook to broaden Phares' scale and develop subscales for measuring additional areas. Items and factor analyses of the resulting 60-item scale indicated that the subscales were not measuring separate areas, and items included to yield subscale measures were dropped. Subsequently, Rotter, Liverant, and Crowne (Rotter, 1966) completed a major revision which reduced the number of items in the scale and eliminated the heavy influence of social desirability. In order to add ambiguity to the purpose of the test, six filler items were added to the 23 remaining items, resulting in the 29-item forced choiced format known as the Rotter Internal–External (I–E) Scale (Rotter, 1966). The scale is of particular importance because of its use in the bulk of locus of control research with adults. The scale is not, however, applicable to children and it has been necessary to turn to other scales when conducting research with this population.

Bialer (1961), studying children's conceptualizations of their successes and failures, hypothesized that as a child grows older, he is more likely to note that he can influence outcome by his actions. That is, there should be a shift from external to internal locus of control with increasing age. As part of his research, Bialer adapted the scales by James (Rotter, 1966) and Phares (1957) into a 23-item questionnaire for children. These items, which comprise the Bialer Scale, require simply a "yes" or "no" response. Standardization data were obtained from a sample of normal and mentally retarded children of both sexes between the chronological ages of 6 and 14 years and mental ages ranging from $3^{1}/_{2}$ to 16 years.

A second I–E Scale for use with children is more projective in nature.

Devised by Battle and Rotter (1963), the Children's Picture Test of I–E Control (CPT) presents the subject with six situational pictures. The child is given a statement by one of the figures in the cartoon and is told to write what he wants the other figure to reply. Responses are scored along a seven point scale according to how the child attributes responsibility for the picture situation. According to Nowicki and Strickland (1973), reliability information for the CPT is incomplete. Its validity appears questionable as the cartoons used in the final version were selected after analysis of only 38 protocols. The use of the CPT in research is limited by its lack of suitability for group administration.

According to Sale (Note 2) the Intellectual Achievement Responsibility Questionnaire (Crandall, Katkovsky and Crandall, 1965), a widely used locus of control scale for children, differs from other children's measures in several ways. Primarily, this instrument is intended to measure children's beliefs in internal versus external locus of control in intellectual academic achievement situations rather than their general beliefs across wide areas of experience. On the Intellectual Achievement Responsibility Questionnaire (IAR), the source of external control is limited to teachers, parents, and peers. The influence of luck or fate is not considered. Another major difference lies in its sampling of both positive and negative events. In addition to a total self-responsibility score (I), the questionnaire yields separate subscores related to responsibility for one's successes (I+) and responsibility for one's failures (I−).

The IAR, which is composed of 34 forced choice items each describing a positive or negative experience, was standardized on a sample of 923 elementary and high school students. Methodically developed and widely used, the test has been said to yield a more stable relationship with criterion measures than the Bialer Scale (Milgram, 1971). It is applicable to a wide age range, but dull or very young children may have difficulty understanding the items. Because of its specificity to academic situations, the test is not suitable for evaluation of locus of control as a general construct. Reimanis (1973) stated that certain I–E measures cannot be used interchangeably in all situations and that the IAR scale is better suited to assess locus of control with respect to children's school activities than are the Bialer or Battle Scales.

The Children's Nowicki–Strickland Internal–External Scale (Nowicki and Strickland, 1973) was developed to provide a generalized measure of locus of control for children over a wide age range. Items in the Children's Nowicki–Strickland Internal–External Scale (CNS-IE) were constructed on the basis of Rotter's (1966) definition of locus of control, and they describe reinforcement situations in a variety of areas such as affiliation, achievement, and degendency. The original 102-item scale was refined to yield 40 questions which were administered to 1017 mostly caucasian children representing all socioeconomic levels from the third through twelfth grades who did not differ significantly in IQ. Children's "yes" or "no" responses are scored in an external direction so that high scores indicate an external orienttion.

A number of other instruments and techniques for assessing locus of control inihildren have been developed. Attempting to avoid the pitfalls of verbally loaded formal questionnaires, some researchers have used structured interviews (Shore, *et al.*, 1971; Stephens and Delys, 1973), or questioning tchniques (Coleman *et al.*, Note 3). Gruen, Korte, and Baum (1974) have developed a group measure of locus of control. Standardized on a large sample of moderately disadvantaged black, white, and Spanish children from grades two through six, the taped test questions are augmented by pictorial representations in the test booklet. While the scale shows promise, it is limited by the marked skewedness of responses. Apparently, it has had little use beyond the standardization study. The bulk of work with school age children has been done with the Bialer and IAR. However, in a discussion of varous measures, MacDonald (1973) wrote that the CNS-IE appears to be the best measure of locus of control as a generalized expectancy presently available for children.

Scales have also been devised to measure locus of control in preschoolers. Mischel, Zeiss, and Zeiss (1974) have patterned their test after the IAR, and Nowicki and Duke (1974) have constructed a downward extension of the CNS-IE suitable for children as young as 4 years. As the focus of this paper is on school age children, these preschool scales will not be discussed in greater detail.

Other measures of locus of control for children are available and new ones should be and are continually being developed. For example, Milgram and Milgram (1975) have recently published a locus of control scale designed to measure 3 dimensions of locus of control—content, time, and orientation. While other measures of locus of control are available, the present authors have presented those scales which are most commonly found in the current literature.

PERSONALITY AND SITUATIONAL FACTORS

Developmental Change

Much of the locus of control literature regarding children is related to variables involved in their development (Sale, Note 2). One factor is age.

Standardization data from the CNS-IE indicate that both male and female subjects become more internal with age (Nowicki and Strickland, 1973). Gruen *et al.* (1974), working with second to sixth graders, reported that responses of older chilren are more internal than those of younger ones. As predicted, Bialer (1961) found a significant tendency to perceive locus of control as more internal with increasing age regardless of whether the child was normal or mentally retarded. Bialer's findings have been replicated by others using his scale (Riedel and Milgram, 1970; Hawkins, Note 7; Beebe, 1971; Pawlicki, 1974). Beebe (1971) reports a leveling off of movement toward internality at adolescence which suggests that subjects of this age may have reached a point in their development where internal or external locus of control is mainly a function of past experiences and maturation alone is no longer a critical variable. These findings suggest that children develop an increasing belief in personal control to age 18.

Studies with the IAR suggest a more complex relationship between control orientation and age when responsibilities for success and failure are introduced. There is evidence that young children are more inclined to take credit for their successes but less likely to assume responsibility for their failures (Newhouse, 1974). Crandall *et al.* (1965) found general tendencies for I+, I−, and total I scores to increase only slightly with age, but found girls' scores, especially from the sixth grade up, to be slightly higher than boys. There was a shift to greater externalization among twelfth graders which the authors interpreted as related to anxiety over approaching graduation. In that same study, age was found to combine with both intelligence and social class to affect IAR scores. Younger children's total I and I− scores and older children's I+ scores were predicted by intelligence test scores, but not by socioeconomic status. However, both IQ and social class contributed significantly to younger children's I+ scores and older children's total I and I− scores. These opposing patterns suggest that children of varying intellect and social background respond to their academic successes and failures in quite different ways, as they grow older.

There appear to be significant differences in the extent to which individuals will accept responsibility for success as compared with responsibility for failure. In the intellectual–academic sphere, it was this hypothesis that led to the subscores of the IAR as previously described (Crandall *et al.*, 1965). The progression from externality to the highest levels of internality is as yet speculative and may, indeed, differ somewhat among individuals. Still, based on the evidence to date, Lawrence and Winschel (1975) have postulated five stages of development of locus of control orientation.

1. Stage I—The child attributes the events of his life, particularly failure, to forces beyond his control.
2. Stage II—Internality for success begins to emerge while externality for failure, though still evident, begins to fade.
3. Stage III—The maturing child becomes essentially internal, although this belief is principally evident in self responsibility for success.
4. Stage IV—The previous stage of development appears to be reversed as a growing awareness of responsibility and a sense of courage in the face of difficulty lead to high internality for failure coupled with a new modesty for one's successes.
5. Stage V—With the onset of genuine self reliance, the individual accepts equally the responsibility for his successes and failures.

In conclusion, there is strong support for conceptualizing locus of control as a maturational variable, but a simple linear relationship does not hold when specific cues, such as those elicited by the IAR, are present.

Socioeconomic/Ethnic Variables

The same general relationships found between the I–E Scale and socioeconomic/ethnic variables with adults reappear in studies of children; that is, an internal orientation is associated with middle class white values and external control is associated with lower classes and minority groups (Sale, Note 2). Assessing locus of control with the CNS-IE, Ludwigsen and Rollins (1973) found subjects of low socioeconomic status to be more external than high socioeconomic status subjects, and Nowicki and Strickland (1973) concluded that internality, especially in males, is significantly related to parents' higher occupational level.

Jessor, Graves, Hanson, and Jessor (1968) used their own measure of locus of control in a tri-ethnic study of Anglo-Americans, Spanish-Americans and American Indians. Among adults in these groups, Anglo-Americans exhibited the greatest internality; Spanish-Americans exhibited the greatest externality; and the American Indians were in between. Most of the significance of the obtained differences were from both the Anglo-American and Indian groups. In a similar sample of tri-ethnic high school groups, by Jessor et al., no such ethnic differences in locus of control beliefs were found. Jessor and colleagues suggested that their I–E measure may not have been valid. It is possible, however, that a rise in externality occurs as one leaves high school. At this point in one's life, there is the first massive encounter with the dominant culture and all its implications as regards job discrimination, prejudice, etc. The child faces leaving the security of home and the institutionalized support of the school system and perhaps realizes that he or she now must adopt greater independence than ever before.

Gruen *et al.* (1974), whose pictorial test (CPT) was developed for disadvantaged children, reported that white children made more internal responses than either black or Spanish children. They also found some sex differences, i.e., black females were more internal than black males. Milgram, Shore, Riedel, and Malasky (1970), using the CPT, found disadvantaged children to be more external, but found no differences between racial scores in the disadvantaged group itself. Subsequently, Milgram (1971), using the Bialer Scale and studying black and white children of comparable social class from a parochial school, found no racial differences on control orientation.

There is some evidence that differences in control orientation as a function of social class do not appear until after children have entered school. Using the Bialer Scale, Bartel (1971) found no significant differences in locus of control between lower and middle class children at first and second grade levels, but found significant differences in children from the fourth and sixth grades. Bartel also noted that lower class children did not make the expected gains in internality from the first through sixth grades, and attributed this failure to factors in the school environment that are detrimental to the development of internality in disadvantaged children.

Battle and Rotter (1963), using both the CPT and Bialer Scale, found that middle class children were significantly more internal than lower class children. They also found class differences between races, i.e., lower class blacks were more external than middle class blacks or whites. Furthermore, lower class blacks with high IQ's were more external than middle class whites with lower IQ's. These authors suggest that bright, lower class blacks, who come from deprived backgrounds, may develop external attitudes defensively (and perhaps realistically) because they perceive their opportunities for rewards as quite limited.

Crandall *et al.* (1965) reported only moderate relationships between the IAR and social class in their standardization study and explained this finding in terms of the purpose of the test. According to these authors, the IAR is limited to intellectual/academic situations where children from all social backgrounds have been subjected to similar admonitions from teachers, such as, "Work hard and you'll pass." Therefore, children who did not differ on the IAR as a function of social class might differ with a broader band of situations in which previous experiences is measured. Accordingly, generalized measures, such as the CNS-IE, Bialer, or CPT should be (and have been) more sensitive to social class differences.

A study by Garrett and Willoughby (1972) supports the idea that control orientation and socioeconomic/ethnic variables are more highly related in the academic situation than Crandall's *et al.* (1965) work indicates. Garrett and Willoughby compared a large, urban, low socioeconomic, black population to Crandall's *et al.* sample which contained more middle-class than lower-class children. The black children in general, and sixth grade girls in particular, assumed less responsibility for their failures than subjects in Crandall's *et al.* standardization group, the fifth grade boys and girls assumed less responsibility for their successes. Perhaps the failure of the IAR to appear sensitive to social class and ethnic variables in locus of control, as the more general measures appear to be, is a function of its standardization sample in addition to the situational-specificity of the test itself.

In conclusion, most of the research suggests that events common to disadvantaged groups, particularly throughout early and middle school years, promotes a belief in external causality regardless of race or sex. The implication is that those social and ethnic groups that have relatively little access to significant power, social mobility, opportunity, or material advantages will manifest relatively higher external scores. While these statements seem reasonable, one should remember the nature of the data on which they are based. Once again, most of the work is correlational in nature and conveys little about the exact mechanisms that mediate these relationships. Such work also may encourage a kind of stereotyped approach to research that obscures rather than illuminates these mechanisms.

At least two possibilities emerge as potential reasons for the typically obtained external scores for blacks. One is direct teaching. The children's parents or older siblings and peers may coach them quite directly about the "true reality." When they make internal type statements based on their limited experiences, their older, "wiser" peers may laugh at them or flaunt their superior experience. This would quickly teach them not to verbalize such beliefs about internal control and also might lead to significant changes in locus of control beliefs with increasing experience. A second, equally plausible reason is the reality they face. Members of any ethnic minority quickly learn that, at times, they are restricted in terms of jobs, promotions, housing, etc. Such experiences teach them in vivid terms how little real power they possess.

In this connection, it is interesting to speculate about the development of locus of control orientation. The evidence suggests that as children become older and move out of the period of childhood helplessness and total reliance on the family, their locus of control becomes more internal. It seems unlikely that favored and deprived groups would show the same growth curve. One might hypothesize that for a deprived group there would be an increase in internality up to a point at which individuals face the dominant culture on their own. This experience might result in an interruption in the growth of internality. Specifically, one might expect that black children, going to black schools with black teachers and tested in black settings, might well show the typical increase in internal scores over time (in the absence of any marked parental coaching to the contrary). But what will happen when those children transfer later to a larger school with many white students and teachers? Certainly this area needs increased attention to help resolve these issues.

Another point involves the nature of typical I–E scales. Most such scales are related mainly to the white culture. This being the case, I–E scores obtained from blacks may be somewhat misleading. For example, an individual could easily be external in the areas tapped by the CNS-IE or the IAR but internal in other life areas. The point is, we should not generalize too far beyond the specific nature of the scale as it interacts with the specific nature of the test population. As noted before, these scales, having some degree of generality, are subject to error when predicting relatively narrow classes of situations.

Personality and Emotional Factors

Personality and emotional factors have been investigated as variables related to and effected by locus of control. Literature regarding locus of control in children and psychological adjustment does not show apparent patterns as a function of the measuring scale used; however, the majority of work has been done with the IAR (Sale, Note 2). In general, the literature is consistent with that relevant to adults; that is, internals are considered the better adjusted. Internality has been found to correlate with interpersonal distance (Duke and Nowicki, 1972; Kendall *et al.*, 1974) and more appropriate classroom behavior and attitudes (Buck, 1970), while externality has been found to correlate with Machiavellianism (Deysack *et al.*, 1975) and heightened anxiety in boys (Bauer, 1975). Finch and Nelson (1974), measuring locus of control with the CNS-IE and Bialer Scale, also found locus of control and anxiety related in the predicted direction when the Children's Manifest Anxiety Scale was used as a dependent measure, but not when either the A-State or A-Trait portion of the State-Trait Anxiety Inventory for children was used.

In a comparison of CNS-IE scores from normal versus emotionally disturbed children, Kendall, Finch, and Mahoney (1976) found that the two groups did not differ on overall locus of control scores. However, when scores were compared on CNS-IE factors which had been isolated in a previous study (Kendall, Finch, Little, Charico, and Ollendick, in press), the two groups differed on the helplessness factor. Scores of emotionally disturbed children were more external on this factor than those of normal, suggesting that these children are indifferent to creating change and view events as unalterable to a greater degree than did the normal group.

Patterns of responsibility for success (I+) and failures (I−) have been examined in connection with adjustment. "Problematic" children raised in a Kibbutz were not unequivocally external, but between the ages of 10 and 14, they accepted more blame for failure than normal children (Lifshitz, 1973). However, inner city Negro boys of approximately the same age (10 through 13) attributed failure more than success to external causes (Epstein and Komorita, 1971). These studies suggest that "normals" in this age group may defensively disown responsibility for failures.

Ducette, Wolk, and Soncar (1972) found that children referred for treatment possessed unbalanced patterns of I+ and I− (I+ significantly higher or lower than I− compared to nonreferral groups whose I+ and I− scores were essentially equal). They reasoned that unbalanced children were not influenced in their behavior by the usual negative or positive environment agents. Wolk and Elliott (1974), testing that hypothesis, predicted that unbalanced subjects would respond more selectively to information because they would "filter out" segments of information perceived as being inconsistent with their unbalanced locus of control pattern. Contrary to their predictions, they found unbalanced subjects more easily influenced and balanced subjects less easily influenced. Thus, unbalanced I+ and I− patterns may be correlated with a general tendency to be overly influenced by information, particularly when few cues can be classified. Locus of control, as measured by the IAR, tends to remain stable across both success and failure situations (Allen, 1971).

Dweck and Reppucci (1973) examined the differential effects of failure on performance of fifth graders differing in locus of control. Externals demonstrated the largest decrement in performance when confronted with failure. Among internals, those who related failures to effort rather than lack of ability were most persistent in the task at hand. When internals and externals were compared on their performance on a conceptual task following failure, externals outperformed internals, and following success, internals performed better than externals. This finding supports the hypothesis that externals tend to disown the "forget" failures, while internals seem to perceive them more intensely.

Considered as a whole, data from studies with children are consistent with the hypothesis that children develop external views of causality particularly with regard to failure experiences as defensive measures (Lawrence and Winschel, 1975; McGhee and Crandall, 1968; Rotter, 1975). One would expect to find corresponding low self-esteem in individuals who hold an external orientation. Supporting such an hypothesis is Bryant's (1974) study of teacher–child interperceptual experiences in a population of sixth grade males. External locus of control subjects attributed significantly more negative qualities to themselves than did internal locus of control subjects and they also attributed more negative qualities towards themselves than teachers attributed to them. More direct support comes from two studies that report a positive relationship between internality and self-concept. One assessed locus of control in fourth through tenth graders with the Bialer Scale (Beebe, 1971), and another assessed third graders via the CNS-IE (Roberts, 1971). Epstein and Komorita's (1971) study with inner city black boys between 10 and 13 years of age is of particular interest. They divided subjects into groups on the basis of low, moderate, or high self-esteem scores on Coopersmith's Self-Esteem Inventory. They found that both low and moderate self-esteem subjects were significantly more external than high-esteem subjects. The authors of the study believe that negative self-image is characteristic of a stigmatized ethnic group and gives rise to external attributions of casuality. However, intrinsic self-esteem (found in varying degrees in these children) may cushion the consequences of stigmatized group membership.

In summary, data support the assumption of relationships between control orientation and adjustment, the concept of externality as a defensive measure, and a strong association between locus of control and self-esteem.

Parent–Child Relationships

Attention has been given to the role of parent–child relationships in the development of locus of control orientation in children. Loeb (1975), measuring locus of control in children with the Bialer Scale and in adults with Rotter's I–E, substantiated earlier work with adults by his finding that parents of externals are more often highly directive. Loeb theorized that an optimal level of directiveness best fosters internality in children. Accordingly, an internal son would be more likely than an external son to have a mother who helps rather than abandons or overdirects. The opposite would be true for externals. Epstein and Komorita (1971) came to similar conclusions, measuring locus of control with a scale designed specifically for their study. They concluded that parental discipline characterized by excessively hostile control and inconsistency related to externality in the child, particularly with regard to accepting responsibility for successes.

Several studies with the IAR support Loeb (1975) in principle. They suggest that protective, nurturing, approving, nonrejecting parental behaviors foster an internal orientation (Chance, Note 4; Katkovsky et al., 1967). Perhaps such behaviors are more difficult to accomplish when a family has only one child, as suggested by Newhouse's (1974) finding that only-born children assume credit for fewer positive events than do first or later borns. Additional siblings change the picture, according to Nowicki and Roundtree (1971) who reported that the more one moves from being a first born, the more likely he is to be an external (if a male) or internal (if a female).

Regarding the relationship of I–E to parental attitudes, Tolor (1967) did not find any relationship between the I–E Scale and the Maryland Parent Attitude Survey. Davis and Phares (1969), using a population of college students, found that internals reported their parents to be less rejecting and to exert less hostile control and more positive involvement. In the same study, parents' self-reported attitudes showed no direct relationship to the child's I–E orientation. Additionally, there was no correlation between internality and externality in parents and their own children. However, Davis and Phares did note that when children's and parents' I–E attitudes are similar, parents are less disciplinary and more indulgent. In a subsequent study which included both adults and children as subjects, Davis (Note 5) reported parents of externals to be more controlling and dominating in addition to being inconsistent. In contrast with Davis' and Phares' (1969) findings, Davis did not find parents of externals more rejecting or parents of internals encouraging greater self-reliance when judged on behavioral tasks in an experimental setting. In conclusion, one can only agree with Phares that locus of control antecedents are not clearly defined, perhaps due to a lack of sophistocated research methods that takes the complexity of the construct into account.

To summarize, parental attitudes and behaviors are recognized as influential in the development of locus of control in children; however, one could scarcely go beyond very general terms in defining what the optimal attitudes and behaviors are. Research that employs behavioral rather than pencil and paper measures may prove fruitful.

Educational Influences

Although a number of writers have addressed the issue of the influence of educational institutions on locus of control, few have studied it systematically. Wooster's (1974) results, obtained from a population of mentally retarded school children, are consistent with those from parental attitude studies. Using the IAR to assess locus of control, he found support for his hypothesis that mentally retarded children who are educated in an informal supportive setting in which they can make choices and experience the outcomes arising from them will be able to accept more responsibility for their own successes and failures in school. Stephens and Delys (1973), assessing locus of control via interview techniques in subjects from Headstart classes and nondisadvantaged control group, concluded that less structured programs where children are consciously encouraged to accept personal responsibility also enhance internality in preschool children. Internals professed greater satisfaction with an open setting as opposed to a traditional one (Arlin, 1975).

The failure of Bartel's (1971) sample of sixth grade disadvantaged subjects to show significant gains in the direction of internality over his first grade subjects would be contrary to expectations if Crandall's *et al.* (1965) belief that school experiences provide a leveling effect is correct. Bartel is of the opinion that teacher's insistence that lower class children conform prohibits their opportunities to control their environment and may actually foster an external orientation. Bauer (1975) expresses similar views when he points to the example in externality set by school authorities in their excessive reliance on test scores for decision-making. Lawrence and Winschel (1975) warn that overzealous use of praise in the classroom may also promote externality. By its repetitiousness, it may appear to the child to be unrelated to his efforts and consequently attributed to the chance actions of a powerful outsider, the teacher.

In general, research suggests that opportunities for choices at school promote internality just as they do in the home situation. Furthermore, it appears that some of the common practices in elementary schools may be detrimental to the development of an internal control orientation. The finding that disadvantaged children, whose control orientations do not differ significantly from those of middle class children when they begin school, tend to become more external as they go through school is of particular concern. Currently, data are too speculative to evaluate fully the effects of school practices on locus of control development. Systematic investigation is clearly needed.

MODIFICATION OF LOCUS OF CONTROL

As the preceding literature indicates a large body of research has accumulated that shows locus of control to be especially relevant to those in our society who need help. The locus of control construct has been related to physical and emotional disorders, behavioral problems, job related attitudes and behaviors, interpersonal relationships, school achievement, social disengagement, and other variables. For example, research has shown that minority-group status, ethnic and social class difference, and physical disability is related to one's locus of control orientation. The poor, the minorities, the young, and the disabled have been found to be more external.

It is evident from the literature that externals see themselves as having little control over their lives and environment and, as a result, fail to take the necessary steps to effect changes in their environment. The external's low expectancy for success leads the individuals to withdraw from social action involvement (Gurin *et al.*, 1969), to fail to obtain relevant information about life situations and to be less amenable to the effects of a remedial education program (Phares *et al.*, 1968). Internals, on the other hand seem to acquire more knowledge about their problems on the task before them (Dua, 1970; MacDonald, 1973). Consequently, they are in a better position to cope with the problems they may have. Externals may want to try to change but believe their effects will not be successful. This does not say that they do not want to change or cannot do so; it simply means they have a negative expectancy for success.

The majority of locus of control research has focused on personality and situational correlates of this construct. It is quite appropriate to focus on these correlates and to emphasize their importance but, at the same time, it is necessary to move beyond this state of research to the realm of intervention. We know that externals are more likely than internals to have problems in interpersonal, academic, and psychological areas. The next step is to discover the means whereby externals can become more effective in this day to day functioning.

In the past 5 years, locus of control researchers have shifted their attention, from the correlates of locus of control to its modification. The paragraphs below will summarize several of the methods utilized to modify locus of control in children.

Several studies which experimentally manipulated I–E have implications for changes in control. In a game against a white opponent, Lefcourt and Ladwig (1966) told highly external blacks that they were being studied as jazz musicians. These blacks persisted in competing despite continuous losses while two control groups not given the same set failed to show the same persistence. The blacks were felt to have persisted because they had been previously successful in the area of jazz. Lefcourt and Ladwig believe that external control expectancies could be altered if new goals are cognitively linked to individuals prior to successes. The study suggested that attempts at altering I–E should make use of an individual's history of reinforcement.

In a second study, Lefcourt (1967) gave directions which varied in number of cues utilized in defining the reinforcements which were available in a level of aspiration task (Rotter's Level of Aspiration Board). The external subjects increased in internal behavior as measured by appropriate patterns on the level of aspiration task. The internal subjects did not vary their aspiration behavior as a result of the different cue conditions. The increased availability of cues regarding reinforcement possibilities successfully altered external control expectancies. This raised the possibility that a lack of goal striving behavior might be more adequately predicted on the basis of cognitive and perceptual deficiencies than from lack of motivation. Lefcourt concluded that external subjects were less aware of cues which could inform them of the probability for success experiences in different situations. Roth and Bootzin (1974) successfully induced expectancies of external control in a group of college students by administering random reinforcement for performance on conceptual learning tasks.

Feather (1968) demonstrated that task performance is related to locus of control but is more heavily influenced by history of success and failure for internally and externally oriented subjects under skill conditions. As a test of their verbal intelligence, subjects who differed in locus of control were required to solve five easy anagrams (success condition) or five very difficult anagrams (failure condition) before attempting to answer 10 common anagrams of moderate difficulty level. It was found that internal subjects made more typical changes in confidence than external subjects over the entire 15 trials. Typical changes were defined as upward shifts after success and downward after failure. Feather explained this finding by suggesting that internal subjects perceived themselves as having control over their reinforcement outcomes in the situations, and that they could rely on their previous experiences in similar situations to anticipate outcomes on the presented task. Furthermore, internal subjects also could use their present task experiences on each trial as a means of anticipating outcomes on the next trial. On a strictly chance-determined task, reliance on previous experiences would presumably not be helpful in anticipating success or failure outcomes on the next trial because these outcomes would occur randomly (Phares, 1957). Previous research (Feather, 1966) also had indicated that subjects who experienced initial success on a task involving the use of individual skills were more confident than subjects who experienced initial failure. Searcy (Note 6) hypothesized correctly that a skill task which would enable a child to view his own personal efforts rather than chance as responsible for his successes and failures would be effective in increasing a sense of internality. Luginbuhl, Crowe, and Kahan (1975) reported that subjects who experienced success on a task attributed the success to a factor over which they had control (effort) while those subjects who failed on a task attributed their failure to a factor over which they had no control (ability).

The preceding alterations in locus of control were the result of manipulations in specific situations and presumably are operative only as long as that situation exists. However, they are expected to influence generalized expectancies in subsequent situations to the degree that those situations resemble the experimental one. The following paragraphs of this chapter are concerned with changes in the generalized expectancy itself.

That changes in the direction of internality occur as a function of normal maturation is clearly established (Bialer, 1961; Hawkins, Note 7; Nowicki and Strickland, 1973). Changes also may occur spontaneously with life experiences. Results from three studies indicated that success in coping with difficulties would change one in the direction of more internal control orientation (Gottesfield and Dozian, 1966; Levens, 1968; Bilker, 1970). In Levens' study of welfare mothers who were members and nonmembers of a welfare client's organization greatly increased political activism on the part of the members and reduced their feeling of powerlessness. Another study (Gottesfield and Dozian, 1966) observed indigenous people who were trained and returned to work in poverty areas as community organizers. Significant support was obtained for the hypothesis that community organizers who had been trained and had been working felt less external than those who were still in training. Bilker (1970) found that participation in an educational program was effective in changing indigent mothers' locus of control expectancy in an internal direction.

For a period of 3 years, Eitzen (1974) studied young male offenders living in a group home where the stated goal was to teach the necessary social skills for successful community participation. Behavior was controlled by a token economy system. Each subject was given the CNS-IE on entering, after 4 months and 9 months of residence, and again at the end of his stay. Although the 21 subjects were initially more externally oriented than a control group of junior high school boys, they were more internally oriented than controls at the end of their stay. In a study of disadvantaged black and white high school students participating in Upward Bound programs, Hunt and Hardt (1969) reported significant increases in internality for subjects of both races following 8 weeks of intensive educational emphasis in a residential setting. Using the IAR to assess locus of control, Rutledge (1972) found a significant shift toward internality among children participating in a special 4-H Club project designed for disadvantaged youth. Nowicki and Barnes (1973) administered the CNS-IE to a group of inner city teenagers entering a structured camping experience that emphasized working together to accomplish goals and where social reinforcement was given for successes. Retest scores at the end of 1 week indicated greater internality. Although there was no control group, results are strengthened by replications with successive groups of campers for the next 8 weeks. Of the eight groups studied, subjects in seven became more internal, and changes reached significance in six.

Also researchers have attempted to alter locus of control through specific skills training. In an 18-hour training program, Martin and Shepel (1974) instructed female nursing students, who functioned as lay counselors, in skills expected to increase their effectiveness as counselors. Pre- and posttraining I–E scores indicated a highly significant shift toward internality. However, Page (1975), who hypothesized that mastery of a skill previously thought beyond reach, would alter control orientation, was unsuccessful in changing locus of control among black youths as a function of success in flight training in a summer aviation program. He did find improved self-esteem in some subjects. Perhaps programs that tap a wide range of skills are more successful in altering a generalized expectancy than those concentrating on one specific area unless that skill is relevant to a critical life role.

Attention has been given also to changes in locus of control in educational settings. Johnson and Croft (1975) examined control orientation in a group of college students enrolled in a psychology course taught according to a Personalized System of Instruction (PSI). According to the authors, the PSI allows individual students pacing and mastery of material before proceeding. Therefore, it sets up a sequence of situations in which the participant's control is demonstrated to him, and should foster attitudes of internality. As predicted, pre- and posttreatment I–E scores of all subjects, including those high on externality at the beginning of the course, indicated a significant shift in the internal direction.

The effectiveness of a sequential instruction program in altering locus of control in a group of educable mentally retarded children, aged 9 through 12, was tested by Wicker and Tyler (1975). Subjects participated in daily sessions for 12 consecutive weeks during which instructional games and dramatized conflict situations were presented via role-playing, pictorial illustrations, and group discussions. These activities were designed to emphasize the connections between behavior and consequences. Mean pretreatment scores on the Bialer and IAR indicated no difference between experimental and control groups, but mean post-treatment scores on both measures indicated that the experimental group had become significantly more internal than a randomly assigned control group of children from the same class.

In a related issue, White (1971) compared the effects of self vs. peer vs. adult evaluations of school performance on belief in locus of control. He reported that external control orientations among a group of school children tended to become more internal in a nonthreatening school environment that permitted children to practice self-evaluation of their own performance. Evaluations from positive self-assuring adults were also effective in promoting internality. White's findings lend support to the idea that school environments which are too rigid in their demands for conformity may contribute to the failure of some children to develop the expected internal orientation. According to Lawrence and Winschel (1975), nondiscriminated use of praise may be another source of promoting externality in the classroom. These writers also suggest that opportunities for both success and failure must be realistically available in the classroom in order to provide an optimal environment for fostering internality. Neither of the last two hypotheses has been tested, but they both, nevertheless, contain provocative implications for educators.

Some attempts have been made to alter locus of control via behavior modification. Dua (1970) compared the effectiveness of behaviorally oriented action programs with psychotherapy reeducation in two groups of female university students who had expressed concern about ability to relate in interpersonal situations. He hypothesized that, because of the positive relationship between locus of control and interpersonal anxiety, the more effective program would lead to greater internal control, reflected in post treatment testing on Rotter's I–E scale. Subjects attended two $^1/_2$-hour weekly therapy sessions for a period of 8 weeks. Those in the action group were helped to establish specific behaviors for improving interpersonal relationships, and those in the reeducation groups focused on attitudinal changes via cognitive processes and verbal interaction. Results indicated that both experimental groups became more internal than the control group, but changes in the action group were significantly greater than those in the reeducation group.

Reimanis (1973) trained regular classroom teachers (via weekly counseling sessions) to use behavior modification techniques to make children aware of behavior consequences and contingencies in their environment. Subjects from the first and third grades were selected on the basis of teachers' ratings of low internality and met in weekly sessions with the experimental teachers who focused on the use of reinforcement to emphasize behavior-effect contingencies. Comparison of pre- and posttreatment CPT scores indicated that the experimental subjects increased significantly in internal control while no changes were noted in the control group. Also, teachers informally rated the experimental subjects behavior as more typically internal. However, teachers knew which children were in the treatment group and gave them extra attention in the classroom as time permitted. Therefore, results are probably contaminated. Reimanis' approach appears to have promise, but his methodology was poor. Replication with a larger number of subjects and adequate controls is needed.

While group psychotherapy has been the most popular mode for experiments designed specifically to alter locus of control, this approach has been utilized primarily to investigate changes in locus of control with adult or college-aged subjects. Felton and Biggs (1972), Felton (1973), Foulds (1971), and Felton and Davidson (1973) all found increases in internality following experiences in Gestalt oriented group psycho- therapy.

Changes in I–E orientation were a secondary focus in group discussion designed to modify delinquent behavior in boys aged 15–16 years, who had been placed on probation after being convicted of felonies (Ostrom et al., 1971). Treatment consisted of seven 2-hour group sessions extending over a 2 month period conducted by lay persons trained to lead these particular groups. Techniques included discussion, role-playing, emphasis on common group goals, and activities. Leaders were directed to respond to any incidents of behavior indicating control and to augment this emphasis. In addition they wrote a letter to each subject following each session, noting and praising any internal behavior observed during the meeting. Although effects of the program on delinquent behavior began to dissipate 2 to 4 months after termination of group sessions, subjects were found to be significantly more internal 9 months later (measured by a modified form of the I–E) than a group of matched controls. As premeasures of I–E were not obtained, actual change cannot be verified. Furthermore, it is questionable that greater internality had generalized to a behavioral level.

Majunda, Greever, Holt, and Friedland (1973) conducted a field study with disadvantaged high school male and female students, aged 14 through 16 years, to test the effectiveness of counseling techniques patterned after those used by Reimanis (1973) in altering locus of control. Basically, this method consists of confronting external statements and having the subjects restate them in internal terms, rewarding internal statements, and requiring subjects to focus on behavioral contingencies. Subjects participated in one individual and two group counseling sessions each week for 5 weeks. Comparisons between I–E counseled, noncounseled, and nonI–E counseled controls indicated that the I–E counseled group showed significantly greater increases in internality on posttreatment scores than the nonI–E counseled groups or the noncounseled groups. There was no significant difference between the noncounseled and nonI–E counseled groups. In attempts to alter locus of control, the methods developed by Reimanis (1973) and Felton (Felton and Biggs, 1973) in particular depend on cognitive awareness of responsibility. Other research, to which we now turn, has focused on cognitive restructuring related to the locus of control construct.

Searcy (Note 8), working with a sample of 84 racially mixed boys and girls from the first grade in a southern public school system, examined the effect of a cognitive training program designed to improve concept formation and ability to generalize. Subjects were given training in one $1/2$-hour group sessions daily for 19 days. Pre- and posttreatment measures of locus of control on the Stanford Preschool I–E Scale indicated a significantly higher posttreatment internal orientation for experimental groups, but no changes occurred for controls. Replication also yielded positive results. The children were found to maintain their gains in a follow up check 20 days after program completeion.

To summarize, the research that has been carried out in the area of alteration of locus of control suggests that I–E can be modified. This alteration of I–E can be accomplished through the appropriate environment or situational conditions such as explicit cues for reinforcement opportunities and success experiences in a skill task. The results of such attempts to modify locus of control have been to increase internality as measured by paper and pencil measures. Clearly, more research in the area is needed. For example, the data is unclear at this point as to whether there are concomitant behavioral changes resulting from increased internality as measured by locus of control scales. Furthermore, if behavior does change in a manner consistent with locus of control scores, are these changes enduring or will they extinguish once the modification program is terminated? Additionally, research must be directed at the refinement of these change procedures as well as continued demonstration of their effectiveness. Until then, it appears that the research done in the last several years is sufficient to begin to help those in the mental health and education professions to consider adopting one or more of the procedures outlined above.

REFERENCE NOTES

1. James, W. H. (1957). *Internal versus external control of reinforcement as a basic variable in learning theory.* Unpublished doctoral dissertation, Columbus, Ohio State University.
2. Sale, M. J. F. (1976). *The effect of self-instructional training on locus of control in sixth grade boys.* Unpublished doctoral dissertation, Richmond, Virginia Commonwealth University.
3. Coleman, J. J., Campbell, E. Q., Hobson, C. J., Mapartland, J., Mood, A. M., Weinfield, F. D., and York, R. L. (1966). *Equality of Educational Opportunity.* (Superintendent of Documents, Catalogue No. FS5 238 38001) Washington, D.C.: U.S. Government Printing Office.
4. Chance, J. E. (1965). *Internal control of reinforcements and the school learning process.* Paper presented at society for Research in Child Development, Minneapolis.
5. Davis, W. L. (1969). *Parental antecedents of children's locus of control.* Unpublished doctoral dissertation, Manhattan, Kansas State University.
6. Searcy, J. D. (1972). *Modification of locus of control among male school children using a skill-chance task.* Unpublished master's thesis, Greenville, East Carolina University.
7. Hawkins, J. E. (1972). *Developmental trend of locus of control.* Unpublished master's thesis, Greenville, East Carolina University.
8. Searcy, J. D. (1975). *Modification of locus of control and related variables with first grade children in a public school setting.* Unpublished doctoral dissertation, Raleigh, North Carolina State University.

REFERENCES

Allen, L. J. (1971). A study of some plausible origins and sources of I–E control orientation in children. *Dissertation Abstracts International* 32(4-B):2390–2396.
Arlin, M. (1975). The interaction of locus of control classroom structure, and pupil satisfaction. *Psychology in the Schools* 12:279–286.
Bartel, H. R. (1971). Locus of control and achievement in middle class and lower class children. *Child Development* 42(4):1099–1107.
Battle, E., and Rotter, J. B. (1963). Children's feeling of personal control as related to social class and ethnic group. *Journal of Personality* 31:482–490.
Bauer, D. H. (1975). The effect of instructions, anxiety and locus of control on intelligence test scores. *Measurements and Evaluation in Guidance* 8:12–19.
Beebe, J. S. (1971). Self-concept and internal-external control in children and adolescents. *Dissertation Abstracts International* 31(8-B):4966-4967.
Bialer, I. (1961). Conceptualization of success and failure in mentally retarded and normal children. *Journal of Personality* 29:303–320.
Bilker, L. M. (1970). Locus of control expectancy and expectancy changes of disadvantaged mothers. *Dissertation Abstracts International* 31(11-B):6839.

Bryant, B. K. (1974). Locus of control related to teacher-child interperceptual experiences. *Child Development* 45:157–164.

Buck, M. L. R. (1970). The culturally disadvantaged child and levels of school achievement as related to the internal versus external control of reinforcement, personality construct, deviant classroom behavior, and parental attitudes. *Dissertation Abstracts International* 30(8-A):3312.

Coven, A. B. (1970). The effects of counseling and verbal reinforcement on locus of control of the disabled. Unpublished Doctoral Dissertation, Tucson, University of Arizona.

Crandall, V. C., Katkovsky, W., and Crandall, V. S. (1965). Children's beliefs in their control of reinforcements in intellectual-academic achievement situations. *Child Development* 36:91–109.

Davis, W. L., and Phares, E. J. (1969). Parental antecedents of internal–external control of reinforcement. *Psychological Reports* 24:427–436.

Deysack, R. E., Keller, H. R., Roes, A. W., and Hieous, T. G. (1975). Social decentering and locus of control in children. *Journal of Psychology* 90:229–235.

Dua, P. S. (1970). Comparison of the effects of behaviorally oriented action and psychotherapy re-education on interversion–extraversion, emotionality, and internal–external control. *Journal of Counseling Psychology* 17(6):567–572.

Ducette, J. P., Wolk, S. and Soncar, E. (1972). Atypical and nonadaptive patterns in locus of control and nonadaptive. *Journal of Personality* 40:289–297.

Duke, M., and Nowicki, S. (1972). A new measure and social learning model for interpersonal distance. *Journal of Experimental Research in Personality* 6:119–132.

Dweck, C. S., and Reppucci, N. D. (1973). Learned helplessness and reinforcement responsibility in children. *Journal of Personality and Social Psychology* 25:109–116.

Eitzen, D. S. (1974). Impact of behavior modification techniques on locus of control and delinquent boys. *Psychological Reports* 35:1317–1318.

Epstein, R., and Komorita, S. S. (1971). Self-esteem, success–failure and locus of control in Negro children. *Developmental Psychology* 4:2–8.

Feather, N. T. (1966). Affects of prior success and failure of expectations of success and subsequent performance. *Journal of Personality and Social Psychology* 3:287–298.

—— (1968). Change in confidence following success or failure as a predictor of subsequent performance. *Journal of Personality and Social Psychology* 9:38–46.

Felton, G. S. (1973). Teaching internalization to middle-level mental health workers in training. *Psychological Reports* 32:1279–1282.

——, and Biggs, B. E. (1972). Teaching internalization behaviors to collegiate low achievers in group psychotherapy. *Psychotherapy: Theory, Research and Practice* 9:281–283.

——, and Davidson, H. R. (1973). Group counseling can work in the classroom. *Academic Therapy* 8:461–468.

Finch, A. J., and Nelson, W. M. (1974). Locus of control and anxiety in emotionally disturbed children. *Psychological Reports* 125:273–275.

Foulds, M. L. (1971). Changes in locus of I–E control: a growth group experience. *Comparative Group Studies* 2:293–300.

Garrett, A. M., and Willoughby, R. H. (1972). Personal orientation and actions to success and failure in urban Black children. *Developmental Psychology* 7:92.

Gottesfield, H., and Dozian, A. (1966). Changes in feelings of powerlessness in a community action program. *Psychological Reports* 19:978.

Gruen, G. E., Korte, J. R., and Baum, J. F. (1974). Group measure of locus of control. *Developmental Psychology* 10:683–686.

Gurin, P., Gurin, A., Lao, R., and Beattie, M. (1969). Internal–external control in motivational dynamics of Negro youth. *Journal of Social Issues* 25:29–53.

Hunt, D. E., and Hardt, R. H. (1969). The effect of Upward Bound programs on the attitudes, motivation, and academic achievement of Negro students. *Journal of Social Issues* 25:117–129.

Jessor, R., Graves, T. D., Hanson, R. C., and Jessor, S. (1968). *Society, Personality, and Deviant Behavior.* New York: Holt, Rinehart & Winston.

Johnson, W. G., and Croft, R. D. (1975). Locus of control and participation in a personalized system of instruction course. *Journal of Educational Psychology* 67:416–421.

Katkovsky, W., Crandall, V. C., and Good, S. (1967). Parental antecedents of children's belief in I–E control of reinforcements in intellectual achievement situations. *Child Development* 38:765–776.

Kendall, P. C., Deardorff, P. A., Finch, A. J., Jr., and Graham, L. (1974). Proxemics, locus of control, anxiety, and type of movement in emotionally disturbed and normal boys. *Journal of Abnormal Child Psychology* 4:9–16.

——, Finch, A. J., Jr., Little V. A., Charico, B. M., and Ollendick, T. H. (in press). Variations in a construct: Quantitative and qualitative differences in children's locus of control. *Journal of Consulting and Clinical Psychology.*

——, Finch, A. J., Jr., and Mahoney, J. (1976). Factor specific differences in locus of control for emotionally disturbed and normal children. *Journal of Personality Assessment* 40:42–45.

Lawrence, .E. A., and Winschel, J. F. (1975). Locus of control: implications for special education. *Exceptional Children* 41:483-489.

Lefcourt, H. M. (1967). Effects of our explications upon persons maintaining external control expectancies. *Journal of Personality and Social Psychology* 5:372–378.

—— and Ladwig, G. W. (1966). The effect of reference group upon Negroes task persistence in a biracial competitive game. *Journal of Personality and Social Psychology* 1:668–671.

Levens, H. (1968). Organization affiliation and powerlessness: A case study of the welfare poor. *Social Problems* 16:18–32.

Lifshitz, M. (1973). Social locus of control dimensions as a function of age and the socialization milieu. *Child Development* 44:538–546.

Loeb, R. (1975). Concomitants of boys' control examined in parent–child interactions. *Developmental Psychology* 11:353–358.

Ludwigsen, K., and Rollins, H. (1973). Recognition of random forms as a function of cue, perceived locus of control and socioeconomic level. Paper presented at the annual meeting of the Southeastern Psychological Dissociation, Florida, 1971. Cited by S. Nowicki and B. R. Strickland, A locus of control scale for children. *Journal of Consulting and Clinical Psychology* 40:148–154.

Luginbuhl, J. E. R., Crowe, D. H., and Kahan, J. D. (1975). Causal attribution for success and failure. *Journal of Personality and Social Psychology* 31:86–93.

MacDonald, A. P. (1973). Internal–external locus of control change-techniques. *Rehabilitation Literature* 33(2):44–47.

McGhee, P. E., and Crandall, V. C. (1973). Beliefs in internal–external control of reinforcements and academic performance. *Child Development* 39:91–102.

Majunder, R. K., Greever, K. B., Holt, P. R., and Friedland, B. U. (1973). Counseling techniques: field study shows effective internal-external counseling. *Journal of Rehabilitation* 39:19–22.

Martin. R., and Shepel, L. (1974). Locus of control to discrimination ability with lay counselors. *Journal of Consulting and Clinical Psychology* 42:741.

Milgram, N. A. (1971). Locus of control in Negro and white children at four age levels. *Psychological Reports* 29:459–465.

——, and Milgram, R. M. (1975). Dimensions of locus of control in children. *Psychological Reports* 37:523–538.

——, Shore, M. F., Riedel, W. M., and Malasky, C. (1970). Level of aspiration and locus of control in disadvantaged children. *Psychological Reports* 27:343–350.

Mischel, W., Zeiss, R., and Zeiss, A., Internal-external control and persistence: Validation and implications of the Stanford Preschool Internal-External scale. *Journal of Personality and Social Psychology*, 1974, 29, 265–278.

Newhouse, R. (1974). Reinforcement-responsibility differences in birth-order, grade level, and sex of children in grades 4, 5 and 6. *Psychological Reports* 34:699–705.

Nowicki, S. D., and Roundtree, J. (1971). Correlates of locus of control in secondary school age students. *Developmental Psychology* 4:477–478.

——, and Barnes, J. (1973). Effects of a structured camp experience on locus of control orientation. *Journal of Genetic Psychology* 122:247–252.

——, and Strickland, R. W. (1973). Personality correlates to locus of control scale. *Psychological Reports* 33:267–270.

——, and Duke, M. P. (1974). A preschool and primary internal–external control scale. *Developmental Psychology* 10:874–880.

Ostrom, T. M., Steele, C. M. Rosenblood, L. K., and Mirels, H. L. (1971). Modification of delinquent behavior. *Journal of Applied Social Psychology* 1:118–136.

Page, W. F. (1975). Self-esteem and internal versus external control among black youths in a summer aviation program. *Journal of Psychology* 89:307–311.

Pawlicki, R. E. (1974). Locus of control and the effectiveness of social reinforcers. *Journal of General Psychology* 125:153–159.

Phares, E. J. (1957) Expectancy changes in skill and chance situations. *Journal of Abnormal and Social Psychology* 54:339–342.

——, Ritchie, D. E., and Davis, W. L. (1968). Internal–External control and reaction to threat. *Journal of Personality and Social Psychology* 10:402–405.

Reimanis, G. (1973). School performance, intelligence, and locus of control scales. *Psychology in the Schools* 10:207–211.

Riedel, W. W., and Milgram, N. A. (1970). Level of aspiration, locus of control and nonachievement in retardates and normal children. *Psychological Reports* 27:551–557.

Roberts, A. (1971). The self-esteem of disadvantaged third and seventh graders. Unpublished doctoral dissertation, Emory University, 1971. Cited by S. Nowicki and B. R. Strickland. A locus of control scale for children. *Journal of Consulting and Clinical Psychology* 40:148–154.

Roth, S., and Bootzin, R. (1974). Effects of experimentally induced expectancies of external control: an investigation of learned helplessness. *Journal of Personality and Social Psychology* 29:253–264.

Rotter, J. B. (1954). *Social Learning and Clinical Psychology*. Englewood Cliffs, N.J.: Prentice Hall.

Rotter, J. B. (1966). Generalized expectancies for internal versus external control of reinforcement. *Psychological Monographs: General and Applied* 30(1):1–28.

—— (1975). Some problems and misconceptions related to the construct of internal versus external control of reinforcement. *Journal of Consulting and Clinical Psychology* 43:56–67.

——, Chance, J. E., and Phares, E. J. (1972). *Applications of a social learning theory of personality*. New York: Holt, Reinhart & Winston.

Rutledge, L. L. (1972). Selected socio-psychological behavior changes occurring in boys and girls involved in the Arkansas special 4-H project. *Dissertation Abstracts International* 32(7-A):3880–3881.

Shore, D., Milgram, N. A., and Malasky, M. (1971). Evaluation of an enrichment program for disadvantaged young children. *American Journal of Orthopsychiatry* 41:442–449.

Stephens, M. W., and Delys, P. (1973). External control expectancies among disadvantaged children at preschool age. *Child Development* 44:670–674.

Tolor, A. (1967). An evaluation of the Maryland Parent Attitude Survey. *Journal of Psychology* 67:69–74.

White, K. (1971). The effect of source of evaluation on the development of internal control among young boys. *Psychology in the Schools* 9:56–61.

Wicker, P. L., and Tyler, J. L. (1975). Improving locus of control through direct instruction: a pilot study. *Education and Training of the Mentally Retarded* 10:15–18.

Wolk, S., and Elliott, J. (1974). Information generated influence as a function of locus of control patterns in children. *Child Development* 45:928–934.

Wooster, A. D. (1974). Acceptance of responsibility for school work by educationally subnormal boys. *British Journal of Mental Subnormality* 20:23–27.

Chapter Five

Hyperactivity in Children

SAMUEL A. SAXON

Numerous areas of scientific investigation exist that simply cannot proceed without a very exacting, even computerizable, theory upon which to make projections (e.g., space flight). Medical, social, and behavioral scientists should rejoice that this is not the case with the study and investigation of the construct of "hyperactivity." For with the study of hyperactivity these scientists have demonstrated their tenacity to proceed unabatedly in their effort to define, describe, measure, and control something without the extreme utility that a good theory can offer.

Probably because of Kahn's and Cohen's (1934) description, most pre-World War II clinicians took hyperactivity to be a sign of organicity. Then, as a result of more speculation and observation, clinicians began to assume that hyperactivity was not necessarily a sign of some kind of organic pathology but that it was instead an entity in its own right and as such was diagnosable, treatable, and probably of organic etiology! The juxtaposition of these two last sentences exemplifies the careless way in which scientists and clinicians have confused cause and effect and reified hypothetical constructs.

It is not the purpose here to make the theories of such constructs as hyperactivity, minimal brain dysfunction (MBD), and similar such entities look any more theoretically ludicrous than Ross (1976) has already very poignantly done. Instead, an attempt will be made to specify a rather

103

simple model for conceptualizing the causes, behaviors, and treatments of hyperactivity. While not intended to be explanatory, the model will allow for the categorization of various research efforts in this area and will, hopefully, lend itself to the formulation in the reader's clinical judgement of a process for conceptualizing a series of hypotheses to entertain when working with the management of the hyperactive child and his (and in fewer instances *her*—Stewart, Pitts, Craig and Dieruf, 1966) parent(s). Several fairly palatable assumptions are going to be made. They are specifically: (1) There is a qualitative and quantitative aspect of behavior that can be called, with more than a modicum of consensual validation, hyperactivity. (2) There are numerous identifiable and demonstrable or potentially demonstrable causes that result in this type of behavior. (3) There are specific treatment techniques or potential treatment techniques for this type of behavior that will correspond in some logical fashion to the particular contributing causes of the behavior. This chapter is devoted to (1) specifying the nature of what is meant by "hyperactivity," (2) a very cursory review of relevant research and clinical speculation relative to four interrelated but somewhat distinct contributory factors in the behavior and corresponding treatment intervention techniques, and (3) a summary of the efforts of this laboratory in its attempt to assess and treat the hyperactive child.

THE BEHAVIOR

In the last decade, and even more recently, there has been a tendency to focus more on the symptomatology (e.g., level of locomotion and duration of attending behavior) of the hyperactive child and to become decreasingly confused concerning hyperactivity as a hypothetical construct or disease entity. More specifically, there are increasing efforts to describe the quantity and quality of the motor activity of the hyperactive child and to describe some of the behavioral and psychosocial characteristics of the hyperactive child (Werry and Sprague, 1969). Werry and his associates (Werry, 1968; Werry *et al.*, 1964; Werry *et al.*, 1966) have been the primary proponents of viewing hyperactivity as a behavioral or personality trait or dimension. They maintain, then, that the hyperactive child is simply one who is at the upper end of the distribution of this behavioral trait in the general population. However, their observation is, apparently, a more clinically reliable one than experimentally. Investigators such as Cromwell, Baumeister, and Hawkins (1963) found little support for viewing activity level as being very stable. Similarly Schulman,

Kaspar, and Thorne (1965), using actometers* as a measure of activity level, found marked variations both with groups and with children when measuring activity level. It would be premature, however, at this time to suggest that a lack of experimental evidence should negate speculations as to the existence or nonexistence of level of behavioral output as a viable dimension in the concept of hyperactivity. The measurement of hyperactivity in terms of a quantitative dimension is plagued by several difficulties. Foremost among these is, of course, the type of measurement used and its reliability.

With regard to the Schulman, Kaspar, and Thorne (1965) study, one difficulty is obviously a question of the reliability of the actometers. There have been a variety of different types of actometers devised, and these show varying levels of reliability both in terms of within and between-group measurement and in terms of the mechanical reliability of the device. Additional studies using actometers which should be cited for purposes of comparison are Massey, Lieberman, and Batarseh (1971) and Saxon, Dorman, and Starnes (1976).

A second type of assessment technique used in assessing the quantity and quality of hyperactive behavior can be called direct observation of motor activity. Under these circumstances the child is generally observed for a specified period of time in a room divided into subsections or quadrants in order to obtain a quantitative score on activity level. Usually the structure of such situations is that of the ordinary free-field types where the child is allowed to engage in regular activities. The work of Donald Routh represents a good description of the measurement and assessment of the quantity of activity level under this type of circumstance (Routh, Note 1). The kinds of behaviors observed and recorded under these free-field type of environments range from that of simple locomotion (Cromwell *et al.*, 1963) to the inclusion of many different kinds of motor behaviors (e.g., Becker *et al.*, 1967; Hutt *et al.*, 1965; Werry and Quay, 1969; Patterson *et al.*, 1965). The procedure reported by Cromwell and his associates and by Routh was simply to draw squares or grids on the floor of the playroom or waiting room and count the number of these squares or quadrants crossed or entered in a particular period of time. Patterson and his associates, on the other hand, specified seven categories of behaviors which they observed and on which they attempted to obtain reliability measures. These behaviors consisted of

---

*Actometers in most instances have been, and in this author's work are, wrist watches that have been modified so as to provide a free swinging movement of the minute and hour hands when the watches are moved. Inter and intra actometer reliability is quite high (upper 0.90's) when assessed on a standard mechanical movement device.

things like movements directed toward the body, movements in the chair, distracting movements (turning of the head), gross movements of the legs and feet, fidgeting, communicative activities, and walking or standing. Consequently, even with direct observation assessment, there are a variety of ways in which to simply observe aspects of hyperactive behavior. It will continue to be difficult to generate high reliabilities in the assessment of the quantity, much less the quality, of hyperactive behavior unless more clearly defined and generally more widely used assessment and observation techniques are used.

Another type of assessment technique consists of the use of movies or video recording to assess the quality and quantity of the behavior under observation. Although potentially and initially a costly procedure for assessment, it does have the advantage of some permanence. Photoelectric counters (Ellis and Pryer, 1959) and ultrasonic sound generators (McFarland *et al.*, 1966) share similar advantages and disadvantages with some of the other assessment techniques. While they allow for monitoring of movement of children in relatively uninhibiting environments without the child's awareness, they are costly and require specially equipped laboratories while making no provisions for qualifying the behaviors. All of the above-mentioned types of assessment techniques do allow for the child to behave in a relatively unrestricted environment with the possible exception of simply having the child restrained or confined to a particular laboratory or waiting room. Several other kinds of assessment techniques used to measure hyperactivity restrict even more severely the behavioral activity level possible for the child. These are, specifically, the balistocardiographic chair and the stabilimetric cushion (Christensen and Sprague, 1973).

Although the laboratory here at the Center for Developmental and Learning Disorders has used primarily an ultrasonic sound system device to measure quantities of activity level (Saxon and Starnes, Note 2; Saxon *et al.*, 1976), it is obvious to us that another type of assessment technique will in the long run necessarily be the most widely used. That technique will be the rating scale. The reasons for its rather wide use in the past are obvious. Rating scales can easily be reproduced and used by a variety of personnel including clinicians, teachers, parents, physicians, and work-study students alike. With sufficient pretraining, a moderate interrater reliability can be obtained. Several of these scales, for example, that of Bell, Waldrop, and Weller (1972), of Davids (1971), and of Conners (1969), have additionally shown some sensitivity to presumed changes in the quality and quantity of hyperactive behavior in children under certain circumstances (for example, pre- and postdrug treatment).

It is felt then that if there is one type of assessment technique that will be generally accepted it will very likely be some type of rating scale assessment. One scale in particular that holds some attractiveness is that which resulted from the work of Bell, Waldrop, and Weller (1972). Its attractiveness results from three specific characteristics. First, it has some experimental validation literature that accompanies it. Second, it is comprised of six distinct behavioral categories which receive different weights in terms of their predictive quality. Third, the six components of the behavior rating scale consist of behaviors that easily elicit vivid recollections on the part of any individual who has ever seen a really hyperactive (in every sense of the word) child. The specific behaviors which the parent or teacher is asked to rate the child on are the following:

(1) The amount of frenetic play in which the child engages. [In each instance the child is rated on a scale from 1 (no frenetic play) to 11 (extreme, inordinate amounts of frenetic play), etc. Additionally, the rater is given bench marks between points 1 and 11 to serve as references.]

(2) The frequency of intervention in the child's behavior by adults.

(3) The amount of nomadic play exhibited by the child.

(4) The amount of age-appropriate spilling and throwing that the child exhibits.

(5) The ability or lack of ability of the child to delay gratification.

(6) The frequency with which the child expresses some type of emotional aggression.

Despite the economical aspects of rating scales and particularly those that have shown some sensitivity to behavior change and some potential for interrater reliability, rating scales as such do suffer from a number of disadvantages such as their subjective nature and rater biases. It is consequently felt that where at all possible both the more objective assessment techniques, such as the actometers, videotaping, stabilimeters, natural observation of free field play, and ultrasonic sound rooms, should be used in addition to rating scales. This should be done not only to extend the reliability and potentially consensual validity data that can be obtained but also to continue to assess both quantitative and qualitative aspects of behavior.

Common to all of the above measurement instruments, however, is the concept of movement or activity level as the primary dependent variable. Also, movement is the lowest common denominator identifiable in the rating scale developed by Bell, Waldrop, and Weller (1972). Consequently, it is suggested that a good operational definition at this point in time is the amount and frequency of behaviors exhibited that comprise the Bell *et al.* scale. Although this particular laboratory has been singularly uneventful in demonstrating good reliability with this particular rating scale, there have been a number of instances of other laboratories having reported substantial reliability coefficients. In addition, however, the interpretation of some of the data gathered in this laboratory does suggest that the Bell *et al.* scale has some therapeutic predictive validity.

THE CAUSES

There is no doubt a variety of different factors or classes of events which can or do contribute to the heightened level of motor output in youngsters called hyperactive. One way of classifying or categorizing such etiological events is to say that there are at least four distinct facets of the cause that may or may not interact with each other in an individual child to produce hyperactive behavior. These factors are organic, developmental, emotional, and intellectual.

Organic Factors

As early as 1923, hyperactivity in children was viewed (Ebaugh, 1923; Strecker and Ebaugh, 1924) as resulting from some kind of brain damage occurring in the developmental period. Such *structural* damage could result from diseases like encephalitis, anoxia, or some kind of head trauma. The organic view of the etiology of hyperactivity was then very much expounded upon by the work of Strauss and Lehtinen (1947) who wrote about the concept of brain damage and its being indicated in children by the level of activity they exhibited. Although in recent years many terms such as hyperkinesis, hyperkinetic syndrome, and minimal brain dysfunction have replaced what they were originally calling brain damage, the position still holds that the hyperactivity evidenced by a child is primarily a result of a generalized central nervous system dysfunction. Teuber (1960) in particular calls this the hard neurological point of view, and it is a perspective frequently held by the pediatric neurologists who see many multiply handicapped retarded children.

The second distinctly different organic perspective is a *functional* one which is currently receiving a great deal of attention from Satterfield and his associates (Satterfield and Dawson, 1971; Satterfield *et al.*, 1974). This perspective holds that in many hyperactive children diffuse impairment of higher cortical centers simply is not suspected. Instead, very subtle signs of lack of optimal reticular activating system (RAS) functioning are apparent in these children. They have demonstrated, for example, using such techniques as electroencephalograms, visually evoked potential responses, reaction time tasks, psychophysical tasks of various natures, and the concept of response to Ritalin, a type of youngster exhibiting hyperactivity who shows either under or possibly over-arousal of the RAS. One of the studies to be reported later will further explicate this particular psychophysiological theory of hyperactivity.

Developmental Factors

A second perspective is that hyperactivity is in some ways like all psychopathology, i.e., at any given period during the life span development any behavior in the adult that is conceivably considered pathological has at some time been evidenced in the life history of the organism. With regard to hyperactivity, such individuals as, for example, Routh (Note 1) would suggest that the hyperactive child is simply evidencing a level of motor activity output more commensurate with that of a chronologically younger child. Consequently, it is maintained that when one sees a child who is 6 or 7 years of age who is evidencing hyperactivity, in fact the child is probably displaying the quality and quantity of behavior of a child closer to 2 or 3 years of age. Routh's (Note 1) data, as well as the observations of Klinkerfuss, Lange, Weinberg, and O'Leary (1965), have demonstrated substantial correlations between activity level and age. Knowledge of human development in general would, of course, suggest that the third and fourth years of life would be a period of time of relatively high levels of motor output, since the first 2 years of life were spent in acquiring a skeleton and musculature at a very rapid rate. According to this conceptualization, then, hyperactivity in children is evidence that they are late developmental maturers and that the child is evidencing a concomitant delay in that neurological development.

Emotional Causes

There are a number of factors which contribute to overactivity in children which can be summarily classified as reflecting acquired emotionality. Kennedy's (1971) book probably gives one of the best descriptions of how classical conditioning, operant conditioning, and modeling combine to contribute to the way certain emotional behaviors are acquired and evidenced. In addition to the evidence that children are born with certain predispositions in the area of emotionality, tempera- ment states, and activity level, it is relatively easy to understand a given child's inordinate amount of, say, emotional aggression if his/her anger episodes are either reinforced, punished, attended to by the parents in some other manner, or if they are modeled from the behavior of the parent. Similarly frustration—a presumably natural consequence of early child development and what Piaget calls "decentration"—and how a child learns to cope with or handle frustration is going to very much affect the extent to which adults, parents, and teachers alike feel the need to either tolerate or intervene in the child's conduct.

Intellective Factors

A fourth organismic variable which has not received a great deal of attention in the literature but which does contribute to overactivity and which is not unrelated to the other causative variables under considera- tion, is intellect. On the heels of over half a century of controversy surrounding the nature, nurture, and measurement of "intelligence," it is not the purpose here to add to the already large body of confusing information. Instead, just two distinct possible relationships which exist between intellect and activity will be discussed.

The first relationship between intellect and activity level is in regard to the behavior of the exceptionally bright or gifted child. The parents of these children very frequently report a restlessness and heightened level of curiosity that operationally might easily be confused with nomadic play or frenetic behavior. Although the quantity of the behavior output at times may be similar, qualitatively and functionally the behaviors take on quite a different meaning with the gifted child. The difference, of course, is that the gifted child might in fact learn objects and their functions with such efficiency as to appear to be constantly on the move and flitting from subject to subject, when in fact he is actually habituating or learning the tasks and doing so quite efficiently.

Because of the level of activity output of the gifted child, however, parents frequently do have many complaints and frequently are called upon to intervene in the child's activity. Additional clinical reports suggest that the gifted child, upon the parents' awareness of the giftedness, is likely to become an indulged individual, and a dominant sequela of over-indulgence is frequently the inability to delay gratifica- tion. This, of course, is another one of the qualities of behavior of the so-called hyperactive child, as defined by Bell, Waldrop, and Weller (1972). Although the above discourse represents much clinical impression and, to date, insufficient experimental observation, it would be a relatively easy observation on which to obtain experimental or naturalistic validity data.

At the other end of the intellectual dimension is the slow or mentally retarded child, and here too a relationship to activity level is frequently found. Many people speculate that one of the best predictors of brain damage as such in a child is the level of intellectual functioning. Certainly to some extent this is no doubt reflecting a very real correlation. Much of the earlier work in the 20's and 30's and 40's concerned itself with the multiply handicapped, hyperactive child who had experienced known central nervous system injury or impairment. However, in many instances with the mildly retarded child, neurological evidence, psychological test evidence, as well as social and developmental history evidence cannot be obtained to support with a great deal of certainty generalized central nervous system dysfunction. If we assume only that the child "may perhaps" be organically predisposed to engage in hyperactivity because of a component of the Strauss–Lehtinen syndrome, we are still left to assume that there are other causative factors involved in the heightened activity level of the mentally retarded or slow-learning child. There are several examples used to demonstrate that measured lower levels of intellectual functioning can quite easily be transformed into heightened levels of behavioral output reminiscent of hyperactivity. The first example is that of the retarded child who shows generalized lack of mental and motor development. Parents and, potentially, professionals with no evidence to the contrary have expectations for, and make demands on, the 5-year-old child which are commensurate with his age, size, and generally well-dressed demeanor. Unfortunately, this child, whose mental age is perhaps more like that of a $3^1/_2$-year-old child, is not maturationally ready for comprehension of "shoe-tying," "form discrimination," and "appropriate table manner acquisition behavior." Consequently, more than a child's share of stress is placed on the child, long before he has developed more appropriate cognitive and/or language behaviors to adapt to the level of stress. The result is that the child begins to act out in response to the stress; the behavior is frequently termed "tantrum behavior," "lack of frustration tolerance," and going from task to task simply because they are incomprehensible.

A second example of the relationship between lack of certain abilities and heightened hyperactivity, with a similar set of dynamics present, is that of the child with primary expressive aphasia. High instances of behavior problems and hyperactivity are seen in these children as well. The aphasic child, unable to express what he or she comprehends, is put in a position of acting out and engaging in a lot of physical interaction with his environment that might easily be interpreted as overactivity.

Besides intellect, emotion, organic, and developmental factors, there are a number of incidental factors that have been reported by various individuals to be either causative or associated with the occurrence of hyperactivity and over-activity in children. Such things as being male and not female would tend to predispose one to engage in hyperactive behavior. First-born children are generally more active than later-born children. Others report that there is a relationship between hyperactivity and certain kinds of nutrient or nonnutrient intakes that the child experiences. Elsewhere it is reported that there is the possibility of an allergic reaction to some kinds of substances that results in heightened activity levels. Despite the literally hundreds of possibilities to which hyperactivity can be or has been attributed, most writers generally specify factors that fall into one of the four above-described categories of causative agents: brain pathology of some type; a developmental maturational lag of some type; learned emotionality; and intellective factors.

HYPERACTIVITY: THE THERAPIES

A number of procedures to modify and control the behavioral output of the hyperactive child have been tried and their effectiveness assessed. In keeping with our model of causative factors, the intervention techniques tried to date will also be organized in this chapter around the same four components: organic factors, maturational factors, emotional factors, and intellective factors. Some aspects of the modification of hyperactive behavior have received rather significant and, in many instances, well-designed studies (for example, those dealing with learned emotionality), while others' attempts to modify the behavior have involved more clinical observation and speculation than experimentation (for example, psychoeducational therapy).

Organic Therapies

Generally the treatment of the hyperactive child with drugs consists of the use of either amphetamines or, to a lesser extent, the phenothiazines (see Chapter Eleven). The stimulant drugs, including both methylphenidate (Ritalin) and dextroamphetamine (Dexedrine), have been the most used and consequently represent the class of drug with tne best documentation in terms of effectiveness in treating hyperactivity (Conners and Eisenberg, 1963; Burks, 1964). Estimates to date suggest (Millichap, 1968; Conners, 1970) that as many as 60–80% of all hyperactive children respond with the paradoxical effect to the stimulant drugs. However, both of these investigators also indicate that there are a number of side effects, including irritability, anorexiá, and insomnia, which very frequently are treated with atarax. In addition to the side effects, Safer, Allen, and Barr (1972) also document that dextroamphetamines, and to a lesser extent methylphenidate, can cause a suppression of growth in height and weight when used for periods of 2 or more years. It should be pointed out, however, that the suppression of weight and height, although statistically significant, represented what in actuality were very small diminutions of height and weight.

The locus of the effect of the stimulant drugs which introduce the paradoxical effect in the hyperactive child is not precisely known. However, it is generally accepted that the primary locus of effect is at the reticular activating system, that functional component of the central nervous system primarily concerned with arousal. Summarily, it is felt that many hyperactive children who do respond effectively to Ritalin are for some reason showing a dysfunction at the level of the reticular activating system which puts them in a rather constant state of "unawareness" or "diminished attending ability," a state of affairs which could very easily be interpreted to result in (1) heightened levels of agitation and (more speculatively even) (2) a need to keep one's own cortex more alert by engaging in physical activity in order that the reticular activating system might be stimulated by proprioceptive stimuli in the joints sending afferent impulses to it. Here again, the work of Satterfield and his colleagues represents probably the best explication of this effect.

As indicated, other clinically popular drugs for the treatment of hyperactivity are the phenothiazines. Generally several studies (Freeman, 1966; Alderton and Hoddinott, 1964; Werry et al., 1966; Garfield et al., 1962) have been inconclusive in their attempt to find evidence for the effectiveness of the phenothiazines in the treatment of hyperactivity. Some have found the tranquilizing phenothiazines such as Chlorpromazine helpful, while others have found them no better than the placebos used. Here again, the number of side effects, which seem to occur somewhat more often when using phenothiazines than with the amphetamines, included such things as sleepiness, the possibility of seizures, and extrapyrimedial reactions and alteration in pigment metabolism (Freeman, 1966).

As de Long (1972) has pointed out, it is frequently difficult to evaluate studies of drug treatment because many of them have been poorly designed, omitting such necessary features as blind procedures, placebo controls, random assignment of subjects to groups, and precise definition of the criteria by which the children were diagnosed. Consequently it is felt that, although lacking in experimental design, the studies using pharmacological therapy probably do very validly suggest the beneficial effect of the drugs but have not resulted in sufficient data to indicate when they will be most effective and with what type of youngsters, etc. It should be mentioned in passing that our experience with parents who are considering having their child placed on Ritalin has been that they are also somewhat concerned about the addictive quality of the stimulants. A review of the literature suggests but one instance of any kind of abuse of Ritalin with these youngsters and this was on the part of the mother, who potentially can use the drug for its weight-reducing qualities.

Developmental Therapeutic Implications

Although there are a number of correlates between development and hyperactivity and activity level in general, there is no specific therapeutic intervention technique that can be called primarily developmental in nature. However, one does suspect that there is a tremendous parent–child interaction problem potential that exists in instances where children and their abilities are misjudged. Elardo, Bradley, and Caldwell (1975) have recently published evidence to suggest that the age-appropriateness of the toys provided to a child is probably a better predictor of later intellectual development than early (6–12 months of age) evaluation with the Bayley Scales of Infant Development. What is suggested here is that if it is developmentally appropriate that a child with a delayed development or maturation be engaging in more activity output, then intervention on the part of parents would simply serve as a way of perpetuating or perhaps exacerbating symptomatology. There is also another example of the way in which a lack of developmental stage consideration on the part of the parents and professionals can exacerbate the behavior present. For example, absent-parent anxiety (a very hypothetical construct) has been reported to occur during a brief period of time (about six to eight months) approximately when a child enters school. In single-parent homes, regardless of the reason for its being a single-parent home, children when they hit this age very frequently show heightened levels of emotional behavior and particularly emotional aggression. As this seems to be the case whether the parent is divorced or never had a spouse, and since it seems to be somewhat unrelated to the ego integrity of the child prior to that period of time, it would seem to be developmentally an event which will simply "run its course." This is potentially another kind of developmental episode much like activity level that can best be ignored for its quickest recovery. Eisenberg (1966) also makes some suggestions which are appropriate to the consideration of hyperactivity as a developmental phenomenon. He suggests that parents, when giving instructions to children, should make them brief, unambiguous, and in words the child can comprehend easily. He also suggests making for and demanding of a child activities that are brief and in order with the particular child's ability for sustained attention (also see Chapter Six).

Learned Emotionality: Therapeutic Implications

It is quite easy to view all of those behaviors listed by Bell, Waldrop, and Weller (1972) in their definition of hyperactivity as being operants. Consequently it is only logical that many people have approached hyperactivity therapeutically by using and suggesting the techniques of some form of operant conditioning as a basis of therapy for these children. Indeed, Eisenberg (1966), mentioned above, suggested that it was necessary to promptly reinforce children when they did respond to brief instructions and that it was quite appropriate to provide children with time-out periods when impending tantrums were detected. Werry (1968) and Werry and Sprague (1969) have probably argued best for the use of behavior modification as a primary technique for the treatment of hyperactivity. They maintain this position because behavior modification (1) relies less on verbal mediation than do some other types of potential therapies, (2) is a problem-oriented therapy for those complaining of the child's behavior, (3) is based on a concept of assessment by which the effect of the technique can be quite easily measured for treatment outcome purposes, and (4) does lend itself to use by third-party agents to carry out daily therapeutic routines. Because Werry believed that hyperactivity is an externalized or acted-out type of behavior, there is no doubt that he would be very much taken primarily with the use of behavior modification techniques involving counter-conditioning of incompatible, nonhyperactive behaviors. Because of their potential utility, several good examples of the implementation of operant procedures with the hyperactive child will be given.

Patterson, Jones, Whittier, and Wright (1965) conditioned attending behavior in a brain-injured hyperactive boy in a classroom. Preconditioning of an associative nature, pairing auditory stimulus with pennies or candy, resulted in the secondary reinforcement qualities of auditory stimulus. During class the boy was given an auditory stimulus during each specified time interval in which one of the high-rate nonattentive responses did not occur, and at the end of the class period he was given a corresponding amount of pennies or candies. After eight trials varying in length from 8 to 15 minutes, the child showed a significant decrease in nonattending behavior. Additionally the reduction in nonattending behavior was maintained over the entire next week during the removal of the program.

Doubros and Daniel (1966) maintained a most intriguing perspective, that hyperactivity consisted of a series of wrong responses that were often maintained by many unspecified environmental consequences and originated from many different etiologies. In their treatment they employed an operant differential reinforcement procedure in a playroom setting. The children in their study were reinforced with a token which was associated with a buzzer and a light flash for each 30-second period of time of continued absence of overactive behavior. They employed 20-minute periods and ran the children for 30 trials. Doubros and Daniel found that not only was the total frequency of hyperactive behavior reduced but the procedure also reduced the variability of activity level output during the 14 days of extinction and follow-up.

Quay, Sprague, Werry, and McQueen (1967) worked with a group of five hyperactive children simultaneously in an attempt to modify the individual subjects' visual orientation. All five youngsters were of normal intelligence and had been placed in a special class for behavior-problem children. The subjects were seated at desks in a semicircle around the teacher with a small box containing a light mounted inside the box on top of each desk. Each young subject was observed for fifteen 10-second segments during each experimental session and was reinforced on a variable-ratio schedule by having the light flash, which was followed by candy and/or social reinforcement. The behavior reinforced was a ten-consecutive-second observation of the child looking continuously at the teacher as she read a story. Orienting responses or looking at the teacher significantly increased under the candy-plus-social-reinforcement and the social-reinforcement-alone conditions and significantly decreased under reversal procedures. Quay and his associates concluded that their study demonstrated the feasibility of simultaneously conditioning an academically relevant response in a group of hyperactive youngsters in a classroom-type setting.

Christensen and Sprague (1973) administered reinforcement contingent upon reduced seat movement to two groups of children, one receiving placebo and the other group receiving methylphenidate. Their interest was primarily in whether or not methylphenidate would enhance the effect of the behavior modification techniques by producing faster, greater, or longer-lasting reductions in measured activity level (seat fidgeting behavior). The reinforcements were indicated by a flashing light and a counter on the desk top. Activity level was measured by a stabilimetric cushion attached to each chair. Contingent reinforcement resulted in seat activity reduction in both groups; however, the drug treatment group displayed consistently lower rates of movement. Christensen and Sprague also observed that the placebo subjects showed an immediate increment in moving once the reinforcement contingencies were removed. Their results strongly suggest that in some ways drug-plus-behavior-therapy treatment combinations may be superior to behavior modification alone.

Kauffman and Hallahan (1973) reported their attempts to control the aggressive and disruptive behaviors of a 6-year-old boy with multiple problems using novel contingencies and directive teaching. The teacher provided the child with social reinforcement for each specified time interval that was free of rough physical behavior. The teacher allowed the child to turn over a card in the special deck, with different reinforcements available depending on the symbol on the chosen card. Halfway through the experiment reinforcement was discontinued and a highly structured directive teaching program was instituted. In this procedure the child was taught as part of a small group of four to six youngsters and was expected to respond according to the rules established and modeled by the teacher. The children were socially reinforced for appropriate behavior and all misbehaving children were ignored. Their data, relative to the 6-year-old boy with many of the behaviors listed by the Bell, Waldrop, and Weller (1972) definition, suggest that both the reinforcement using the novel contingencies and the directive teaching procedure were effective in controlling his aggression and hyperactivity.

Another study involving operant conditioning which certainly merits consideration is that of Meichenbaum and Goodman (1971). Meichenbaum was concerned with the construct of impulsivity (see Chapter Six for further discussion), a very frequent complaint about the hyperactive child. Their work suggested very strongly that impulsive (another of the behaviors indicative of hyperactivity) children are deficient in controlling their motor behavior by using self-commands. However, they do provide evidence that a child can develop control over operant motor behavior by employing verbal operants to do so. Summarily, the technique employed was that the child learned to internalize or silently verbalize the rules regulating the necessary motor output via means of reinforced practice. By imitating the examiner as he draws geometric designs and talks out verbal equivalents of the motor behavior, the child then reproduces the geometric design by mouthing the necessary rules and then reproduces the design again simply by thinking through the necessary verbal directions. Over a period of a very few sessions Meichenbaum demonstrated the ability of a child to drastically improve in his reproductions and performance on Bender Visual–Motor Gestalt type tasks.

Several of the studies cited above, of course, will also be relevant to the section on therapeutic implications below, dealing with psychoeducational procedures. In particular, the work of Meichenbaum and his associates and of Eisenberg (1966), as well as the work of Quay, Sprague, Werry, and McQueen (1967), holds a great deal of significance for psychoeducational considerations in the treatment of hyperactivity or that component of hyperactivity that can be a result of intellective factors or correlated with intellectual ability.

Psychoeducational Therapeutic Implications

The last complement of treatment techniques suggested for use in managing the hyperactive child concerns those techniques that would seem to be a primary consideration when the child's hyperactivity is at all related to substantially inferior or superior levels of intellectual functioning, as measured by standardized individual intelligence tests. Of the four areas of therapeutic implications considered, this one has no doubt received the least amount of experimental attention as well as clinical speculation; nonetheless, it is felt to present a significant component of treatment and management of the hyperactive child, and several of the already cited instances are very pertinent to this area of treatment.

The gifted child's insatiable appetite and curiosity frequently do result in an activity level and a type of demanding behavior pattern which tend to irritate parents and teachers who have to contend with them for long periods of time. These children become "bored" apparently very quickly and seek additional stimulation. One procedure that has been proposed to manage this level of activity is to alter their curriculum in such a manner as to make it more challenging. For example, educators (Kirk, 1972) suggest that, instead of the usual content-oriented curricula, it would be more interesting and challenging, and would be more likely to hold the attention of the gifted youngster, if the curriculum stressed process more and content less. Although this suggestion makes intuitive sense, there is not sufficient experimental evidence to suggest that this procedure is any more or less efficient than accelerating a child or providing more and more difficult content for him to master.

In the event that a child's hyperactivity is associated with some retarded mental ability, there does appear to be a series of activities that would result in less emotional strain being placed on the child and consequently less of an opportunity for reaction in a stressful, frustrated manner on his part. In the event of lowered levels of intellectual functioning, traditional group reading, which requires not only an internal locus of motivation but also very selective listening skills, is contraindicated because of the high probability of over-stressing the child (Kirk, 1972). Although comparative empirical data has yet to be obtained, programmed instruction, with its very precise, stepwise progression involving stimuli, responses, and consequences, which are quite specifiable and observable, should be much more effective in the instruction of these children. Also it should result in more efficient learning and reduce the amount of hyperactivity in the classroom. Materials such as the Edmark Reading Program and the Sullivan Programmed Reading Series* can be especially useful in teaching the educable mentally retarded child to read under conditions of diminished demand and stress and consequently the display of less disruptive behavior.

In the instance of an intellectually impaired child with expressive aphasia when attempting speech therapy, McGinnis (1963) has demonstrated that acquisition of speech can proceed in almost the reverse order of the normal acquisition of speech and subsequently produces much less stress and results in more efficient behavior change. The speculations of Eisenberg regarding brief unambiguous instructions and orderly activities and the contention by individuals such as Strauss and Lehtinen (1947) and Laufer and Denhoff (1957) concerning a restructuring of the child's environment so as to optimize regularity of routine, the avoidance of over-excitement, and maximal consistency are all pertinent to the psychoeducational treatment of the hyperactive child. These procedures are as relevant to the child with lowered intellectual functioning as a primary contributor to his hyperactivity as they are to a child whose hyperactivity is perhaps associated with some form of organic involvement. In the same vein, the use of certain psychoeducational therapeutic

---

*The Edmark Reading Program is published by Edmark Associates, 655 South Orcas Street, Seattle, Washington, 98108; and the Sullivan Programmed Reading Series is published by Webster Division, McGraw-Hill Book Company, 1221 Avenue of the Americas, New York, New York, 10020.

interventions that have been specified for use with children showing no intellective correlates of overactivity, but in whom rather minimal brain dysfunction is a suspected contributor (for example, the use of booths to facilitate knowledge acquisition under conditions of reduced environmental stimuli, as suggested by Cruickshank, Bentzen, Ratzburg, and Tannhauser, 1961) has not received sufficient experimental investigation to warrant uncritical use despite the procedures' popularity (Kirk, 1972).

In summary, then, the working assumption of the author is that "hyperactivity" is a term that describes both quantitative and qualitative aspects of behavior and therefore every attempt should be made to measure it along both dimensions. In the first instance, rating scales will give one an idea of the qualitative aspects of the behavior (for example the Bell, Waldrop, and Weller definition), and in the second instance a variety of objective measurement devices can give one an idea of the quantity of activity level output of a child. It is further felt that hyperactive behavior emanates from one or more of four not inseparable but somewhat distinct categories of etiological factors. They are (1) organic, (2) developmental, (3) learned emotionality, and (4) intellective. It is also felt that the therapeutic attempts to date to deal with the overactive child can similarly fall under four related categories: (1) pharmaceutical control, (2) fostering of growth and maturation, (3) operant conditioning learning techniques, and (4) psychoeducational procedures.

STUDIES OF RATING SCALE VALIDITY, PARENT TRAINING EFFECTS, PUNISHMENT EFFECTS, AND PREDICTING RESPONSE TO RITALIN

During the past 2 years several studies related to hyperactivity have been conducted in the Division of Psychology in the Center for Developmental and Learning Disorders. Some of these have been reported previously (Saxon and Starnes, Note 2; Saxon, Dorman, and Starnes, 1976) and will only be reported here briefly. The first study concerned the reliability and validity of the more prevalently used rating scales for assessing hyperactivity (Saxon et al., 1976). The basic assumption made was that "activity" is a basic component of the construct of "hyperactivity." This study, the results of which are summarized in Table 1*, was based on data obtained from 50 children ranging in age from $3^1/_2$ to nearly

---

*Reproduced with permission of the *Journal of Pediatric Psychology*.

Table 1. Correlation Coefficients between Rating Scales and Objective Measures of Activity

	Chronological age	Arm motion	Leg motion	Room activity	Scale A	Scale B
Arm motion	−0.18					
Leg motion	−0.06	0.64^a				
Room activity	0.03	0.45^a	0.51^a			
Scale A	0.23	0.19	0.34^b	0.06		
Scale B	0.24	-0.32^b	−0.18	−0.05	−0.09	
Scale C	−0.27	0.20	0.27	0.14	0.74^a	0.08

$^a p < 0.01.$
$^b p < 0.05.$

$8^1/_2$ years with a mean age of 5.8 years and standard deviation of 1.4 years. The rating scales employed were Davids' (1971) scale (Scale A), Conners' (1970) scale (Scale B), and the Bell *et al.* (1972) scale (Scale C). The arm and leg measures were made by the use of Timex Model 32 self-winding calendar watches whch had been converted to motion recorders (actometers) by the Timex Corporation. A room activity measure was obtained by a Mallory-produced burglar alarm system which was used to detect the amount of time a child was in motion. The movement detection device was activated by 200 cubic inches of mass moving one foot per second, and it would stay activated until less mass movement occurred. All movement measures were taken in a 7 ft × 9 ft playroom.

A perusal of the table should suggest a modicum of concurrent validity that exists among the objective measures and at least a concurrent reliability coefficient of some substance between the David scale and the *Bell et al.* scale. Although the analyses do not permit it, one can assume that the results are not inconsistent with the conceptualization that hyperactivity, like activity in general, varies both in terms of quantity (the criterion measure) and quality (the rating scales) and that the two need not necessarily correlate. The results also strongly suggest that, despite the many advantages of using rating scales, one should if at all possible use more objective measures in addition to them. This admonition, of course, comes from the fact that little evidence for construct validity was found.

The next study, a treatment study, was conducted based on several assumptions: (a) If a child were on amphetamine treatment it would not impede the child's response to operant conditioning therapy. (b) The hyperactive child is amenable to direct behavior modification intervention using principles of learning. (c) Since the author had previously used a parent as an effect mediator of behavior change in children (Garrard and Saxon, 1973), it is possible to do the same with a hyperactive child. Because of the increasing number of children referred as hyperactive and because of the author's inability to glean from the literature or his experience a universal description of the "hyperactive" child, it was decided that a *group* of children would be the target population. This way it was assumed that different types of "hyperactivity" would be represented. This study, then, was an attempt to reduce or alter the quantity and quality of behavioral activity exhibited by 16 kindergarten and first grade children of average ability diagnosed as hyperactive by (1) their pediatricians and (2) the three aforementioned rating scales through counseling the parents in behavioral management techniques. The parent group training sessions met for eight consecutive Wednesday nights for 2 to 3 hours. The eight sessions consisted of didactic discussions concerning hyperactivity, viewing videotapes of hyperactivity being extinguished and taught by unsuspecting psychology interns, reading assignments in Smith and Smith (1970) and Krumboltz and Krumboltz (1972), and discussion of specific individual attempts on the part of parents to effect behavior change in their children. All of the children were assessed before and after the parent training sessions in the same room using the activity measure referred to in the previously mentioned study. The activity level of the children was measured and expressed as the number of minutes out of 20 that the children were in motion under one of four conditions (alone, with a female experimenter, alone, with mother) in a randomized order both before and after treatment. The data were analyzed according to the pattern of activity level of the youngsters before the initial group meeting. By visualizing distinct patterns of activity, three groups of children were identified. One group of eight youngsters was called the mother-stimulated hyperactive group (MSH). These youngsters before parent training were basically twice as active with their mothers as they were under any other condition. The second group was identified as the field independent hyperactives (FIH). There were 5 of these youngsters and they showed no significant variation across stimulus conditions in the pretreatment assessment. The third group identified in this *post hoc* manner was a small group of 3 youngsters who were called the externalized aggression hyperactives (EAH). These 3 youngsters prior to treatment demonstrated three times the amount of activity by themselves and with the female experimenter as they did with their mothers.

When the counseling sessions were terminated measures were repeated on all of the youngsters. The mother-stimulated hyperactive youngsters reduced their level of activity output in the presence of the mother to a statistically significant extent. The externalized aggression hyperactives (EAH) also showed a significant change in that they were more active with their mothers, which the authors interpreted to mean that they were less inhibited around their mothers. Unfortunately, these three youngsters did not show a diminution of generalized activity level by themselves or with the female examiner. The field independent youngsters (FIH), although no more or less active in a quantitative sense than the other two groups, showed absolutely no variability across time under any of the conditions or pre- and postparent group training. It is worthwhile to note that even with this small number of children, the rating scales completed by the mothers of the FIH group prior to the training sessions suggested that these 5 youngsters were extremely hyperactive.

The impression drawn from this study is that parent training may be useful in helping to reduce the activity level of some types of hyperactive children. It is also felt that the particular measure employed may have some utility in behaviorally assessing the pattern of hyperactivity in hyperactive youngsters and this could contribute to some predictive statement regarding the utility of parent effectiveness training. Although the earlier study had questioned the construct validity of rating scales, this study strongly suggests that the scales may have some predictive validity. What was observed *post hoc* was that most hyperactives with moderately high rating scale scores showed lower activity output after parent training, and none of the hyperactives with very high rating scale scores showed quantitatively less activity after parent training.

A third study involving modification of the activity level of hyperactive children employed punishment (Thomas, Note 3). The utility of positive reinforcement has been amply demonstrated in its ameliorative effect on hyperactive behavior. Equally important, although less frequently studied, is the use of negative reinforcement and/or punishment in the control of children's behavior. Several investigators (Solomon, 1964; Walters and Parke, 1967; Baer, 1970) have challenged the view that punishment, as a form of aversive stimulation applied contingent upon a specific behavior, is both ineffective for changing behavior and likely to produce harmful side effects. An extensive review of the literature (Walters and Parke, 1967) on the influence of punishment on the social behavior of children indicates that *consistent* and *intense* aversive stimulation can effectively *suppress* undesirable behavior, especially if *judiciously* timed.

The use of the aversive stimulus in this study with humans, which was conducted by Dr. Diane Starnes Thomas as part of her doctoral dissertation research, does of course raise many ethical concerns. However, this particular study was designed to fulfill all the requirements of each of the principles listed in the 1973 APA *Ethical Principles in the Conduct of Research With Human Participants.* The specific hypothesis which Thomas tested was that the use of contingent punishment would significantly reduce the activity level of hyperactive children when compared to the use of noncontingent punishment or no punishment. The aversive stimulus applied was a 2-second, 90 dB, 1000 Hz narrow-band noise administered contingent upon stepping outside of a specified play area.

Twenty-one children with a mean age of 9 years and a mean WISC Intelligence Quotient of 93 were rated as hyperactive on the Bell *et al.* (1972) scale (2.5 standard deviations above the mean) and the Conners (1969) scale (a score greater than or equal to 24). The children exhibited only minor signs of neurological damage as judged by the Klonoff, Robinson, and Thompson (1969) inventory. All children were assessed to determine that hearing was within normal limits and that they had sufficient tolerance for the aversive auditory stimulus. None of her subjects were on any medication at the time of the study.

After an initial 1-hour evaluation the procedure for the following nine 20-minute experimental sessions was the same. Each child was taken to the experimental room, which was equipped with a small table and chair and a one-way viewing mirror. Before entering the playroom each child was allowed to select three toys from a cart and was told to play with his toys at the table within the play area marked off on the floor by black tape and to wait until the experimenter returned for him in 20 minutes. The experimenter then took her place behind the mirror and recorded three behaviors used as dependent measures: (1) the number of times the child placed his foot on or outside of the line marking the play area, (2) the number of times the change took place, and (3) the amount of time he spent unoccupied with toys.

The nine sessions were divided into three stages. During the assessment-baseline stage (sessions 1 through 3), each child was allowed 20 minutes of free play per day with his toys. Following this stage the children were then randomly assigned to one of three groups, the only restriction being that the groups did not differ with respect to mean activity level during the first segment. During the treatment phase (sessions 4, 5, and 6), all children were instructed at the beginning of session 4 that they might hear a loud noise or sound while playing, and they were given two demonstrations of the noise. A child in the contingent punishment group heard 2-second bursts of the noise, separated by 2 seconds of silence as long as he remained outside the play rectangle. When the child stepped back inside the play area marked by the black tape on the floor, the noise ceased. For every child in the contingent punishment group there was a child in the noncontingent punishment group who served as a yoked control. This child heard the same number of presentations of the noise, presented at the same time as to his contingent punishment control partner but not contingent upon any specific behavior. During the follow-up or recovery phase (sessions 7, 8, and 9) the children in all three groups were then allowed 20 minutes of free play with their toys and heard no presentation of the noise. The total time spent outside of the rectangle was used as a dependent measure of the activity level and it is the one reported here. The main finding of this study relative to the activity level measure is reported in Fig. 1, which shows for the three groups the mean amount of time spent outside the play area over the nine sessions. The rather large amount of variability in the noncontingent punishment group and the nopunishment group as well as the reduction during baseline hampers to some extent the conclusions that could be drawn. Of some significance were the results of the contingent punishment group itself. For this group there were some significant changes in activity level observed over the three blocks of trials ($F = 9.15$, $df = 2,12$; $p < 0.05$). Figure 1 illustrates the significant reduction

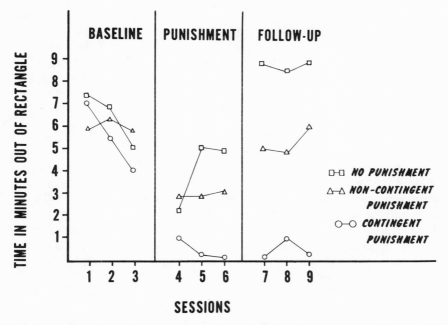

Fig. 1. Mean number of minutes of out-of-seat behavior of three groups of hyperactive children in response to noncontingent, contingent, or no punishment. Follow-up represents return to baseline.

in the amount of time spent outside the play area during the period when the contingent punishment procedure was instituted and shows that this significant reduction, as compared to baseline measure, was maintained through the three immediate follow-up trials. In contrast to the other two groups, subjects in the contingent punishment group did not vary significantly among themselves ($F = 1.06$; $df = 6,12$; NS). This homogeneity may reflect the instructional or feedback component of the aversive noise.

When the results of each group were analyzed individually, only the contingent punishment group showed a significant reduction in activity level over trials. This finding tends to support the hypothesis that a contingent punishment procedure using loud noise as an aversive stimulus more effectively suppresses the activity level of a hyperactive child, as defined by the selection criteria of this study, than does a noncontingent or nopunishment procedure. Although additional studies are necessary to determine some of the parameters of this particular noxious stimulus that contributed to the suppressive effect on activity level, the effect was quite obvious. There are several questions that certainly need to be investigated. For example, one relates to the fact that the noxious stimulus was not that aversive in a painful sense and that quite conceivably part of its effect could have been the cue value of the auditory stimulus, which simply facilitated attending or acquisition of a predictable rule in these particular youngsters. Additionally, of course, it would be of much utility to determine if the same results of punishment would be obtained when children were or were not taking pharmacological treatment, as well as whether punishment was used with or without positive reinforcement for more appropriate behavior.

A fourth study (Saxon *et al.*, Note 4) consists of determining the pattern of activity level within trials of hyperactive children who are good or poor responders to amphetamine treatment. Satterfield and Dawson (1971) have made extensive observations about level of arousal and organic etiology of hyperactivity. "Arousal" is used basically to refer to the level of alertness, depending on or determined by the integrity of the reticular activating system and the central nervous system as assessed by various electrodermal activity measures and psychophysical abilities. By and large, good and poor responders in the Satterfield study, as well as ours, were determined simply by reports of parents and teachers using rating scales of improved behavior while taking Ritalin. What is meant by "poor responders" is that the Ritalin either caused a great many side effects such as irritability, anorexia, or further overactivity, or had absolutely no effect on the behavior of the child. Satterfield, Cantwell,

Lesser, and Podosin (1973) reported about a number of "good responders" that they demonstrated very low skin conductance and consequently they suggested that good responders are by and large underaroused hyperactive children. This observation was made at least in part as a result of an early observation by Satterfield and Dawson (1971) that, under conditions of running and obtaining electrodermal measures on some good responders, 2 of the 11 youngsters, when restrained or inhibited from movement for the purpose of obtaining the measures, fell asleep. Based on these observations, as well as additional observations that many of the poor responders to Ritalin did not show indications of under-arousal, it was hypothesized that good and poor responders to Ritalin show a different pattern of motor activity output from each other and from control subjects.

The Saxon, Magee, and Siegel (Note 4) study used 15 children ranging in age from 4 to 6.8 years of age. They were all of at least average intellectual ability (IQ equal to or greater than 80, as assessed by the WPPSI or Stanford–Binet) and all had been in some kind of prekindergarten, kindergarten, or first grade situation. The 15 youngsters represented 5 subjects in each of three groups (Factor A). The first group (A_1) consisted of children diagnosed as hyperactive on whom Ritalin had been used for varying lengths of time during the previous 9 months and for whom it was, according to the parents and pediatricians, effective in reducing motor output. This group was called the "good responder to Ritalin" group. The second group (A_2) consisted of 5 youngsters all of whom had been labeled as hyperactive by their parents and pediatricians according to rating scales and, in applicable instances, by the first-grade or kindergarten teachers. These youngsters had not responded to or had not shown the paradoxical effect of stimulant (Ritalin) treatment. In addition, both groups A_1 and A_2 had rating scale scores on the Conners (1969) and Bell, Waldrop, and Weller (1972) scales which suggested hyperactivity in all 10 of these youngsters. The third group of 5 youngsters (A_3) were normal control subjects of similar age, size, and intellectual functioning who were not suspected by anyone of being overactive or hyperactive. Additionally, according to the rating scales employed, none of their rating scores suggested the presence of significant hyperactive symptomatology. The good responders were not on any medication at the time of the study.

Besides Factor A (groups), two more independent variables were employed. The second variable was Factor B and represented two trials (B_1 and B_2). The two trials were run during either the same morning or the same afternoon and were separated by variable intervals of time. The third independent variable analyzed was Factor C (four consecutive 5-minute blocks within each trial). Consequently a $3 \times 2 \times 4$ analysis of variance designed with repeated measures on the last two factors was employed. The dependent variable was the number of minutes during each 5-minute period that the child spent in a measurable amount of motion as detected by the ultrasonic sound system. This is the same dependent variable referred to as "room activity" and specified in greater detail in Saxon, Dorman, and Starnes (1976).

Each child was placed in a 7 ft × 9 ft playroom which contained a cart with six sedentary toys (for example puzzles and Play-Doh) which, subjectively speaking, would not tend to elicit much physical activity in children. Each child was taken to the room and instructed to stay there until the experimenter returned. They were told that they could do anything they wanted to do but that they were not to leave the room or open the door. The subject's activity level was measured by the aforementioned ultrasonic sound movement detection system which was adjusted so that it would detect 200 cubic inches or more of mass moving one foot per second in any quadrant of the room. The amount of time spent in motion for each of the 5-minute periods was automatically clocked by a Lehigh Valley Data Pac System with appropriate backup logic equipment. The results of the analysis are reported in Table 2. As can be seen, there were no significant main effects and only one significant interaction effect. The lack of main effect particularly between the hyperactive and control subjects supported our previous finding (Saxon *et al.*, 1976) regarding the rather small relationship between rating scale scores and quantified activity level. The group-times-segments effect was significant, $F(6,36) = 7.09$, $p < 0.01$, and supports the hypothesis that good

Table 2. Analysis of Variance

Source	df	MS	F
Groups (A)	2	0.27	<1
error$_a$	12	1.60	
Trials (B)	1	0.02	<1
A × B	2	0.43	<1
error$_b$	12	0.912	
Segments (C)	3	0.06	<1
A × C	6	1.49	7.09^a
error$_c$	36	0.21	
B × C	3	0.15	<1
A × B × C	6	0.36	<1
error$_{bc}$	36	0.59	

[a]$p < 0.01$.

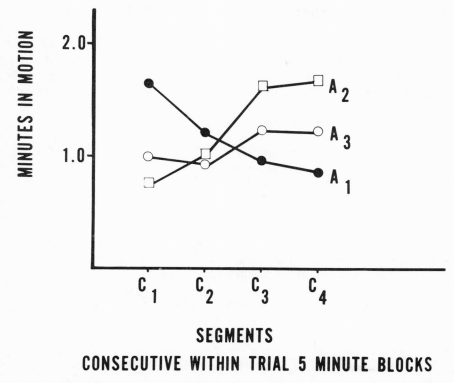

Fig. 2. Mean number of minutes in motion by Groups (Factor A) and by 5-minute segments (Factor C) of the trials (A_1 = responders; A_2 = Nm − responders; A_3 controls).

and poor Ritalin responders show significantly different patterns of motor activity level. This interaction is plotted in Fig. 2. *Post hoc* analyses resulted in the significant interaction effect being a function of significant differences in Group A_1 and Group A_2 at C_1, $t(8) = 2.19$, $p < 0.05$; at C_3, $t(8) = 2.13$, $p < 0.05$; and at C_4, $t(8) = 2.94$, $p < 0.01$. Of the 5 good responders, all show the same trend toward lowered levels of motor output across time. All of the poor responders showed the increased motor output.

The fact that the good Ritalin responder or the so-called "under-aroused" hyperactive child moved about less and less in the playroom certainly supports the probable contention of Satterfield and Dawson (1971) that hyperactives with lowered levels of RAS excitation would become more and more sedate under condition of lowered level of sensory input. It should be pointed out, of course, that this study did not experimentally lower sensory input. It did, however, attempt to minimize and make constant the external stimuli available.

The other aspect of the interaction effect, however, was not as consistent with what was predicted, i.e., that the poor responders (or more aroused) would become progressively more active across treatment segments. As with the explanation of the under-aroused or good responder, the explanation for the poor responder's increase in activity would most feasibly center around the reticular activating system (RAS) and its role in arousal.

Although observed by Bradley (1937), it was the work of Killam (1962) that suggests an explanation for the paradoxical effect of stimulant treatment. The stimulant drug tends to raise RAS excitability by enhancing impulse control, so that need to seek proprioceptive or kinesthetic sensory feedback to enhance the level of RAS arousal is reduced. One could easily speculate, then, that (a) the hyperactive poor responder is already aroused or over-aroused at the level of the RAS, (b) higher cortical processes (not just subcortical ones) are dysfunctional, and/or (c) the RAS' interaction with higher cortical processes is impaired. Walley and Welden (1973) cite studies from both human and infrahuman research which suggest that the construct of cortical inhibition and arousal vary together. From this it can be postulated that there are hyperactive children who are so over-aroused at the level of the RAS that certain response systems become cortically more inhibited and consequently other systems disinhibited. Unable to cortically inhibit or restrain their responding, the child then sends more and more proprioceptive stimuli to further increase their level of arousal, thereby setting up a cyclic reaction that drives the child in a spiraling fashion into more and more activity. This is, of course, a highly speculative explanation for the tendency of the poor-responding hyperactives in the present study to become more and more active and would deserve further observation. In fact, if one compares the work of Zahn, Abate, Little, and Wender (1975) with that of Satterfield *et al.* (1973), he will likely see that the status of arousal level of the good responders is not known for certain.

A recent review by Barkley (1976) concludes that one in four hyperactive children is nonresponsive to amphetamine treatment. His findings also suggest that hyperactive children vary among themselves in level of central nervous system arousal. One apparent possibility is that perhaps the youngsters who are over-aroused and/or poor amphetamine responders are the ones who would respond better to the CNS depressants and tranquilizers.

This present study (Saxon *et al.*, Note 4) has several very significant implications. For one, it is conceivable from Satterfield's several statements and the present one that some hyperactive children, under certain conditions (for example, the barren walls of a testing chamber) will show an organically determined activity level output. Any comment subsequent to this by the clinician that he or she was able to bring the child's behavior under stimulus control should therefore be highly suspect. If indeed the under-aroused hyperactive is the good responder and the good responder is the one to most likely show reduced motor output, then many wrong clinical impressions and treatment might accrue.

Also of some importance is the idea that studies designed to assess the reliability and validity of rating scales which take place in waiting rooms and in the confines of playrooms should seek to control for the "arousal level" or, more appropriately, the responsiveness of the hyperactive child to Ritalin, in the subjects they employ. A third implication of this present study is, of course, that research in the behavioral child could conceivably proceed in a less haphazard manner if beforehand more predictive information were known about the child's arousal level and activity level pattern. For example, if the above findings bear replication, then perhaps the pediatrician or child psychiatrist who attempts to use Ritalin or dextroamphetamine in the treatment of hyperactivity can increase the probability of positive responses from 60 to 70% to 90 or 100%. There is, of course, the same type of implication for psychoeducational experience for these children. Perhaps an external-stimuli-inhibiting booth is the best place for certain types of behaviorally assessed hyperactive youngsters to learn, but in other instances of hyperactivity a learning booth may be found to be quite ineffective.

CLINICAL IMPLICATIONS

This chapter represents a rather meager review of a voluminous amount of research attempting to observe, measure, define, and modify hyperactive behavior. Additionally, the author does not pretend that the research reported here represents in all instances the most rigorous experimental research. It does, however, represent this clinician's attempt to learn more about and to learn how to more effectively deal with a developmental disability that apparently has become either "popular" or more prevalent. As a result of his experience and the studies conducted here at the Center for Developmental and Learning Disorders, the author now has a relatively systematic procedure for handling referrals for hyperactivity. The task, simply, is to attempt identification of the relative contribution of organic, developmental, learned, emotional, and/or intellective factors to a child's hyperactivity and consequently to its management. In many instances relative contributions cannot be assessed; however, it can frequently be determined if a factor is miniscule in its effect or if the factor can be ruled out, so to speak. The last three factors can be assessed rather directly by answering three questions via the usual clinical observation, interviewing, and testing.

The first question that needs answering is, to what extent have the parents taught (if the child is fairly physically healthy and of average skills and ability) the child to be overactive by either modeling or inappropriate attending? Or, to what extent are the parents maintaining, on typically a very thin schedule of reinforcement, a variety of hyperactive behaviors (for example, those specified by the Bell *et al.* scale) that may have been age-appropriate but shocking and attention-getting to the parents when they initially occurred? One must remember, and feel free to remind parents, that the quantitative and qualitative aspects of hyperactivity are all age-appropriate at certain developmental stages. These hyperactive children get moderately high ratings on the scales of hyperactivity, show more hyperactive behavior when with parents than when with others or by themselves, do not have an unusually high number of hospitalizations, and have parents that report high levels of inconsistency and conflict over discipline (Saxon and Starnes, Note 2). On both rating scales and the measure of observable movement we employed, these children showed significantly improved behavior after eight didactic parent training group meetings.

A second question asked is: To what extent does this child show a developmental lag significant enough to suggest that, in terms of skills and various abilities, he/she is functioning much more like a 2 or 3-year-old child than a 5 or 6-year-old child? Here one should observe primarily the amount of motor activity in which the child engages. If the assessment reveals developmental lags, it is not felt that they will necessarily be facilitated greatly by direct intervention. However, intervention with the parents in regard to their expectations and a universal parental propensity to project feelings onto unsuspecting children should be beneficial counseling. If the parents have other children or are familiar with the content of other children's behavior, they can with assistance be helped to see the similarity between the content and amount of motor behavior of their child showing a maturational lag and that of younger children. By altering parents' expectations in this regard, what is avoided is the potential on the part of the parents to intervene in such a manner as to either exacerbate or reinforce, and consequently maintain, hyperactive behaviors once a child has continued to develop and would otherwise be no longer engaging in these behaviors.

The third question is answered with the administration of standardized intelligence tests. The youngster may be of very superior intellectual skills and be very appropriately non task-oriented or inattentive in class. On the other hand, the child may be of sufficiently low average or borderline intellectual skills as to be under continuous and undue stress because of his not comprehending what is demanded of him. Appropriate educational strategies should be implemented with these children.

A fourth concern is in regard to organic factors and their treatment, i.e., drugs. Most hyperactive children do respond to amphetamine treatment. The data to this end are becoming more and more impressive. In the practice of child clinical psychology, then, the psychologist is generally referred the nonresponsive child. In this instance an attempt is typically made to ascertain the extent to which intervention regarding the other three factors may be of use in helping alleviate school and parental concerns.

With increasing popular awareness of drugs and drug abuse and a more informed population of pediatricians, psychologists may become increasingly useful to the pediatrician in his attempts to pharmaceutically treat hyperactivity. If greater skills are developed and knowledge obtained regarding psychophysiologic and sociobehavioral predictors of response to amphetamine treatment, then the behavioral scientists can become very instrumental to the pediatrician as well as to the parent in the pediatrician's attempt to pharmaceutically treat hyperactivity. Although the psychophysiologic theory behind the Saxon, Magee, and Siegel (Note 4) study is tenuous, this author has successfully predicted four positive responders and two nonresponders to amphetamine treatment in his clinical practice since those data were collected. With Barkley's (1976) recent review, additional research concerning predicting the response of hyperkinetic children to stimulant drugs will no doubt be initiated, and hopefully a less trial-and-error approach to treatment will eventuate.

REFERENCE NOTES

1. Routh, D. K. (1975). Validity of open field locomotion as a measure of hyperactivity. Paper presented at the meeting of the American Psychological Association, Chicago, September.
2. Saxon, S. A., and Starnes, K. D. (1975). Hyperactive children. Paper presented at the annual meeting of the American Psychological Association, Chicago, September.
3. Thomas, D. S. (1976). The effects of punishment on the activity level of hyperactive children. Unpublished doctoral dissertation, University of Arkansas.
4. Saxon, S. W., Magee, J. T., and Siegel, D. S. (1977). Activity level patterns in the hyperactive Ritalin responders and nonresponders. Manuscript submitted for publication.

134   CLINICAL CHILD PSYCHOPATHOLOGY

REFERENCES

Alderton, H. R., and Hoddinott, B. A. (1964). A controlled study of the use of Thioridazine in the treatment of hyperactive and aggressive children in a children's psychiatric hospital. *Canadian Psychiatric Association Journal* 9:239–247.

Baer, D. M. (1970). A case for the selective reinforcement of punishment. In C. Neuringer and J. L. Michael, eds., *Behavior Modification in Clinical Psychology*. New York: Appleton-Century-Crofts.

Barkley, R. (1976). Predicting the response of hyperkinetic children to stimulant drugs: a review. *Journal of Abnormal Child Psychology* 4:327–347.

Becker, W. C., Madsen, C. H., Arnold, C. K., and Thomas, D. R. (1967). The contingent use of teacher attention and praise in reducing classroom behavior problems. *Journal of Special Education* 1:287–307.

Bell, R. Q., Waldrop, M., and Weller, G. M. (1972). A rating system for the assessment of hyperactive and withdrawn children in preschool samples. *American Journal of Orthopsychiatry* 42:23–24.

Bradley, C. (1937). The behavior of children receiving Benzedrine. *American Journal of Psychiatry* 94:577–585.

Burks, H. (1964). Effects of amphetamine therapy on hyperkinetic children. *Archives of General Psychiatry* 11:604–609.

Christensen, D. E., and Sprague, R. L. (1973). Reduction of hyperactive behavior by conditioning procedures alone and combined with methylphenidate (Ritalin). *Behaviour Research and Therapy* 11:331–334.

Conners, C. K. (1969). A teacher rating scale for use in drug studies with children. *American Journal of Psychiatry* 126:884–888.

—— (1970). The use of stimulant drugs in enhancing performance and learning. In W. L. Smith, ed., *Drugs and Cerebral Function*. Ft. Lauderdale: Charles C. Thomas.

——, and Eisenberg, L. (1963). The effects of methylphenidate on symptomatology of learning in disturbed children. *American Journal of Psychiatry* 120:458–464.

Cromwell, R. L., Baumeister, A., and Hawkins, W. F. (1963). Research in activity level. In N. R. Ellis, ed., *Handbook of Mental Deficiency*. New York: McGraw-Hill.

Cruickshank, W., Bentzen, S. A., Ratzeberg, S. H., and Tannerhouser, M. (1961) *A teaching method for brain injured and hyperactive children*. New York: Syracuse University Press.

Davids, A. (1971). An objective instrument for assessing hyperkinesis in children. *Journal of Learning Disabilities* 4:499–501.

de Long, A. R. (1972). What have we learned from psychoactive drug research on hyperactives? *American Journal of Diseases of Children* 123:170–180.

Doubros, S., and Daniels, G. (1966). An experimental approach to the reduction of overactive behavior. *Behaviour Research and Therapy* 4:251–258.

Ebaugh, F. (1923). Neuropsychiatric sequelae of acute epidemic encephalitis in children. *American Journal of Diseases of Children* 23:89–97.

Eisenberg, L. (1966). The hyperkinetic child and stimulant drugs. *Developmental Medicine and Child Neurology* 8:593–598.

Elardo, R., Bradley, R., and Caldwell, B. (1975). The relationship of infants' home environments to mental test performance from six to thirty-six months: a longitudinal analysis. *Child Development* 46:71–76.

Ellis, N. R., and Pryer, R. S. (1959). Quantification of gross bodily activity in children with severe neuropathology. *American Journal of Mental Deficiency* 63:1034–1037.

Freeman, R. (1966). Drug effects on learning in children: a selective review of the past thirty years. *Journal of Special Education* 1:17–44.

Garfield, S. L., Helper, M. M., Wilcott, R. G., and Muffly, R. (1962). Effects of chlorpromazine on behaviour in emotionally disturbed children. *Journal of Nervous and Mental Disorders* 135:147–154.

Garrard, K. R., and Saxon, S. A. (1973). Preparation of a disturbed deaf child for therapy: a case description in behavior shaping. *Journal of Speech and Hearing Disorders* 38:502–509.

Hutt, C., Hutt, S. J., and Ounsted. C. (1965). The behavior of children—with and without CNS lesions. *Behavior* 24:246–268.

Kahn, E., and Cohen, L. H. (1934). Organic driveness: A brainstem syndrome and an experience. *New England Journal of Medicine* 210:748–756.

Kauffman, J. M., and Hallahan, D. P. (1973). Control of rough physical behavior using novel contingencies and directive teaching. *Perceptual and Motor Skills* 36:1225–1226.

Kennedy, W. A. (1971). *Child Psychology.* Englewood Cliffs, N.J.: Prentice-Hall.

Kirk, S. A. (1972) *Educating Exceptional Children.* Boston: Houghton-Mifflin.

Klinkerfuss, G. H., Lange, P. H., Weinberg, W. A., and O'Leary, J. L. (1965). Electroencephalographic abnormalities of children with hyperkinetic behavior. *Neurology* 15:883–891.

Klonoff, H., Robinson, G. C., and Thompson, G. (1969). Acute and chronic brain syndromes in children. *Developmental Medicine and Child Neurology* 11:198–213.

Krumboltz, J. D., and Krumboltz, H. (1972). *Changing Children's Behavior.* Englewood Cliffs, N.J.: Prentice-Hall.

Laufer, M. W., and Denhoff, E. (1957). Hyperkinetic behavior syndrome in children. *Journal of Pediatrics* 50:463–474.

McFarland, J. N., Peacock, L. J., and Watson, J. A. (1966). Mental retardation and activity level in rats and children. *American Journal of Mental Deficiency* 71:381–386.

McGinnis, M. A. (1963). *Aphasic Children,* Washington, D.C.: Alexander G. Bell Association for the Deaf.

Massey, P. S., Lieberman, A., and Batarseh, G. (1971). Measure of activity level in mentally retarded children and adolescents. *American Journal of Mental Deficiency* 76:259–261.

Meichenbaum, D., and Goodman, J. (1971). Training impulsive children to talk to themselves: a means of developing self-control. *Journal of Abnormal Psychology* 77:115–126.

Millichap, J. G. (1968). Hyperkinetic behavior and learning disorders. III. Battery of neuropsychological tests in controlled trial of methylphenidate. *American Journal of Disorders of Children* 116:235–244.

Patterson, G. R., Jones, R., Whittier, J., and Wright, M. (1965). A behavior modification for the hyperactive child. *Behaviour Research and Therapy* 2:217–226.

Quay, H., Sprague, R., Werry, J., and McQueen, M. (1967). Conditioning visual orientation of conduct problem children in the classroom. *Journal of Experimental Child Psychology* 5:512–517.

Ross, A. O. (1976). *Psychological Aspects of Learning Disabilities and Reading Disorders.* New York: McGraw-Hill.

Safer, M. A., Allen, R., and Barr, E. (1972). Depression of growth in hyperactive children on stimulant drugs. *New England Journal of Medicine* 287:217–220.

Satterfield, J. H., Atoian, G., Brashears, G., Burleigh, A., and Dawson, M. E. (1974). Electrodermal studies of minimal brain dysfunction. In *Clinical Use of Stimulant Drugs in Children. Excerpta Medica* 87–97.

——, Cantwell, D. P., Lesser, L. I., and Podosin, R. L. (1973). Response to stimulant drug treatment in hyperactive children: prediction from EEG and neurological findings. *Journal of Autism and Childhood Schizophrenia* 3:36–48.

——, and Dawson, M. E. (1971). Electrodermal correlates of hyperactivity in children. *Psychophysiology* 8:191.

Saxon, S. A., Dorman, L. B., and Starnes, K. D. (1976). Construct validity of three rating scales for hyperactivity. *Journal of Clinical Child Psychology* 5:56–58.

Schulman, J. L., Kaspar, J. C., and Thorne, F. M. (1965). *Brain Damage and Behavior: A Clinical Experimental Study.* Springfield, Ill.: Charles C. Thomas.

Smith, J. M., and Smith, E. D. (1970). *Child Management: A Program for Parents and Teachers.* Ann Arbor, Mich.: Ann Arbor Books.

Solomon, R. L. (1964). Punishment. *American Psychologist* 19:239–253.

Stewart, M. A., Pitts, F. M., Craig, A. G., and Dieruf, W. (1966). The hyperkinetic child syndrome. *American Journal of Orthopsychiatry* 36:861–867.

Strauss, A. A., and Lehtinen, L. E. (1947). *Psychopathology and Education of the Brain-Injured Child.* New York: Grune & Stratton.

Strecker, E. A., and Ebaugh, F. G. (1924). Neuropsychiatric sequelae of cerebral trauma in children. *Archives of Neurology and Psychiatry* 12:443–453.

Teuber, H. (1960). The premorbid personality and reaction to brain damage. *American Journal of Orthopsychiatry* 30:322–327.

Walley, R. E., and Welden, T. D. (1973). Lateral inhibition and cognitive masking: A neurological theory of attention. *Physiological Review* 80:284–302.

Walters, R. H., and Parke, R. D. (1967). The influence of punishment and related disciplinary techniques on the social behavior of children: theory and empirical findings. In B. A. Maher, ed., *Progress in Experimental Personality Research,* Vol. 4. New York: Academic Press.

Werry, J. S. (1968). Diagnosis, etiology and treatment of hyperactivity in children. In J. Helmuth, ed., *Learning Disorders,* Vol. 3. Washington, D.C.: Special Child Publications.

———, and Quay, H. C. (1969). Observing the classroom behavior of elementary school children. *Exceptional Children* 35:461–470.

———, and Sprague, R. L. (1969). Hyperactivity. In C. G. Costello, ed., *Symptoms of Psychopathology.* New York: John Wiley & Sons.

———, Weiss, G., and Douglas, V. (1964). Studies on the hyperactive child: I. Some preliminary findings. *Canadian Psychological Association Journal* 9:120–130.

———, Weiss, G., Douglas, V., and Martin, J. (1966). Studies on the hyperactive child: III. The effect of chlorpromazine upon behavior and learning ability. *Journal of the American Academy of Child Psychiatry* 5:292–312.

Zahn, T. P., Abate, F., Little, B. C., and Wender, P. H. (1975). Minimal brain dysfunction, stimulant drugs, and autonomic neurosystem activity. *Archives of General Psychiatry* 32:381–387.

Chapter Six

Impulsive Behavior: From Research to Treatment

A. J. FINCH, JR. and PHILIP C. KENDALL

One of the most common, yet most difficult, behavior patterns referred for mental health care in children is that of the hyperactive child syndrome. According to Cantwell (1975), the hyperactive child syndrome is characterized by the behavioral components of hyperactivity, distractibility, impulsivity, and excitability. Hyperactivity refers to the amount of motor behavior engaged in by the child. Generally, parents and teachers report that the child exhibits an excessive amount of motor behavior and has done so for a number of years. However, when actual objective measures of activity level have been obtained Cantwell (1975) states that

> there is serious question whether hyperactive children actually have a clearly greater amount of daily motor activity or a different type of motor activity than non-hyperactive children (Cantwell, 1975, p. 5).

Further discussion of the actual amount of motor behavior is provided in Chapter Five.

Distractibility refers to the child's inability to maintain his attention focused on a given task for more than a brief period of time. Teachers report that the child is more interested in what is going on around him than in the work he is supposed to be doing. Observation of such children

137

indicates that the slightest sound, movement, or other type of stimulation tends to immediately capture their attention only to be abandoned shortly for another stimuli.

Impulsivity is characterized by the individual rapidly selecting one possible response without considering all of the available alternatives and consequently making many mistakes. Frequently instructions or directions are completely ignored and the child will begin responding without having learned what is expected of him. For example, when given mazes, the child will enter the first turn without considering whether there is an exit available. Likewise he may reach for the first available toy that he sees without considering that a more desirable one is next to it. Accidents and injuries frequently result from impulsive behavior when the child fails to consider the potential consequences of his actions.

Finally the excitability of the hyperactive child syndrome is manifest in the child becoming easily overly excited in stimulating situations. Those who know hyperactive children are all too familiar with their difficulty in controlling themselves at birthday parties, Christmas, circuses, and school outings. At times it appears that the child becomes driven and beyond control when stimulation is high.

Given the relatively high incidence of the hyperactive child syndrome and the poor prognosis of these children (see Cantwell, 1975), a concerted research effort into the determination of etiology and the efficacy of treatment would certainly appear warranted. It is our opinion that the highest probability of success can be obtained by examining in detail the various behavioral components of this syndrome. Therefore, the research in this section focuses on the behavioral component of impulsivity. Approximately $4^{1}/_{2}$ years of research will be discussed with the resulting treatment program for impulsivity presented and evaluated. We do not consider our work in this area complete. Nor do we feel that the treatment program which has evolved from our research is a "cure-all" for impulsivity. Rather we believe we have made some initial findings, made some inferences from these findings, forced our inferences into a treatment program, and evaluated our initial attempts at treatment. One may question our dependence on developmental psychology for measurements or our nearly exclusive use of emotionally disturbed youngsters as subjects. To these questions we have very little response. Children are in the midst of development and we believe the exactness of the measures provided by development psychology best reflect these changes. Whenever possible children other than those catagorized as emotionally disturbed have been employed as subjects. However, our main commitment has been to children with emotional problems because of the severe service needs of these children and because of their availability to us.

BACKGROUND

While working with a group of brain damaged youngsters, the problem of "carelessness" was brought to the attention of the first author. According to their teacher, these youngsters were constantly making mistakes in their school work because of their failure to follow directions. After close observation it became apparent that this "carelessness" was very similar to Kagan's developmental impulsivity (Kagan et al., 1966). Reflection-impulsivity is the cognitive dimension employed by Kagan and his colleagues (Kagan, 1965a; 1965b; 1965c; Kagan and Kogan, 1970; Kagan et al., 1966) to describe differences in children's approaches to problem solving. Whenever a number of response alternatives are available and uncertainty exists as to the correct response, impulsive children respond quickly without thorough consideration of the available alternatives and consequently make many mistakes. On the other hand reflective children withhold responding until they have explored the available alternatives and consequently make few errors.

The "carelessness" of these brain damaged children was very similar to that of the impulsive child. When given math problems, they frequently ignored the sign; when reading they frequently attended only to a portion of the word; and when interacting with other children their responses frequently were of an impulsive nature. At that point it seemed logical to suspect that the determinants of an impulsive cognitive style should provide some information about impulsive behavior. The first series of studies were conducted to determine if cognitive impulsivity as defined by Kagan was related to behavioral impulsivity seen in disturbed children.

IMPULSIVE BEHAVIOR AND COGNITIVE IMPULSIVITY

Given the similarity between the impulsive behavior of disturbed children and the cognitive impulsivity in Kagan's developmental work, it was somewhat surprising to find little research relating them. After quickly (and as was later learned incompletely—perhaps inpulsively) reviewing the literature, it was felt that a more direct relationship needed to be demonstrated. Ollendick and Finch (1973) compared the performance of a group of brain damaged children with that of a group of normal children, matched on mental age, on Kagan's (Kagan et al., 1966) Matching Familiar Figures Test (MFF). This test is a match to sample task which involves presenting the child a picture of an object and having him select from an array of six variants the one picture which is exactly like the standard. Latency to first response and the number of errors are the usual measures. An impulsive cognitive style is defined operationally as falling below the median on latency and above the median on errors. In contrast a reflective cognitive style is defined operationally as falling above the median on latencies and below the median on errors.

Ollendick and Finch (1973) predicted that brain damaged children would be more impulsive than the normal children and would thus obtain shorter latencies and make more errors on the MFF. This prediction was based on the fact that brain damaged children are described as being more behaviorally hyperactive and impulsive. They found that the brain damaged children did have shorter latencies and more errors than did the normal subjects. Their findings suggested that a behaviorally more impulsive group was cognitively more impulsive also.

Montgomery (Note 2) attempted to extend these findings to a group of emotionally disturbed children. He compared the performance of emotionally disturbed children with a group of normals on the MFF. Results indicated that there were no differences between the two groups on latencies but that the emotionally disturbed child made significantly more errors. In discussing his results Montgomery suggested that it was not surprising that the two groups did not differ on both measures since the emotionally disturbed group was not selected on the basis of their being behaviorally impulsive. It seemed logical to suspect that some emotionally disturbed children would be overly inhibited while others were impulsive.

It seemed reasonable to suggest that those emotionally disturbed children who were behaviorally inhibited should differ on the MFF from those who were behaviorally impulsive. Montgomery and Finch (1975) obtained locus of conflict ratings on a group of cognitively impulsive and reflective children. Internalization of conflict is between impulses and their inhibition. Externalization of conflict suggests that the child's impulses are freely discharged into the environment and the conflict is between the child's behaviors and the reactions they bring about in others. Montgomery and Finch (1975) found that the cognitively impulsive emotionally disturbed children were more likely to be rated as exhibiting externalization of conflict while the cognitively reflective group was more likely to be rated as exhibiting internalization of conflict. These findings were consistent with predictions and suggested that cognitive style was important in determining behavior in emotionally disturbed children.

Finch and Nelson (1976) extended the investigation of the relationship between cognitive style and behavior in emotionally disturbed children by obtaining behavioral ratings from parents on a group of impulsive and reflective boys in residential treatment. They found that impulsive emotionally disturbed boys were more likely than reflectives to talk of others blaming them unfairly, threaten to injure themselves, hit and bully other children, and be excessively rough in play. In contrast reflectives were more likely to be reluctant to talk with adults outside the family. Finch and Nelson (1976) suggested that these results add additional support for the importance of cognitive style in determining behavior in emotionally disturbed children.

Continuing along these lines, Finch, Kendall, Deardorff, Anderson, and Sitarz (1975a) hypothesized that less persistence behavior would be exhibited by impulsive emotionally disturbed children than by reflective EDC. They administered the MFF and a persistence task to a group of 78 children in residential treatment for emotional problems and found a significant positive relationship between MFF latencies and persistence time but a nonsignificant relation between MFF errors and persistence. In other words, cognitively impulsive children did not persist as long on a behavioral measure as did reflective ones. Again these results were interpreted as demonstrating the importance of cognitive style in determining overt behavior.

A rather interesting study which supports the importance of cognitive style in determining behavior was conducted by Finch, Pezzuti, Montgomery, and Kemp (1974b). They suggested that cognitive style should be related to academic achievement since many academic tasks involve problem solving. After obtaining MFFs and academic achievement scores on a group of emotionally disturbed youngsters, they found that reflectives and impulsives did not differ. That is, on academic achievement as measured by standard achievement tests there were no differences between impulsive and reflective children. However, when actual grade placement was compared, it was found that the reflective emotionally disturbed children were placed *two* grade levels higher than the impulsives despite similar achievement and age. They suggested that some behavioral difference in the classroom must account for their different grade placement.

Given the results reviewed in this section it seems reasonable to state that cognitive impulsivity is related to impulsive behavior. A one to one relationship is not being suggested but rather a strong relationship. We feel this relationship is strong enough to allow us to learn about impulsive behavior by studying children with an impulsive cognitive style. Cognitive style is easier to study than behavior since it requires fewer measures. The desire for ease in measurement is prompted by limited resources which simply prohibit our spending either the money or the time required to adequately sample the other overt behaviors. We recognize this as a weakness but also recognize it as a reality of our situation.

The next section of this chapter deals with our attempts to determine some of the contributors to an impulsive cognitive style.

CONTRIBUTIONS TO AN IMPULSIVE COGNITIVE STYLE

What factors are responsible for whether a child is impulsive or reflective? Kagan and Kogan (1970) have suggested that cognitive style most likely is determined by several factors. They feel the literature best supports a fear of failure model as the major contributor. The greater the child's fear of making a mistake, the more reflective he will be in his approach to problem solving. On the other hand, the impulsive child is felt to have minimum anxiety over failure and consequently responds without evaluation of alternatives. Correspondingly, fear of failure has been hypothesized as an important determinant of anxiety (Atkinson, 1964; Spielberger, 1966; 1972). According to the State-Trait theory of anxiety (Spielberger, 1966; 1972) the greater the individual's fear of failure and the greater the number of situations which elicit the fear of failure response, the higher the individual's trait anxiety.

Montgomery (Note 2), noting the importance ascribed to fear of failure in the explanations of both reflectivity–impulsivity and trait anxiety, hypothesized that if reflective children have a greater fear of failure as suggested by Kagan and Kogan (1970), it should be expected that they would exhibit more trait anxiety than would impulsive children. To test this hypothesis he compared impulsive and reflective emotionally disturbed and normal children on their responses to the State-Trait Anxiety Inventory for Children (STAIC) (Spielberger, 1973). His results indicated that for both populations there was no difference in the trait anxiety level of impulsive and reflective children. Furthermore, the impulsive and reflective groups did not differ on their responses to the statement "I worry about making mistakes" from the trait portion of the STAIC.

Having found that anxiety was not a significant factor in the determination of cognitive style, attention was directed to other possible contributors. During the observations of impulsive and reflective children, it was noted that reflective children employed more verbalizations while problem solving than did the impulsive children. Finch and Montgomery (1973) reasoned that since impulsives rarely verbalize while problem solving, they may lack the symbolic skills necessary for considering alternatives. Specifically they hypothesized that reflective children employ a more mature form of thinking than do impulsives and that this more mature thinking would be demonstrated on their superior performance on an information seeking task designed to indicate maturity of thinking. Their results indicated that impulsive children think in pictures (less maturely) while reflective children think in words (more maturely) which was as predicted.

To extend the findings of Finch and Montgomery (1973) that impulsive children think in pictures while reflective children think in words, Stein, Finch, Hooke, Montgomery, and Nelson (1975) compared the responding of impulsive and reflective children to an equivalence task which, again, was designed to indicate maturity of thinking. Even though less clear than those of Finch and Montgomery (1973), their results tended to support the contention that reflectives think in words while impulsives think in pictures. Given the results of these two studies, we have come to believe that one of the contributing factors in an impulsive cognitive style is thinking in pictures rather than in words. We believe that this form of thinking is less efficient and a handicap in problem solving situations which require the consideration of several alternatives.

In order to determine what other variables might be important in determining cognitive style Finch, Nelson, Montgomery, and Stein (1974a) hypothesized that a child with an internal locus of control would be expected to assume more responsibility for his behavior and thus exhibit a more reflective approach. This hypothesis was tested by comparing the responses of a group of impulsive and reflective emotionally disturbed children to the Nowicki–Strickland Locus of Control Scale for Children (Nowicki and Strickland, 1973). Although the obtained differences were in the predicted direction, they were not significant. Pointing to the limited number of subjects in each group (10) Finch *et al.* (1976) examined the relationship between locus of control and cognitive style in emotionally disturbed children again. Employing a larger sample ($n = 78$), they found a significant relationship between the two variables with impulsive children tending to attribute event outcomes to external sources while reflective children attributed them to internal ones.

The final study to be reviewed in this section was concerned with the relationship between a child's need for achievement and his cognitive style. Finch, Crandell, and Deardorff (1976) hypothesized that reflective children would have a higher level of need for achievement than would impulsive ones. In order to test this hypothesis they obtained need for achievement and MFFs on a group of emotionally disturbed children. Their results indicated that children with a high need for achievement delayed significantly longer before responding than did children with a low need for achievement. However, there was not a significant difference in the number of errors made by the two groups. Thus, it would appear that although need for achievement is important in at least one of the two criteria used to determine impulsivity, other factors are important in the determination of the other.

In this section we have discussed our attempts to determine some of the factors contributing to an impulsive cognitive style. Essentially we have concluded that impulsive children are *not* more anxious than reflectives; tend to employ pictures when they think rather than words; see event outcomes as *not* being under their control; and possibly have a lower need for achievement than reflective children.

MODIFICATION OF IMPULSIVE RESPONDING

In this section a number of studies will be presented in which an attempt is made to modify an impulsive mode of responding. The varied focus of these studies indicates the progression of our thoughts on the importance of the different components of impulsivity.

Previously the importance placed on fear of failure by Kagan and Kogan was discussed. Montgomery (Note 2) hypothesized that if fear of failure was the primary determinent of a reflective cognitive style, impulsive children would be expected to exhibit a more reflective problem solving approach following a failure experience. To test this hypothesis he exposed a group of impulsive emotionally disturbed and a group of normal children to a failure experience and then readministered the MFF. There was not a significant change in either latencies or errors and Montgomery (Note 2) concluded that increasing an impulsive child's fear of failure through a failure experience did not modify his response style.

Finch, Wilkinson, Nelson, and Montgomery (1975b) reasoned that if impulsives do employ less words in thinking than do reflectives, as suggested by Finch and Montgomery (1973) and Stein *et al.* (1975), then training designed to teach impulsive children to employ words in their thinking should be effective in modifying their cognitive style. Employing a training program modeled after a verbal self-instructions procedure introduced by Meichenbaum and Goodman (1971) Finch *et al.* (1975b) assigned impulsive emotionally disturbed children to one of three groups; (1) cognitive training, (2) delay training, and (3) control.

In the *cognitive training group* each subject was seen individually for six one-half hour sessions distributed over a 3-week period. In the first session the experimenter performed one of the training tasks and talked aloud to herself. Specific step by step self-instructions were verbalized and repeated frequently. An error was deliberately made and the trainer stated to herself that she should have proceeded more carefully. After the experimenter completed the task, the subject was asked to perform the task and to verbalize the self-instructions to himself. If any difficulty was encountered the subject was assisted in self-instructions to himself. If any difficulty was encountered the subject was assisted in self-instructing. During sessions five and six, subjects were instructed to continue giving themselves self-instructions but to do so covertly. The day following the sixth training session the subjects were re-administered the MFF.

In the *delay training group* the subjects had the same number of sessions, were exposed to the identical materials, and engaged in the same activities as the cognitive training group. However, this group did not receive training in verbal self instructions, but rather were instructed to respond more slowly. Again following the sixth session, the MFF was re-administered.

The *control group* was a simple test–retest control group which was administered the MFF at the beginning and end of a 5-week period that corresponded to the passage of time in the other two groups. No contact with the experimenter took place between test administrations.

The results of their training indicated that the group receiving the *cognitive training* procedure emphasizing verbal self-instructions was more reflective on the second administration of the MFF with both latencies and errors being significantly improved. The group which received the *delay training* exhibited significantly longer latencies on the second MFF but no change in the number of errors while the *control* group did not change. Finch *et al.* (1975b) concluded that their results indicated the potential usefulness of verbal self-instructions in modifying impulsivity.

Focusing upon the motivational aspects of cognitive style, Nelson, Finch, and Hooke (1975) suggested that the reflection–impulsivity dimension might involve a motivation for success component as well as a fear of failure one. They suggest that the impulsive emotionally disturbed child might already have the behavior necessary for a reflective response style but lack the motivation to do so. Continuing their arguments, they suggest that a comparison of the effectiveness of a reinforcement and response-cost procedure should provide some indication of the relative merits of the success seeking versus the fear of failure explanation of the reflection–impulsivity dimension. According to Nelson *et al.* (1975) response cost can be viewed as maximizing fear of failure since losing a reinforcer can be avoided only by not making a mistake. In contrast reinforcement is given only after the correct response has been emitted. They state that the fear of failure hypothesis would predict a more reflective approach under response cost conditions. This hypothesis was tested by randomly assigning a group of 40 emotionally disturbed boys, after initial testing, either to a response-cost, reinforcement, or control condition. In the response-cost condition the boys were given 12 tokens and shown a number of attractive prizes which could be purchased. Next they were instructed that they would lose a chip immediately after they made a mistake on the MFF. The reinforcement group was shown the prizes and told that for each correct response on the MFF they would earn a chip which could be traded in for a prize at the completion of the test. The control group was simply readministered the MFF and given a reinforcer for participating.

The Nelson *et al.* (1975) results indicated that both reinforcement and response cost produced an increase in latencies and a decrease in errors while the control group remained unchanged. Next they compared the relative efficacy of response cost and reinforcement for impulsive and reflective children. For impulsive children the response-cost procedure was more effective than the reinforcement condition although both were more effective than the control. On the other hand, the reinforcement condition was more effective with the reflective group. Nelson *et al.* (1975) concluded that their results support the fear of failure hypothesis with impulsive emotionally disturbed boys in that increasing an impulsive's fear of failure reduces his impulsiveness. However, these authors noted that although the impulsive children responded more reflectively under the increased motivation, their performance was still different than the originally reflective children's. This finding would tend to suggest that other variables than the motivational ones are also important in determining cognitive style.

Given the improvement exhibited by the impulsive children in both the verbal self-instructions group in the Finch, *et al.* (1975b) study and the response-cost group in the Nelson *et al.* (1975) study, our attention was next focused on the combining of these procedures into a treatment package for impulsive children. In doing this we would need to look also at actual behaviors in order to determine if the gains obtained could be seen in "real life" problem behaviors. In other words, we were ready to see if the procedures we developed in our research laboratory were useful for treatment of actual clinical problems.

Our first attempt at clinical application was in the form of a case study (Kendall and Finch, 1976). A 9-year-old boy with a history of classroom behavior problems which resulted in his demotion was referred to the Virginia Treatment Center for Children for out-patient treatment. During the initial interview he was constantly in motion—climbing on the furniture, talking rapidly about many different topics, rapidly changing the purpose and direction of behavior without observable reason, etc. During this initial interview several potential target behaviors were noted and recorded during the next two sessions. For example, while playing cards the youngster would be talking about the rules of the game and then quickly gather the cards to be reshuffled and dealt for a second game with different rules before the first game was completed. Also while playing cards, he jumped up and began to throw darts before the game was completed. These behaviors along with initial MFF testing (mean latency = 4.59 sec.; first response errors = 9) were considered impulsive.

Before beginning treatment it was decided that a systematic evaluation was to be conducted on the specific problem behaviors, MFF performance, and the generalization of the results. A multiple baseline design was selected to evaluate change in the inappropriate and untimely "switches" in (1) topics of conversation, (2) games played with, and (3) rules of play. In order to increase the probability of generalization and to assess its occurrence, three variations in the context or situation of treatment were employed: (a) the therapy room was changed, (b) the array of games was varied, and (c) the therapist was changed.

Following baseline observations, consisting of seven 10-minute segments of two therapy sessions, treatment was initiated. During the first portion of each session, training in verbal self-instructions was provided. These instructions consist of the therapist modeling reflective responding while talking aloud to himself. Next the therapist had the patient perform the task and assisted the patient in emitting the verbal self-instructions. The therapist next modeled whispering verbal self-instructions to himself while problem solving and then had the patient whisper while engaging in the same activity. Finally the therapist had the patient problem solve while talking covertly to himself.

The response-cost portion of treatment consisted of the therapist giving the patient a number of dimes at the beginning of each session. It was explained to the client that he could keep these dimes unless he committed a switch. Each switch would cost him one dime. Care was taken to insure that the "rules" were understood. Immediately after each switch response, a dime was taken by the therapist and a thorough explanation given of why the dime was lost.

The effectiveness of this treatment program was surprising even to us. The frequency of switches in topic of conversation, games played with, and rules for play across 10-minute segments of the therapy sessions is presented in Fig. 1. As can be seen the reduction in the frequency of target behaviors occurs systematically following the introduction of specifically tailored verbal self-instructions and response-cost training for each area.

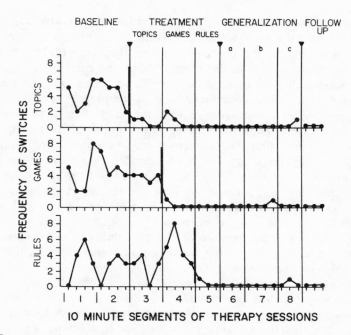

Fig. 1. Frequency of switches in topics, games, and rules across 10-minute segments of therapy sessions as a function of treatment and generalization tests. *Copyright 1976 by the American Psychological Association. Reprinted by permission.*

In addition, generalization of the treatment effectiveness was successful as indicated in several ways. First, generalization assessment was built into the treatment program and can be seen in Fig. 1. In section "a" of Fig. 1 the room in which therapy had been taking place was changed without a marked increase in switches. Likewise in section "b," the array of available games was altered without marked increase and finally the therapist was changed in section "c" without marked increase.

An even more impressive demonstration of generalization is suggested in Table 1 which presents a summary of school behavior from the patient's report card. The patient's teacher was aware neither of the form of treatment in which he was involved nor the specific target behaviors. The format of the report card was such that it allowed us to have available pretreatment information as well as information during and after treatment. As can be seen, the study skills categories of "listens attentively," "completes work on time," "uses spare time well," and "begins promptly," all went from I (needs improvement) to S (satisfactory) with this change occurring concomitantly with treatment. In addition the pretreat-

Table 1. Summary of School Behavior from Report Card*

| Report No. | Study Skills Category | | | | | | |
	Listens attentively	Follows directions	Completes work on time	Works carefully	Uses spare time well	Begins promptly	Considerate of others
1. (pre-treatment)	I	S	I	S	I	I	S
2.	S	S	S("better")	S	S("better")	I	S
3.	S	S	S	S	S	S	S
4.	S	S	S	S	S	S	S

Report No.	Teacher's Overall Comments
1. (pretreatment)	...not attentive, not participating.
2.	...has been more attentive.
3.	...continues to improve.
4.	...working harder, participates often.

*I and S were the only two grading codes available for use in the reporting of behavior. I = needs improvement, S = satisfactory.

ment comments of the teacher were negative while during and after treatment they were progressively more positive.

A posttreatment MFF resulted in a mean latency of 18.73 seconds and 5 errors which is a more reflective approach than pretreatment. Likewise a 6-month follow-up administration of the MFF was more reflective with a mean latency of 24.7 seconds and only 4 errors. The follow-up data for switches is presented in Fig. 1. The total absence of inappropriate switching behavior during the 6-month follow-up is particularly interesting since the specific treatment program was discontinued from the point of termination of the experimental procedures to the follow-up and the program was not being conducted at home.

The success of the treatment employed in the case study was highly encouraging and suggested that the combination of response cost and verbal self-instructions might have considerable treatment application. However, we felt that the clinical utility of this treatment program needed to be demonstrated further employing a clinic population in a group comparison study. In other words, while case studies are suggestive, we felt that a demonstration of treatment effectiveness with groups was necessary before conclusions could be drawn as to the effectiveness of the program. Our next study (Kendall and Finch, 1978) was designed with this need in mind.

Our first step in conducting a group-comparison study was to screen all the newly admitted children during their first 10 days at the Treatment Center and identify those that were impulsive. This screening process was continued for approximately 9 months until a total of 20 impulsive children were isolated. The 20 impulsives who were divided into a treatment and a control group, included male and female, and black and white children. It should be noted that the admission rate of children was not tampered with but rather the study was conducted in accordance with the naturally occurring rate of appearance of impulsive children. This meant that the number of subjects varied in the two groups from time to time and that at some times several subjects were controls, and at other times several subjects were being treated. This was due to the random assignment procedure and fortunately, was helpful in keeping behavioral raters (teachers and unit staff) blind as to the group any particular child was assigned.

When subjects were initially screened, they completed two self-report measures (Impulsivity Scale, IS; Sutton-Smith and Rosenberg, 1959; Impulse Control Categorization Instrument, ICCI; Matsushima, 1964) and the MFF. Impulsiveness was determined by the latency and error criteria of the MFF. Behavioral ratings were also obtained from the child's teacher (Impulsive Classroom Behavior Scale, ICBS; Weinreich, Note 4; Locus of Conflict; Armentrout, 1971) and from unit staff members (Locus of Conflict).

Once subjects were identified as impulsive and assigned to one of the groups, they met individiually for six 20-minute sessions with the therapist. Aside from the cognitive-behavioral training prescribed for the treatment group, both the treated and control subjects received an identical experience. The treatment group received training in verbal self-instructions and a response-cost contingency for errors on the training tasks. The controls were exposed to the training materials, received equal time and attention, and were able to select a noncontingent reward at the end of each session.

After the completion of the six 20-minute sessions, the MFF and self-report measures were readministered, and the post-treatment ratings were obtained from the teacher and unit staff. These measures were again collected at a 2-month follow-up.

An examination of the dependent measures for all children who went through the screening, posttreatment, and follow-up assessments ($n = 51$) indicated that both the latency and error scores on the MFF were reliable (correlations ranging from 0.62 to 0.92) and that the self-report measures were reliable (correlations ranging from 0.33 to 0.70). The ICBS reliability was high (0.85) for a sample of students rated by teacher pairs as were the reliabilities of the LOC overall scores (correlations ranging from 0.84 to 0.95). These reliabilities were considered acceptable and partially indicative of the utility of the measures.

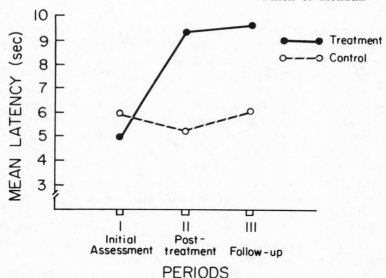

Fig. 2. Mean latency in seconds for the treatment and control groups at the initial assessment, posttreatment, and follow-up periods. Copyright 1978 by the American Psychological Association. Reprinted by permission.

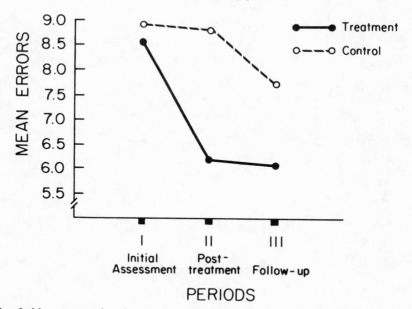

Fig. 3. Mean errors for the treatment and control groups at the initial assessment, posttreatment, and follow-up periods. Copyright 1978 by the American Psychological Association. Reprinted by permission.

The most important outcome was based upon the comparisons of the treatment and control groups. These results indicated that the treatment group exhibited significantly longer latencies and fewer errors on the MFF than the control group at posttreatment *and* follow-up (see Figs. 2 and 3). As can be seen in both figures, there was a significant change in the predicted direction for subjects in the treatment group. In addition, the treatment group was rated as less impulsive by their teachers than were the controls (see Fig. 4). It should be noted that controls showed an increase in teacher-rated impulsiveness. This increase may be due to the dynamic theoretical model of the treatment center as a whole in which the expression of feelings is emphasized. While this may or may not be the best approach for inhibited children, it would not appear to be the treatment choice for children who exhibit problems of impulse control. Moreover, these findings illustrate the efficacy of examining differential treatment effectiveness for distinct groups of children (Kendall and Finch, see Chapter One).

In summary of the group comparison study we may conclude that while the self-report measures and unit staff ratings did not reflect

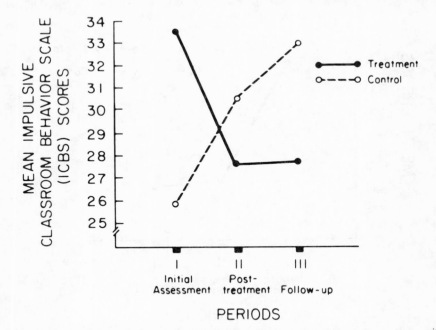

Fig. 4. Mean Impulsive Classroom Behavior Scale (ICBS) Scores for the treatment and assessment, posttreatment, and follow-up periods. Copyright 1978 by the American Psychological Association. Reprinted by permission.

treatment effects, the dramatic and lasting changes in MFF latencies and errors and classroom impulsive behavior were impressive. Indeed, these results support those found in some of our earlier studies (e.g., case-study) and, taken together, indicate the efficacy of a cognitive-behavioral treatment for modifying impulsivity and attaining generalization to the classroom. The cognitive-behavioral strategy would thus appear to have considerable potential usefulness in the development of self-control in children. A limited amount of training is needed to implement the program and it appears that such training could be conducted by paraprofessionals. Our hopes for the eventual applicability of this procedure are high.

RECENT EVENTS

Most recently efforts have been made to evaluate the individual components in the treatment program. Nelson (Note 3) randomly assigned a group of 50 second and third grade normal children identified as impulsive to one of five groups. Group 1 was a response-cost plus verbal self-instructions group which received training in verbal self-instructions and under response cost conditions. It was essentially the same procedure employed in the case study and in the treatment group of the Kendall and Finch (1978) study. Group 2 was a response-cost training group which received training under response-cost conditions but did not receive training in verbal self-instructions. Group 3 received verbal self-instructions training but not response-cost training while Group 4 was a test control group which received no treatment but was tested along with the other groups. Finally, Group 5 was a response-cost contingency group which was administered the MFF under response-cost contingencies during the second testing and under standard conditions otherwise. Each group was pretested, posttested after training or after that period of time, given follow-up testing $2^1/_2$ weeks after posttesting and 6 weeks after posttesting.

Results indicated that at posttesting all treatment groups (Groups 1, 2, 3, and 5) significantly increased their latency scores but only the verbal self-instructions training, response-cost plus verbal self-instructions training, and the response-cost contingency groups significantly decreased their error rate. At the $2^1/_2$ week follow-up testing the performance of the response-cost verbal self-instructions training group (Group 1) and the verbal self-instructions training group (Group 3) were significantly more reflective when compared to the control group in terms of both latencies and errors while the response-cost training and response-cost contingencies groups differed from the control group only in terms of latencies. At the 6 week follow-up, the increased latencies and decreased errors were maintained for the response-cost plus verbal self-instructions training and the verbal self-instructions only groups while the response-cost contingency group maintained only increased latencies.

The results suggested that the verbal self-instructions portion of the treatment package produced the most enduring decrease in impulsiveness while the gains obtained from the response-cost training were more short lived. However, it should be noted that the greatest gains were made by the group receiving training in both verbal self-instructions and response cost even though this difference was not significant.

Broad-Spectrum Treatment Implications

Having been intimately involved with impulsive children for several years one major point stands out in our minds—these children and their problems are somewhat unique. So too, as our research has demonstrated, treatment should be designed with this uniqueness in mind. Indeed, our cognitive-behavioral treatment does just that. But what about the many and varied child therapists who follow other philosophies or theoretical ideals? Do our findings have any palatable use within other models?

It is our position that there are certain major tactical approaches to dealing with impulsive children. These tactics, we feel, will be maximized if they conform to our outlined treatment program. But they can also be useful within other treatment approaches. What is being suggested is that, philosophy and theory aside, the impulsive child will benefit from the therapists' emphasis on all possible alternatives before responding, the prevention of fast guessing, clear modeling of appropriately paced behavior (both overt and covert), and the assimilation of verbal mediation or self-task. Qualified child therapists of treatment persuasion other than the cognitive-behavioral bent can undoubtedly utilize these tactics and such utilization should prove most beneficial.

At this point we feel that we are beginning to gain some understanding of impulsiveness and to develop a treatment plan for it. Much has been learned and our work continues in this interesting area. Presently we are examining the effects of impulsivity on long and short-term memory in the hope of gaining some insights into the frequently reported difficulty these children have in profiting from experience. In addition we hope to be able to replicate the Nelson (Note 2) study with emotionally disturbed children to determine if their response to the various treatment components is the same or different from the normal group. We suspect that the response-cost training may prove more important with this group. Finally, we hope to be able to break the verbal self-instructions training program down into a number of components and evaluate the relative effectiveness of each of these. Our efforts are limited by service demands and lack of funds but these are the problems present in most applied research programs.

REFERENCE NOTES

1. Montgomery, L. E. (1974). *Reflection-Impulsivity in Emotionally Disturbed and Normal Children.* Unpublished docteral dissertation, Hattiesburg: University of Southern Mississippi.
2. Nelson, W. M., III (1976). *Cognitive Behavioral Strategies in Modifying an Impulsive Cognitive Style.* Unpublished docteral dissertation. Richmond: Virginia Commonwealth University.
3. Weinrich, R. J. (1975). *Inducing Reflective Thinking in Impulsive Emotionally Disturbed Children.* Unpublished masters thesis, Richmond: Virginia Commonwealth University.

REFERENCES

Armentrout, J. A. (1971). Parental child-rearing attitudes and preadolescents' problem behaviors. *Journal of Consulting and Clinical Psychology* 37:278–285.

Atkinson, J. W. (1964). *An Introduction to Motivation.* Princeton, New Jersey: Van Nostrand-Reinhold.

Cantwell, D. P. (1975). *The Hyperactive Child.* New York: Spectrum Publications, Inc.

Finch, A. J., Jr., and Montgomery, L. E. (1973). Reflection-impulsivity and information seeking in emotionally disturbed children. *Journal of Abnormal Child Psychology* 1:358–362.

——, and Nelson, W. M., III (1976). Reflection-impulsivity and behavior problems in emotionally disturbed boys. *Journal of Genetic Psychology* 128:271–274.

——, Nelson, W. M., III, Montgomery, L. E., and Stein, A. B. (1974a). Reflection-impulsivity and locus of control in emotionally disturbed children. *Journal of Genetic Psychology* 125:273–275.

——, Pezzuti, K. A., Montgomery, L. E., and Kemp, S. R. (1974b). Reflection-impulsivity and academic attainment in emotionally disturbed children. *Journal of Abnormal Child Psychology* 2:71–74.

——, Kendall, P. C., Deardorff, P. S., Anderson, J., and Sitarz, M. A. (1975a). Reflection-impulsivity, persistence behavior, and locus of control in emotionally disturbed children. *Journal of Consulting and Clinical Psychology* 43:748.

——, Wilkinson, M. D., Nelson, W. M., III, and Montgomery, L. E. (1975b). Modification of an impulsive cognitive tempo in emotionally disturbed boys. *Journal of Abnormal Child Psychology* 3:47–51.

——, Crandell, C., and Deardorff, P. A. (1976). Reflection-impulsivity and need for achievement in emotionally disturbed children. *Journal of Genetic Psychology* 129:329–331.

Kagan, J. (1965a). A developmental approach to conceptual growth. In H. J. Klausmeier and C. W. Harris, Eds., *Analysis of Concept Learning.* New York: Academic Press.

—— (1965b). Impulsive and reflective children: Significance of conceptual tempo. In J. D. Krumboltz, ed., *Learning and the Education Process.* Chicago: Rand McNally.

—— (1965c). Individual differences in the resolution of response uncertainty. *Journal of Personality and Social Psychology* 2:154–160.

——, and Kogan, N. (1970). Individual variation in cognitive processes. In P. H. Mussen, ed., *Carmichael's Manual of Child Psychology.* New York: Wiley.

——, Pearson, L., and Welch, L. (1966). Conceptual impulsivity and inductive reasoning. *Child Development* 34:583–594.

Kendall, P. C., and Finch, A. J., Jr. (1976). A cognitive-behavioral treatment for impulsive control: a case study. *Journal of Consulting and Clinical Psychology* 44:853–857.

—— (1978). A cognitive-behavioral treatment for impulse control: a group comparison study. *Journal of Consulting and Clinical Psychology* 46:110–118.

Matsushima, J. (1964). An instrument for classifying impulse control among boys. *Journal of Consulting Psychology* 28:87–90.

Meichenbaum, D. H., and Goodman, J. (1971). Training impulsive children to talk to themselves: a means of developing self-control. *Journal of Abnormal Psychology* 77:115–126.

Montgomery, L. E., and Finch, A. J., Jr. (1975). Reflection-impulsivity and locus of conflict in emotionally disturbed children. *Journal of Genetic Psychology* 126:89–91.

Nelson, W. M., III, Finch, A. J., Jr., and Hooke, J. F. (1975). Effects of reinforcement and response–cost on cognitive style in emotionally disturbed boys. *Journal of Abnormal Psychology* 84:426–428.

Nowicki, S., Jr., and Strickland, B. L. (1973). A locus of control scale for children. *Journal of Consulting and Clinical Psychology* 43:148–154.

Ollendick, T. H., and Finch, A. J., Jr. (1973). Reflection-impulsivity in brain-damaged and normal children. *Perceptual and Motor Skills* 36:654.

Spielberger, D. C. (1966). Theory and research on anxiety. In C. D. Spielberger, ed., *Anxiety and Behavior.* New York: Academic Press.

—— (1972). The effects of anxiety on complex learning and academic achievement. In C. D. Spielberger, ed., *Anxiety: Current Trends in Theory and Research,* Vol. I. New York: Academic Press.

—— (1973). *Preliminary Manual for the State-Trait Anxiety Inventory for Children ("How I Feel Questionnaire").* Palo Alto, California: Consulting Psychologists Press.

Stein, A. B., Finch, A. J., Jr., Hooke, J. F., Montgomery, L. E., and Nelson, W. M., III (1975). Cognitive tempo and the mode of representation in emotionally disturbed and normal children. *Journal of Psychology* 90:197–201.

Sutton-Smith, B., and Rosenberg, B. G. (1959). A scale to identify impulsive behavior in children. *Journal of Genetic Psychology* 95:211–216.

Part II

Treatment in Child Psychopathology

Chapter Seven

Training Parents
to Modify the Noncompliant
Behavior of their Children*

REX FOREHAND and STEVE PEED

A frequent complaint of parents is that their children fail to comply to their commands. Such noncompliance may occur when the parent calls the child to dinner, asks the child to pick up his/her blocks, commands that two children stop fighting, and demands a host of other behaviors from a child.

The psychological literature clearly supports the contention that noncompliance is a frequent problem. Among children who are referred to clinics for treatment of deviant behavior, noncompliance is consistently reported to be the most prevalent problem. Taplin and Reid (1975) state that noncompliance was reported to be a problem by 24 of 25 parents who referred their children to the Oregon Research Institute for treatment. Other research-oriented clinicians (e.g., Christophersen *et al.*, 1976; Tavormina *et al.*, 1976) have reported similar results after surveying

*Much of the research reported in this chapter was supported in part by a grant from the University of Georgia Research Council to the first author.

the various behavior problems of children referred to them for treatment. Not only is noncompliance a frequent complaint about clinic-referred children, but, according to Johansson (1971), it traditionally has been a primary characteristic of several classifications of child psychopathology. Furthermore, the frequent occurrence of noncompliance is not limited to clinic-referred children. In extensive naturalistic observations in the home setting of 33 nonclinic "normal" children, Johnson, Wahl, Martin, and Johansson (1973) found that among 13 deviant behaviors (e.g., crying, tantrums, etc.) noncompliance was the most frequent response and occurred among more children than any other deviant behavior.

Obviously, noncompliance is a child behavior problem for which clinicians need to develop effective and efficient treatment procedures. Recent reviews of the literature (Berkowitz and Graziano, 1972; Johnson and Katz, 1973; O'Dell, 1974) indicate that parent behavioral training programs are effective in teaching parents to modify behavior problems of their children. Many of these programs have focused on measures of general child deviance (e.g., Patterson, 1974) because deceleration of *total* deviant behavior is probably the goal of most behavior therapists who train parents to modify their children's behavior problems. However, combining various child behaviors into a total deviant behavior category can produce data interpretation and treatment evaluation problems. (See Forehand, 1977, for a discussion of such problems.) Consequently, investigators such as Hanf (1970) have devised programs designed specifically for the modification of child noncompliance.

The Hanf program is designed for children between the ages of 2 and 8. Work with young children in this age range is viewed as particularly important in order to prevent later problems in adolescence. Hopefully, by teaching parents child management skills early, potential problems can be "nipped in the bud."

The purpose of this chapter is to outline the program which was developed by Hanf and subsequently modified by Forehand and his associates (e.g., Forehand and King, 1977). Furthermore, a series of investigations examining various components of the program and treatment outcome data resulting from applications of the program will be presented. The treatment procedures, to which we now turn, will be delineated by describing the following aspects of the program: the behavioral interview, clinic observations, the program outline, the content of each session, and a detailed description of one session.

TREATMENT PROGRAM

Behavioral Interview

The first session at the clinic (e.g., Psychology Clinic at the University of Georgia) includes a behavioral interview with the parent(s) of the identified problem child. The purpose of this initial interview is to establish the nature of typical parent–child interactions which are problems as well as to elicit a description of settings in which problem behaviors occur and the consequences which accompany such behaviors. The parent(s) are asked to specify how they react to noncompliance in various situations. For example, the mother of a 4-year-old would be asked if her child were a problem in the following situations: bedtime, mealtime, grocery store, car, visiting in a friend's home, and bath time. For each area in which the mother reports a problem, the therapist will examine how the parent reacts to the problem and, subsequently, how the child reacts to the parent's intervention. A continued analysis of both the parents' and child's behavior in each problem situation allows the therapist to examine the nature and pattern of child noncompliance to parental commands. Other relevant information concerning noncompliance in the above-mentioned situations, including the frequency and duration of the problems and the role of the other parent and siblings in facilitating or inhibiting solutions to the problem, is elicited. Information gathered during the interview with the parents serves as one important source of data in helping the therapist determine if the child is appropriate for the program.

Clinic Observations

Following the initial interview with the parent(s), each parent–child pair is observed in a clinic playroom equipped with a one way mirror and wired for sound. The playroom contains various age appropriate toys such as building blocks, toy trucks and cars, dolls, marbles, puzzles, crayons, and paper. An observer codes the parent–child interaction from an adjoining observation room.

Prior to each clinic observation, the parent is instructed to interact with his/her child in two different contexts. In the first context (hereafter referred to as Child's game), the parent is instructed to engage in any activity that the child chooses and to allow the child to determine the nature and rules of the interaction. The Child's game is essentially a free play situation. In the second context (hereafter referred to as Parent's game), the parent is instructed to engage the child in activities whose rules and nature are determined by the parent. The Parent's game is essentially a command situation. Each clinic observation consists of coding the parent–child interaction from behind a one way observation window for 5 or 10 minutes in both Child's and Parent's games. (The observed behaviors are defined in the Early Treatment Outcome Studies section and in the Recent Treatment Outcome Studies section.) Three clinic observations occur prior to treatment and three clinic observations occur after treatment is completed. Only one clinic observation occurs on any given day.

Program Outline

Following the three baseline clinic observations, treatment is initiated and carried out in a clinic playroom similar to the one used for clinic observations. The treatment room is also equipped with a bug-in-the-ear communication system (Farrell Instruments) which gives the therapist the ability to unobtrusively talk to the parent while the parent interacts with the child.

The treatment program consists of two phases. During the reinforcement phase of treatment (Phase I), the parent is taught to be a more effective reinforcing agent. In the context of the child's game, the parent is trained to increase the frequency and range of his/her social rewards and to eliminate verbal behavior, such as commands and criticisms (Forehand and Scarboro, 1975; Johnson and Lobitz, 1974), that is associated with deviant child behavior. First, the parent is taught to attend to the child's behavior. Moreover, he/she is required to eliminate all commands, questions, and criticisms directed to the child during the clinic training session. The second segment of Phase I consists of training the parent in the contingent use of rewards, particularly praise statements in which the parent labels the child's desirable behavior (e.g., "You are a good boy for picking up the blocks."). Throughout Phase I, the therapist emphasizes the use of contingent attention to increase child behaviors that the parent considers desirable. In the home, the parent is required to structure daily 10 minute Child games to practice the skills that she/he learned in the clinic. With the aid of the therapist, the parent formulates lists of rewards and lists of child behaviors that she/he wishes to increase. The contingent use of alternative rewards, such as television time, social outings, and treats, is also discussed. The parent is required to develop programs for use outside of the clinic to increase at least two child behaviors using her/his new skills.

The second phase of the treatment program (Phase II) consists of training the parent to use a time-out (TO) procedure to decrease noncompliant behavior exhibited by the child. The parent is trained in the context of the Parent's game to give direct, concise commands and to allow the child sufficient time to comply. If compliance is initiated within 5 seconds of the command, the parent is taught to reward the child with contingent attention. If compliance is not initiated, the parent is trained to use a time-out procedure involving the following event sequence. A warning is given that labels the time-out consequence for continued noncompliance. ("If you do not ——, you will have to sit on the chair in the corner."). If compliance does not occur within 5 seconds following the warning, the child is placed in a chair in the corner of the room. If the child leaves the chair, a warning is given that a spanking will occur if she/he leaves the chair again. The child is then returned to the chair. If the child leaves the chair after this warning, two quick spanks are administered on the child's rear by the parent and the child is returned to the chair. This procedure is repeated until the child remains quietly on the chair for 2 to 3 minutes. The child is then returned to the uncompleted task and given the initial command. Compliance is followed by contingent attention from the parent. In practice with the child during Parent's game, the parent is instructed to give a series of commands designed to evoke noncompliance. With the aid of the therapist, the parent is required to develop a list of nonclinic situations in which child noncompliance and deviant behavior occur. The parent is instructed how to use the time-out technique in each setting.

Treatment Session Outline

The number of treatment sessions which is necessary for the completion of each phase of treatment depends upon the speed with which the parent(s) demonstrate competence in the skills being taught and the child's response to this intervention. The number of treatment sessions per client necessary for the completion of the entire treatment program has ranged between five and twelve sessions. The mean number has been approximately nine treatment sessions. Each treatment session is approximately one hour in length and consists of the following steps:

(1) a 5-minute data gathering period in which the therapist observes the parent and child playing either Child's game (Phase I) or Parent's game (Phase II);

(2) discussion with the parent about her/his use of reinforcement (Phase I) or time-out (Phase II) during the preceding observation period and at home;

(3) modelling of additional reinforcement (Phase I) or time-out (Phase II) techniques for the parent by the therapist;

(4) practice of the reinforcement (Phase I) or time-out (Phase II) techniques in a role playing situatior with the therapist acting the part of the child;

(5) a practice period for the parent in either the Child's game (Phase I) or Parent's game (Phase II) in which she/he wears a bug-in-the-ear and receives instructions and feedback from the therapist.

Treatment Session Description

In order to provide a further description of the treatment procedures, the third treatment session for one client (Mrs. M. and John) is presented (originally presented in Forehand and King, 1977). The session initially consisted of a 5-minute assessment observation of Mrs. M. and John engaging in whatever activity the child wished (Child's game). During the observation, Mrs. M. emitted 21 praise statements, 10 attending statements, one command, and no questions. Subsequently, John was sent to another playroom and the therapist talked with Mrs. M. about her use of attending and praise statements during the immediately preceding observation. Mrs. M. reported that she believed she had attended to or praised most of John's desirable behaviors. The therapist agreed and praised Mrs. M. for her performance. Mrs. M. then was asked about her use of reinforcement with John at home. She reported using attending and praise statements frequently and indicated that John appeared to be responsive to such statements as his behavior was becoming less aversive to her. Mrs. M. then was asked to suggest one of John's behaviors which she might increase by the use of attending and praise statements. Mrs. M. indicated that she wanted to increase the length of time that John remained in his room and did not demand attention by asking for various items during a 1-hour rest and quiet play period after lunch. Mrs. M. was asked how she might accomplish such a goal by her use of praise. She replied that she could praise him for periods of time that he did not demand attention and remained quietly in his room. The therapist agreed and suggested that she tell John to rest or play quietly in his room and, after he remained quietly in his room for 5 minutes, she should go and praise him. She was told initially to praise him for each 5-minute period that he emitted the desired behavior. She also was told that after 1 week she could lengthen the interval between praise statements to approximately 10 minutes. She was informed that during subsequent weeks, she could continue to lengthen the time interval between praise statements but never to fade it out entirely for John resting or playing quietly during this hour of the day. Mrs. M. agreed to the intervention strategy and planned to implement it the following day.

The importance of Mrs. M.'s attention to John was reviewed next and she was reminded to make her attention and reinforcement to John contingent on his emission of desirable behaviors. Subsequently, Mrs. M. was told that the therapist wanted her to practice her use of praise statements with John. She was given the bug-in-the-ear, John was returned to the therapy room, the therapist left the room, and, for approximately 10 minutes, Mrs. M. and John played activities chosen by John. During this time, the therapist prompted Mrs. M. by way of the bug-in-the-ear regarding what praise statements she could use and when to use them. The therapist also verbally reinforced Mrs. M. for the use of praise statements that she emitted without being prompted by the therapist. Following the parent–child interaction, Mrs. M. was praise for her performance and again encouraged to use praise statements for John's appropriate behaviors at home.

LABORATORY INVESTIGATIONS

In order to specify the parameters and variables in the parent training package which are effective in modifying noncompliance, various components of the program have been investigated in a laboratory setting. These studies were conducted with children who were not referred to clinics for treatment. The selection of nonclinic children for these studies was a function of experimenter convenience and the desire for experimental control. Extraneous variables that may systematically or unsystematically affect child compliance in the home were controlled since the studies were conducted in a laboratory setting. Furthermore, more closely supervised withdrawal as well as introduction of treatment conditions (e.g., ABAB designs) was possible. Additionally, subjects were more easily recruited and could be paid for their participation. Finally, ethical questions concerning research with subjects who are seeking treatment were eliminated.

All of the studies described in this section were conducted in laboratory settings equipped with observation windows and adjoining observation rooms. Children in all the studies were 4 to 6 years old. In all cases, the experimenter used a bug-in-the-ear to cue the parent how to respond to the child.

In an effort to investigate the effects of number of parental commands upon child compliance as well as investigating certain parameters of the compliant act itself, Forehand and Scarboro (1975) had mothers issue 12 standard commands to their children in a laboratory setting. Presence or absence of compliance was coded for each of 15 ten second intervals following each command. A comparison of child compliance to the first six versus the second six commands indicated significantly less compliance to the latter commands. Furthermore, children demonstrated significantly less compliance in each of the first 3 ten second intervals following a command than in the latter (4–15) intervals. The first result suggests that as the number of parental commands increases, the amount of child compliance decreases. Such a finding lends support for the first component of the parent training program in which parents are initially taught to reduce the number of commands to their children. The second finding suggests that failure to initiate compliance rather than failure to continue or complete the compliant act is a major factor in the occurrence of noncompliance. Thus, attempts to increase compliance should focus on the initiation of compliance. Furthermore, observation systems should include measures of the initiation of compliance.

In another study, Bernhardt and Forehand (1975) examined the effects of different types of parental social reinforcement upon the child's response. A game which involved dropping marbles in a hole was used. Forty mothers and their children were assigned to one of two groups. Following a baseline in which the mother simply observed her child drop marbles in either of two holes (designated as the red and green holes) for 3 minutes, the mother was cued by an experimenter to reward the child on a FR 2 schedule during a 6-minute period for dropping a marble in the hole least preferred during baseline. For one group, each mother used unlabeled verbal rewards (e.g., "very good") whereas in the second group mothers used labeled verbal rewards (e.g., "Very good, you put another marble in the red hole"). Relative to baseline, both reward conditions were associated with increases in the number of marbles dropped in the rewarded hole; however, the labeled reinforcement was associated with a significantly greater increase from baseline to treatment than the unlabeled condition. These results suggest the importance of labeling verbal reinforcement given to children and support the efficacy of teaching parents the use of labeled verbal rewards in Phase I of the treatment program.

The majority of our laboratory studies has examined the effects of timeout (a period of time in which one or more reinforcers are removed) on child noncompliance to maternal commands (e.g., Gardner et al., 1976; Scarboro and Forehand, 1975). The studies were undertaken after a review of the literature indicated that most investigators utilizing time-out have not employed adequate experimental methodology (Forehand and MacDonough, 1975) and that most parameters of time-out (e.g., location of time-out, presence versus absence of a verbalized reason for time-out prior to its onset) have not been examined (MacDonough and Forehand, 1973). As time-out is the primary mode of treatment in Phase II of the parent training program, it was judged that a systematic examination of the procedure and its various parameters was needed.

Scarboro and Forehand (1975) compared a within-room (ignoring) and an out-of-room (isolation) time-out procedure. After a baseline, mothers assigned to the within-room procedure were instructed to issue a warning ("If you do not ——, I am not going to play with you for awhile.") if the child did not initiate compliance within 5 seconds after a maternal command. If the child did not initiate compliance within 5 seconds after the warning, the mother moved away from the child and withdrew all her attention from him/her for 2 minutes. After 2 minutes, the mother returned her attention to the child when the child was quiet for 5 seconds (5 second quiet contingency). The procedure for the out-of-room time-out was similar except for the warning ("If you do not ——, I am going to take the toys and leave the room.") and the actual time-out administration, which involved the mother taking the toys and leaving the room for 2 minutes plus the 5 second quiet contingency. During training, mothers in both groups were cued by way of the bug-in-the-ear as to when and how to issue commands and warnings and to implement time-out. Relative to a control group in which the mothers issued the same commands but did not use time-out, both time-out procedures significantly increased initiation of compliance to maternal commands. The two procedures did not differentially affect compliance. However, the within-room procedure required significantly more administrations of time-out than the out-of-room procedure, suggesting that the latter is more efficient than the former. Efficiency is particularly important when one considers that potential sources of reinforcement are being lost with multiple administrations of time-out. Finally, in a post-training period, without cueing from the experimenter regarding when to issue warnings or implement time-out, the mothers in both time-out groups maintained child compliance at the levels previously achieved during training.

The efficacy of including a verbalized reason (e.g., "You did not do what I said, so I am going to take all the toys and not play with you") in the time-out procedure was examined by Gardner *et al.* (1976). A comparison of groups receiving time-out only, verbalized reason followed by time-out, and time-out followed by a verbalized reason failed to reveal any significant differences; however, all three were associated with less noncompliance than a control group for which time-out was not implemented. During a posttraining period, without cueing from the experimenter about when to implement time-out, the mothers in the time-out groups maintained their children's compliance at the level obtained during training.

Hobbs, Forehand, and Murray (in press) have produced results which suggest that the length of time-out is a critical variable in the effectiveness of time-out in suppressing noncompliance. In this study, children were assigned to a control group or one of three experimental groups: 10 seconds, 1 minute, or 4 minutes of time-out (standing in a corner) for each noncompliance to a series of maternal commands. The four minute time-out was more effective in reducing noncompliance than the 10 second or 1 minute time-outs and all were more effective than a control group in which time-out was not implemented. Interestingly, during a subsequent treatment withdrawal period (return to baseline), the non-compliance of the subjects in the 4 minute time-out group was significantly lower than that of the 10-second or 1-minute time-out groups. The results indicate that a time-out period as brief as 1 minute is not as effective as a time-out of moderate duration (i.e., 4 minutes) in suppressing and maintaining noncompliance.

An earlier study by Hobbs and Forehand (1975) suggested that contingent release from time-out is also important when modifying noncompliance. A comparison of contingent release (15 seconds of quiet were required prior to the mother re-entering the room in an out-of-room time-out procedure) and noncontingent release (subjects were yoked to those in the contingent release group in terms of the total length of time-out, but no quiet contingency was employed) groups indicated that less disruption occurred during time-out for the contingent release group. Furthermore, the results suggested that contingent release was associated with less noncompliance to maternal commands than noncontingent release.

These time-out studies suggest that the most effective and efficient time-out condition is one in which the mother isolates the child rather than just ignores him/her, uses a time-out duration longer than 1 minute (but for ethical reasons under 5 minutes), and releases the child from time-out when he/she is being quiet. A verbalized reason for time-out is optional as it neither adds to nor subtracts from the effectiveness of time-out in suppressing child noncompliance. Furthermore, if the parent wishes to increase compliance, the other laboratory studies indicate that he/she should limit the number of commands issued, use labeled verbal rewards, and insure the initiation of compliance. Research has just been completed examining the interactive effects of two of these factors on noncompliance. Roberts, McMahon, Forehand, and Humphreys (in press) trained one group of parents in "good command issuing skills" (i.e., clear commands plus allowing the child 5 seconds to initiate compliance) and one group in command giving plus time-out training. The results indicate that both types of training increased child compliance relative to a placebo control condition. However, the combination of command training and time-out training was more effective than command training alone, suggesting the importance of consequences and antecedents in modifying child noncompliance.

EARLY TREATMENT OUTCOME STUDIES

In addition to the examination of the various components of the treatment program in the laboratory setting, several early studies were conducted in which the effectiveness of the entire parent training program was evaluated. The behaviors, the attitude measures which were employed, the therapists who treated the clients, the procedures which were used in each study, and the results of the studies will now be described.

Behaviors Observed

In each study, one child behavior and three parent behaviors were recorded in the clinic setting. For outcome evaluation purposes, these behaviors were coded in three pretreatment (baseline) sessions as well as in all treatment sessions. The recorded child behavior was compliance and the parent behaviors were commands, questions, and rewards. Compliance was defined as the child's initiation of obedience to the parental command within five seconds. For example, the mother states "put the blocks in the box." If the child begins to pick up the blocks and place them in the box within 5 seconds, compliance is scored. Completion of compliance (e.g., placing all the blocks in the box) was not scored. Maternal commands were orders (e.g., "Pick up the blocks."), directions (e.g., "Color inside the lines.") or suggestions (e.g., "Why don't you erase the line?") that required a motor response from the child. Questions were any interrogation (e.g., "What did you do at school today?") or suggestion (e.g., "Wouldn't you like to talk?") that required a verbal response from the child. Maternal rewards were defined as attention to the child by describing his activity (e.g., "You are stacking the blocks high."), by praising his/her behavior (e.g., "You are a good boy for picking up the blocks." "Great job."), or by using positive physical contact (e.g., a hug or kiss). Reliability on each of these categories was obtained in approximately 20% of the sessions in each study. Reliability was above 80% for each behavioral category in all the early treatment outcome studies.

Attitude Measure

In addition to behavioral measures, the Parent Attitude Test (PAT) (Cowen *et al.*, 1970) was administered to each mother who participated in two studies (Forehand and King, 1977; Forehand *et al.*, 1975). The PAT is a set of four measures (School Attitudes, Home Attitudes, Behavior Rating Scale, and Adjective Checklist Scale) of parent attitudes and perceptions of child behavior. The School and Home Attitude measures consist of 4 and 7 item scales, respectively, which reflect the parent's perception of the child's adjustment at school and home. The Behavior Rating Scale consists of 25 items, each of which refers to a behavior problem, while the Adjective Checklist Scale consists of 34 adjectives, each describing a child behavior or personality characteristic. Cowen *et al.* (1970) have presented evidence demonstrating the reliability and validity of the measures. The School Attitude scale was not utilized in any of the studies reported in this chapter as frequently the children were not of school age.

Therapists

The therapists for the treatment studies (Forehand and King, 1974, 1977) were either Ph.D. clinical psychologists (the authors of those studies) or graduate students in clinical psychology working under the supervision of the two authors. The therapist in all cases also collected the outcome data used to evaluate the program's effectiveness.

Procedures and Results

A comparative study which investigated differences between a group of "normal" mother–child pairs and a group of mothers and noncompliant children was perceived as an important first step in evaluating the validity of the behavioral measures used in the program. Consequently, Forehand *et al.* (1975) examined the interactions of 20 mothers and their 4 to 6 year old noncompliant children referred to a clinic for treatment and 20 mothers and their nonclinic children. The latter group was recruited from kindergartens and neighborhoods to match the former group in terms of age, sex, and socioeconomic status. A 20 minute behavioral observation in the clinic setting consisting of 10 minutes of Child's game and 10 minutes of Parent's game was performed for each mother–child pair. In addition, all mothers completed the Parent Attitude Test (Cowen *et al.*, 1970). As one would expect, results indicated that the interactions of noncompliant clinic children and their mothers differed from those of nonclinic children and their mothers. During the Child's game the mothers of the noncompliant clinic children issued significantly more commands than the mothers of the nonclinic children; yet, the two groups of mothers did not differ in the number of rewards emitted. In the Parent's game the clinic children complied to significantly fewer of their parent's commands than did the nonclinic children. Furthermore, on all three of the Parent Attitude Test scales the mothers of the clinic children perceived their children as significantly more maladjusted than the mothers of the nonclinic children perceived their children. These results provided supportive data for the notion that the sample of children treated in the program are less compliant than "normal" children and that their mothers differ on at least one important parenting behavior (number of commands) from mothers of nonclinic children.

In one of the early outcome studies, Forehand and King (1974) successfully used the parent training program to treat eight preschool noncompliant children and their mothers in a mean of 6.2 sessions. In the Child's game, mothers significantly increased their use of rewards and significantly decreased their use of commands and questions from baseline to treatment. In the Parent's game, maternal rewards again increased significantly from baseline to treatment as did child compliance. These results suggest that both parent and child behaviors changed in the desired and predicted direction with treatment.

Forehand and King (1977) subsequently used the program in the treatment of 11 physically normal, preschool children and their mothers. Parent attitude measures (Parent Attitude Test) as well as observational data on the mother–child interaction in the clinic were obtained. Results of the attitude measures indicated that after treatment the mothers perceived their children as significantly better adjusted than prior to treatment. The results of the observational measures were similar to those obtained by Forehand and King (1974); parents significantly decreased their use of commands and questions, parents significantly increased their use of rewards, and children increased their compliance to commands. Both the mother's attitude and the mother's and child's behaviors were maintained at a 3 month follow-up. Relative to a nonclinic "normal" sample of 11 mother-child pairs, the treated children were less compliant prior to treatment and more compliant after treatment. Furthermore, prior to treatment parents of the clinic children perceived their children as less well adjusted than parents of the nonclinic children perceived their children. However, following treatment, the two groups of parents did not differ significantly in their perception of their children.

The program's effectiveness is not limited to modifying the interactional patterns of physically normal children and their parents. Although they defined their behavioral categories slightly different, Hanf and Kling (1973) have used the same procedures to alter the interactions between 40 pairs of mothers and their severely physically handicapped, noncompliant children. A comparison of baseline to treatment data indicated that the mothers significantly increased their use of verbal rewards and decreased their use of commands and questions. There also was a significant increase in child compliance. All gains were maintained at a 3 month follow-up. In a case study, Forehand, Cheney, and Yoder (1974) reported similar effects in the treatment of a noncompliant, deaf child.

RECENT TREATMENT OUTCOME STUDIES

The studies reviewed in the preceding section offer support for the training program. However, a number of problems exist with the previously reviewed studies which limit the conclusions one can draw about the overall effectiveness of the treatment package. First, demonstration of generality of treatment effects from the clinic to the home is needed. Forehand's review (1977) of a number of studies in which parent behavior training in the clinic failed to change parent or child behavior in the home effectively demonstrates that the therapist cannot *assume* generality in the absence of data. Furthermore, child compliance in a clinic setting is not an effective predictor of compliance in the home (Forehand *et al.*, 1978); this result suggests that changes in child behavior in the clinic may not reflect changes in the behavior in the home. Second, the earlier behavior coding system was not designed to measure a number of critical parent and child behaviors. Important behaviors which were not coded included: (a) parental reinforcement contingent on child compliance (total parental reinforcement was measured in the early studies; such measurement did not allow an assessment of how much parental reinforcement was actually contingent on child compliance); (b) parental commands to which compliance was not possible (earlier studies measured parental commands; such measurement did not allow differentiation between commands to which compliance was possible and commands to which compliance was not possible); and (c) child deviant behaviors other than noncompliance. Third, objective treatment criteria concerning the appropriate timing of movement from one segment of treatment to another were not established and available for therapists. The absence of such criteria allows clients to acquire varying degrees of the skills taught in each segment of the program which in turn can effect the outcome data. Fourth, the data collected in the earlier studies were not collected by independent observers but rather by the therapists. Fifth, proper experimental control was not demonstrated in the earlier studies as an untreated control group was not included to control for maturational processes, nonspecific environmental events, and the effects of observation. Thus, the following studies were undertaken to systematically evaluate the treatment program by taking each of the above issues into consideration.

Home Observations

In order to assess generality of treatment effects from the clinic to the home, trained observers conducted home observations in each of the studies described in this section. For each home observation, the mother was instructed to adhere as much as possible to her daily routine and to interact normally with the child. No situations analogous to those used in the clinic (i.e., Child's game and Parent's game) were introduced. The mother was instructed to remain in two adjoining rooms with the child, to ignore the observer, and to avoid having visitors, telephone calls, or the television on during the observation. Family members other than the mother and child were allowed to be present during the observation.

The observer, equipped with a cassette tape recorder, earphone, and coding sheets, stationed himself so that he could observe the mother–child interaction in either of the two adjoining rooms. The tape recorder signalled the observer, via the earphone, at one minute intervals. The observer collected data in sets of 10 consecutive minutes followed by a 1-minute nonrecording period. Forty minutes of data were collected for each home observation.

Behaviors Observed

In order to include additional important parent and child behaviors in the analysis of the effectiveness of the parent training program, the revised coding system permitted the recording of the following seven classes of parent behaviors and four classes of sequential child–parent behaviors:

Parent Behaviors

1. *Rewards:* praise, approval, or positive physical attention which refers to the child or the child's activity; verbal rewards include both specific (labeled) and nonspecific (unlabeled) reference to "praiseworthy" behavior.
2. *Attends:* descriptive phrases that follow and refer to (a) the child's ongoing behavior; (b) objects directly related to his play; (c) his spatial position; or (d) his appearance.
3. *Questions:* interrogatives to which the only appropriate response is verbal.
4. *Commands:*
   (a) *Alpha Commands:* an order, rule, suggestion, or question to which a motoric response is appropriate and feasible.
   (b) *Beta Commands:* commands to which the child does not have the opportunity to demonstrate compliance. Beta commands include parental commands which are (a) so vague that proper action for compliance cannot be determined; (b) interrupted by further parental verbage before enough time (5 seconds) has elapsed for the child to comply; or (c) carried out by the parent before the child has an opportunity to comply.
5. *Criticisms:* negative evaluations or disapproval of the child or his activities.

6. *Warnings:* statements that describe aversive consequences to be delivered by the parent if the child fails to comply to a parental command.

7. Time-out: any procedure used by the parent that removes the child from positive reinforcement.

Sequential Child–Parent Behavior

1. *Child Compliance:* an appropriate motoric response initiated within 5 seconds following a parental alpha command.

2. *Child Noncompliance:* failure to initiate an appropriate motoric response within 5 seconds following a parental alpha command.

3. *Child Deviance:* behavior, excluding noncompliance, classified as deviant by Patterson, Ray, Shaw, and Cobb (1969) which occurs immediately prior to a scoreable parent behavior. These behaviors include crying, tantrums, and demanding attention plus nine other child behaviors.

4. *Contingent-Attention:* a Reward or Attend presented by the parent within the 5 seconds following the initiation of Child Compliance.

In two treatment outcome studies, reliability for the coding system was assessed by means of reliability checks conducted on the primary observer's data by a second (calibrating) observer. The calibrating observer obtained reliability checks on 20% of the observation sessions in the home and 33% of the observation sessions in the clinic. Reliability between observers averaged 75%.

Treatment Criteria

In order to provide objective criteria upon which therapists could base their decisions regarding movement from one segment of treatment to another, behavioral and time (number of sessions) criteria were established for each segment of treatment. These criteria were based upon data gathered on "normal" mother–child interactions by Forehand *et al.* (1975) and Johnson *et al.* (1973).

The behavioral criteria for the successful completion of the attending segment of Phase I was at least one 5-minute observation of Child's game in which the mother obtained: (1) an average of four or more attends per minute, 75% of which were contingent upon nondeviant child behavior; and (2) an average of 0.4 or less commands plus questions per minute. Training in the attending segment of Phase I was limited to no more than four treatment sessions.

The behavioral criteria for the successful completion of the reward segment of Phase I was at least one 5 minute observation of Child's game in which the mother obtained an average of four rewards plus attends per minute. Of this sum, at least two rewards per minute were required. A minimum of 75% of these statements had to be contingent upon nondeviant child behavior. Training in the use of rewards was limited to no more than four sessions.

The behavioral criteria for the successful completion of Phase II was at least one 5 minute observation of the Parent's game in which: (1) a 75% child compliance ratio (child compliance/total maternal commands) was obtained; and (2) a 60% reward ratio (contingent parent rewards/child compliances) was obtained. Training in Phase II was limited to no more than six sessions, and total treatment (Phase I and II) was limited to no more than 12 therapy sessions.

The therapists in the recent treatment outcome studies applied the above listed criteria to data which they collected during the data gathering period of each clinic treatment session. When criteria were met, movement to the next segment of treatment ensued. Cotherapists conducted reliability checks on the therapists data during 36% of the data gathering periods. These checks revealed 83% overall agreement between therapist and calibrater.

Therapists and Observers

Seven graduate students with experience in using the parent training program served as primary therapists in the studies. Graduate students inexperienced in the parent training program served as cotherapists.

Six undergraduate and five graduate students served as observers. Each observer spent at least 12 hours of training in the use of the coding system during the 4 weeks preceding the initiation of the studies. After the initial training sessions, biweekly 45-minute training sessions were held in order to maintain the accuracy of the observers.

Procedures

In order to evaluate the effectiveness of the treatment program in comparison to a no treatment control group and to investigate the generality of treatment changes from the clinic to the home, Peed, Roberts, and Forehand (1977) undertook a study which compared six mother–child pairs who received treatment by way of the noncompliance training program to six mother–child pairs who constituted a waiting list control group. (The children who served as subjects in the study were eight boys and four girls who ranged in age from 2 years, 9 months to 8 years, 8 months; their family socioeconomic status ranged from lower class to upper middle class.) Each mother–child pair was randomly assigned to either the treatment or control group after the mother contacted the psychology clinic (University of Georgia) expressing concern over her child's noncompliance. Each mother–child pair then underwent three clinic observations as well as five home observations. Following treatment which averaged 9.5 treatment sessions or a waiting period that averaged 33 days, each mother–child pair again underwent three clinic observations and five home observations.

The results from the Peed *et al.* (1977) study indicated that in the Child's game in the clinic setting the mothers in the treatment group significantly decreased their frequency of questions and significantly increased their frequency of attends and rewards from pre- to posttreatment assessments. In the Parent's game in the clinic setting, the treatment group mothers decreased their use of beta commands (those to which the child couldn't comply) and increased their use of contingent attention for child compliance from pre- to posttreatment. The children demonstrated a significant increase in compliance in the Parent's game. In the home observations, significant increases from the pre- to posttreatment assessments occurred for child compliance and for maternal rewards, attends, and contingent attention to compliance. Significant decreases occurred for maternal use of beta commands. For the control group significant changes did not occur from the pre- to postwaiting period, providing support for the notion that the treatment program rather than the passage of time was responsible for the mother and child behavior change in the treatment group. The influence of the treatment program on several behaviors (i.e., criticisms, warnings, time-outs, and child deviance) could not be examined because these behaviors occurred too infrequently.

The Parent Attitude Test (Cowen *et al.*, 1970) was also administered to the mothers in each group at the pre- and postassessments. In general, mothers in *both* groups saw their children as better adjusted at the post- than at the premeasure, suggesting that the changes in attitudes of the mothers in the treatment group did not result from treatment per se. This finding suggests that an attitude measure *alone* may not be an adequate criterion upon which to base judgements concerning the effectiveness of parent training programs.

The Peed *et al.* (1977) study provided convincing data concerning the immediate effectiveness of the training program in changing parent and child behavior in both the clinic and home. However, data were not provided concerning whether changes in parent and child behaviors maintained longer than immediately after treatment. Thus, a study by Forehand, Sturgis, McMahon, Aguar, Green, Wells, and Breiner (in press) was undertaken to examine temporal generality resulting from the training program. The client sample consisted of 10 mother–child pairs, including the six mother–child pairs from the treatment group in the Peed *et al.* (1977) study. Data gathered in five home observations which were performed both before and after treatment indicated that the subjects demonstrated pre- to postchanges in the same parent and child behaviors as reported in the Peed *et al.* (1977) study. The *temporal* generality of the treatment program was assessed by means of data gathered from the 10 mother-child pairs at 6 and 12 months following treatment. Observations in the home revealed that the changes in mother and child behaviors observed immediately after treatment were maintained, and mothers continued to report the positive attitude changes concerning their children (as measured by the Parent Attitude Test) which were evident immediately following treatment.

In addition to data concerning generality of treatment effects from the clinic to the home and over time, data also have been obtained on the generality of treatment effects from the home to the school and from one sibling to another. The effect of the treatment program on child behavior in the school as well as in the home is of concern because Johnson, Bolstad, and Lobitz (1976) have reported data suggesting that children may increase their deviant behavior in school when deviant home behavior is treated by parent training programs. In order to examine if such a "behavioral contrast" effect or if setting generality (decrease in deviant school behavior when noncompliance decreases in the home) occurs with the compliance training program, Forehand *et al.* (in press) also measured the total amount of child deviant behavior in the school (e.g., cry, demand attention, tantrum, negativism) during four observation sessions both before and after treatment for eight children in their study. In addition, the classroom deviant behavior of eight randomly selected "normal" school children was measured before and after a time interval which was equivalent to the one that separated the treated children's pre and post measures. The results indicated that three of the eight children treated for home noncompliance decreased their deviant school behavior and five increased such behavior from pre to post measures. For the randomly selected control children, four increased and four decreased their school deviant behavior. Statistical analysis of the data revealed no systematic changes in school behavior.

Humphreys, Forehand, McMahon, and Roberts (in press) have examined the generality of treatment effects from one sibling to another. During four to eight pretreatment home observations and four posttreatment home observations, the interactions of the mother and clinic-referred child and of the mother and a sibling of the clinic-referred child were observed. In all eight cases, both the clinic-referred child and the sibling were 3 to 8 years old and the sibling was within 3 years of the clinic child's age. The results indicated that from pre- to posttreatment the mothers increased their use of attention contingent on compliance, rewards, and attends and decreased their use of beta commands toward the *untreated* child. In addition, the untreated children increased their compliance. These results suggest that parents can generalize their skills for dealing with noncompliance to other children in the family and that the untreated children respond by increasing their compliance.

In summary, treatment outcome studies have gathered data from over 75 noncompliant children and their parents in three different clinical settings (University of Oregon Medical School, University of Georgia Psychology Clinic, and Emory University Medical School). Data from subsamples of these subjects were obtained to investigate setting, temporal, and sibling generality of treatment effects. Furthermore, change in parental attitude toward the noncompliant child was included as an outcome measure in a significant number of cases. The treatment outcome data have been consistent in demonstrating the effectiveness and efficiency of the parent training program for the treatment of child noncompliance.

Future research will address several issues relating to the work reported above. First, procedures to facilitate generality of treatment effects will be examined. For example, will the requirement that parents learn general social learning principles, in addition to acquiring the particular skills taught in our training program, promote generality of treatment effects to different child behaviors, different settings, and untreated siblings? Will a procedure by which treatment is gradually faded out facilitate temporal generality over terminating treatment without fading? The latter procedure (no fading) is typically practiced now and is more efficient than fading of treatment; however, its effectiveness in terms of maintenance of treatment effects may be more limited. A second area for future research concerns the development and evaluation of written instructional packages to modify child noncompliance. Can the skills in our parent training program be communicated effectively to parents in brochures? Obviously, such a treatment method is efficient; however, we are again faced with the question of effectiveness versus efficiency. Our future research efforts will be directed toward addressing these issues.

CONCLUSIONS

Noncompliance is a behavioral category which includes a significant percentage of the deviant behaviors exhibited by children referred to professionals for psychotherapeutic intervention. The importance of noncompliance in childhood behavior problems is illustrated by the fact that noncompliance is a primary characteristic of several classifications of child psychopathology. Clinicians have long been concerned with effective and efficient means for the treatment of noncompliance. This chapter described a program which utilizes parents as the primary agents of change in the treatment of their children's noncompliance. Training parents to modify noncompliance exhibited by their children is an attractive treatment approach because parents are quite frequently the most powerful social agents in their children's environment, are the persons most often confronted with instances of child noncompliance, and are vested by society with control of their children's behavior.

The current parent training program is the result of 10 years of development and research. One area of research over the past 5 years focused upon the identification of components of the treatment program which are most effective in the modification of noncompliance. Laboratory studies with nonclinic subjects indicated that compliance was increased most effectively by limiting the number of commands issued and using *labelled* verbal rewards to consequate the *initiation* of compliance. Furthermore, noncompliance was decreased most effectively by using an isolation type of time-out of moderate duration (greater than 1 minute; less than 5 minutes) with release from time-out contingent upon a period of quiet by the child. These techniques are incorporated as important components in the parent training program.

The second area of research focused upon investigating the effectiveness of the total treatment package and evaluating its usefulness in a clinical setting. One consideration in this area of research is the *specificity* of the parent training program in identifying clients most likely to benefit from the particular treatment as well as detailing the treatment procedure itself. The parent training program was designed for and has been used almost exclusively with children aged 2–8 years whose parents identify noncompliance as a major problem. The program has been used successfully with physically and mentally handicapped children as well as children of normal physical and mental capacities. Children labelled "psychotic" or "autistic" have been excluded from treatment. Specification of characteristics of parents most suitable for the program has not been undertaken. Parents successfully included in the treatment program have ranged from lower to upper middle class. The specificity of treatment procedures is such that the content of treatment sessions is outlined step by step and decisions concerning movement from one stage of treatment to the next are made on the basis of data based criteria.

A second consideration is the *effectiveness* of the treatment program in making predicted changes for a sufficient number of clients to suggest the power and reliability of the treatment effects. To date, data have been gathered from over 75 noncompliant children and their parents who underwent treatment. The data are remarkable for the consistency with which they demonstrate clinically significant changes in predicted parent and child behaviors. Additionally, data have demonstrated that observed changes for a subsample of these cases were the result of the parent training program rather than some other variable such as the mere passage of time.

Another consideration is the *generality* of treatment effects across settings, siblings, and time. A primary concern for the parent training program under consideration is the generality of treatment effects from the clinic to the home. Data from a subsample of 10 subjects indicate that such setting generality occurs. Data concerning the generality of child behavior changes to other settings, such as the school, indicate that home treatment is not associated with any systematic child behavior change in these secondary settings. Data are available to indicate that parents generalize the skills taught to them to siblings of the treated child and that significant changes occur in the siblings' behavior. An important consideration concerning the effectiveness of any intervention is the temporal generality of treatment effects. To date, data have been gathered at 6 and 12 month follow-ups on a subsample of 10 subjects. The data resulting from these posttreatment checks provide evidence of continued treatment effects over the time intervals examined.

Yet another consideration in judging the effectiveness of a treatment program is the *quality* of the supporting data. Most of the early data concerning the effectiveness of the parent training program consisted of behavioral data collected by therapists. In an attempt to overcome some of the obvious limitations of such data, observers other than therapists or parents were used in later studies. These observers were trained to acceptable levels of reliability, training sessions were conducted throughout the studies to maintain reliability, and frequent reliability checks were conducted by "calibrating" observers. Furthermore, the coding system was expanded to include relevant behaviors that were not coded in earlier studies. Finally, parent attitude measures were collected to increase the number of sources of data concerning the effects of treatment and, thus, increase the validity of outcome assessment.

The *efficiency* and difficulty in carrying out any treatment program are important considerations for the clinician. This parent training program achieved desired levels of compliance in an average of nine 1-hour treatment sessions per client. In our more recent work (Humphreys *et al.*, in press), we have reduced the number of treatment sessions to five. Our preliminary data suggest our treatment effectiveness is being maintained. The effort required to carry out the treatment program in terms of personnel and equipment appears acceptable for most clinical settings. Cotherapists used a one-way mirror, bug-in-the-ear, sound system, and toys to conduct the parent training program for cases reported in this chapter. However, the use of cotherapists does not appear to be a necessity as single therapists have reported informally the successful use of the treatment program. Furthermore, it is conceivable that paraprofessionals could be trained to conduct the treatment program and that innovative clinicians could devise methods of observation and communication that circumvent the need for a one-way mirror, bug-in-the-ear, and sound system. Obviously, data are needed to evaluate what effects such changes in the treatment program would produce before such recommendations are made. Nevertheless, even without such changes, the parent training program does not require an inordinate amount of personnel or equipment for implementation.

Finally, the responsible clinician needs to consider the overall effect that any intervention has upon the *parent–child relationship*. Data indicate that parents' attitudes toward their children improved following participation in the parent training program although the changes in attitudes could not be attributed to treatment per se. We think that these attitude changes are important in restoring balance and harmony to what is often a negative relationship based upon coercion by the time the parent brings her/his child to the professional therapy. This parent training program requires the parent to focus upon the positive aspects of the parent–child relationship and learn ways to increase the quality and quantity of positive interactions. Only after the parent has demonstrated the ability to interact with the child and increase appropriate behavior (compliance) through positive means are direct methods to control deviant behavior (noncompliance) introduced. The emphasis throughout the treatment program upon positive interaction often sharply reduces or obviates the need to use aversive procedures (time-out) to reduce noncompliance. Even when aversive procedures are employed, parents appear better able to use them to *teach* their children appropriate behavior rather than as a means to *vent* angry emotions and *coerce* the- child into appropriate behavior. The consistency which the parent displays in his/her actions toward the child after treatment as well as her/his change in attitude toward the child seems to result in a sounder, more positive parent–child relationship. Obviously, further data are needed to support or reject these impressions but the absence of such data does not negate the importance of the change in the overall parent–child relationship.

REFERENCES

Berkowitz, B. P., and Graziano, A. M. (1972). Training parents as behavior therapists: a review. *Behaviour Research and Therapy* 10:297–317.
Bernhardt, A., and Forehand, R. (1975). The effects of labeled and unlabeled praise upon lower and middle class children. *Journal of Experimental Child Psychology* 19:536–543.
Christophersen, E. R., Barnard, J. D., Ford, D., and Wolf, M. M. (1976). The family training program: improving parent-child interaction patterns. In E. J. Mash, L. C. Handy, and L. A. Hamerlynck, eds., *Behavior Modification Approaches to Parenting.* Pp. 36–56. New York: Brunner/Mazel.
Cowen, E. L., Huser, J., Beach, D. R., and Rappaport, J. (1970). Parental perceptions of young children and their relation to indexes of adjustment. *Journal of Consulting and Clinical Psychology* 34:97–103.
Forehand, R. (1977). Child noncompliance to parental commands: behavioral analysis and treatment. In M. Hersen, R. M. Eisler, and P. M. Miller, eds., *Progress in Behavior Modification,* Vol. 5. Pp. 111–147. New York: Academic Press.
——, and King, H. E. (1974). Pre-school children's noncompliance: effects of short-term behavior therapy. *Journal of Community Psychology* 2:42–44.
——, and King, H. E. (1977). Noncompliant children: effects of parent training on behavior and attitude change. *Behavior Modification* 1:93–108.
——, and MacDonough, T. S. (1975). Response contingent time out: an examination of outcome data. *European Journal of Behavioral Analysis and Modification* 1:109–115.
——, and Scarboro, M. E. (1975). An analysis of children's oppositional behavior. *Journal of Abnormal Child Psychology* 3:27–31.
——, Cheney, T., and Yoder, P. (1974). Parent behavior training: effects on the noncompliance of a deaf child. *Journal of Behavior Therapy and Experimental Psychiatry* 5:281–283.
——, King, H. E., Peed, S., and Yoder, P. (1975). Mother–child interactions: comparisons of a noncompliant clinic group and a non-clinic group. *Behaviour Research and Therapy* 13:79–84.
——, Sturgis, E., McMahon, R., Aguar, D., Green, K., Wells, K., and Breiner, J. (in press). Generality of treatment effects resulting from a parent-training program to modify child noncompliance. *Behavior Modification.*
——, Wells, K. C., and Sturgis, E. T. (1978). Predictors of child noncompliant behavior in the home. *Journal of Consulting and Clinical Psychology* 46:179.

Gardner, H. L., Forehand, R., and Roberts, M. (1976). Timeout with children: effects of an explanation and brief parent training on child and parent behaviors. *Journal of Abnormal Child Psychology* 4:277–288.

Hanf, C. (1970). Shaping mothers to shape their children's behavior. Unpublished manuscript, University of Oregon Medical School.

——, and Kling, F. (1973). Facilitating parent-child interaction: a two stage training model. Unpublished manuscript, Portland: University of Oregon Medical School.

Hobbs, S. A., and Forehand, R. (1975). Effects of differential release from time-out on children's deviant behavior. *Journal of Behavior Therapy and Experimental Psychiatry* 6:256–257.

——, Forehand, R., and Murray, R. G. (in press). Effects of various durations of timeout on the non-compliant behavior of children. *Behavior Therapy*.

Humphreys, L., Forehand, R., McMahon, R., and Roberts, M. W. (in press). Parent behavioral training to modify child noncompliance: Effects on untreated siblings. *Journal of Behavior Therapy and Experimental Psychiatry*.

Johansson, S. (1971). Compliance and noncompliance in young children. Unpublished dissertation, University of Oregon.

Johnson, C. A., and Katz, R. C. (1973). Using parents as change agents for their children: A review. *Journal of Child Psychology and Psychiatry* 14:181–200.

——, Bolstad, O. D., and Lobitz, G. K. (1976). Generalization and contrast phenomena in behavior modification with children. In E. J. Mash, L. A. Hamerlynck, and L. C. Handy, eds., *Behavior Modification and Families*. Pp. 160–188. New York: Brunner/Mazel.

Johnson, S. M., and Lobitz, G. K. (1974). Parental manipulation of child behavior in home observations. *Journal of Applied Behavior Analysis* 7:23–31.

——, Wahl, G., Martin, S., and Johansson, S. (1973). How deviant is the normal child? A behavioral analysis of the preschool child and his family. In R. D. Rubin, J. P. Brady, and J. D. Henderson, eds., *Advances in Behavior Therapy*, Vol. 4, pp. 37–54. New York: Academic Press.

MacDonough, T. S., and Forehand, R. (1973). Response-contingent time out: important parameters in behavior modification with children. *Journal of Behavior Therapy and Experimental Psychiatry* 4:231–236.

O'Dell, S. (1974). Training parents in behavior modification: a review. *Psychological Bulletin* 81:418–433.

Patterson, G. R. (1974). Interventions for boys with conduct problems: multiple settings, treatments, and criteria. *Journal of Consulting and Clinical Psychology* 42:471–481.

——, Ray, R. S., Shaw, D. A., and Cobb, J. A. (1969). Manual for coding of family interactions. NAPS Document, #01234, New York.

Peed, S., Roberts, M., and Forehand, R. (1977). Evaluation of the effectiveness of a standardized parent training program in altering the interaction of mothers and their noncompliant children. *Behavior Modification* 1:323–350.

Roberts, M., McMahon, R., Forehand, R., and Humphreys, L. (in press). The effect of parental instructional-giving on child compliance. *Behavior Therapy*.

Scarboro, M. E., and Forehand, R. (1975). Effects of two types of response-contingent time-out on compliance and oppositional behavior of children. *Journal of Experimental Child Psychology* 19:252–264.

Taplin, P. S., and Reid, J. B. (unpublished data). Changes in parent consequation as a function of family intervention. Eugene: Oregon Research Institute.

Tavormina, J. B., Henggeler, S. W., and Gayton, W. F. (1976). Age trends in parental assessments of behavior problems of their retarded children. *Mental Retardation* 14(no. 1):38–39.

Chapter Eight

Assessment and Treatment of Childhood Encopresis*

DANIEL M. DOLEYS

INTRODUCTION

Definition and Classification

The term "encopresis" was introduced into the literature in 1926 by Weissenberg as the fecal equivalent of enuresis. As is often the case, however, there has been considerable disagreement as to the definition of encopresis. The type of soiling pattern, the age, and etiological factors considered to be characteristic of the encopretic have varied. A general definition of functional encopresis proposed herein is: the passage of fecal material of any amount or consistency into the clothing or other generally

---

*Preparation of this manuscript was supported in part by Project 910, U.S. Maternal and Child Health, H.S.M.S.A., Department of Health, Education and Welfare, as awarded to the Center for Developmental and Learning Disorders, University of Alabama in Birmingham School of Medicine.

Appreciation is expressed to Ms. Marilyn Hodges and Ms. Linda Nelson for their secretarial and editorial assistance.

unacceptable areas in the absence of any organic pathology and at an age beyond 3 years. This condition has also been referred to as "fecal incontinence" and "psychogenic megacolon."

This definition covers a broad range of encopretic conditions, but several subclassification schemes have been suggested. Gavanski (1971) discriminated encopretics on the basis of retentive, nonretentive, or diverse and mixed types. Excessive retention of bowels was attributed to a "pot refusal" syndrome caused by inappropriate toilet training procedures or a toilet phobia maintained by fear of the commode and bathroom. Anthony (1957) separated encopretics on the basis of demonstrated continence and control. Those children who had never displayed appropriate bowel control were referred to as "continuous" (or primary) encopretics and those who had for at least 6 months been continent and then regressed to soiling were referred to as "discontinuous" (secondary or acquired) encopretics. Woodmansey (1972) made a similar distinction but referred to his groups as "infantile" and "reactive" incontinence. Easson (1960) combined the above systems and talked of (1) primary infantile encopresis (continuous, nonretentive), (2) primary reactive encopresis (continuous-retentive with overflow incontinence), (3) secondary infantile encopresis (discontinuous and nonretentive) and (4) secondary reactive encopresis (discontinuous and retentive). Overflow incontinence refers to the leakage of fecal material about impactions which are created by bowel retention or constipation. Berg and Jones (1964) grouped encopretics into five different categories: (1) training problems with constipation, (2) pot refusal retention, (3) severe constipation with overflow, and (4) uncomplicated functional fecal incontinence, with (a) stress subgroup and (b) distraction-precipitance subgroup. Encopresis for the children in the stress subgroup was related to emotional trauma and disturbance, while the distraction-precipitance group was not well defined and appeared to include those with suspected physiological disorders. In addition Hall (1941) described three groups of encopretics: continuous, discontinuous, and encopresis associated with coprophagia (playing with and smearing of feces on persons or objects).

It is important to be able to discriminate among the various types of encopresis because differential treatment may be called for. Anthony (1957), for example, speculated that the continuous encopretic would benefit most from continuation of basic toilet training, since adequate bowel continence had never been achieved. On the other hand, he postulated that psychotherapy would be most beneficial to the discontinuous encopretic, assuming that regression to soiling was a result of some psychiatric or psychological trauma. The notion of differential treatment is particularly true when excessive bowel retention is noted. Contrary to popular thought, encopresis may or may not be accompanied by bowel retention or constipation. When bowel retention does exist it is often referred to as megacolon because of the resulting dilation of the colon. Children who do retain may demonstrate overflow incontinence. Upon casual examination, this type of incontinence mimics diarrhea and has been referred to as "paradoxical diarrhea" (Davidson, 1958). However, because of the nature of the symptom the use of constipating agents would only serve to exacerbate the condition. Constipation, distention of the colon and passing of feces into the pants are indicative of both psychogenic (of psychological origin) and neurogenic (organic or pathological causal factors) megacolon. Neurogenic megacolon or Hirschsprung's disease (Nixon, 1964; Ravitch, 1958), however, is a congenital disorder due to the absence of ganglion cells in part of the intestine (Myenteric Plexus). Ravitch (1958) cites several instances where misclassification has occurred. Although there is some evidence of successful application of behavioral procedures with Hirschsprung's cases (Kohlenberg, 1973; Epstein and McCoy, 1975), surgery followed by treatment with enemas and drugs is frequently required.

Incidence and Characteristics

The incidence of functional childhood encopresis is estimated to be about 3% of the population (Levine, 1975; Yates, 1970). This figure, however, was obtained from a sample of children referred to or attending psychiatric or general pediatric clinics and is, thus, biased. In a descriptive analysis of 102 cases of encopresis, Levine (1975) noted an age range of 4–13 years with 87 cases. Of these, 85% were male, whereas general constipation without fecal incontinence is found in equal proportion in both sexes. More than half the children were incontinent during the day and night, and none were totally nocturnally incontinent. The absence of sensation to defecate, abdominal pain, poor appetite, and lethargy were commonly noted. About 31% were enuretic and over 75% were found to have stool impactions. Thirty-nine percent were described as primary or continuous encopretics. The presence of personality traits often attributed to the encopretic (compulsively neat, hoarding, withdrawal from peers, and academic failure) was reported in less than 30% of the cases. This rather broad and all-encompassing clinical picture of the encopretic illustrates the necessity for careful assessment with an eye toward differential treatment.

ASSESSMENT

The assessment process for the encopretic child should involve (1) precise measurement and description of the soiling behavior, (2) medical evaluation, (3) treatment history, and (4) parental counseling. The general form of the interview described by Ciminero and Doleys (1976) for enuretic children could be applied to the encopretic. Detailed information-gathering is a must with an emphasis on discovering consequences, such as parental attention or escape from school, which could be maintaining the soiling behavior. Obtaining a 3-week baseline consisting of (a) the frequency of soiling, (b) magnitude of each accident, (c) when and where the episode occurred, and (d) appropriate toileting behavior would not only provide a specific description of the behavior but would also assess the parents' motivation for treatment and the child's compliance. Experimentally, this baseline period would also provide an opportunity to assess the effects of self-monitoring on the frequency of soiling.

It is also important to distinguish between the continuous and discontinuous encopretic. Even though both forms have responded to similar treatment, more emphasis often has to be placed on the acquisition of basic toileting skills for the continuous type. Bowel evacuation is not a simple response but occurs at the end of a sequence of responses, including undressing. If these prerequisite behaviors are not in the child's repertoire they must be established. Azrin and Foxx (1974) and Foxx and Azrin (1973) have provided specific procedures for doing so.

The assessment process should also examine the role of "fear." For example, Ashkenazi (1975), Doleys and Arnold (1975), and Gelber and Meyer (1965) have noted fear of the toilet in several subjects and found modeling and reinforcement of successive approximations to be effective in eliminating such toilet phobias. Gavanski (1971) has also documented the pot refusal syndrome, wherein the child avoids the bathroom and sitting on the commode because of aversive procedures which had been employed during toilet training. Some children have also experienced pain during bowel movements following a period of constipation. This may lead to fear of additional pain and thus further retention, which only magnifies the problem.

An assessment of previous medical, psychological and parental treatment attempts would also provide further information regarding a potential treatment or program. The application of punishment and, less frequently, reinforcement procedures, albeit inconsistent, by the parents may preclude their continued use or suggest the need for a more comprehensive program.

A complete medical evaluation may be necessary to rule out the existence of organic pathology which could be contributing to the encopresis. Raft (1973), however, cautioned against over-examination of the encopretic. It is important for the psychologist and other professionals and paraprofessionals who will be working with the encopretic child and communicating with medical personnel to have some basic understanding of the physiology of fecal incontinence. Gaston (1948) has provided a description of this process. The detection of impactions verifying the presence of retention or of bowel distention, which may be accompanied by a loss of sensation to void and response to normal accumulations of feces, also has implications for treatment and needs to be determined during medical assessment. Purgatives, suppositories, or enemas may be needed in individual cases to assure daily cleansing, thus aiding in the recovery of normal sphincter tone, and will require recommendations of medical personnel. The excessive use of enemas, for example, can result in irritation and should be avoided.

Parental counseling is likewise an important aspect in the assessment process. Oftentimes parents tend to give up or apply undue pressure to their child. In addition, many parents are frustrated at the failure of other treatment procedures and may not fully understand the problem. Guilt feelings resulting from the use of harsh toilet training procedures or over having punished the child without success are also common. It is important from the onset to get the parents to relax about the problem of encopresis and to concentrate on following through with the prescribed program. The lack of parental cooperation and inconsistency in the application of the treatment program are two of the more common reasons for therapeutic failure.

Aside from the parents' reactions to the child, the stability of the marital relationship should be examined. Children can easily become the scapegoat for marital problems. In addition, marital dysfunction can interfere with carrying out the treatment program. A similar caution needs to be issued with regard to parent–child relationships. If this relationship is strained or if the child is extremely noncompliant, it is possible that this difficulty should be treated prior to treating the encopresis. Under these circumstances a positively oriented program would be more appropriate in order to avoid further parent–child confrontations.

THEORIES OF ETIOLOGY

There are at least three categories of theories relating to the development of encopresis: medical, psychoanalytic or psychodynamic, and learning-behavioral. The medical approach tends to adopt a neurodevelopmental model emphasizing the examination of the neural integrity and appropriate functioning of the physiologic and anatomical mechanisms and structures involved in the acquisition and maintenance of bowel control. Although physicians are sensitive to the potential influence of emotional and conditioning factors, these are often not adequately integrated into the medical model and into the treatment procedure.

The psychoanalytically oriented theorist tends to postulate encopresis to be a sign or symptom of some deeper unconscious conflict. Lack of parental love, separation anxiety, fear of loss of feces, pregnancy wishes, fear of castration, aggression against the hostile world, response to familial dysfunction, and traumatic separation from the mother between the oral and anal stages of psychosexual development have been offered in explanation (Pierce, 1975; Silber, 1969; Warson et al., 1954; Yates, 1970). The "power" struggle which often occurs during toilet training is also viewed as a precipitating factor (Hilbrun, 1968). Freud noted girls to be generally less aggressive and defiant and more self-sufficient than boys, thus making them easier to toilet train. Pinkerton (1958) suggested that this may account for the relatively low incidence of functional encopresis in girls.

The learning-behavioral or conditioning formulation gives careful consideration to the toilet training procedures in attempting to account for the presence of soiling behavior. In a case of the continuous or primary encopretic, it would be postulated that appropriate training methods had not been consistently applied. Prerequisite behaviors may not have been firmly established, adequate reinforcement not provided, or excessive punishment may have been used. A study by Madsen, Hoffman, Thomas, Koropsak, and Madsen (1969) clearly documented the differential effects of various toilet training procedures. With regard to the discontinuous or secondary encopretic, the learning theorist would likewise rely on a functional analysis of the behavior, emphasizing the consequences which are maintaining the soiling and the absence of sufficiently strong reinforcement to maintain appropriate toileting behavior.

TREATMENT

Mechanical Devices

The use of mechanical devices in the treatment of encopresis has been most successful with the mentally retarded. These devices are often of two types. One type is designed for immediate detection of soiling episodes and the other for the signaling of elimination while the child is sitting on the commode. In both cases this makes the immediate application of contingencies more plausible. Foxx and Azrin (1973) list several commercially available detection devices. One such device was modified and used by Logan and Garner (1971) in the successful treatment of a partially deaf child. Van Wagenen and Murdock (1966) and Fried (1974) described transistorized devices which allow for the transmission of a signal noting inappropriate elimination to a separate receiver. Watson (1968) and Cheney (1973), on the other hand, described potty chair-type devices designated to detect appropriate elimination and provide immediate reinforcement. Hopkinson and Lightwood (1966) reported on the use of an electrical device surgically implanted in the anal area which, through the delivery of low-level electrical stimulation, maintained normal anal sphincter tone in a patient with retroprolapse (a condition resulting in almost continual passage of feces due to the absence of appropriate anal sphincter contraction). Another type of device for training sphincter control is described by Kohlenberg (1973). This apparatus includes a balloon-like structure which was inserted into the rectum. This assembly was then attached to a tube filled with colored water which was in clear view of the subject. Contractions of the anal sphincter resulted in a rise in the fluid level. The use of this device provided a mechanism for giving the subject immediate feedback as to whether he was displaying the appropriate response or not.

Mechanical devices need to be seen for what they are, technical aids to be used in therapy when needed. They do not and cannot replace a precise analysis of the problem and the consistent application of a systematic procedure. Caution must be exercised so that the use of such devices does not interfere with the therapist's or the parents' interaction with the encopretic child during therapy. Many programmatic changes are based upon information which can only be obtained from first-hand observation and interaction with the child.

Medical Treatments

Standard medical treatments tend to rely on the use of purgatives (laxatives and enemas) and dietary manipulation without due consideration of (1) the obtaining and maintenance of parental and child compliance, (2) the acquisition of appropriate toileting skills, and (3) the long-term maintenance of desirable behaviors once they are established. In some instances imipramine (Tofranil), a tricyclic antidepressant, may be prescribed because of its antispasmodic properties.

Nisley (1976) has outlined the medical procedure and considerations in the assessment and treatment of encopresis which provide a recommended diet for children with fecal impactions. The use of cleansing enemas, stool-softening agents and parental counseling is described by Silber (1969). In addition, it is advised that parents (a) ignore episodes of soiling, (b) do not discuss toileting habits, and (c) do not keep any written or mental records. The intention, of course, is to remove all pressure from the child, hopefully making toileting a more natural and relaxed event and eliminating excessive fear. Silber does not, however, provide any experimental or clinical evidence of the relative efficacy of this procedure. Ravitch (1958) described an outpatient program which involves daily potting without the use of bribes, discussion, threats, or rewards but prescribed the use of enemas if bowel movements did not occur. Hospitalization was recommended if parental cooperation was not obtained. Ravitch provides some anecdotal data on the successful application of this program with seven children. Commenting on the use of enemas and laxatives, Berg and Jones (1964) noted that relief of the symptomatology achieved through these methods tends to be only temporary.

Davidson, Kugler, and Bauer (1963) implemented a three-phase program with 119 encopretics. The first phase of the program was designed to establish regular bowel movements. Hypertonic phosphate enemas were used to eliminate fecal impactions. Mineral oil preparations taken orally were then prescribed to induce regular bowel movements. The second phase began 1 month after the beginning of the first. The goal of the second phase was to achieve and maintain regular bowel movements in the absence of laxatives. The second phase continued for 3 months, during which time laxatives were gradually removed while bowel habits through training were continued. The third phase was intended to be a maintenance and follow-up period during which bowel habits established during the first two phases were maintained and monitored through parental counseling, contacts, and follow-up. The data indicated that, of the 90 patients who completed the program, 80 were identified as successfully treated. While these statistics are quite impressive, the fact that some patients were treated by private physicians and others as part of a clinic does raise some question as to the adequacy of the description of the procedure. It can certainly be assumed, as is always the case, that there was differential support, encouragement, feedback, and counseling applied to parents concerning a wide variety of behaviors of their children. Therefore, while the regimen described in the study may be relatively important, these ancillary factors may also be heavy contributors to the success and require further documentation and analysis.

One study (Gavanski, 1971) examined the use of imipramine (Tofranil) in conjunction with psychotherapy. Imipramine is supposed to have an inhibitory effect upon the internal anal sphincter, thus potentially reducing the frequency of bowel movements. Case descriptions noted the successful application of this treatment with three nonretentive encopretics. Gavanski, however, notes that imipramine should be used only to produce temporary relief from high-rate soiling and is contraindicated with retentive encopretics due to its inhibitory effect upon bowel evacuation. In addition, Gavanski recommends that it be used only as an adjunct to adequate psychotherapy.

The information on the effective treatment of encopresis found in the medical literature suffers from many of the same experimental deficiencies found in other areas. First, there is an inadequate documentation of pretreatment soiling behavior. Second, descriptions of the procedure and subject responses are vague and incomplete. Third, posttreatment follow-up data collection are erratic and nonspecific. Fourth, the frequency of appropriate toileting behavior is often not noted, only a decrease in soiling, which could be a result of retention as well as of more frequent use of the bathroom. Fifth, there is a conspicuous absence of controlled studies.

These studies have, however, shown some success with the use of enemas, laxatives, stool softeners, dietary manipulation, and pharmacological agents. So as not to "throw out the baby with the bath water," we must recognize the potential usefulness of these methods while at the same time realizing that used by themselves they tend to be inadequate. Although it is a discrete behavior, soiling oftentimes does not occur in isolation. That is, there may be a variety of circumstances contributing to the soiling behavior and other behavioral problems with the child or in the family. Therefore, a more comprehensive approach appears to be needed.

Verbal Psychotherapy

A report by Pinkerton (1958) provides a descriptive illustration of the use of psychotherapy with 30 encopretic children. Pinkerton suggested that bowel negativism, which was demonstrated by refusal to defecate or defiant soiling, was at the basis of this disorder. This problem behavior was speculated to be exacerbated by perfectionistic or over-solicitous parents who overemphasize the aversiveness and noxiousness of feces and display an excessive concern over the acquisition of toileting behavior.

This treatment procedure was primarily conducted with and through the parents and emphasized the removal of parental fear and prejudices. Presumably treatment allowed for the development of insight into the emotional origin of soiling, combined with encouraging the parents to become more indifferent to the display of the symptomatology. Therapeutic procedures with the encopretic himself included hospitalization when parental counseling was ineffective. Play therapy was also engaged in and had four definite objectives: (1) to break down the child's "defensive facade and establish adequate depth of contact with him," (2) to help the child come to the realization of what the fundamental problem was through the use of projective play techniques, (3) to encourage and promote the "working through" of difficulties using associated release during play of the child's pent-up hostilities, and (4) to attempt to restore emotional stability to the child following the resolution of the difficulties. Pinkerton noted remission in 17 of the 30 cases with follow-up ranging up to 3.5 years, but he does not provide data on specific treatment duration.

Gavanski (1971) also reported on the use of psychotherapy in conjunction with imipramine. Psychotherapy was applied to three nonretentive secondary encopretics, but the specific form of the psychotherapy and duration of therapy were not indicated. McTaggert and Scott (1959) similarly employed play therapy, clay modeling, and finger painting in an attempt to facilitate the acting out of feelings of their encopretic children. Extensive therapy-counseling was carried out with the parents. They reported that 7 of 12 children were cured and 3 were described as improved.

Berg and Jones (1964), however, reviewed the records of some 70 children who were noted to have been treated for encopresis and interestingly reported similar rates of remission among those children receiving psychotherapy and those who did not. Likewise, Ashkenazi (1975) commented on the failure of psychotherapy and play therapy with three of the subjects in his study who later became continent within eight weeks of being exposed to a behaviorally oriented program which emphasized regular potting, induced defecation, and positive reinforcement.

An adequate evaluation of verbal psychotherapy and play therapy in the treatment of encopresis does not appear plausible at this time. The absence of control studies in which psychotherapy is compared with nontreated groups or with other treatment programs makes such evaluation difficult. In addition, the term "verbal psychotherapy" is frequently used in a very generic fashion. Inadequate descriptions of the treatment procedure have made replication of these studies virtually impossible. Although some success appears to have been derived from the application of what is referred to as verbal psychotherapy, the parameters of such treatment success have not been identified and therefore remain quite nebulous and nonspecific.

Learning-Behavioral

A behavioral or learning theory approach to the treatment of encopresis emphasizes the arrangement of environmental contingencies to encourage the development and maintenance of appropriate toileting skills. A large variety of programs have been attempted. For purposes of the present discussion these studies will be grouped according to their complexity and type of consequences imposed. Generally the studies can be classified as (1) those which primarily employed positive reinforcement with no consequences for soiling, (2) those which specifically punished soiling, and (3) those which combine positive reinforcement and punishment in a more complex, comprehensive program. It should also be noted that several of the programs to be described have employed laxatives, suppositories, and enemas as therapeutic adjuncts in an attempt to produce the desirable behavior so that it can be reinforced and strengthened. Several of the studies which have employed behavioral procedures in the treatment of fecal incontinence are described in Table 1 and will be discussed in this section.

Positive Reinforcement Programs

Treatment programs based on the contingent application of positive reinforcement have generally been of two types. In the first type (Type I) reinforcement was delivered contingent upon bowel movements while the encopretic was sitting on the commode. Bach and Moylan (1975), Young and Goldsmith (1972), Larsen, Larsen, and Hall (1971), Plachetta (1976), and Keehn (1965) each report on the successful application of Type I reinforcement with individual cases. Young (1973), however, applied Type I contingent reinforcement to a group of 24 children (20 males and 4 females) in whom there appeared to be an absence of internal sensation preceding defecation. This state was associated with dilation of internal sphincter which was also noted in each of the children. Young's program involved the initial removal of accumulated feces, administering of a warm drink to initiate the internal reflex bowel activity, and potting of the

Table 1. Characteristics of Studies Using Behavioral Procedures in the Treatment of Encopresis

Study	N(Age and Sex)	Type	Treatment	Outcome	Duration	Follow-up
Tomlinson (1970)	1 (3 y-o-m)	Con. retent.	Pos. reinf. Type I	Increased appropriate defecation		
Neale (1963)	4 (7–10 yrs) males	Discon. retent.	Type I reinf. periodic potting	3 successful 1 not	$\bar{X}$ about 14 weeks	3–6 months
Keehn (1965)	1 (5 y-o-m)	Discon.	Type I reinf.	successful	Immediately	2 months
Larsen, Larsen, and Hall (1971)	1 (3 y-o-m)	Cont.	Type I reinf.	successful	6 weeks	
Young and Goldsmith (1972)	1 (8 y-o-m)	Discon.	Type I reinf.	successful	4 weeks	1 month
Young (1973)	24 (4–10 yrs) 20 males 4 females	14 Cont. 10 Discon.	Type I reinf. potting induced BM	22 successful	19 within 52 $\bar{X}$ = 20 weeks	$\bar{X}$ = 29 months 4 relapsed
Bach and Moylan (1975)	1 (6 y-o-m)	Discon.	Type I reinf.	successful	20 weeks	24 months No relapse
Plachetta (1976)	1 (6 y-o-m)	Discon.	Type I reinf. potting, self-recording	successful	8 weeks	3 mos.—2 accidents 24 mos.—none
Pedrini and Pedrini (1971)	1 (11 y-o-m)	Contin.	Type II reinf.	successful	11 weeks	10 months No relapse
Logan and Garner (1971)	1 (7 y-o-m)	Contin.	Type II reinf. (group consequences)	successful	11 weeks	

Ayllon et al. (1975)	1 (7 y-o-m)		Type II reinf.	successful	12 weeks	11 months No relapse
Conger (1970)	1 (9 y-o-m)	Discon.	extinction	successful	12 weeks	3 months
Balson (1973)	1 (8 y-o-m)	Contin.	extinction play therapy	successful	9 weeks	5 months
Freinden and Van Handel (1970)	1 (7 y-o-m)	Contin.	punishment	successful	20 weeks	6 months No relapse
Edelman (1971)	1 (12 y-o-f)	Contin.	punishment and negative reinforcement	successful	41 weeks	3 months
Gelber and Meyer (1965)	1 (13 y-o-m)	Contin.	Type I reinf., punish. pant-checks	successful	9 weeks	6 months 2 accidents
Doleys and Arnold (1975)	1 (8 y-o-m)	Discon.	Type I and II reinf. FCT	successful	16 weeks	6 months 1 accident/wk.
Doleys et al. (1977)	3 (4–8 yrs) males	Discon.	Type I and II reinf. pant-checks, FCT	successful	6–10 weeks	3–12 months No relapse
Wright (1975)	14 (3–9 yrs) 12 males 2 females	3 Contin. 9 Discon.	Type I and II reinf. punish., enemas	successful	10–38 weeks	6 months 1 relapse
Ashkenazi (1975)	18 (3–12 yrs) 12 males 6 females	Contin. Discon.	Type I reinf., potting, suppositories	16 of 18 successful	3–9 weeks	6 months No relapse

child for ten minutes, during which time bowel movements were reinforced. In addition a laxative/stool-softener (Senokot) was administered nightly. Twenty-two of the 24 subjects were successfully treated, 19 within 12 months. Follow-up of these 19 subjects revealed the reoccurrence of encopresis in only 4 of them. Neale (1963) examined the effects of a program designed to gradually shift responsibility for toileting to the subject with 4 children. Initially the children were potted four times per day. This was later reduced to once a day and the responsibility for toileting passed from the experimenter to the child. Pants were checked periodically but soiling episodes were ignored. Self-initiated bowel movements in the toilet were positively reinforced. Three of the 4 subjects became continent within a 14-week treatment. No relapses were noted during the 3- to 6-month follow-up.

The second type of positive reinforcement program (Type II) involved the delivery of reinforcement contingent upon clean pants rather than just appropriate toileting (Ayllon et al., 1975; Pedrini and Pedrini 1971). Tokens, stars and outings were used to reinforce the absence of soiling during the day. Success was reported in each of the case studies. Logan and Garner (1971) reported on the use of Type II reinforcement with a group reinforcement contingency to eliminate soiling in a 7-year-old, partially deaf child. A pants-alarm was constructed such that a buzzer or alarm sou ided with the occurrence of soiling. The alarm apparatus was so constructed that conditioning could be carried out in the classroom where soiling frequently occurred. The buzzer was placed on the encopretic's desk. When it sounded he was to go to the bathroom, clean himself and his clothes, and return to the class. Each student in the subject's class was awarded a point for each hour the subject kept the buzzer silent (no soiling) during the day. Points could be exchanged for a variety of backup reinforcers which varied in value. For example, one point earned a small piece of candy or gum, while six could be traded for a movie. The program was immediately effective in establishing bowel control which was maintained over a several-month follow-up. Two interesting side effects were noted. First, the children in the class began to respond much more positively toward the subject and, secondly, the teacher began effectively applying reinforcement principles to other classroom activities. Although successful, these reinforcement programs do not provide contingencies for reinforcing appropriate toileting behavior and therefore may not be generally applicable or the best choice for the retentive encopretic.

In contrast to the above studies, Balson (1973) and Conger (1970) examined the effects of extinction upon soiling. In these case studies parental attention to soiling episodes was removed and the child was required to attend to himself. In each case soiling was successfully treated. By virtue of the fact that extinction was effective, it suggests that parental attention to soiling was a major contributing factor. In all probability, however, this is the exception rather than the rule and, although important to consider during assessment and in devising a treatment plan, it is not going to be the *sine qua non* of the etiology of encopresis.

Punishment Procedures

Unlike the above studies which involve the ignoring of soiling episodes and the reinforcement of appropriate behavior, Edelman (1971) and Freinden and Van Handel (1970) relied almost exclusively upon punishment of the soiling behavior. Edelman (1971) used a 30-minute confinement to the bedroom following each soiling episode paired with avoidance of dishwashing if no soiling occurred with a 12-year-old female. Decreased soiling was noted over a 22-week treatment period and was maintained at a 3-month follow-up. Freinden and Van Handel (1970) used the cleaning of soiled clothes and washing with a strong soap and cold water as punishment for soiling. Treatment was reportedly successful within 4 months. Although punishment procedures like these are perhaps promising, in the absence of more extensive research their tendency to elicit emotional responses, promote negative parent–child interactions, and lead to excessive retention suggests that their use should be limited and applied only in conjunction with positive reinforcement.

Complex Programs

A third type of program is more comprehensive or complex and typically involves combined use of punishment for soiling and positive reinforcement for appropriate toileting behavior. Furthermore, these two procedures are often used in conjunction with laxatives or stool-softeners to help promote frequent bowel movements and use of enemas to prevent the accumulation of feces. Gelber and Meyer (1965), for example, report on the successful application of a procedure which combined Type I reinforcement, punishment for soiled pants, and periodic pants-checks with a 13-year-old male. Treatment was successful within 9 weeks and a 24-week follow-up revealed only one accident during each of the last couple of weeks.

Wright (1973, 1975) and Wright and Walker (1976) described the use of a conditioning program which incorporated positive reinforcement, punishment, periodic potting, enemas, and suppositories. Positive reinforcement was delivered for each bowel movement into the commode and for the absence of pants soiling. Punishment in the form of loss of privileges, fines, etc., was given following each soiling episode. In addition the child was potted after each meal. Enemas and suppositories were used to induce defecation on days when it did not occur naturally, but such artifically induced bowel movements were not reinforced. The child was gradually weaned off the program with all contingencies being removed after 1 week of continence. A recent study with 14 subjects 3 to 9 years of age noted success in 100% of the cases with a mean treatment period of 16.9 weeks (range 10–38 weeks). Only one child relapsed during the 6-month follow-up. Wright (1975) interestingly noted that treatment success and duration were related to parental consistency in carrying out the program.

Ashkenazi (1975) reported on the treatment of 18 encopretics. Six were noted to have a "pot phobia" reaction and were treated by reinforcement of successive approximations to sitting on the commode. A second group were willing to sit on the commode but reported having no sensation to defecate. All children were potted following the insertion of a glycerine suppository to promote a bowel movement. Defecation was strongly reinforced as was the absence of soiling during the day. Suppositories were discontinued after 5 consecutive days of defecation in the commode but were reinstated if the child missed a bowel movement. Positive reinforcers were gradually faded out. Sixteen of the 18 subjects were successfully treated and continence was maintained at a 6-month follow-up.

Azrin and Foxx (1971) and Foxx and Azrin (1973) introduced a comprehensive toilet training program for the mentally retarded. Two aspects of this program, full cleanliness training and positive practice, have been shown to be particularly applicable to the treatment of encopresis. Full cleanliness training requires the child to clean himself and his clothes thoroughly following each accident. Foxx and Azrin (1973) proposed that this (a) taught responsibility to the child by having him correct the detrimental effects of his behavior and (b) motivated the child to perform the desirable behavior in order to avoid this negative task. Positive practice requires the child to repeatedly perform the prerequisite toileting behaviors (going to the bathroom, removing clothes and sitting on the commode) for the purpose of strengthening them. Two recent studies (Doleys and Arnold, 1975; Doleys et al., 1977) explored the utility of a three-part program adapted from Foxx and Azrin (1973) which included (a) periodic pants-checks, (b) full cleanliness training contingent upon soiling, and (c) positive reinforcement for appropriate toileting behavior. Initially parents were requested to check the child's pants on a regular schedule, hourly if possible, and to reinforce clean pants. Younger children and frequent soilers were also potted at each pants-check during the first part of treatment. The interval between pants-checks was gradually increased. Full cleanliness training followed each soiling episode and involved (1) parental expression of displeasure, (2) the child washing his underpants and trousers for 20 minutes, and (3) the child taking a bath to clean himself for 20 minutes in cool water. The parents were instructed to be nonchalant during full cleanliness training and to continue to verbalize the reason for full cleanliness training and how it could be avoided. In addition, the child was not to be released from full cleanliness training if he was being disruptive, so as to prevent negatively reinforcing disruptive behavior. The third part of the program consisted of the delivery of tokens or points contingent upon each bowel movement in the toilet. Points could then be exchanged for a variety of backup reinforcers. Soiling was eliminated in four of four subjects in a 4- to 10-week period. One subject relapsed due to parental noncompliance with the maintenance program (Doleys and Arnold, 1975). Another subject had two accidents during a 48-week follow-up. Butler (unpublished manuscript) and Freeman and Priddle (1974) have also applied variations of the Foxx and Azrin program. Butler, for example, successfully treated three children with overcorrection-positive practice within 8 weeks and noted one accident during a 6-month follow-up.

Some studies have concentrated on the direct conditioning of anal sphincter control as a means of achieving fecal continence. Kohlenberg (1973) employed a balloon-like apparatus inserted in the rectum and attached to a tube filled with colored water as a way of providing feedback to the subject. Constriction of the anal sphincter raised the level of the fluid. Monetary reinforcement was used to shape sphincter control. A similar procedure was reported by Engel, Nikoomanesh, and Schuster (1974) with seven patients. Follow-up of 6 months to 5 years revealed maintenance of acquired continence in five of the cases.

There has been some preliminary examination of the relationship between enuresis and encopresis when found in the same child. Doleys *et al.* (1977) and Edelman (1971) both noted these two behaviors to be functionally independent. That is, the elimination of one did not affect the other. In both instances soiling was treated first. Epstein and McCoy (1975), however, noted increased bladder control following increased bowel control in a 3-year-old child diagnosed with Hirschsprung's disease and having had corrective surgery.

SUMMARY

In spite of the relatively high frequency of functional encopresis in children, it does not appear to have gotten the attention of many other childhood disorders. Our analysis and treatment of encopresis appears to be somewhat effective but clearly quite insufficient and primitive. The frequent case studies noting the effects of single procedures like Type I or Type II positive reinforcement are rather misleading in that they do not effectively deal with the potential complexities of the problem and therefore can give a false sense of security about the status of our knowledge. In addition, we have no way of knowing the number of cases in which such simple procedures have failed. The need for more well-controlled group studies is great. Indeed, of the nearly twenty studies using behavioral procedures herein reviewed, only four employed 6 subjects or more and none employed a comparison group.

With regard to specific treatment procedures, it appears that verbal psychoanalytic therapy is minimally effective at best. Systematic replications and comparisons with other procedures have not been carried out. Treatment effects may well be due to demand characteristics, attention to the child or changes in parental behavior. Medical procedures appear moderately successful but often ignore the more nonmedical aspects of the problem such as the development of appropriate toileting skills, the maintenance of appropriate behavior, and the modification of parental response patterns.

Though behavioral procedures have been successful, the reliance upon one single procedure such as extinction, positive reinforcement or punishment seems a rather naive approach (Nilsson, 1976). Several more comprehensive programs have been proposed (Ashkenazi, 1975; Doleys et al., 1977; Wright, 1975) but demand further validation. If we can be assured of one thing it is the necessity and importance of parental cooperation and consistency for the successful treatment of the encopretic child.

We should not be surprised if it turns out that certain procedures are more applicable to some cases than to others. Indeed, this ought to be our expectation, since we should be aware of the vast differences which occur between individuals and their backgrounds. This being so, assessment becomes a critical part of the therapeutic process. Berg and Jones (1964) perhaps made the point best when they noted that incontinence had simply been too exclusively viewed as a mechanical or emotional problem with insufficient consideration given to the needs of the individual child. Examining the individual background behavior and needs of the child is not incompatible with any of the theoretical positions noted in this chapter. It does, however, demand careful documentation of potential etiological influences, current behavior, and their relationship to treatment outcome.

REFERENCES

Anthony, E. J. (1957). An experimental approach to the psychopathology of childhood encopresis. *British Journal of Medical Psychology* 30:146–175.

Ashkenazi, Z. (1975). The treatment of encopresis using a discriminative stimulus and positive reinforcement. *Journal of Behavior Therapy and Experimental Psychiatry* 6:151–157.

Ayllon, T., Simon, S. J., and Wildman, R. W. (1975). Instructions and reinforcement in the elimination of encopresis: a case study. *Journal of Behavior Therapy and Experimental Psychiatry* 6:235–238.

Azrin, N. H., and Foxx, R. M. (1971). A rapid method of toilet training the institutionalized retarded. *Journal of Applied Behavior Analysis* 4:89–99.

——, and Foxx, R. M. (1974). *Toilet Training in Less than a Day.* New York: Simon & Schuster.

Bach, R., and Moylan, J. M. (1975). Parent-administered behavior therapy for inappropriate urination and encopresis: a case study. *Journal of Behavior Therapy and Experimental Psychiatry* 6:147–156.

Balson, P. M. (1973). Case study: Encopresis: a case with symptom substitution? *Behavior Therapy* 4:134–136.

Berg, I., and Jones, K. V. (1964). Functional fecal incontinence in children. *Archives of Disease in Childhood* 39:465–472.

Butler, J. F. (unpublished manuscript). The treatment of encopresis by overcorrection. Lackland Air Force Base, San Antonio, Texas.

Cheney, C. D. (1973). Mechanically augmented human toilet training or the electric potty chair. In R. L. Schwitzgebel and R. H. Schwitzgebel, eds., *Psychotechnology: Electronic Control of Mind and Behavior.* New York: Holt, Rinehart & Winston.

Ciminero, A. R., and Doleys, D. M. (1976). Childhood enuresis: considerations in assessment. *Journal of Pediatric Psychology* 4:17–20.

Conger, J. C. (1970). The treatment of encopresis by the management of social consequences. *Behavior Therapy* 1:386–390.

Davidson, M. (1958). Constipation and fecal incontinence. In H. Bakwin, ed., *Pediatric Clinics of North America.* Philadelphia: W. B. Saunders & Company.

Davidson, M. D., Kugler, M. M., and Bauer, C. H. (1963). Diagnosis and management in children with severe and protracted constipation and obstipation. *Journal of Pediatrics* 62:261–275.

Doleys, D. M., and Arnold, S. (1975). Treatment of childhood encopresis: full cleanliness training. *Mental Retardation* 13:14–16.

——, Ciminero, A. R., Tollison, J. W., Williams, S. C., and Wells, K. C. (1977). Dry bed training and retention control training: a comparison. *Behavior Therapy* 8:541–548.

——, McWhorter, A. Q., Williams, S. C., and Gentry, R. (1977). Encopresis: its treatment and relation to nocturnal enuresis. *Behavior Therapy* 8:77–82.

——, and Wells, K. C. (1975). Changes in functional bladder capacity and bed-wetting during and after retention control training. *Behavior Therapy* 6:685–688.

Easson, W. M. (1960). Encopresis–psychogenic soiling. *Canadian Medical Association Journal* 82:624–630.

Edelman, R. F. (1971). Operant conditioning treatment of encopresis. *Journal of Behavior Therapy and Experimental Psychiatry* 2:71–73.

Engle, B. I., Nikoomanesh, D., and Schuster, M. M. (1974). Operant conditioning of rectosphincteric responses in the treatment of fecal incontinence. *New England Journal of Medicine* 290:646–649.

Epstein, L. H., and McCoy, J. F. (unpublished manuscript). Bowel control in Hirschsprung's disease. Auburn University, Auburn, Alabama.

Foxx, R. M., and Azrin, N. H. (1973). *Toilet Training the Retarded*, Champaign, Ill.: Research Press.

Freeman, B. J., and Priddle, W. (1974). Elimination of inappropriate toileting by overcorrection. *Psychological Reports* 35:802.

Fried, R. (1974). A device for enuresis control. *Behavior Therapy* 5:682–684.

Friedman, A. R. (1968). Behavior training in a case of enuresis. *Journal of Individual Psychology* 24:86–87.

Freinden, W., and Van Handel, D. (1970). Elimination of soiling in an elementary school child through application of aversive technique. *Journal of School Psychology* 8:267–269.

Gaston, E. A. (1948). The physiology of fecal incontinence. *Surgery, Gynecology and Obstetrics* 87:281–290.

Gavanski, M. (1971). Treatment of non-retentive secondary encopresis with imipramine and psychotherapy. *Canadian Medical Association Journal* 104:46–48.

Gelber, H., and Meyer, V. (1965). Behavior therapy and encopresis: The complexities involved in treatment. *Behaviour Research and Therapy* 2:227–231.

Hall, M. B. (1941). Encopresis in children. *British Medical Journal* 2:890–892.

Hilbrun, W. B. (1968). Encopresis in childhood. *Journal of the Kentucky Medical Association* 66:978.

Hopkinson, B. R., and Lightwood, R. (1966). Electrical treatment of anal incontinence. *The Lancet*, Feb., 297–298.

Hunsaker, J. H. (1976). A two-process approach to nocturnal enuresis: preliminary results. *Behavior Therapy* 6:560–561.

Keehn, J. D. (1965). Brief case report: reinforcement therapy of incontinence. *Behaviour Research and Therapy* 2:239.

Kohlenberg, R. J. (1973). Operant conditioning of human anal sphincter pressure. *Journal of Applied Behavior Analysis* 6:201–208.

Larsen, S.C., Larsen, P., and Hall, R. V. (1971). Potty training a 3-year-old boy through systematic reinforcement. In R. V. Hall, ed., *Managing Behavior. Part 3. Applications in School and Home.* Lawrence, Kansas: H & H Enterprises.

Levine, M. D. (1975). Children with encopresis: a descriptive analysis. *Pediatrics* 56:412–416.

Logan, D. L., and Garner, D. G. (1971). Effective behavior modification for reducing chronic soiling. *American Annals of the Deaf* 116:382–384.

McTaggert, A., and Scott, M. (1959). A review of twelve cases of encopresis. *Journal of Pediatrics* 54:762–768.

Madsen, C. H., Hoffman, M., Thomas, D. R., Koropsak, E., and Madsen, C. K. (1969). Comparisons of toilet training techniques. In D. M. Gelfond, ed., *Social Learning in Childhood.* Belmont, Calif.: Brooks/Cole.

Neale, D. H. (1963). Behavior therapy and encopresis in children. *Behaviour Research and Therapy* 1:139–149.

Nilsson, D. E. (1976). Treatment of encopresis: a token economy. *Journal of Pediatric Psychology* 4:42–46.

Nisley, D. D. (1976). Medical overview of the management of encopresis. *Journal of Pediatric Psychology* 4:33–34.

Nixon, H. H. (1964). Hirschsprung's disease. *Archives of Diseases in Childhood* 39:109–115.

Pedrini, B. C., and Pedrini, D. T. (1971). Reinforcement procedures in the control of encopresis: a case study. *Psychological Reports* 28:937–938.

Pierce, C. M. (1975). Enuresis and encopresis. In A. M. Friedman, H. T. Kaplan, and B. J. Sadock, eds., *Comprehensive Textbook of Psychiatry II.* Baltimore: Williams & Wilkins.

Pinkerton, P. (1958). Psychogenic megacolon in children: the implications of bowel negativism. *Archives of Diseases in Childhood* 33:371–380.

Plachetta, K. E. (1974). Encopresis: a case study utilizing contracting, scheduling and self-charting. *Journal of Behavior Therapy and Experimental Psychiatry* 7:195–196.

Raft, D. (1973). Psychologic management of patients with bowel disorders. *American Journal of Family Practice* 8:124–128.

Ravitch, M. M. (1958). Pseudo-Hirschsprung's disease. *Annals of Surgery* 148:781–795.

Silber, D. L. (1969). Encopresis: discussion of etiology and management. *Clinical Pediatrics* 8:225–231.

Tomlinson, J. R. (1970). The treatment of bowel retention by operant procedures: a case study. *Journal of Behavior Therapy and Experimental Psychiatry* 1:183–185.

Van Wagenen, R. K., and Murdock, E. E. (1966). A transistorized signal package for the toilet training of infants. *Journal of Experimental Child Psychology* 3:312–314.

Warson, S. R., Caldwell, M. R., Warrinner, A., Kirk, A. J., and Jensen, R. A. (1954). The dynamics of encopresis. *American Journal of Orthopsychiatry* 24:402–415.

Watson, L. S. (1968). Application of behavior shaping devices to training severely and profoundly mentally retarded children in an institutional setting. *Mental Retardation* 6:21–23.

Weissenberg, S. (1926). Uber enkopresis. *Z Kinderleilkd* 40:674.

Woodmansey, A. C. (1972). Wetting and soiling. *British Medical Journal* 3:161–163.

Wright, L. (1973). Handling the encompretic child. *Professional Psychology* 4:137–144.

—— (1975). Outcome of a standardized program for treating psychogenic encopresis. *Professional Psychology* 6:453–456.

——, and Walker, C. E. (1976). Behavioral treatment of encopresis. *Journal of Pediatric Psychology* 4:35–37.

Yates, A. J. (1970). *Behaviour therapy.* New York: John Wiley & Sons.

Young, G. C. (1973). The treatment of childhood encopresis by conditioned gastroileal reflex training. *Behaviour Research and Therapy* 11:499–503.

Young, I. L., and Goldsmith, A. D. (1972). Treatment of encopresis in a day treatment program. *Psychotherapy: Theory, Research and Practice* 9:231–235.

Chapter Nine

Assessment and Treatment of Childhood Enuresis*

DANIEL M. DOLEYS

INTRODUCTION

Definition and Classification

Functional nocturnal enuresis has been defined as the persistent wetting of the bed during the nighttime in the absence of any neurologic or urologic pathology (Campbell, 1970). Although there are many types of urinary incontinence or enuresis (Lund, 1963), nearly 95% of all cases fall into this category and are also referred to as idiopathic (Campbell, 1951). There is considerable controversy over the age at which a child should be considered enuretic, with the range generally being 3–5 years.

*Preparation of the manuscript was supported in part by Project 910, U.S. Maternal and Child Health, H.S.M.S.A., Department of Health, Education and Welfare, as awarded to the Center for Developmental and Learning Disorders, University of Alabama in Birmingham School of Medicine.

Appreciation is expressed to Ms. Marilyn Hodges and Ms. Linda Nelson for their secretarial and editorial assistance.

Medical-developmental data from Muellner (1960a,b) and Campbell (1970), however, suggest that normal urinary control should be established by 3 years of age. Additionally, Muellner noted potential long-term bedwetting could be identified by this age. The frequency of bedwetting needed to classify a child as enuretic also varies. Most writers, however, refer to children who regularly wet their beds three times or more per week on the average.

Two main types of functional nocturnal enuresis have been identified on the basis of the child's history. The persistent (continuous or primary) enuretic has never displayed nocturnal continence. The acquired (discontinuous, secondary, or onset) enuretic, on the other hand, has demonstrated nighttime continence of 6 months or more. About 85% of all cases of enuresis are of the persistent or continuous type (de Jonge, 1973). This percentage has been noted to decrease as a function of age, with only about 50% of 12-year-old enuretics being classified as continuous.

Incidence and Characteristics

The estimates of the incidence of enuresis vary but recent reports indicate 15–20% of all 5-year-olds are nocturnally enuretic, with males outnumbering females about two to one. This percentage decreases to about 2% of 12- to 14-year-olds (Lovibond and Coote, 1970; Yates, 1970; Oppel et al., 1968). Forsythe and Redmond (1974) followed 1129 enuretics who were not cured by drug therapy or surgery and who were not exposed to the urine alarm. Of these, 56% were primary enuretics and 90% wet their beds 5 or more nights per week during an 8-week period. "Spontaneous" remission was noted in 14% of 5- to 9-year-olds, 16% of 10- to 14-year-olds, and 15% of 15- to 19-year-olds. Three percent of the original sample was still wetting at 20 years of age. The word "spontaneous" is probably a misnomer and only reflects our lack of knowledge as to the actual sequence of events which lead to remission of bedwetting. Although it is apparent that most children become dry, no measurement device has yet been described which reliably identifies these children. In addition, these remissions frequently are not "spontaneous" in the sense that they occur without trauma or active involvement with the environment. Therefore, the problem remains of whom to treat, when, and how.

Enuresis is often regarded as a sign of emotional or psychiatric disturbance. Several attempts have been made to document the presence or absence of associated psychiatric and behavioral problems in enuretic children. One study by Kolvin, Tounch, Currah, Garside, Nolan, and Shaw (1972) described the characteristics of 94 enuretic children. Sixty percent were males who showed a slight delay in attainment of major developmental milestones (e.g., walking) and more than half were from the lower socioeconomic class. Only 30% were rated as psychiatrically disturbed, with emotional problems in one of the parents noted in about 33% of the cases. Shaffer (1973) and Rutter, Yule, and Graham (1973) have summarized much of the earlier work in this area. Shaffer noted no consistent evidence regarding a correlation between enuresis and a specified psychiatric syndrome or other specified deviant behavior (e.g., thumb-sucking). A positive correlation, however, was noted with imma-ture behavior and a tendency toward introversion in boys. While there was some positive association with emotional disturbance, the number of children in that category was relatively small. Evidence does show a consistent relationship between enuresis and family disruptions, long-term enuresis, and low socioeconomic class and the presence of early stress events, as compared to nonenuretics. It is interesting to note that the association between enuresis and behavioral deviance is stronger in females than males (Rutter *et al.*, 1973). Thus, Rutter *et al.* (1973) have suggested that enuresis in boys may tend to be a developmental disorder while in girls it is more likely to be associated with behavioral disturbances and diurnal (daytime) wetting. In any such study, however, it is difficult to separate which characteristics in the child were present before and may have been precipitating factors of the enuresis from those which developed as a result of the enuresis.

PHYSIOLOGY OF MICTURITION

An understanding of the basic physiology of micturition (urination) and the developmental sequence associated with urinary control is helpful in the accurate assessment of problems, the devising of effective treatment and parental counseling. Yeates (1973) has outlined five steps found in the normal functioning of the mature bladder. First, the bladder is filled as a result of the flow of urine from the kidney into the bladder via the ureters. Next, the desire to void appears as the detruser muscle surrounding the bladder stretches and relaxes to accommodate the influx of urine. Third, postponement of voiding occurs as a result of the maintenance of tension and pressure on the sphincter muscles or by the application of perineal pressure. A variety of inhibitory responses are controlled at the subcortical level and involve inhibition of reflexes which ordinarily occur automatically and result in reflexive urination. Fourth, as the bladder achieves its full capacity further filling results in rhythmical contractions of the bladder, opening of the bladder outlet and relaxation of the sphincters, resulting in the outward flow of urine. Fifth, bladder contractions and relaxed sphincters are maintained until the voiding is complete and the bladder is emptied.

Four steps noted in the development of a mature bladder have been outlined by Muellner (1960a,b). First, the child must demonstrate an awareness of bladder fullness, which usually occurs around 1 or 2 years of age. Next, the acquisition of the ability to retain urine is accomplished. This ability is acquired by controlling the levator ani and pubococcygeus muscles at the beginning of the third year. The third step involves the demonstrated capacity to start and stop the flow of urine in midstream and should be developed by about $4^1/_2$ years of age. The fourth and final step is the ability to initiate and terminate the flow of urine at any degree of bladder fullness.

Sleep Findings

There have been several lengthy discussions on the relationship between depth of sleep and enuresis. Intuitively many parents, para-professionals, and professionals alike reason that unusually deep sleep is the causative factor in enuresis. Indeed, most parents readily comment on the difficulty they experience in attempting to arouse their enuretic child during the night. First off, it is important to note the difference between depth of sleep and arousability. The depth of sleep is divided into and described by four stages, each of which is associated with a particular EEG (electroencephalographic) pattern. Rapid eye movement (REM) is a distinctive category of sleep usually associated with dreaming (Kales and Kales, 1974). Arousability refers to how easily a child can be aroused from sleep. Depth of sleep and arousability are not necessarily connected (Graham, 1973).

The research findings in both areas are inconsistent (Graham, 1973; Salmon et al., 1973). With regard to depth of sleep, it appears as though wetting may and can occur in any of the stages of sleep but typically not in REM sleep. Finley (1971) also noted that as age increased wetting tended to occur in lighter stages of sleep. This may partially explain why older children "outgrow" bedwetting, in that they are more likely to be aroused by bladder fullness if the urge to void occurs in light as opposed to heavy sleep. For this reason it has been suggested that enuresis may be an "arousal disorder" (Finley, 1971). Gastaut and Broughton (1965) have described the "enuretic episode" in which the child does not report dreaming if awakened by or shortly after the wetting, but if sleep continues and the child subsequently is awakened during REM sleep he will report dreams which incorporate being wet.

Based on 62 all-night EEG records of 7 males which collectively involved 48 wettings, Ritvo, Ornitz, Gottlieb, Poussaint, Maron, Ditman, and Blinn (1969) described three classes of bedwetting. The first was awake enuresis (10% of the episodes recorded), in which the child was awakened when wetting occurred. Secondly, nonarousal enuresis was described, where there were no recorded physiological "arousal signals" preceding wetting. Thirdly there was arousal enuresis, in which arousal signals emanating from bladder fullness were clearly noted up to 10 minutes before wetting and most frequently 30–60 seconds before. The authors speculated that arousal and awake enuresis were characterized by the presence of other "neurotic symptoms" in the enuretic.

With regard to arousability, two studies (Bostock, 1958; Boyd, 1960) compared enuretics with nonenuretics. Bostock found enuretics to take longer to arouse, while Boyd noted that enuretics waken more quickly than nonenuretics. Differences in arousal stimuli (buzzer vs. calling and physical prompt), however, make a comparison difficult.

In general, it would seem that enuresis cannot be categorically attributed to depth of sleep. It is interesting to note the relative paucity of information on changes of sleep patterns when enuresis is eliminated by any of the various treatment procedures, in spite of the accusations that nighttime conditioning procedures may have an undesirable effect on sleep patterns. In addition, although many of the parents of enuretics describe their children as difficult to arouse, there still appears to be inconsistencies in the data comparing enuretics with nonenuretics.

THEORIES OF ETIOLOGY

Several etiological theories have been postulated to account for enuresis. These can be divided into three main categories: medical-genetic, psychodynamic and learning-behavioral. The medical-genetic approach has several components. First is the physiologic-neuro-maturational component (Crosby, 1950; Gillison and Skinner, 1958; Smith, 1967), which views enuresis as a deficit or lag in cortical control and is exemplified by Crosby's (1950) suggesting that enuresis was a condition "arising from physiological activity and not of anatomical, pathological or psychological origin" (p. 534). Evidence from sleep studies (Finley, 1971; Kales and Kales, 1974; Ritvo *et al.*, 1969) is taken as suggestive of an arousal deficit in some children. A second view is represented by Bakwin (1971), who described the basis of enuresis as "principally genetic," based on his observations of the concordance rate for enuresis in monozygotic twins, which is twice that of dyzygotic twins. A third view emphasizes the maturational-developmental lag. Muellner (1960a,b), for example, identified four stages (described above) in the acquisition of urinary control. The presence of small functional bladder capacities is indicative of immature bladder functioning and represents inadequate or incomplete development of urinary control as a result of faulty or insufficient training and practice.

The psychodynamic approach tends to interpret enuresis as a symptom or sign of some deeper or more fundamental conflict, anxiety, or emotional disturbance (Pierce, 1975; Sperling, 1965). Enuresis is then variously interpreted as regressive behavior, a bid for attention, expression of resentment or anger, a masturbatory equivalent, and a clinging to infancy. Sibling rivalry, expression of feelings of being unwanted, fear of castration, reluctance to grow up, or a need to remain dependent have also been postulated (Pierce, 1975). Additionally, Sperling (1965) has spoken of enuresis as a means of symbolically gratifying erotic and hostile needs, offsetting the mother's control, or exhibiting genitals, and is taken as an indication that the child is sexually precocious. Sperling further postulates an "inability to tolerate instinctual and emotional tension" (p. 28) and the need for immediate discharge and gratification as characteristic of enuretics. Therefore, treatment tends to focus on training the child to tolerate and control his instinctual impulses and feelings without discharging them through urination or on elimination of the underlying disturbance, conflict or anxiety.

The learning-behavioral approach to functional nocturnal enuresis emphasizes the role of appropriate learning experiences and environmental consequences, i.e., conditioning (Atthowe, 1973; Lovibond and Coote, 1970; Yeates, 1973; Young, 1965b). It is generally agreed that micturition control incorporates complex cortical controls involving conditioned inhibition of urination and controlled evacuation. When these skills are absent it may be due to physiological deficits, disorder in neurodevelopment or inadequate learning. Basically the conditioning approach attempts to arrange environmental contingencies such that internal stimulation arising from bladder fullness will begin to initiate the urinary inhibitory response or awaken the child from sleep. The presence of enuresis then suggests that the cues originating from bladder fullness have not acquired such discriminative properties and therefore the child continues to engage in "reflexive" voiding. Another aspect of the learning-behavioral position is the acknowledgement of the importance of the entire behavioral sequence which precedes nocturnal voiding in the toilet, for example, the child's being able to find his way to the bathroom when partially awake, remove his night clothes and void in the appropriate place. These responses are often ignored because they are not part of the physiology of micturition but they can nonetheless be factors in the acquisition and maintenance of enuresis.

ASSESSMENT

Doleys and Ciminero (1976) have listed several different treatment procedures for enuresis, including dietary and fluid restriction, sphincter control exercises, nighttime awakening, parental and child counseling, positive reinforcement, retention control training, urine alarm conditioning, and dry-bed training. This list, of course, is not exhaustive. The selection of one procedure or another is often made on the basis of the therapist's knowledge or bias. To date there has been little attempt at the development of a systematic assessment procedure which would logically lead to differential application of one or more of these treatment procedures. The assessment procedure described below is intended to be a comprehensive one and provide the clinician with a complete description of the problem behavior(s).

The assessment of enuresis should include medical screening for pathology, a clinical interview, and behavioral recording (Ciminero and Doleys, 1976; Doleys *et al.*, unpublished manuscript.) Medical screening is necessary to rule out urological and neurological pathology. Cohen (1975) has suggested a general procedure which includes noting abnormalities in the size and velocity of the urine stream and control of the sphincter. The presence of diurnal dribbling, dysuria (painful urination), and polyuria (frequent urination) or urgency (the inability to refrain from voiding) may be indicative of pathology. Although many urologists request a radiological examination, this is often initially unnecessary (Campbell, 1970). Urine cultures and urinalysis, however, should be standard in order to rule out the presence of infections.

The clinical interview should be extensive and comprehensive, oriented toward obtaining information in five areas. First, information regarding the child's day- and night-time wetting behavior is useful, including estimates of frequency, retention, and sphincter control. Second, the history of the onset of enuresis and prior treatment attempts should also be obtained. Difficulties during toilet training, responsiveness or lack of responsiveness to prior treatment attempts, and whether or not the child had demonstrated any period of continence will affect the choice of a treatment procedure. A brief medical history of the family concerning the presence of renal diseases or diabetes should also be obtained. If the parents or other family members have in the past been enuretic, this may affect their attitudes toward the child and the treatment. For example, they may insist that the problem will pass in time or they may be unusually demanding with regard to the child ceasing the bedwetting. Morgan and Young (1975) have noted a positive correlation between parental tolerance of wetting and treatment success. A fourth area for the clinical interview would be concentration on seeking out the existence of other behavior problems. Although enuresis is not typically accompanied by other pathological behaviors, when other problems, such as noncompliance, do exist they may be severe enough to hamper the treatment of the enuresis and therefore may need to be eliminated first. It has also been noted that some children avoid going to the bathroom at night because they are fearful of the dark or fearful of the toilet. The interviewer should be on the lookout for indications of the presence of such behaviors, which themselves may have a causal relationship to the enuresis. Finally, information should be gathered concerning the home and family environment. Marital and family difficulties may complicate the treatment of enuresis and have been related to treatment failure (Turner et al., 1970).

The behavioral recording portion of assessment can provide precise information regarding the wetting behavior of the child and can serve as a baseline against which to evaluate treatment. A 3-week period of recording is recommended. This not only provides adequate time for stable records to be obtained but also provides an opportunity to assess parental cooperation and motivation for treatment. Frequency of nighttime wetting, bladder capacity, size of wet spot, time of wetting, spontaneous awakening, and arousability should be examined. Some children have been known to respond positively to self-monitoring (Doleys et al., 1977) and to advice and encouragement (Dische, 1971, 1973; White, 1968; Meadow, 1970) which can easily be implemented during this period.

Estimates of the maximum and average bladder capacity should be obtained. Some data have been provided noting smaller bladder capacities in enuretic than in nonenuretic children (Fig. 1; Zaleski et al., 1973). The presence of a small functional bladder capacity may indicate the need to incorporate bladder stretching exercises such as retention control training (Kimmel and Kimmel, 1970) into treatment. The average

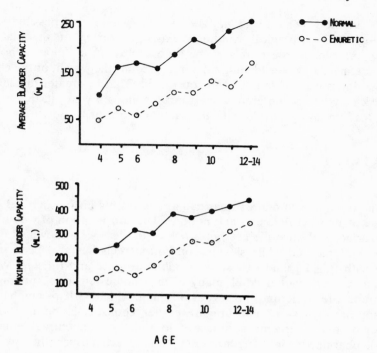

Fig. 1. The maximum (MBC) and average (ABC) bladder capacity for enuretic and nonenuretic children in milliliters (Zaleski *et al.*, in *Bladder Control and Enuresis*, 1973, pp. 96–97).

bladder capacity (ABC) is determined by providing the parents with a measuring cylinder and requesting them to record the amount of urine passed by the child each time he voids over a 7-day period. The mean amount per void is considered the ABC. The maximum bladder capacity (MBC) can be obtained in two ways. The first is by water-loading the child with liquids equivalent to 30 ml per kilogram body weight (one ounce per 2.2 lbs up to a maximum of 500 ml or 17 oz), then asking the child to refrain from voiding until it becomes uncomfortable. The amount of the subsequent two voiding episodes is recorded, with the larger being the MBC. The second method of obtaining MBC is represented by using the largest void obtained while collecting data for the ABC. The water-load procedure for determining the MBC can be carried out in an office or clinic in about 1–3 hours under supervision and thus can be very reliable (Starfield, 1967). However, it may not be as sensitive a predictor or measure of functional bladder capacity as the MBC obtained by the second method (Zaleski *et al.*, 1973) and, where the possibility of pathological or urological condition exists, rupturing of the bladder during water-load procedure may be a possibility. In addition, although the guidelines for water-loading take into account the weight of the child, the age differences have not been considered. That is, greater difficulties and risk may be encountered when water-loading a 5-year-old than when water-loading an 8-year-old with the same amount of liquids.

TREATMENT

The treatment of enuresis has had an interesting history marked with the use of unusual remedies and potions. The consumption of wood lice, swine urine, and mice pie are but a few of the less well-known. Raising the foot of the bed while sleeping on cotton reels has also been tried, along with flogging and exposure to public disgrace and ridicule. While these may sound rather cruel, many of the "home remedies" attempted by parents are sometimes no less astonishing, which perhaps emphasizes the appropriateness of encouraging earlier counseling and treatment. Contemporary treatment approaches to functional nocturnal enuresis include pharmacologic or medical intervention, verbal psychotherapy, and conditioning procedures.

Before describing these major categories, a word should be said about fluid restriction and dietary control. Current data provide no evidence supporting the utility of these procedures in the treatment of enuresis. It perhaps goes without saying that the restriction of fluids is going to modify, if not eliminate, bedwetting in a child. However, under these conditions the child is not given the opportunity to learn how to control urges to void during the night by either inhibiting voiding or arousing and using the bathroom. Therefore it is more than a question of semantics as to whether or not fluid restriction really does provide a "treatment" procedure for enuresis or whether it merely postpones the attacking of the problem.

Pharmacological Intervention

With the variety of pharmacological agents which have been used in the treatment of enuresis, only two (amphetamine and imipramine) continue to be researched. Stimulants like amphetamine are proposed to lower the threshold of sleep, making it more likely that the enuretic will be aroused by the urge to void. The data, however, do not support its effectiveness. McConaghy (1969), Young (1965a) and Forrester, Stein, and Susser (1964) compared amphetamine to a conditioning treatment and imipramine. Successful treatment was reported in 22%, 36% and 23% of the children respectively in the three studies. These results were significantly inferior to other treatments. Amphetamine has reportedly been more effective with children described as deep sleepers (Pooley and Shersby, 1963). In an extensive review of the research literature, Blackwell, and Currah (1973) stated that there was "no control support for the utility of amphetamine" (p. 233).

Imipramine hydrochloride (Tofranil), a tricyclic antidepressant, is reported to have an anticholinergic effect, relaxing the detrusor muscles surrounding the bladder and thus allowing for greater expansion and delaying the onset of contractions and subsequent voiding (Blackwell and Currah, 1973). Therefore, instead of the enuretic child tending to awaken during the night, as with amphetamine, the effects of imipramine increase the probability of his sleeping through the night while retaining urine. Several studies have shown imipramine to be significantly more effective than placebo in reducing the frequency of nighttime wetting (Forsythe and Merrett, 1969; Kardash *et al.*, 1968; McConaghy, 1969; Poussaint and Ditman, 1965; Schaffer *et al.*, 1968). The dosages vary from 25 mg for children under 5 years of age to 75 mg for older children. Although imipramine has been shown to be superior to placebo and amphetamine, the percentage of children who actually achieved dryness continues to be less than 30%. The effects of imipramine are generally noted in the first week or two and show up as a reduction of frequency of wetting. Relapses following removal of the drug are very common, with studies noting only 5–40% of the subjects maintaining continence. Schaffer, Costello, and Hill (1968) pointed out that gradual or sudden withdrawal of medication made no difference. There are some control data (Hagglund and Parkkulainen, 1965) which demonstrate increased bladder capacity and delayed voluntary detrusor contractions, indicating that imipramine may be functioning to inhibit detrusor muscle activity. A recent study by Mahony, Laferte, and Mahony (1973) indicated that imipramine may be most effective with female enuretics of the secondary or acquired type and in more severe cases.

As is the case with many pharmacological agents, negative side effects may appear as a result of their use. Imipramine has been noted in a small number of cases to induce a variety of side effects, primarily disturbances in mood and sleep. In addition, deaths from imipramine toxicity, although few, have also been noted (Meadow, 1970; Rohner and Sanford, 1975).

Some studies have explored the use of amphetamine or imipramine in conjunction with the urine alarm conditioning procedure. A review of these studies by Doleys (1977) noted the addition of drugs did not appreciably affect the outcome data.

Verbal Psychotherapy

Relatively few studies have systematically explored the effects of verbal psychotherapy in the treatment of enuresis. Lovibond (1964) reported on five studies appearing between 1923 and 1961 which noted rates of remission between 25–57%. More recent studies (Werry and Cohrssen, 1965; Novick, 1966; Friedman, 1968; DeLeon and Mandell, 1966) have failed to give evidence of the effectiveness of verbal psychotherapy over no-treatment controls. Novick (1966), for example, noted only 20% of 45 children receiving what was referred to as "routine supportive-symptomatic treatment" to have achieved dryness criteria. Treatment was oriented toward the elimination of the child's guilt, increasing his confidence and becoming his friend, instructing the parents to cease the use of punishment in the treatment of and response to enuresis. No relapse rates, however, were provided in the study. Friedman (1968) reported on the failure of one year of verbal psychotherapy with an 11-year-old enuretic female, and DeLeon and Mandell (1966) noted success in only two of eleven subjects (18%) after twelve sessions of psychotherapy-counseling. Both of these subjects subsequently relapsed, however.

Several studies (Stewart, 1975; Dische, 1971; White, 1968; Meadow, 1970) have documented the effective use of advice and encouragement with enuretic children. This usually took the form of focusing the child's attention on the problem by having him record his wetting behavior and providing stars and praise for dry nights. Additionally, the parents were instructed to be encouraging rather than punitive. Periodic contacts with the therapist or physician were maintained. Dische (1971) noted that up to 37% of her subjects achieved dryness criterion under this simple procedure. Without further description of the specific content of counseling sessions, this procedure very closely mimics self-monitoring and positive reinforcement for dry nights, therefore it may not adequately fall under the category of verbal psychotherapy.

Because of the absence of control studies and the inability to replicate previous studies given the absence of an adequate description of the content of the "verbal psychotherapy," any attempt at an evaluation of this procedure in the treatment of enuresis would be rather fruitless. About all that can be said at this point is that there is no empirical evidence to indicate that verbal psychotherapy can produce a remission rate significantly different from that noted in no-treatment control subjects and clearly it is inferior to some of the data provided with the use of imipramine and conditioning procedures.

Learning-Behavioral Therapies

The learning-behavioral or conditioning approaches to the treatment of enuresis can be classified in three broad categories: first, those which have employed the urine alarm either exclusively or as part of a more comprehensive program; second, treatments which have emphasized the expansion of bladder capacity through the systematic application of retention trials which are reinforced; third, those that have relied on one specific behavioral procedure such as positive reinforcement, punishment, or response cost.

Urine-Alarm

Table 1 summarizes some of the recent studies which have employed the urine alarm. The urine alarm is a mechanical device first applied systematically by Mowrer and Mowrer (1938) to the treatment of enuresis. Basically, the device consists of two foil pads separated by an absorbent sheet upon which the child sleeps. Urine passed by the child is then absorbed by the middle sheet and completes a circuit between the two foil sheets. This completed circuit activates an alarm designed to arouse the child. Doleys (1977) and Meadow (1973) have summarized other types of urine alarms and some of the early and current problems with these alarms. False alarms due to excessive perspiration or movement of the child, allowing the foil pads to make contact, have been troublesome. Wetting off the pads may also occur but is infrequent and does not appear to disrupt the therapeutic process. Buzzer "ulcers" or electrical burns have been a problem in the past. The addition of new guidelines for the construction and use of various alarm systems, however, has significantly reduced the likelihood of burns.

The conditioning procedure first described by Mowrer and Mowrer (1938) and adopted by many others since involves several steps. The urine

Table 1. Characteristics of Studies Using Behavioral Procedures in the Treatment of Enuresis

Author	Subjects (age range)	Treatment	Duration (weeks)	% Arrest (criterion)	Follow-up/ relapse (months)
Young and Turner (1965)	105 (4–15)	Urine-alarm	$\overline{X} = 10$	65% (14)	6–12 (13%)
DeLeon and Mandell (1966)	56 (6–13)	Urine-alarm	$\overline{X} = 7.8$	79% (14)	6 (79%)
Novick (1966)	36 (6–13)	Urine-alarm	$\overline{X} = 5.2$	89% (14)	10 (50%)
Baker (1969)	27 (9–12)	Urine-alarm	50 buzzer operations	74% (28)	6 (20%)
Forsythe and Redmond (1970)	200 (5–15)	Urine-alarm	$\overline{X} = 9.9$	66% (14)	12–36 (23%)
Dische (1971)	79 (4–15)	Urine-alarm	$\overline{X} = 10.1$	89% (21)	19 (30%)
Young and Morgan (1972)	144 (4–15)	Urine-alarm		70% (14)	12–42 (35%)
Finley et al. (1973)	10 (6–8)	Urine-alarm	Max. = 6	90% (7)	3 (44%)
Sloop and Kennedy (1973)	21 (6–18)	Urine-alarm	$\overline{X} = 8$	52% (14)	7.5–11.6 (36%)
Collins (1973)	33 (4–12)	Urine-alarm	Max. = 10	79% (10)	9 (33%)
Taylor and Turner (1975)	21 (4–15)	Urine-alarm	$\overline{X} = 9.7$	62% (28)	15.5 (69%)
Finley et al. (1973)	10 (6–8)	Intermittent Alarm (70%)	Max. = 6	80% (7)	3 (12%)
Finley and Wansley (1976)	87 (6–11+)	Intermittent Alarm	$\overline{X} = 6.5$	96% (14)	3–6 (18%)
Taylor and Turner (1975)	18 (4–15)	Intermittent Alarm (50%)	$\overline{X} = 16.1$	50% (28)	14.3 (44%)
Young and Morgan (1972)	67 (4–15)	Overlearning		82% (14)	12–42 (12.7%)
Taylor and Turner (1975)	22 (4–15)	Overlearning	$\overline{X} = 12.3$	60% (28)	8.5 (23%)
Jehu et al. (1977)	19 (5–15)	Overlearning	$\overline{X} = 11.9$	95% (14)	20+ (30%)
Azrin et al. (1974)	26 (3+)	Dry Bed Training	$\overline{X} + 2.7$	100% (14)	6 (30%)

alarm is placed on the child's bed. When the alarm is activated it must be turned off by the child. The child then is encouraged to rush to the bathroom and finish voiding. Washing the face with cold water is suggested to ensure that the child is awake. The bedding is then changed and the child returned to sleep. Charts are kept noting dry and wet nights. Fourteen consecutive dry nights is the typical criterion for dryness, following which the alarm is removed. Fluid restriction or other modifications in the child's drinking behavior are not encouraged.

Early reviews of the research on the effectiveness of the urine alarm (Lovibond, 1963; Lovibond and Coote, 1970; Turner, 1973; Yates, 1970) noted rates of remission between 80–90%. Relapse rates, however, were approximately 35%. A recent paper by Doleys (1977) examined the studies conducted between 1960 and 1975 using the urine-alarm procedure. Data on 628 subjects treated with the urine alarm revealed success in 75% of the cases with a treatment duration of 5–12 weeks. Of the successfully treated subjects, 41% relapsed during follow-up. Sixty-eight percent of these subjects were exposed to retreatment and achieved dryness.

Several aspects of this urine-alarm procedure have been systematically examined. Collins (1973) and Peterson, Wright, and Harlon (1969) explored the importance of temporal contiguity between wetting and onset of the alarm by delaying the alarm for 3 or 5 minutes. Remission was longer under the delayed procedure and rates of relapse were higher. Similarly Catalina (1976) had parents check their child during the night and arouse him if he was wet. This procedure was less effective than comparison procedures which resulted in immediate arousal contingent upon wetting.

The effects of the urine alarm have been compared to a placebo tablet (White, 1968), no treatment (DeLeon and Mandell, 1966), presence of an inoperative alarm (Baker, 1969), and verbal psychotherapy (Werry and Cohrssen, 1965; Novick, 1966; DeLeon and Mandell, 1966) and were found to be superior in each instance. As noted earlier, the use of central nervous system stimulants (dexedrine and methadrine) or imipramine (Tofranil) as adjuncts to the urine alarm has not proved to be generally beneficial.

There has been some concern on the part of the psychoanalytically and psychodynamically oriented theorists that conditioning procedures are only attacking the symptom and not the problem. Therefore, other symptoms will appear with removal of the enuresis, i.e., symptom substitution. A number of studies have examined this and generally noted the absence of new "symptoms" following the elimination of enuresis (Baker, 1969; Bennett, 1973; Compton, 1968; Dische, 1971; Werry and Cohrssen, 1965). Following a review of the research, Schaffer (1973) reported that new emotional or behavioral symptoms may appear in a minority of children but that they do not persist. Sachs, DeLeon, and Blackman (1974) obtained pre- and post-measures, including a symptom checklist, teacher rating scales, and personality inventories, on 51 enuretic children treated by conditioning or psychotherapy-counseling methods in a control group. Behavioral symptoms decreased following successful treatment in all instances and remained so during 1 year of follow-up.

Two modifications of the standard urine-alarm procedure have been found to be effective in reducing the rate of relapses: intermittent scheduling of the alarm and over-learning. The intermittent alarm procedure involves the presentation of the alarm on a variable rather than a continuous schedule. That is, instead of each wet being followed by an alarm, only a given percentage (usually 50% or 70%) are followed by an alarm. Theoretically, it has been reasoned that if attainment of nighttime continence is achieved by conditioning then relapses are essentially a result of extinction (removal of the alarm). According to learning principles, then, the use of an intermittent schedule during conditioning strengthens the response (increases resistance to extinction). A controlled study by Finley, Besserman, Bennett, Clapp, and Finley (1973) compared an intermittent alarm schedule (alarm followed approximately 70% of the wetting episodes) to a continuous (100%) schedule and placebo (no alarm) group over a 6-week treatment period. Figure 2 clearly shows both treatment groups to be superior to the control group. There was also some trend toward slower conditioning in the intermittent group, but as Table 1 indicates the relapse rates were much lower in the intermittent group (15% versus 44%). A subsequent report by Finley and Wansley (1976) noted only 3 of 87 children treated failed to achieve dryness under the intermittent procedure, and the relapse rate was 17%. The data provided by Taylor and Turner (1975) are not as impressive. This, however, may be due to the use of a 50% schedule, a different apparatus, and different population and follow-up duration.

The second innovation in the standard urine-alarm procedure is referred to as "over-learning." Briefly this requires the child to increase his intake of liquids just before bedtime after he has achieved dryness under the usual urine-alarm procedure. The child is encouraged to drink 10–32 oz of liquid depending upon his age and size. Young and Morgan (1972) suggested this procedure as a means of reducing rates of relapse. They propose that relapses were a result of the absence of generalization of conditioning to levels of bladder fullness other than those experienced during treatment. Increased liquid intake, theoretically, would extend control to higher levels of bladder fullness. Three studies have employed the overlearning procedure (Young and Morgan, 1972; Taylor and Turner, 1975; Jehu et al., 1977). In general the treatment duration was noted to be longer but the extended follow-up data are encouraging. The study by Jehu et al. (1977) is particularly noteworthy because it was

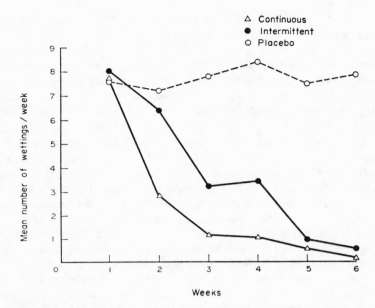

Fig. 2. Mean number of wets per week across the 6-week treatment period for continuous, intermittent and placebo reinforcement groups (Finley *et al.*, *Behaviour Research and Therapy*, 1973, 11:293).

conducted in residential homes for children by staff and aides. Of the 19 children treated within the overlearning paradigm, 95% became dry. Thirteen remained dry during follow-up, while four became dry after being retreated; no data were available on another child. Therefore, if one includes those subjects successfully retreated in the dryness category, then 18 of 19 children could be said to have achieved and maintained dryness under this procedure.

A cautionary note regarding overlearning is appropriate. Young and Morgan (1972) did note severe regression to baseline wetting in some children when they were exposed to the overlearning procedure. These children did not appear to be able to tolerate excessive liquid intake prior to bedtime and perhaps needed to be gradually introduced to it. Giving too much liquid and causing renewed bedwetting after it has been eliminated can be upsetting to the parent and the child. Both need to be fully prepared for this eventuality. One possibility would be to delay the onset of overlearning for several weeks after initial training and then gradually increase the amount of liquid given at nighttime.

The dry-bed training procedure was introduced by Azrin, Sneed, and Foxx (1973, 1974) as a multidimensional approach to enuresis which incorporated positive practice, positive reinforcement, retention control training, nighttime awakening, negative reinforcement, and full cleanliness training. The procedure called for the placing of the urine alarm or buzzer in the parents' bedroom for the purpose of alerting the parents to any wetting episode that occurred so that appropriate consequences could be imposed. The procedure was initiated by one night of "intensive training" in which trained therapists came into the home to introduce the program to the parents and the child. During this night the child was first informed of all aspects of the program and then carried out twenty positive practice trials. The child was then encouraged to drink his favorite liquid, repeat the training instructions, and allowed to retire for the night. Minimal prompts were used to awaken the child each hour, direct him to the bathroom and encourage him to void (if under 6 years of age) or to inhibit urination for an additional hour. Positive verbal reinforcement was given for a dry bed, followed by more liquids. Each wetting episode was followed by cleanliness training, which involved the child changing his bedding, his night clothes, cleaning himself and engaging in twenty positive practice trials. "Posttraining supervision" began the second night, in which full cleanliness training and positive practice were still imposed contingent upon wet nights. The child was, however, awakened only once, usually in late evening. This awakening was gradually faded out. Parents were strongly encouraged to reinforce the child after each dry night and to invite relatives and friends to do the same. The "normal routine" was the third phase and began after seven consecutive dry nights. During this phase the alarm was taken off the child's bed and cleanliness training conducted the morning after a wet. Positive practice was carried out the following evening. Posttraining supervision was reintroduced any time two or more wets occurred within any seven-day recording period.

The results from the initial study examining the effectiveness of this procedure (Azrin, Sneed, and Foxx, 1973) were quite impressive. One hundred percent of the 24 subjects achieved the 14-day dryness criterion. Seven of these children were noted to display frequent enough wetting to involve the reinitiation of the posttraining supervision. While specific follow-up data are not given, the authors note that none of the subjects relapsed to pretreatment rates of wetting during the 6-month follow-up period.

There is only one systematic replication reported of dry-bed training (Doleys *et al.*, 1977). In this study 13 subjects were exposed to a 6-week period of dry-bed training. Substantial decreases in wetting were noted for each of the subjects. Of the 11 subjects, 7 who completed the training program met the dryness criterion within the 6-week period and 6 of these remained dry during follow-up. Although these data are clearly not as impressive as those of Azrin *et al.* (1974), they do indicate the potential utility of dry-bed training and suggest the need for further research.

The single most common reason cited for failure of the urine-alarm procedure appears to be lack of parental cooperation (Doleys, 1977). One of the difficulties of the Azrin *et al.* (1974) program, for example, is its complexity and time demands on the parents. The author has found several parents who are willing to use a potentially less effective procedure for this reason. Other parents are willing to try anything but may become inconsistent in their implementation of a complex program once they experience the necessary time commitment. The use of instructional manuals, regular office and telephone contacts, behavioral recording, and proper training in how to carry out the procedures can each enhance parental cooperation and success rates.

It is also clear that there are a number of "nonspecific" factors operating in the treatment of enuresis with the urine alarm. For example, although the number was small, Baker (1969) noted some decrease in wetting frequency by simply placing an inoperative alarm in the child's room. Doleys *et al.* (1977) and others have documented positive changes resulting from self-recording. Attention from parents and the therapist is also a factor to consider. The author recently talked with a parent who found that keeping only the alarm in the child's room with the pad off the bed served to eliminate periodic wetting which appeared during posttreatment follow-up. The child said that the alarm reminded him that he had to keep trying to stay dry.

Bladder Expansion Training

Studies on the physiology of micturition in enuretics (Muellner, 1960a,b; Vincent, 1964) have noted a tendency for voiding to occur in response to relatively small degrees of bladder fullness or distention. The data provided by Zaleski *et al.* (1973, Fig. 1) and Starfield and Mellits (1968) also showed the average amount of urine per void to be lower for many enuretics than nonenuretics. These data, in combination with a search for a treatment procedure which can be conducted during the day rather than at night, have provided the impetus for the development and exploration of bladder expansion or retention control training procedures. Generally, these procedures require the enuretic to increase the intake of liquids so as to produce an urge to void. Refraining from voiding until it is uncomfortable or for a predetermined time interval is then reinforced. It is speculated that this procedure would facilitate and strengthen urinary inhibitory control mechanisms. Furthermore, once these control mechanisms are established they would begin to operate during the night while the child is asleep. This then would allow the accommodation of a large enough volume of urine in the bladder to allow the child to sleep through the night or increase the intensity of the stimulus which arises from a greater degree of detrusor muscle distention, thus arousing the child.

The studies using bladder expansion training have provided mixed results (Doleys, 1977). Starfield and Mellits (1968) examined changes in wetting frequency and bladder capacity after a 6-month treatment program involving one retention trial per day. The children were asked to refrain from voiding until it became very uncomfortable. Increased bladder capacity was noted and was positively correlated with decreases in nocturnal wetting. Only 6 of 83 children, however, became dry during the 6-month treatment period.

Kimmel and Kimmel (1970) described a procedure called retention control training (RCT). Liquid intake was increased and the child asked to refrain from voiding whenever the urge appeared. The retention interval was gradually increased to 30 minutes and positive reinforcement was delivered for successful retention. Two of the three children placed on the regimen achieved dryness within 7 days and the third within 14 days. A subsequent study with a larger sample (Paschalis, Kimmel, and Kimmel, 1972) noted that 40% of the subjects became dry over a 20-day treatment period. Although relatively impressive, these data have not been replicated in other studies (Allen, 1976; Doleys et al., 1977; Harris and Purohit, 1976; Hunsaker, 1976).

A recent study by Doleys and Wells (1975) represents one of the few attempts to document changes in bladder capacity during training. In addition, an effort was also made to measure nighttime bladder capacity. Fig. 3 shows the immediate change in bladder capacity which resulted from the application of a variation of retention control training. However, it should be noted that dry nights did not begin to appear until some time later.

There continues to be some controversy over the role of bladder capacity in nocturnal continence. Allen (1976), for example, suggested that bladder control and not bladder enlargement is necessary for nighttime continence. Hunsaker (1976), Muellner (1960a,b) and Zaleski et al. (1973), implicate a more direct relationship between bladder capacity and enuresis. It may be that increased bladder control is a by-product of bladder expansion exercises or vice versa, making it difficult to separate the two effects.

Clinically, Hunsaker (1976) has recommended differential application

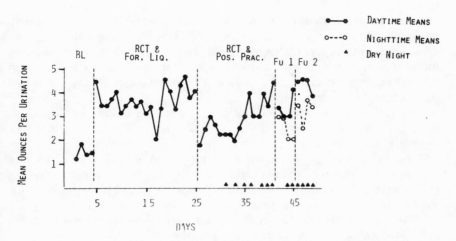

Fig. 3. The mean number of ounces voided per urination for each day of the program. The various experimental conditions are indicated: baseline (BL), retention control training with forced liquids (RCT-For.Liq.), retention control training and positive practice with no forced liquids (RCT-Pos.Prac.), 2-week follow-up (FU1), and the 6-week follow-up (FU2). The closed circles indicate mean volumes voided per daytime urination. Mean ounces voided per nighttime urination are denoted by the open circles. Solid triangles indicate dry nights (Doleys and Wells, *Behavior Therapy*, 1975, 6:687).

of retention control to those children who demonstrate low functional bladder capacities. Kimmel and Kimmel (1970), however, appear to be more in favor of its general utility as a daytime treatment for enuresis. The use of bladder expansion exercises as an adjunct to the urine alarm procedure has not been explored and may provide an effective, comprehensive program which attacks bladder capacity, bladder control and nighttime toileting.

Other Behavioral Procedures

Other behavioral and nonbehavioral procedures have been attempted with limited or small numbers of children. Many of these procedures are relatively simple and certainly less complex than the above ones. Allgeier (1976), for example, reported on the successful use of a response cost program with 8- and 11-year-old enuretics. The two subjects (sisters) monitored their nighttime wetting daily and were fined for not recording daily or for lying. After 5 weeks withdrawal of privileges followed wet nights. Wetting was eliminated within 18 weeks in both subjects, but follow-up data are not provided.

Punishment and differential reinforcement were applied by Tough, Hawkins, McArthur, and Ravensway (1971) to eliminate enuresis in an 8-year-old multiply-handicapped child and his brother. Each wetting incident was followed by the child being "dipped" into a tub of cold water. Wetting was eliminated in 22 and 16 nights, respectively, but it had to be retreated in one child.

Nighttime awakenings and potting at fixed or random time intervals have been studied (Creer and Davis, 1975; Samaan, 1972; Young, 1964). Young (1964) reported a reduction in wetting frequency in 67% of 58 children on a random awakening procedure. Only 10%, however, became dry with extended treatment. Lovibond (1963) and Morgan and Young (1975) have cautioned against the use of nighttime awakening procedures, suggesting that it would promote compulsive nighttime wetting. In addition, the child could learn to become dependent on the parent to be awakened rather than attending to internal cues.

Charting, self-monitoring, positive reinforcement, and advice and encouragement appear to be effective with some children (Collins, 1973; Dische, 1971; Meadow, 1970; White, 1968) and can be used in baseline to prevent the application of more comprehensive, time-consuming and complex procedures for those children who do not require them.

SUMMARY

A single theoretical and practical solution to the problem of functional nocturnal enuresis has not yet been achieved. But nor are we helpless in providing relief from such a troublesome behavior. The need for a thorough and precise evaluation and description of the characteristics and pattern of nocturnal wetting in the enuretic himself is a necessity. Extended baseline recording may eliminate those children who will be responsive to less complicated procedures, and also assess the motivation and cooperation of parent and child. Substantial research has indicated the general absence of significant pathology in most enuretics and has evidenced positive changes following its remission. The treatment of enuresis in children under 5 years of age remains somewhat questionable, but after this age treatment should be viewed as necessary. Although many children do become dry "spontaneously," the variety and magnitude of psychological trauma (harrassment and ridicule from parents and peers) suffered is unpredictable.

In light of the documented etiological factors responsible for enuresis, verbal psychotherapy appears to be a rather fruitless endeavor as a treatment procedure, particularly when compared to pharmacological and behavioral intervention. The use of drugs in the treatment of enuresis has a relatively unimpressive track record; nonetheless, the potential for bringing about immediate, temporary relief from high-rate wetting would appear to have therapeutic value for some children but should be used in conjunction with proven behavioral procedures such as the urine alarm to help insure total remission of wetting and maintenance during follow-up and after drug withdrawal. Several behavioral-conditioning procedures have been proven successful in treating functional enuresis. The standard urine-alarm method as described by Mowrer and Mowrer (1938) is certainly the most extensively researched. Frequently noted 75–90% rates of remission and 25–40% relapse rates may reflect the maximum efficiency of this method. The use of over-learning and intermittent alarm schedules seem to be clinically significant as procedural modifications. Other procedures such as dry-bed training, though apparently effective, require further validation.

The role and effects of bladder expansion exercises continue to be in question. They would seem useful with children who void frequently but at low volumes. The development of bladder and sphincter control mechanisms, although perhaps not sufficient for engendering nighttime continence, may be a very important by-product of this type of training.

Baseline recording, self-monitoring, positive reinforcement, advice and encouragement, frequent contacts with the therapist, use of a modification of the urine-alarm procedure, and periodic retention exercises as a comprehensive program would appear to be justified. Such a multifaceted approach would greatly increase the likelihood of successful treatment, maintenance of parental cooperation, and the reduction of relapse rates.

REFERENCES

Allen, R. B. (1976). Bladder Capacity and Awakening Behavior as Outcome Variables in the Treatment of Enuresis. Unpublished dissertation, Burlington: University of Vermont.
Allgeier, A. R. (1976). Minimizing therapist supervision in the treatment of enuresis. *Journal of Behavior Therapy and Experimental Psychiatry* 7:371–372.
Atthowe, J. M. (1973). Nocturnal enuresis and behavior therapy: a functional analysis. In R. B. Rubin, J. Henderson, H. Fensterheim, and L. P. Ullman, eds., *Advances in Behavior Therapy*, Vol. 4. New York: Academic Press.
Azrin, N. H., Sneed, T. J., and Foxx, R. M. (1973). Dry bed: a rapid method of eliminating bedwetting (enuresis) of the retarded. *Behaviour Research and Therapy* 11:427–434.
——, Sneed, T. J., and Foxx, R. M. (1974). Dry bed: rapid elimination of childhood enuresis. *Behaviour Research and Therapy* 12:147–156.
Baker, B. L. (1969). Symptom treatment and symptom substitution in enuresis. *Journal of Abnormal Psychology* 74:42–49.

Bakwin, H. (1971). Enuresis in twins. *American Journal of Diseases in Childhood* 121:222–225.

Bennett, L. F. (1973). Psychological concomitants of enuresis nocturna before and after conditioning treatment. *Dissertation Abstracts* 34:23928B.

Blackwell, B., and Currah, J. (1973). The pharmacology of nocturnal enuresis. In I. Kolvin, R. C. MacKeith, and S. R. Meadow, eds., *Bladder Control and Enuresis*. Philadelphia: W. B. Saunders.

Bostock, J. (1958). Exterior gestation, primitive sleep, enuresis and asthma: a study in aetiology. *Medical Journal of Australia* 149:185–192.

Boyd, M. M. (1960). The depth of sleep in enuretic school children and in non-enuretic controls. *Journal of Psychosomatic Research* 4:274–280.

Campbell, M. F. (1951). *Clinical pediatric urology*. Philadelphia: W. B. Saunders.

—— (1970). Neuromuscular uropathy. In M. F. Campbell and T. H. Harrison, eds., *Urology*, Vol. 2. Philadelphia: W. B. Saunders.

Catalina, D. A. (1976). Enuresis: the effects of parent contingent wake-up. *Dissertation Abstracts* 37:28025.

Ciminero, A. R., and Doleys, D. M. (1976). Childhood enuresis: considerations in assessment. *Journal of Pediatric Psychology* 4:17–20.

Cohen, M. W. (1975). Enuresis. In S. B. Friedman, ed., *The Pediatric Clinics of North America*. Philadelphia: W. B. Saunders.

Collins, R. W. (1973). Importance of the bladder-cue buzzer contingency in the conditioning treatment of enuresis. *Journal of Abnormal Psychology* 82:299–308.

Compton, R. D. (1968). Changes in enuretics accompanying treatment by the conditioned response technique. *Dissertation Abstracts* 29:2549A.

Creer, T. L., and Davis, M. H. (1975). Using a staggered-wakening procedure with enuretic children in an institutional setting. *Journal of Behavior Therapy and Experimental Psychiatry* 6:23–25.

Crosby, N. D. (1950). Essential treatment: successful treatment based on physiological concepts. *Medical Journal of Australia* 2:533–543.

de Jonge, G. A. (1973). Epidemiology of enuresis: a survey of the literature. In I. Kolvin, R. C. MacKeith, and S. R. Meadow, eds., *Bladder Control and Enuresis*. Philadelphia: J. B. Lippincott.

DeLeon, G., and Mandell, W. (1966). A comparison of conditioning and psychotherapy in the treatment of functional enuresis. *Journal of Clinical Psychology* 22:326–330.

Dische, S. (1971). Management of enuresis. *British Medical Journal* 2:33–36.

—— (1973). Treatment of enuresis with an enuresis alarm. In I. Kolvin, R. C. MacKeith, and S. R. Meadow, eds., *Bladder Control and Enuresis*. Philadelphia: W. B. Saunders.

Doleys, D. M. (1977). Behavioral treatments for nocturnal enuresis in children: a review of the recent literature. *Psychological Bulletin* 84:30–54.

——, and Ciminero, A. R. (1976). Childhood enuresis: considerations in treatment. *Journal of Pediatric Psychology* 4:21–23.

——, Ciminero, A. R., and Tollison, J. W. (1975). Considerations in the behavioral assessment and treatment of childhood enuresis. Unpublished manuscript, Athens: University of Georgia.

——, and Wells, K. C. (1975). Changes in functional bladder capacity and bed-wetting during and after retention control training. *Behavior Therapy* 6:685–688.

——, Ciminero, A. R., Tollison, J. W., Williams, C. L., and Wells, K. C. (1977). Dry bed training and retention control training: a comparison. *Behavior Therapy* 8:541–548.

Finley, W. W. (1971). An EEG study of sleep of enuretics at three age levels. *Clinical Electroencephalography* 1:35–39.

——, and Wansley, R. A. (1976). Use of intermittent reinforcement in a clinical-research program for the treatment of enuresis nocturna. *Journal of Pediatric Psychology* 4:24–27.

——, Besserman, R. L., Bennett, L. F., Clapp, R. K., and Finley, P. M. (1973). The effect of continuous, intermittent, and "placebo" reinforcement on the effectiveness of the conditioning treatment for enuresis nocturna. *Behaviour Research and Therapy* 11:289–297.

Forrester, R. M., Stein, Z., and Susser, M. W. (1964). A trial of conditioning therapy in nocturnal enuresis. *Developmental Medicine and Child Neurology* 6:158–166.

Forsythe, W. I., and Merrett, J. D. (1969). A controlled trial of imipramine ("Tofranil") and nortriptyline ("Allegron") in the treatment of enuresis. *British Journal of Clinical Practice* 23:210–215.

——, and Redmond, A. (1970). Enuresis and the electric alarm: study of 200 cases. *British Medical Journal* 1:211–213.

——, and Redmond, A. (1974). Enuresis and spontaneous cure rate: study of 1129 enuretics. *Archives of Diseases in Childhood* 49:259–276.

Friedman, A. R. (1968). Behavior training in a case of enuresis. *Journal of Individual Psychology* 24:86–87.

Gastaut, H., and Broughton, R. (1965). A clinical and polygraphic study of episodic phenomena during sleep. In J. Wortis, ed., *Recent Advances in Biological Psychiatry*, Vol. 7. New York: Plenum Press.

Gillison, T. H., and Skinner, J. L. (1958). Treatment of nocturnal enuresis by the elective alarm. *British Medical Journal* ii:1268–1272.

Graham, P. (1973). Depth of sleep and enuresis: a critical review. In I. Kolvin, R. C. MacKeith, and S. R. Meadow, eds., *Bladder Control and Enuresis*. Philadelphia: W. B. Saunders.

Hagglund, T. B., and Parkkulainen, K. (1965). Enuretic children treated with imipramine. *Annales Pediatriae Fennae* 2:53.

Harris, L. S., and Purohit, A. P. (1976). Bladder training and enuresis: a controlled trial. Unpublished manuscript, Queens University, Kingston, Ontario.

Hunsaker, J. H. (1976). A two-process approach to nocturnal enuresis: preliminary results. *Behavior Therapy* 6:560–561.

Jehu, D., Morgan, R. T. T., Turner, A., and Jones, A. (1977). A controlled trial of the treatment of nocturnal enuresis in residential homes for children. *Behavior Research and Therapy* 15:1–16.

Kales, A., and Kales, J. D. (1974). Sleep disorders. *New England Journal of Medicine* 290:487–499.

Kardash, S., Hillman, E, and Werry, J. (1968). Efficacy of imipramine in childhood enuresis: A double-blind control study with placebo. *Canadian Medical Association Journal* 99:263–266.

Kimmel, H. D., and Kimmel, E. C. (1970). An instrumental conditioning method for the treatment of enuresis. *Journal of Behavior Therapy and Experimental Psychiatry* 1:121–123.

Kolvin, I., Tounch, J., Currah, J., Garside, R. F., Norlan, J., and Shaw, W. B. (1972). Enuresis: a descriptive analysis and a controlled trial. *Developmental Medicine and Child Neurology* 14:715–726.

Lovibond, S. H. (1963). Intermittent reinforcement in behavior therapy. *Behaviour Research and Therapy* 1:127–132.

—— (1964). *Conditioning and enuresis*. New York: Pergamon Press.

——, and Coote, M. A. (1970). Enuresis. In C. G. Costello, ed., *Symptoms of psychopathology*. New York: John Wiley & Sons.

Lund, C. J. (1963). Types of urinary incontinence. In C. J. Lund, ed., *Clinical obstetrics and gynecology*. New York: Harper & Row.

Mahony, D. T., Laferte, R. O., and Mahony, J. E. (1973). Observation on sphincter-augmenting effect of imipramine in children with urinary incontinence. *Urology* 1:317–323.

McConaghy, N. (1969). A controlled trial of imipramine, amphetamine, pad-and-bell conditioning and random wakening in the treatment of nocturnal enuresis. *Medical Journal of Australia* 2:237–239.

Meadow, R. (1970). Childhood enuresis. *British Medical Journal* 4:787–789.

Meadow, S. R. (1973). Buzzer ulcers. In I. Kolvin, R. C. MacKeith, and S. R. Meadow, eds., *Bladder Control and Enuresis*. Philadelphia: W. B. Saunders.

Morgan, R. T. T., and Young, G. C. (1975). Parental attitudes and the conditioning treatment of childhood enuresis. *Behaviour Research and Therapy* 13:197–199.

Mowrer, O. H., and Mowrer, W. M. (1938). Enuresis: a method for its study and treatment. *American Journal of Orthopsychiatry* 8:436–459.

Muellner, S. R. (1960a). Development of urinary control in children: a new concept in cause, prevention and treatment of primary enuresis. *Journal of Urology* 84:714–716.

—— (1960b). Development of urinary control in children. *Journal of the American Medical Association* 172:1256–1261.

Novick, J. (1966). Symptomatic treatment of acquired and persistent enuresis. *Journal of Abnormal Psychology* 71:363–368.

Oppel, W. C., Harper, P. A., and Rider, R. V. (1968). The age of obtaining bladder control. *Pediatrics* 42:614–626.

Paschalis, A. P., Kimmel, H. D., and Kimmel, E. (1972). Further study of deirenal instrumental conditioning in the treatment of enuresis nocturan. *Journal of behavior therapy and experimental psychiatry* 3:253–256.

Peterson, R. A., Wright, R. L. D., and Harlon, C. C. (1969). The effects of extending the CS-UCS interval on the effectiveness of the conditioning treatment for nocturnal enuresis. *Behaviour Research and Therapy* 7:351–357.

Pierce, C. M. (1975). Enuresis and encopresis. In A. M. Friedman, H. T. Kaplan, and B. J. Sadock, eds., *Comprehensive textbook of psychiatry II*. Baltimore: Williams & Wilkins.

Pooley, J. M., and Shersby, B. J. (1963). Enuresis: a new idea and a new way with an old treatment. *The Practitioner* 190:494.

Poussaint, A., and Ditman, K. (1965). A controlled study of imipramine (Tofranil) in the treatment of childhood enuresis. *Journal of Pediatrics* 67:283–290.

Ritvo, E. R., Ornitz, E. M., Gottlieb, F., Poussaint, A. F., Maron, B. J., Ditman, K. S., and Blinn, K. A. (1969). Arousal and nonarousal enuretic events. *American Journal of Psychiatry* 126:77–84.

Rohner, J. J., and Sanford, E. J. (1975). Imipramine toxicity. *Journal of Urology* 114:402–403.

Rutter, M., Yule, W., and Graham, P. (1973). Enuresis and behavioral deviance: some epidemiological considerations. In I. Kolvin, R. C. MacKeith, and S. R. Meadow, eds., *Bladder Control and Enuresis*. Philadelphia: W. B. Saunders.

Sachs, R., DeLeon, G., and Blackman, S. (1974). Psychological changes associated with conditioning functional enuresis. *Journal of Clinical Psychology* 30:271–276.

Salmon, M. A., Taylor, D. C., and Lee, D. (1973). On the EEG in enuresis. In I. Kolvin, R. C. MacKeith, and S. R. Meadow, eds., *Bladder Control and Enuresis*. Philadelphia: W. B. Saunders.

Samaan, M. (1972). The control of nocturnal enuresis by operant conditioning. *Journal of Behavior Therapy and Experimental Psychiatry* 3:103–105.

Schaffer, D., Costello, A. J., and Hill, I. D. (1968). Control of enuresis with imipramine. *Archives of Disease in Children* 43:665–671.

Shaffer, D. (1973). The association between enuresis and emotional disorder: a review of the literature. In I. Kolvin, R. C. MacKeith, and S. R. Meadow, eds., *Bladder Control and Enuresis*. Philadelphia: W. B. Saunders.

Sloop, E. W., and Kennedy, W. A. (1973). Institutionalized retarded nocturnal enuretic treated by a conditioning technique. *American Journal of Mental Deficiency* 77:717–721.

Smith, E. D. (1967). Diagnosis and management of the child with wetting. *Australian Pediatric Journal* 3:193–205.

Sperling, M. (1965). Dynamic considerations and treatment of enuresis. *Journal of the American Academy of Child Psychiatry* 4:19–31.

Starfield, B. (1967). Functional bladder capacity in enuretic and nonenuretic children. *Journal of Pediatrics* 70:777–782.

——, and Mellits, E. D. (1968). Increase in functional bladder capacity and improvements in enuresis. *Journal of Pediatrics* 72:483–487.

Stewart, M. A. (1975). Treatment of bedwetting. *Journal of the American Medical Association* 232:281–283.

Taylor, P. D., and Turner, R. K. (1975). A clinical trial of continuous, intermittent, and overlearning "bell-and-pad" treatments for nocturnal enuresis. *Behaviour Research and Therapy* 13:281–293.

Tough, J. H., Hawkins, R. P., MacArthur, M. M., and Ravensway, S. V. (1971). Modification of enuretic behavior by punishment: a new use for an old device. *Behavior Therapy* 2:567–574.

Turner, R. K., Young, G. C., and Rachman, S. (1970). Treatment of nocturnal enuresis by conditioning techniques. *Behaviour Research and Therapy* 8:367–381.

Vincent, S. A. (1964). Treatment of enuresis with a perineal pressure apparatus: The irritable bladder syndrome. *Developmental medicine and Child Neurology* 6:23–31.

Werry, J. S., and Cohrssen, J. (1965). Enuresis: an etiologic and therapeutic study. *Journal of Pediatrics* 67:423–431.

White, M. (1968). A thousand consecutive cases of enuresis: results of treatment. *The Medical Officer* 120:151–155.

Yates, A. J. (1970). *Behaviour therapy*. New York: John Wiley & Sons.

—— (1975). *Theory and practice in behavior therapy*. New York: John Wiley & Sons.

Yeates, W. K. (1973). Bladder function in normal micturition. In I. Kolvin, R. C. MacKeith, and S. R. Meadow, eds., *Bladder Control and Enuresis*. Philadelphia: W. B. Saunders.

Young, G. C. (1964). A "staggered-awakening" procedure in the treatment of enuresis. *The Medical Officer* 111:142–143.

—— (1965a). Conditioning treatment of enuresis. *Developmental Medicine and Child Neurology* 7:557–562.

—— (1965b). The aetiology of enuresis in terms of learning theory. *The Medical Officer* 113:19–22.

——, and Morgan, R. T. T. (1972). Overlearning in the conditioning treatment of enuresis. *Behaviour Research and Therapy* 10:419–420.

——, and Turner, R. K. (1965). CNS stimulant drugs and conditioning of nocturnal enuresis. *Behaviour Research and Therapy* 3:93–101.

Zaleski, A., Garrard, J. W., and Shokier, M. H. K. (1973). Nocturnal enuresis: the importance of a small bladder capacity. In I. Kolvin, R. C. MacKeith, and S. R. Meadow, eds., *Bladder Control and Enuresis*. Philadelphia: W. B. Saunders.

Chapter Ten

Learning Disabilities

RUDOLPH F. WAGNER Ph.D.,
Associate Professor
Valdosta State College, GA.

BRIEF HISTORICAL OVERVIEW

Perhaps no other field has made such rapid strides in the past than the Learning Disabilities (LD) movement, both in this country and abroad. Interestingly enough, the movement has gained momentum only in the past 2 decades after having remained dormant for many years with only initial efforts to define the conditions under various terms.

The first mention of definite reading problems was made by a German physician, Adolf Kussmaul, in 1877, who studied aphasia cases and had paid special attention to speech pathology and related brain functions. He wrote about his observations and decided to call his special cases *Worttaubheit und Wortblindheit*, e.g., word deafness and word blindness (Kussmaul, 1877). In England in 1896, W. A. Morgan described a case of congenital word blindness in the medical literature. He mentioned that obviously children he had examined could see with their eyes, but they acted as if they were blind to words on the printed page. They could see a cat running, but they could not read the word cat. Still later, in 1896, James Hinshelwood, an ophthalmologist in Glasgow, also

235

made an important contribution to the study of reading disability and wrote about word blindness and visual memory, and remained a "torchlighter" in this field for over 2 decades.

Another opthalmologist, Rudolf Berlin in Germany, coined the word *dyslexia* to describe the poor taste his patients had developed for reading. Dyslexia is derived from Greek *dys-*, faulty or impaired, and *lexis*, meaning speech, from *legein*, to speak, but pertaining to words. In Europe today, the word *legathenia* is widely used, a Latin derivative, referring to a weakness in reading. The first bridges to education were laid by the American neurologist, Dr. Samuel Orton (1937), who thought of the inability to read as a laterality problem, that is, confusion between the two hemispheres of the brain. The short circuits characteristic of LD might be caused by a lack of hemispheric dominance in the brain, possibly producing mixed-up letters and words, a condition Orton called *strephosymbolia*, a Greek combination meaning "scrambled symbols."

Orton's pioneer work in the United States was perpetuated in the formation of the Orton Society, an association devoted to the diagnosis and treatment of dyslexia which they see as a language disorder. Orton's coworker, Anna Gillingham, a psychologist, worked out a remedial approach, the so-called Orton-Gillingham method, which emphasizes a tactile-kinesthetic approach to the problem.

With the advent of strong sentiments about handicapped children and Special Education programs in this country, often sponsored by sizeable financial grants, the LD movement gained an unprecedented momentum. New leaders have emerged in the field of research, some of them to be mentioned in this chapter. For a comparison of the early pioneer work done by Kussmaul, Berlin, and Orton, the reader is referred to an article by Wagner (1976a) which analyzes the contributions of these three men in the field of LD and makes comparisons as to etiology, symptoms, and diagnostic terminology.

CONCEPTS AND DEFINITIONS RELATED TO RESEARCH

The term Learning Disability (LD) eventually emerged from a need to identify and serve a group of children and adolescents who experienced school failures but eluded the traditional categories of exceptionality. Three concepts now seem to have evolved in the field of LD, as follows: (1) The term brain injury was primarily promoted by the pioneer work of Strauss and Lehtinen (1947), Cruickshank *et al.* (1961), and others who sought etiology for LD in the brain and its neurological mechanisms. (2)

The term minimal brain dysfunction, (MBD) became popular very rapidly after it was promoted by a three-phase project headed by Clements (1966) and jointly sponsored by the U.S. Department of Health, Education and Welfare and the National Society for Crippled Children and Adults. (3) Finally, Kirk's (1962) coining of the term learning disability along with the development of the Illinois Test of Psycholinguistic Abilities (ITPA) by the Kirks (1966) made the term acceptable to parents and educators, if not popular.

Speculation as well as serious hypotheses regarding the etiology of LD have become proliferated in recent years. Wagner (1971a) has proposed a task-oriented model in which two systems, namely the learner and the task, are seen as incompatible in LD children and can only be made compatible through modification or remediation of either system. Recently, Mercer, Forgnone, and Wolking (1976) have focused on the various definitions of LD used in the United States by examining them in a systematic manner and in an analytic framework. They came up with definitional components in relation to the definition of the National Advisory Committee on Handicapped (NACHC) of the U.S. Office of Education (USOE). This definition reads as follows:

> Children with special learning disabilities exhibit a disorder in one or more of the basic psychological processes involved in understanding or in using spoken or written languages. These may be manifested in disorders of listening, thinking, talking, reading, writing, spelling, or arithmetic. They include conditions which have been referred to as perceptual handicaps, brain injury, minimal brain dysfunction, dyslexia, developmental aphasia, etc. They do *not* include learning problems which are due primarily to visual, hearing or motor handicaps, to mental retardation, emotional disturbance, or to environmental disadvantage (USOE, 1968, p. 34).

Mercer *et al.*, came up with 15 components of LD definitions, among them intelligence, primary exclusions, neurological impairment, affective, etc., and conclude: "It is possible that the medical versus educational issue will be minimized, and definitional factors can be evaluated in terms of their usefulness in identifying and serving learning disabled persons." They go on to say that "Traditionally, attempts to formulate definitions of LD have focused on the use of characteristics, e.g., hyperactivity, perceptual impairment, perseveration, emotional liability." This implies that the problem is within the individual. However, a study of functional relationships between behavior and environmental conditions would focus on conditions outside the individual and could, perhaps, enlighten our understanding of the behavioral manifestations. This view is in line with work done by Haring (1974) and Wagner (1971a).

Today LD is often seen as an "umbrella concept" not only including reading (dyslexia) as the primary area of dysfunction, but also including spelling, handwriting, arithmetic, comprehension and speech. These areas can show up behaviorally in one area alone, or they may appear in clusters and combinations. A commonly observed combination is reading and spelling low, with arithmetic relatively intact. The umbrella concept is shown in Fig. 1.

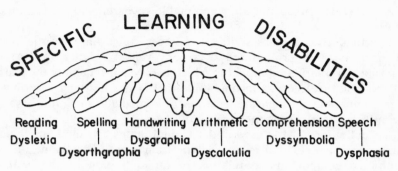

Fig. 1. The "umbrella concept" of specific learning disabilities.

More so than in any other field, research in LD is truly interdisciplinary and has harmoniously combined many scientific disciplines in the search for answers to pinpoint the causes of LD and remedial intervention techniques.

BEHAVIORAL CHARACTERISTICS

Children with Specific Learning Disabilities show definite behavioral characteristics. While some authorities simply list these characteristics and state that they may occur in various combinations with not all of them present necessarily, others speak of an LD syndrome which implies a cluster of specific symptoms. The characteristics can also be divided into primary and secondary. Among the secondary characteristics, emotional reactions to continuous academic failures are cited. Poor academic performance, significantly below expectancy for age and intelligence, is another.

Among the most often stated behavioral characteristics in LD conditions are:

1. Poor visual discrimination
2. Poor auditory memory for words and/or visual sounds
3. Persistent reversal errors, found in single letters or words

4. Reversal of sequence in words, numbers, or events
5. Weakly established handedness
6. Clumsiness and poor hand control
7. Hyperactivity and distractibility
8. Poor concentration

The above list is not complete. A simple check list is reproduced in Table 1 to give the reader some idea of the different behavioral syndrome in LD children (Wagner, 1971). Speech characteristics are also included in this list.

While psychological and educational professionals have their set of characteristics, pediatricians, neurologists, and psychiatrists have their own set of guides (see Richardson, 1966). Here is a partial list:

1. Mild tremor, especially on effort; mild choreaform or athetoid movements
2. Hyper-reflexia
3. Excessive clumsiness
4. Monocular vision or minor ocular imbalance
5. Disturbance of body image, including right–left confusion
6. Impaired form perception
8. Hyperkinesis with distractibility, short attention span, irritability, and emotiona! lability.

Again, the symptoms do not necessarily have to be present *in toto* to establish a diagnosis of LD, but an isolated symptom would not be sufficient.

No diagnosis should be complete without a social history which would include developmental milestones and "red flags" in the child's history. Pre-, peri-, and postnatal trauma are often significant in their occurrence, and so are postnatal diseases and accidents resulting in damage to the nervous system.

The subject of lateral dominance has received much attention in the past in connection with LD conditions. However, more recent studies indicate that "crossed dominance" in and by itself is not a cause, nor indication, of an LD condition, but may contribute to the severity of the condition if it does exist as observed by other characteristics that allow for an establishment of the diagnosis.

LD children usually show secondary emotional reactions to their primary learning problems due to continuous failure in school, with social concomitants such as rejection by teachers or teasing from peers, not to mention parental disapproval and discipline. These secondary reactions may show up behaviorally as defense and avoidance mechanisms, compensatory mechanisms, aggressiveness, and anxiety and withdrawal (Wagner, 1970c).

Table 1. Characteristic Signs of Specific Learning Disabilities
Rudolph F. Wagner, Ph.D.

GENERAL OBSERVATIONS

	Yes	No
1. Is the student's intelligence within the broad range of "average" or above, based on observations, group test results, comparisons, and other indications?	☐	☐
2. Does the school record indicate reading difficulties from the first grade? Do teachers' comments include statements such as, "He could do it if he tried"? or, "He seems to have higher potential"?	☐	☐
3. Has he ever received special tutoring with conventional teaching methods for reading, but shown little or no improvement afterwards?	☐	☐
4. Is his reading level two years or more below expectancy with respect to his mental ability and educational opportunities? (In children aged 5–7, this discrepancy would be less than two years.)	☐	☐
5. Does he forget previously learned words some days, but remember them on other days?	☐	☐
6. Is there evidence of similar reading difficulties in other male members of the family line?	☐	☐
7. Does he show emotional reactions to the reading problem, such as strong aversion to reading, feelings of inferiority, aggressive tendencies or behavior problems?	☐	☐
8. Does he feel "stupid," not smart, because he cannot read like others in his class?	☐	☐
9. Were there any injuries or significant incidents before, during, or after birth?	☐	☐
10. Has he ever been seen by a medical doctor because of hyper-activity or nervousness?	☐	☐

PERCEPTUAL ABILITIES AND ORIENTATION

	Yes	No
11. Does he have difficulties in following a series of detailed directions? Does he mix up yesterday and tomorrow?	☐	☐
12. Is he unable to recall with reasonable accuracy a series of events in proper time sequence?	☐	☐
13. In his reading of text, does he omit words and phrases, skip lines, or lose his place?	☐	☐
14. Does he have difficulty in school copying words correctly from the board?	☐	☐
15. Does he frequently ignore parts of words, both in copying and in reading? For example, does he read "stilt" for slit, "cover" for clover, or "plot" for pilot?	☐	☐
16. Does he often and persistently read some words from right to left, such as "was" for saw, "pot" for top, or "no" for on?	☐	☐
17. Does he have mixed dominance, i.e., does he use the eye opposite his dominant or preferred hand? Can he use both hands equally well when writing? Does he kick with the foot opposite his writing hand?	☐	☐
18. Does he show evidence of poor orientation in space? Does he experience difficulty in telling left from right during games and activities? Are directional concepts confusing in general, e.g., east and west, before and behind, days of the week?	☐	☐

Table 1. (*Continued*)

PERCEPTUAL—MOTOR ACTIVITIES

	Yes	No
19. Does he show poor ability to reproduce rhythm in sequence?	☐	☐
20. Is his handwriting cramped, slowly done, or very messy? Does his written work show many erasures, mark-outs, or mistakes in general? Is his work poorly spaced in general, such as words too far apart or running together?	☐	☐
21. Does he frequently miscopy a work in one place and copy it correctly in another? For example, he may spell house as hous, hose, horse, or hours all on the same page of work.	☐	☐
22. Does he often make letter and number formation from down to up or from right to left, starting at the wrong place, but perhaps ending with the correct symbol?	☐	☐
23. Does he habitually and persistently reverse some of his letters and/or numbers? For example, b for d, 6 for 9, 12 for 21, or p for q?	☐	☐
24. Is his motor coordination poor, either in using play equipment or in manipulating smaller objects in the classroom or at home? Does he hold his pencil in a clumsy way when writing? Is he considered awkward by others? Does he drop things easily?	☐	☐
25. Does he appear clumsy when hopskipping? Does he throw a ball with his right arm but write with his left, or vice-versa?	☐	☐

SPEECH AND LANGUAGE BEHAVIOR

	Yes	No
26. Is his speech immature, like baby talk? Was he slow in learning to talk?	☐	☐
27. Does he sometimes confuse the order of syllables in multisyllabic words, such as "japama" for pajama, "pasghetti" for spaghetti, and "aminals" for animals?	☐	☐
28. Does he have difficulty pronouncing words which contain consonantal clusters, such as episcopal, statistics, or crisp biscuits?	☐	☐
29. Does he have difficulty in hearing sound difference between similar words, such as pin/pan, lease/leash, bend/bent, or his/hiss?	☐	☐
30. Does he show a poor ability to associate sounds with letter symbols? Or, can he give the proper sounds of letters individually while he is unable to blend the sounds into words?	☐	☐
31. Is his comprehsnsion of materials greatly influenced either by oral or by silent reading; i.e., is there significant improvement in understanding when one or the other method is employed?	☐	☐
32. Does he rely heavily on pictures in the book when reading? For example, he may look at the picture of a duck but read the printed word bird as "duck."	☐	☐
33. Is his spelling particularly poor or even bizarre in original compositions? Does he make errors such as "cud" for could, "luns" for lunch and "wuns" for once?	☐	☐
34. Did he ever develop a stutter, possibly after attempts were made to change his handedness?	☐	☐
35. Did he have a significant delay in speech or show difficulty with certain sounds which persisted for a while, especially the r, w, and th sounds?	☐	☐

DIAGNOSTIC EVALUATION

While a complete psychological evaluation is necessary in LD condition, and usually mandated by state regulations, the diagnosis must include an educational assessment. This combined evaluation has become known as a psychoeducational evaluation. It can be done by a psychologist who is familiar with educational procedures, or it is executed separately by an educator and a psychologist.

Evaluation includes an estimate of the child's intelligence level, carried out with acceptable instruments such as the Wechsler tests. A test which yields subtest patterns is preferable here because a wide scatter is considered significant and of diagnostic value, as is the difference between verbal and performance scales. In addition to the intelligence measures, the following tests are usually included in the battery:

Bender Visual–Motor Gestalt Test;
Tests of Visual–Perceptual Ability (e.g., Frostig);
Tests of Auditory Discrimination (e.g., Wepman);
Lateral Dominance (hand, eye, foot);
Personality (e.g., House–Tree–Person);
Academic Skills (e.g., WRAT by Jastak).

Among the more educationally oriented tests, the Illinois Test of Psycholinguistic Abilities (ITPA) has received much attention as a means of evaluating learning disabilities. The test is described by Kirk and Kirk (1973). However, there are still controversies regarding the ITPA that need further clarification. For example, Hammill et al. (1975) investigated the relationship of the ITPA subtests to measures of academic performance and found that "the results failed to support the hypothesis that psycholinguistic abilities, with one exception, are related to academic proficiency. Another study (Waugh, 1975), is titled: The ITPA: Ballast or Bonanza for the School Psychologist, and shows, inter alia, that remediation directed towards strengths and weaknesses in sensory or perceptual processing, as measured by the ITPA subtests, has not been effective. Waugh also states that the ITPA is not a test of psycholinguistics since it does not yield information about the units of natural language The controversies seem to persist.

Secondary emotional reactions can be measured by the Draw-A-Person Test or commonly used projective instruments. This author has found the Zulliger Test (Zulliger, 1969), an abbreviated Rorschach-type test, and the Kahn Test of Symbol Arrangement (Kahn, 1957; Wagner, 1970a, 1971c) very helpful devices. It should be pointed out that a diagnosis for learning disabilities primarily addresses itself to disabilities in the academic and learning realm, and only uses evaluations of emotional stability in the peripheral or secondary areas. This does not exclude the fact that after the evaluation is completed, a diagnosis of primary emotional disturbance may result based on test data and observations.

From an interdisciplinary standpoint, a thorough diagnosis should also include a physical, ophthalmological, and neurological evaluation, to rule out organic conditions.

REMEDIAL/THERAPEUTIC INTERVENTION TECHNIQUES

Remedial therapies are primarily educational in nature unless strong secondary emotional reactions accompany the LD condition in which case a trained professional such as the psychologist or psychiatrist would conduct the sessions. Psychoeducational and psychotherapeutic intervention approaches will be taken up separately below.

Educational intervention approaches and techniques usually are based on certain theories or theoretical assumptions advanced by various professionals in the different disciplines. Almost all approaches specify that the one-to-one relationship is important as LD children are distractible and cannot learn in groups. This means one tutor to every child. Because such relationship is costly, frequent use is made of volunteers and peers who are trained by specialists to do certain routine teaching jobs.

Among the proponents of perceptual-motor approaches to remediation are Strauss and Lehtinen (1947) who took two sources as starting points for their own work, e.g., Goldstein and his work on brain-injured adults, and Seguin's work with the retarded. Strauss also drew on Gestalt psychology to explain perceptual defects. His approach was essentially to reach brain-injured children in special classes as interim environments, but his techniques foreshadowed today's remedial approaches to learning disabilities.

When Kephart (1960) wrote his book on slow learners, the term "LD" had not been coined. Kephart dealt with marginal children, not normal, and not severely handicapped. He emphasized a logical approach to teaching basic skills which his children were lacking, e.g., form perception and discrimination, ocular control, or sensory-motor coordination, to name a few.

Among the proponents with a neurophysiological flavor is Delacato (1963) whose theory has been subject to much debate and criticism.

Delacato shows how the brain has become organized over the years, the ontogenic development, and established levels in the brain according to the physiological development. His remedial approaches include the patterning technique where the nervous system is taught certain stage patterns of earlier development which the child has not yet mastered or skipped for some reason.

Among the more unusual methods is Heckelman's (1966) Neurological-Impress Remedial-Reading Technique. The individual method consists of the instructor and the student meeting for approximately 15 minutes a day in consecutive daily sessions. The child is seated slightly in front of the instructor, both reading the same text out loud. The student hears his instructor pronounce the words, can follow the rhythm, and is corrected only by hearing the differences between his and the instructor's pronunciation. There are no interrogations or testing. Heckelman considers his technique multi-sensory in nature and part of an audioneural-conditioning process whereby the incorrect reading habits of the child are suppressed and then replaced with correct, fluid reading habits.

This author has used the method in conjunction with other remedial approaches, leaving the Heckelman approach to the parents while during the day a remedial reading teacher conducts the actual lessons on a regular basis, e.g., twice or three times per week for 1 hour.

Finally, Barsch (1965) belongs to the group of theorists who promoted a perceptual-motor approach to remediation. He maintains that whatever impediment stands in the way of the child must be corrected. Barsch has a physiologic curriculum with a well worked out movement theory derived from *movigenics*, the study of movement patterns leading to learning efficiency. He has worked out a series of activities which are too detailed to be described here.

The second category of remedial approaches is developmental in nature, with an emphasis on visual perception. Among the early proponents of this approach was Marianne Frostig who first emphasized assessment and remediation techniques in the area of visual perception. The five areas of her well-known Developmental Test of Visual Perception (Frostig, 1963) contains the following sub-areas:

    I. Eye-Motor Coordination
   II. Figure–Ground
  III. Constancy of Shape
  IV. Position in Space
   V. Spatial Relationships

If and when deficits in these areas are found, they are remediated with specifically prepared exercises. Frostig is also interested in helping the child with social and emotional adjustment. Factor analyses of the five tests have shown overlaps, as can be expected.

Another representative in this category is Getman (1965) with a program of visuomotor training assuming that visual perception is learned. Getman includes four processes in his training, namely anti-gravity, centering, identification, and speech–auditory. Getman's work is primarily based on the ocular mechanism and visual perception, but he goes much beyond this.

Among other approaches are the linguistic one, spearheaded by the American neurologist/psychiatrist Samuel Orton who assumed some hemispheric interference as the cause of learning disabilities. The mixed-up products of his LD subjects were called "strephosymbolia," Greek for scrambled symbols. Together with Gillingham and Stilman he developed an educational method by which the child is retrained primarily through the tactile and kinesthetic sensory avenues. The approach is popular to this day and has contributed much to the advance of the LD movement in this country.

Finally, Fernald (1943) should be mentioned in this array of remedial theories and approaches as diagnostic-remedial in nature. She advocates to monitor constantly the child's progress through testing, with subsequent remediation of the needed or deficient areas.

In more recent years, many people have combined "the best of everything" and developed their own, eclectic, unorthodox method, suspended in a tutorial relationship. This unique relationship is worth exploring further.

While remediation in LD condition has had much attention in the literature, the actual tutorial relationship has had little attention. Granted, it is a type of counseling or psychotherapy technique, but then it is only one aspect of the entire situation called tutorial relationship. What is being done here is work on two levels, Cognitive or Skill, and Affective or Emotional. Wagner (1976b) has suggested a simple model that shows how the two levels are covered by the remedial teacher. The normal child needs little attention on the affective level; he is taught primarily on the cognitive level and in larger groups, e.g., the classroom situation. On the other hand, the LD child will need a lot of personal attention, on the affective level, with some work done on the cognitive level, until his deficiencies are corrected and the teacher can return to the skill level. Figure 2 illustrates the model.

Adjuncts to remedial work with LD children can enhance the process. For example, behavioral modification can be used to make the LD child more motivated by working for rewards (reinforcers), or make him produce more.

The Two Levels of Teaching in a Tutorial Model

Affective Level

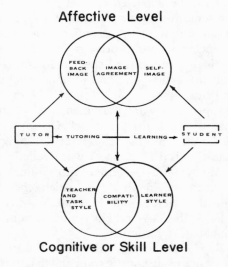

Cognitive or Skill Level

Fig. 2. The two levels of teaching in a tutorial model. From: Wagner, R., Helping the word-blind. The Center for Applied Research in Education, N.Y., 1976b.

Another adjunct to therapy with the LD child is medication. There are some pharmaceutical drugs on the market that are prescribed by physicians particularly where lack of concentration, distractibility, or hyperactivity is part of the LD syndrome. Drugs like Ritalin, Phenobarbital, and Mellaril are examples.

While emotional reactions in LD children are regarded secondary to the learning disability, they frequently reflect their feelings of inferiority and aggression in their drawings of a human figure (see Fig. 3, for example). In addition to the one-to-one tutorial situation which is often sufficient to reduce the secondary emotional reactions, more effective or specific therapuetic intervention techniques can be used. For example, individual and group counseling can be an effective adjunct to overall therapy with these children. Small group counseling likewise can be effective. If the LD condition is seen as a family problem, or affects the entire family including siblings, family therapy is indicated. This author has experimented with a series of thematic situation cards (see Fig. 4) where the LD child can project his feelings onto the situations and abreact his emotions in a therapeutic situation, e.g., with the counselor in his school or classroom.

Fig. 3. Human figure drawings by learning disabled children. (A) *Aggressive Stance*. Drawing by a boy aged 14, IQ 107, eighth grader reading on fourth grade level, with numerous reversals of words. Note aggressive stance as a secondary emotional reaction to his learning problem. (B) *Insecurity*. Drawing by a boy aged 13, IQ 125, eighth grade, reading on late sixth grade level. Handwriting dysgraphic. Note interrupted line drawings suggestive of feelings of insecurity.

CURRENT ISSUES AND PROBLEMS

Due to the fact that LD conditions are relative newcomers in psychological research, problems and issues exist in specific areas.

Early Identification

It would be impossible to imagine in the medical field that a disease is known and can be diagnosed, but nobody would bother about early detection until the case comes to the physician's attention or the patient dies from the disease. While LD is not considered a disease as such, the analogy of early detection and prevention holds. Why is it possible that young men and women in high school and college are "suddenly"

Fig. 4. Thematic situation card developed by author. Artwork by Whitney Hardy.

discovered as having a dyslexic condition, when this condition must have been quite visible in earlier school years and even before school entrance? Precisely this is the problem today, a lack of systematic means of identifying youngsters in our schools with LD who, if found early, could be remediated at once and prevented from suffering agony and failure in later years. Many states make early identification mandatory, within the confines of Special Education programs, but the mandate is not consistent in all states and all schools.

Validity of Diagnostic Instruments

There are still some unresolved questions as to reliability and validity of test instruments used in the diagnosis of LD. For example, while the subtest scatter of the Wechsler Tests is supposedly of great diagnostic significance, some professionals attach importance to differences of 2 or 3 points which, statistically, are not significant. As in other areas of psychological practice, clinical judgement prevails and may present hazards. The suitability of the ITPA as an assessment instrument has been discussed above. At this point the use of the ITPA as the sole instrument in diagnosing LD is not feasible, nor does it appear valid to base educational prescriptions on single ITPA subtests.

Lack of Treatment Facilities

Educators often lament that in LD we are long on diagnosis but short on treatment. There is truth in the statement, no doubt. In this country, we lack an adequate number of treatment facilities for LD. If they exist, they are forbiddingly expensive as far as tuition is concerned and are available only for an affluent few. Special Education programs for LD children are becoming more frequent throughout the country, but if the child is not in a public school but in the private sector, the dilemma is great. While urban areas usually have adequate facilities, rural areas are in want of them. The present strategies of dealing with LD children is to "mainstream" the milder cases, give resource help to the moderate cases, and only isolate the severe cases. Isolation of LD children brings about a "hothousing effect" (Wagner, 1976c) which overemphasizes the weak areas of the child's LD condition while at the same time he is not offered regular fare of the curriculum and suffers by it, often lowering the IQ as a concomitant.

Plight of Adolescents and Young Adults

There is a tremendous shortage of facilities that treat LD conditions of older students. Once out of the public school system, very little is available to help the grown-up man or woman when LD is discovered. These people also have suffered vocational setbacks since they cannot read, write, or do arithmetic, sufficiently proficient to hold a job, however menial. Careful vocational planning will have to be an important element in the basic curriculum of LD children. Handwriting in some LD cases is often so atrocious that the employer will reject their application forms before they ever get to their personal interview. The sample handwriting of a dysgraphic boy tells the story (Fig. 5).

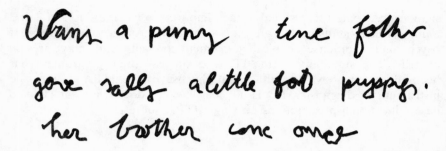

Fig. 5. Sample of dysgraphic handwriting: Boy, age 12, dysgraphic. Note phonetic spelling, "m" written as "n", inconsistency of directionality (slant), loops in o's and a's, inconsistency in pressure and spacing.

Delinquency and LD Conditions

The correlation in studies done on delinquent populations regarding LS is alarmingly high, yet a mere correlation does not allow the researcher to make inferences as to causality: Is the boy delinquent because he cannot read? Or, are children who are criminally inclined destined to become poor readers? Many penal institutions and detention homes have incorporated reading instructions and remedial reading in their rehabilitative programs.

Terminology and Diagnostic Labels

The labyrinthine confusion in LD terminology exists to this day. Early labels, such as dyslexia, *amnesia verbalis visualis*, strephosymbolia, word blindness, etc., have given no way to controversies over definitions and terms. The literature still is abundantly cluttered with terms such as phonetic dyslexia, spatial dyscalculia, figure alexia, primary developmental dyslexia, dysphonetic and dyseidetic dyslexia, etc., *ad nauseam*. No real clarification appears in sight. Governmental regulations do not always clarify the situation but add perplexity in terms of formulae for LD conditions, diagnostic straight jackets determined by financial funding of projects and LD classes rather than professional concern for clarity.

REFERENCES

Barsch, R. H. (1965). *A Movigenic Curriculum*. Madison, Wisc. Bureau for Handicapped Children.

Berlin, R. (1887). *Eine Besondere Art der Wortblindheit* (Dyslexia). Private Publication: Wiesbaden.

Clements, S. D. (1966). *Learning Disabilities-who*? Paper presented at the *44th Annual Convention of the Council for Exceptional Children*, Washington, D.C.

Cruickshank, W. M. (1961). *A Teaching Method for Brain Injured and Hyperactive Children*. Syracuse: Syracuse University Press.

Delacato, C. H. (1963). *The Diagnosis and Treatment of Speech and Reading Problems*. Springfield. Thomas.

Fernald, G. (1943). On certain language disabilities: nature and treatment. Baltimore, Md.: Williams & Wilkins.

Frostig, M., and Horne, D. (1964). *The Frostig Program for the Development of Visual Perception*. Chicago: Follett.

Getman, G. N. (1965). The visuomotor complex in the acquisition of learning skills. In J. Hellmuth, ed., *Language Disorders*. Seattle, Wash. Special Child Publications of the Seattle Seguin School, Inc.

Hammill, D., Park, R., and Newcome, P. (1975). Psycholinguistic correlations of academic achievement. *Journal of School Psychology* 13:248–254.

Haring, N. A. (1974). Systematic instructional procedures: an instructional hierarchy. In S. A. Brainard, ed., *Learning Disabilities: Issues and Recommendations for Research*. Washington, D.C.: U.S. Dept. of Health, Education and Welfare, 1974.

Heckelman, R. G. (1966). Using the neurological impress remedial-reading techniques. *Academic Therapy* Summer:235–239.

Hinshelwood, J. (1896). A case of Dyslexia: A peculiar form of word blindness *Lancet* 2:1451–1454.

Kahn, T. (1957). The Kahn test of symbol arrangement. *Perceptual and Motor Skills*, Monograph Suppl. 1.

Kephart, N. C. (1960). *The Slow Learner in the Classroom*. Columbus, Ohio: Charles E. Merrill.

Kirk, S. (1962). *Educating Exceptional Children*. Boston: Houghton Mifflin.

—— (1966). *Diagnosis and remediation of Psycholinguistic Abilities*. Urbana, Ill.: University of Illinois Press.

——, and Kirk, W. (1973). *Psycholinguistic Learning Disabilities: Diagnosis and Remediation*. Urbana, Ill.: University of Illinois Press.

Kussmaul, A. (1877). Disturbance of speech. In H. von Ziemssen, ed., *Encyclopedia of the Practice of Medicine*. New York: William Wood.

Mercer, C., Forgnone, C., and Wolking, W. (1976). Definitions of learning disabilities used in the United States. *Journal of Learning Disabilities* 9:376–386.

Morgan, W. P. (1896). A case of congenital word-blindness. *British Medical Journal* 2:1378.

Orton, S. (1937). *Reading, Writing and Speech Problems in Children*. New York: Norton.

Richardson, S. (1966). *Learning Disabilities: An Introduction*. Proceedings of the *3rd Annual International Conference of the ACLD*, An International Approach to Learning Disabilities of Children and Youth, Tulsa, Okla. (March 3–5, 1966).

Strauss, A., and Lehtinen, L. (1947). *Psychopathology and Education of the Brain-Injured Child*. New York: Grune and Stratton.

Wagner, R. F. (1970a). Form symbolization in normal readers and dyslexics based on a modified pattern recognition theory. *International Journal of Psychology* 1(3):51–56.

—— (1970b). Secondary emotional reactions in children with learning disabilities. *Mental Hygiene* 54:577–579.

—— (1970c). *Dyslexia and Your Child*. New York: Harper and Row.

—— (1971a). Specific reading disabilities: The incompatibility of two systems. *Journal of Learning Disabilities* May:260–263.

—— (1971b). Symbolization deficits in dyslexic conditions. *Academic Therapy* 6:359–365.

—— (1976a). Three early pioneers in the diagnosis of specific reading problems: Adolf Kussmaul, Rudolf Berlin, and Samuel Orton. *Reading in Virginia*, March:14–16.

—— (1976b). *Helping the Wordblind*. New York: The Centers for Applied Research in Education.

—— (1976c). *Cognitive loss and perceptual gain over a substantial time space in children with learning disabilities*. Unpublished Manuscript, Richmond, Virginia.

Waugh, R. P. (1975). The I.T.P.A.: Ballast or bonanza for the school psychologist. *Journal of School Psychology* 13(3):201–208.

Zulliger, H. (1969). *The Zulliger Individual and Group Test*. New York: International Universities Press.

Chapter Eleven

Early Infantile Autism
and Theraplay

AUSTIN M. DESLAURIERS

The present chapter will describe a specific treatment approach to the developmental and behavioral disturbances present in early infantile autism. We call this treatment method: Theraplay. It is specific to the autistic syndrome because it was derived from a conceptual understanding of the nature of the autistic disturbance of infancy and developed as a methodological design to assess the validity of this understanding.

What is early infantile autism? Since Kanner defined and circumscribed this syndrome in 1943, this behavioral syndrome has undergone a variety of modifications and vicissitudes related mostly to the tendency of observers and scientists to reduce an obscure and mysterious condition to a more known and familiar one. Some viewed it as a type of mental retardation of organic origin; others declared it to be a form of early childhood psychosis of the schizophrenic variety; others again saw it as an essentially aphasic disorder or a severe and ill-defined speech and learning disability. To avoid these confusions, many researchers today refer to early infantile autism as "Kanner's syndrome" which is intended to refer to a behavioral "autistic disturbance of affective contact" which is present in early infancy and possesses specific characteristics that are neither those of mental retardation as such, nor those of childhood schizophrenia.

Rutter (1971), who has given this matter of differential diagnosis a considerable amount of attention, characterizes the syndrome in the following terms: "Autism (as used in this context) was shown by appearance of aloofness and distance and apparent lack of interest in other people, failure to join in group play, the avoidance of eye to eye gaze, little variation in facial expression, infrequent exhibition of emotions or humor, and a relative lack of sympathy or empathy for other people . . .. The ritualistic and compulsive phenomena took any or all of four forms: a morbid attachment to unusual objects, peculiar preoccupations, a resistance to changes of any kind, and a variety of other quasi-obsessive rituals and compulsions. These features are closely similar to those outlined in Kanner's original paper (1943). In the present state of knowledge it appears that the diagnosis of infantile autism should be restricted to children who show autism (as defined above) *and* delays in speech and language development, *and* ritualistic and compulsive phenomena. One further diagnostic criterion also necessary is onset in infancy. Kanner stated that the onset is during very early infancy but that it may occasionally occur as late as 2 years of age (Eisenberg and Kanner, 1956; Kanner and Lesser, 1958). In particular, as Eisenberg (1968) has stressed, it is important to differentiate autism from the disorder in which the child develops perfectly normally at first and then, usually after a period of vague illness about the age of 3–5 years, loses speech, becomes incontinent, generally regresses, and is often very overactive."

The following passage was written by the mother of an autistic child and provides an excellent description:

The first year. We were unaware of anything wrong with Kathryn. In fact we were very happy and content to have such a sweet and good baby. We did not realize she was too good to be true. We had an older child—Mark. As an infant he was active, restless, and a continual case of hunger. Kathryn was so content and good that it was sheer joy to have such a baby. People looked shocked and probably doubted the veracity of my statement that Kathryn had never cried for food or milk since she was three months old. She never cried at all! This did cause me some concern as I had heard that crying strengthens the lungs, and I was sure she would have weak lungs.

Another sign of trouble during her first year that should have alarmed us, but didn't, was that she never cried for attention. She had no need to be held or cuddled as a normal baby does.

Still another warning sign was Kathryn's ever-increasing fear of anything, anyone, or any place new to her. She would cry and not be consoled until she was safely home again. Just getting in the car frightened her, and she would cover her eyes. This fear of change or newness began around six to eight months as she became aware of her environment. We couldn't go to church, to the grocery store, or anywhere as a family because poor little Kathryn would cry the whole time. We catered to her fears and went on errands singly, always taking Mark so he didn't miss out on so much.

Her fears included our dog, which surprised me. Children are often afraid of dogs but usually not if they have a dog, and certainly not of their own dog. Bessy was quite a large and clumsy dog so I thought perhaps her size explained Kathryn's fear. She was so small compared to Bessy.

Kathryn's physical development went along very normally. She sat, crawled, stood holding on, and walked holding on to furniture all within a normal range. She started to crawl at seven and a half months and was a very proficient little girl. She was walking around the furniture by 9 to 10 months. But she was still walking by holding on to the furniture at 16 months. It was during this interim that we began to have apprehensions about her. Why wouldn't she let go and try to walk? She wasn't hanging on for balance, only touching for security.

I took her to our former family doctor for her first year physical checkup. I told him of her fear of everything. To my chagrin he just chuckled and commented that he had no pill for that, and we would have to let time take care of it. Of course, she was crying all the time in his office. He told me to bring her back another day when she wasn't crying because he couldn't examine her while she was so upset. That was the last time I ever went to that doctor. I came home and immediately called the pediatrician to whom we had always taken Mark and made Kathryn's first appointment. I knew she would cry no matter when I took her, so there was absolutely no point in waiting for a day when she wouldn't. Dr. L. examined her thoroughly and pronounced her in fine health. On the day of our appointment the doctor's waiting room was so crowded that I decided to save my questions of her fears for the time being.

Feeding became more of a problem as each month passed. She showed no interest in food at all, and even less in feeding herself. I just brought her to the kitchen at mealtime, and she ate passively as I gave her each spoonful. I never knew for sure when or if she was full. When the food on the plate was gone that was okay with her. I did get a rather wry chuckle out of a statement in Dr. Spock's book. He said that no child would starve to death if food was in front of them. I thought to myself—he just hasn't seen Kathryn, because I know she would. I even skipped two meals one day in hopes she would accept new food. It failed completely and I didn't have the courage or strength of determination to starve her any more. It was clear that she wasn't aware of being hungry anyway.

For her first birthday her Daddy gave her a small pink animal. We all called it Fuzzy. Fuzzy became Kathryn's constant companion. He seemed to give her some sort of warmth and security that we couldn't give her. He slept with her, and she carried him and hugged him most all of the time. Not until we began her therapy sessions at nearly three years of age did she part with her beloved Fuzzy.

She made no sounds or coos as a baby, and there was no hint of the beginnings of speech. At this time I wasn't concerned since Mark was slow to start talking, but certainly made up for it once he started. I am not the kind of mother who talks to babies. I feel uncomfortable and even silly carrying on a one-sided conversation with a baby. I knew very well that the sound of mother's voice is pleasant to the baby and probably did encourage the baby to mimic at an earlier age, but I still couldn't do it.

During her second year my husband and I faced the fact that something was wrong with our little girl, but we were at a complete loss to know what. We decided to try and do something about it ourselves. This job was largely up to me, since my husband, of course, was gone all day.

The second year. The first thing I decided to do was to make her realize that I was her mother and I wanted to hold her. I would pick her up and carry her out to the living room and sit in my rocking chair. She would cry and try to get off my lap, but I held her close and talked to her. In a surprisingly short time she stopped rejecting this form of attention and acted as though she enjoyed it. I was greatly encouraged.

Next on the list of problems was her eating. She was still drinking milk from a bottle, and we thought she should use a cup now. We tried offering her a cup and were met with total rejection. We then took the bottle away completely, hoping that a physical need or craving for milk would work on our side and make her try the cup. It didn't, so we took a rather drastic step which upset us both quite a lot. It seemed so cruel. One of us held her head and the other gave her milk from the cup. Again this effort was successful in a very short time. After only two or three crying and fighting sessions she found out that it was really okay to drink from a cup and she drank readily thereafter. However, she insisted on drinking from only one cup, her cup, limiting her drinking only to mealtimes, and only to milk or orange juice. She would never drink any water.

From these two experiences we concluded that we couldn't be gradual about necessary changes. We had to decide what was right to do, and then do it amid her screams of fear and protest.

She got too big for her little plastic bathtub as we knew she would, but she screamed when I put her in the bathtub. This time I felt it was unnecessary to force her to accept this change. I just couldn't do it. She hung on to me so tightly and was so frightened that we both ended up crying. After that I put her in the kitchen sink. She was frightened, of course, the first time, but after that she was fine.

She stayed withdrawn in her own room and we either went in there or carried her out if we were to see her. She spent hours curled up on her bed clutching her beloved pink Fuzzy animal, scratching at the wall or flickering her fingers in front of a light. When in bed she often rocked with such vigor as to move her bed halfway across the room.

The third year. After her second birthday we faced the problem more realistically and knew we needed help. We had to know what was wrong. I was emotionally torn apart as it was so difficult to face these changes. I was in constant fear that I would make her worse. I was certain that her problem, whatever it was, was psychiatric in nature and that she needed professional help.

This was a period of extreme anguish for us. My first step was to consult Kathryn's pediatrician, Dr. L. I told him of her problems and difficulties, and he suggested that we take her to the Pediatrics Evaluation Center of a hospital in a large metropolitan area. He mentioned the possibility of a personality change. That was the only clue I needed to assure myself that her problem was indeed psychiatric. I consulted with Dr. L. in September, and we immediately applied to the Evaluation Center. It was not until February that we started the evaluation, and these months were indeed black ones for us. I went over in my mind, until I could no longer, everything that I could think of that could have affected her emotionally. I was sure it was my fault that she was disturbed. I became psychosomatically ill myself during these months. This was never diagnosed, only my own opinion, but it seemed accurate. A few weeks after talking to Dr. L. I became hoarse and could barely talk. This condition lasted during these months of anxiety and disappeared completely once we started the evaluation process. I knew it was psychosomatic, but that didn't help at all.

Once the evaluation started, a calm of sorts settled down on us and we didn't feel the anxiety and dread so intensely. We were frightened but it didn't gnaw at us anymore. We had confidence in the people who would examine Kathryn, and we were sure that we would have positive answers to our questions. Knowing the truth, no matter how bad, is always easier than fearing the unknown. During her evaluation she was tested in every conceivable way—eyes, hearing, neurology, EEG, brain X-ray, pediatrics, occupational therapy, speech therapy, psychology, psychiatry, etc.

Throughout all the tests she cried and there was no cooperation at all. She would start to cry as soon as we walked in the door of the clinic and didn't stop until we left. During brief times in the waiting room she would quiet down and walk around a little, seemingly intrigued by the different floor tiles, but mostly she sat on my lap and clung to me in fear. The worst ordeal of all was the X-ray. We had to lay her on the X-ray table while she screamed in terror. We had to tape her to the table and forcibly hold her down. I was so upset and felt so sorry for her that I came very near grabbing her and running out. It was a dreadful ordeal for both of us, but I stuck it out and she had no other choice.

Anecdote: One doctor came in to examine her reflexes and brought two interns along. He was telling them how to get a baby's attention and keep the baby happy. Well, with Kathryn his method was a total failure and he looked a bit foolish. She cried and threw his "objects of interest" on the floor.

We had to cancel our first appointment for our final conference at the Evaluation Center. Mark was sick; John called Mrs. G. to cancel and arrange for a new time. He told me that Mrs. G. seemed quite anxious to see us soon and reassured John that they had something planned to help us. We had no idea what she meant, and she didn't volunteer any information. During the time of Kathy's evaluation I had become rather puzzled and uncertain. It seemed at times that the various ways they examined her had little to do with her problems. I knew her eyes and ears and muscles and reflexes were okay so I suppose I was mostly impatient. I was very anxious for the psychologist to see her, and when he did I deluged him with questions. He couldn't answer them so he was evasive and noncommital. This bothered me a little but I rather thought he wished I would keep quiet so he could observe Kathryn. All I could think of was why?-why?-why? Why won't she chew her food? Why does she throw everything down? Why can't I hold her on my lap? Why is she so afraid of everything? and so on ad infinitum. A little later we were called and asked to bring Kathy in again because a psychiatrist wanted to see her. I was sure now that they were on the right track. When we took her up for the final visit she was in better shape and didn't cry and cling to me. When the psychiatrist came in she was standing on the floor studying the tile. He tried to hug her and she pulled away instantly. He asked me if she let us hug her. I said, "No, she only clings to me if she is afraid." He said that was all he needed to know. He had evidently satisfied himself, but I was a little disappointed that the whole thing was over in so short a time. From then on until our conference I was bewildered about Kathy's problem. I had seen a number of children with various problems all getting the same tests as Kathy, but none seemed at all like Kathy.

Everyone there was so nice to us and seemed extra nice to Kathy. I wondered if her problem, whatever it was, had any hope for help.

Finally the conference day came and I was not only relieved that at last we would know what the problem was but also very frightened of the truth. I felt that I could accept any problem, no matter how serious, if there was just some way to help her.

We had to wait only a few minutes, and then Mrs. G. led us into Mrs. A.'s office. I had scarcely sat down when Mrs. A. said, "Kathy has a very serious problem." I went numb all over and just sat there staring at her. (Reprinted from DesLauriers and Carlson, 1969.)

Early infantile autism, thus defined, is not, as now recognized by most specialists (Bender, 1967; DesLauriers, 1962; Rimland, 1964; Kanner, 1965) an early form of childhood schizophrenia or an intriguing variety of mental deficiency.

The behaviors characteristic of childhood schizophrenia include affective inappropriateness in human contacts; lack of realistic integration between what is behaviorally intended and what is actually attempted; arbitrary and unpredictable responses to familiar social situation; and autistic (in the Bluererian sense of dereistic, and not in the Kannerian sense of self-referent or self-stimulating) preoccupations, speech, ideation, or action. This cluster of characteristics usually apparent in a child at the age of 3 or 4 and following what had appeared to be a normal development until then, constitutes what clinicians over the years have usually associated with the term "psychotic." Childhood schizophrenia is a psychosis; early infantile autism is more appropriately described as a developmental arrest.

Mental deficiency, in its essential features, as these have been recognized over the years by most specialists in this field, can best be characterized by the term: mental subnormality (Sarason, 1958; Tredgold & Soddy, 1970; Menolascino, 1970). What this term emphasizes of this behavioral condition is its *limitations* in relationship to normal human functions as opposed to distortions or vicissitudes. The mentally defective child has the ability to establish and maintain appropriate affective contacts with his human environment, but in a limited way; he has the ability to acquire and learn acceptable patterns of social skills, but in a limited way; his interest in himself and in the world about him is present, but limited. All this is in relationship to what we observe as the usual mode of development in a normal child and, thus, we refer to him as subnormal. His behaviors reflect no glaring or florid psychotic qualities like in childhood schizophrenia—thought it is possible for a child to be both mentally defective and schizophrenic, in the same clinical sense that it is possible for a schizophrenic child to be an intellectual genius! Within the limits of his understanding of a situation, the behaviors of the mentally defective are not affectively inappropriate, or intentionally arbitrary and unpredictable. The mentally defective enjoys people, likes to be with people, and seeks out people. The autistic infant does not.

Observe Becky, for instance. She was born the second of three children; her brother, 4 years her senior, is an intelligent, easygoing youngster, alert and interested in the normal activities and pleasures appropriate to his age. Her little brother, 8 months old, is an active and responsive child. Becky, as her parents report, was "out of it" from early infancy. Though she is a well formed and physically healthy child, her beautiful brown eyes have a distant and somewhat blurry gaze; she seems to see no one and never tries to look at anyone. She avoids people and, left to her own devices, occupies all of her time, crouched on the floor, looking at the patterns of shadows created by the sun or any other light on her fingers. When she is interrupted in this activity she ignores the interruption, and, if the interruption is insistent, she becomes rigid in her body, bites her thumbs, and strikes out blindly and indiscriminately at her surroundings. She will eat only mushy foods and will not tolerate any change in her sleeping habits. At the age of 3, she has no interest in playing with toys or in exploring her home. She makes a few babbling noises but says no words. Her parents have recognized very early that Becky was not really with them; the mother, a warm and patient person, spends a great deal of time intruding on this child, trying to elicit some interested response from her; the father, a hard-working engineer, "adores" his little girl, rough-houses with her when he comes home from work, and is puzzled and worried by her aloofness and her distance. Developmentally, Becky's functioning can be estimated to be between 6 and 9 months.

Now look at Christopher. The first born of three children, he behaves, at the age of four, as if the world around him did not exist, except possibly as it provides him with balls or round objects in which he absorbs himself every moment of his waking life. He looks at nobody and appears to see no one; he makes grunting sounds but does not speak. When he is spoken to, he remains indifferent, and when he is prevented from manipulating (rolling, tapping, tossing in the air, etc.) round objects, he wails and whines like a lost soul. He becomes very upset also when anything in the physical arrangement of his home is changed or whenever any button on his shirt is unbuttoned. His mother, a homemaker, is very gentle and patient with him, and his father, a systems analyst for an engineering firm, plays ball with his son and tries to involve him in social interactions. Christopher responds with annoyance to all these intrusions and wants no part of any such involvements. Developmentally, Christopher's functioning can be estimated to be between 2 and 3 years of age.

Becky and Christopher are autistic children. Their behaviors reflect in a most striking way a lack of interest in or enjoyment of human contacts, communications, or relationships. There is no joy in their lives, and they hardly give any pleasure to anyone around them. They live in a "circle of silence" or in a "glass hall"; Bettelheim described their staunch rejection of their human environment as having the cold and solid quality of an "empty fortress."

Our research work (DesLauriers and Carlson, 1969) led us to see the autistic child's affective isolation with its consequent arrest in human growth and development a very special instance of sensori-affective deprivation. The evidence, however, did not support the view that such a deprivation could be a result of parental rejection, as Bettelheim (1967) had suggested, or of environmental lack of stimulation, such as that reported by Spitz (1945) in his studies on hospitalism and marasmic children. On the contrary, the behavioral manifestations of autism seem to suggest a basic deficiency in the child's capacity to monitor the affective components of the sensory stimulations provided by the environment, as if the child's *threshold for such affective input were too high* or as if, centrally, the brain functions involved in processing these affective qualities (midbrain-limbic regions) *never became sufficiently excited or aroused* to allow for the decoding of such affective components.

Additional support for this tentative conclusion was derived from investigations (Routtenberg, 1968) on the neurophysiological mechanisms underlying human sleep functions and in the evidence adduced which suggested an intimate and crucial functional relationship between two Arousal systems in the Central Nervous System. The Ascending Reticular Formation, traditionally viewed as the primary mechanism of cortical arousal (System No. 1) was also given essential primacy in the emission of behavioral responses to sensory stimulations; the Midbrain-limbic processes (System No. 2) were discovered to constitute a second arousal mechanism directly implicated in the affective and emotional qualities of sensory-stimulations and to the stabilization, consolidation and fixation of such stimulations through short-term and long-term memory functions. Between the two Systems, a functional balance appeared required such that each had a dampening effect on the other: when System 1 (responses being behaviorally produced) was in ascendancy, System 2 remained in a relatively quiet, unaroused, condition; conversely, when System 2 (affective-sensory stimulations being processed, decoded, and analyzed) was in ascendancy, System 1 became relatively inactive, allowing emitted behavioral responses to acquire meaningfulness and become fixated or retained. Learning, thus, appeared to be a function of a proper balance between these two Arousal systems, any dysfunction in either one bringing about an imbalance and, therefore, a barrier or obstruction to the acquisition of any learned responses. (For a detailed elaboration of this neurophysiological model see DesLauriers and Carlson, 1969.) This neurophysiological hypothesis, we felt, allowed for an understanding of the totality of the autistic syndrome of infancy since it gave a rationale to the essential behavioral features of this syndrome.

First it accounts for the striking affective and emotional isolation of the child present from birth: the autistic infant is never affectively responsive because of the high threshold (or barrier) to affective sensory inputs preventing arousal System 2 from becoming intensely involved in the sensori-affective experiences stimulated by environmental contacts.

Second, the hypothesis helps to explain the sterile repetition of ritualistic and compulsive-like behaviors which at best appear to have some self-stimulating value to the child, but which, at worst are meaningless and useless; the absence of the inhibiting effect of Arousal System 2 on the response-emitting effects of the unending activities of System 1 leaves this latter System in a constant state of arousal, producing the same responses over and over, whether they are appropriate, meaningful, or of rewarding value.

Third, the postulated imbalance between the two Arousal Systems (with System 1 in constant ascendancy) makes understandable the great difficulty which the autistic child demonstrates in learning, that is, in acquiring stable and appropriate responses to environmental situations and in developing adaptive (through accommodation and assimilation in the Piagetian sense) problem-solving patterns of behaviors. Lacking in any interesting value, because of their dull and drab affective qualities, environmental stimulating situations have no appeal or motivating force. The child has no incentive in mastering an environment that makes no sense to him because it has none of the meaningfulness for him which would be derived from the felt exciting qualities associated with the arousal of System 2.

Finally, the learning having such a central function in the totality of human development, its absence would obviously face the autistic child with a severe developmental arrest. All areas of functioning would suffer, especially those related more specifically to the acquisition of skills differentially human, such as language and speech, abstract ideation, and reflective consciousness. The autistic child's isolation, his total indifference to interactions with his human environment, his lack of interest or curiosity in any new situation, his deep absorption in the endless repetition of his rituals and stereotypes, and the colorless and joyless aspects of most of his activities, all those features which constitute the "autistic disturbance of affective contact," also close the child's experience to the excitement of discovery, to the mastery of new and novel situations, to the value of initiative and curiosity in expanding his "possession" of his surrounding world, and to the pleasures and satisfactions of human attachments and relationships.

The same rationale which gives us an understanding of the total behavioral syndrome of early infantile autism provided us also with a methodological design to test its validity. What was central to the autistic child's development arrest and impairment? Not a defect in receiving sensory stimulations: available evidence showed the child to have an intact sensorium; the child could see, hear, taste, respond to touch, and to smell. Neither was it an intellectual limitation as such, since many autistic children show unusual skills at solving intricate and complex problems. Nor could it be delusional preoccupations occupying constantly the focus of the child's attention and concentration; no autistic child has been reported to act as if he were acting out the part of Cinderella, Jenny in the magic lamp, or Ali Baba of the Thousand Nights. The central factor of the autistic syndrome was seen as an affective defect not a cognitive one.

The test of this hypothesis would have to be a treatment method which addressed itself directly to this central factor and, through it, to the totality of the autistic child's problems. If a situation could be set up in which each stimulating experience for the child could be imbued with a forceful quality of pleasure and excitement; if, in other words, all contacts and communication with the child could have on the child a high affective impact, would it then be possible to transgress the barrier created by the child's high threshold of affective receptivity and, thus, arouse and excite him in the experience of the meaningfulness for him of such contacts and interactions? If such an approach could provide successful, as evidenced in the child's eagerness to want these interactions repeated and expanded, would we not witness the emergence of a learning process in the child, and, with learning, new growth and development in his awareness of his human environment and in his capacity to master his surrounding world?

The experimental situation we decided upon to accomplish this was simple: the autistic child in a room with an adult would be bombarded repeatedly with a wide variety of close physical contacts of an excitingly pleasurable quality (high affective impact) until his spontaneous response to the situation reflected clearly his awareness and experience of the situation and his need to have it continued and maintained. Play, i.e., playful and fun interactions, thus, constituted the independent variable of this controlled situation, where only the child and his human environment would be allowed to interact; other objects in the room would be limited to such things as may be progressively needed to introduce variety or to expand the human interactional contact.

The immediate goal of this situation is to elicit from the autistic child a response of interest, of attention, of pleasure, clearly indicative of the child's awareness of the stimulations received from the therapist. Implicit in this goal is the idea that the child should be made to feel, above anything else, that it is fun to be a child, part of the human race, and that it is good to be with an adult whose entire form of intrusion is to insure that the child feels pleased, happy, gratified.

A second goal has to do with the first level of learning which we hoped the child would reach: the child should learn how to play, how to seek interactions of a fun and pleasurable affect, how to invent such situations, and how to discover new and surprising ways of having fun with another human being. As we have mentioned earlier, the most noteworthy aspect of these children's behaviors would appear to be their total lack of playful interactions; these children do not know how to play. In truth they seem to be missing out on one of the most constant and important ingredients present in any normal child's development from infancy: the need or the ability to interact playfully with their human environment.

This reference to the importance of play in the normal child's development has been recognized by parents and by all observers and researchers in the field of children's growth and maturation. It is for this reason that we chose play as the most effective instrumentality in our efforts at breaching in the autistic child, the solid walls of the empty fortress of his affective isolation. Play comes naturally to a child; it is nearly instinctual. It is in Lovaas' view, the most powerful agent of "reinforcement" to a child's activity. In a playful interaction nothing need be contrived or artificial; spontaneity, initiative, imagination, pretend, make-believe are all part of the fun, without fear of consequences but with a multisplendored variety of opportunities to discover and master new and important problems of living. We call our therapeutic experimental design: Theraplay.

Just recently a book was published on "The Therapeutic Use of Child's Play (C. E. Schaefer, ed., 1976) in which Ann Jernberg describes in a few pages the essence of Theraplay (Jernberg, 1976). The rest of the book is devoted to various forms of play therapy. Theraplay is not play therapy. It is neither interpretive nor analytical, Kleinians or Axlinian, of story telling or of dollhouse conflict-resolving intent. Theraplay is simply the adventure of two human beings having fun with each other, and, in the process, learning about each other as well as about any number of other useful things in this world. Theraplay is direct, physical, noisy, exciting, and happily human. It can be exhausting but it is always exhilarating.

Theraplay begins slowly. You cannot enter into the isolation of the autistic child's life with the insensitive brutishness of a bull in a china shop. Yet you have to intrude with the confidence and assurance derived from the conviction that, given a chance to have more fun than what he now has, the child will seek it and want it. Thus, in entering the child's autistic world, one should "fit" this intrusion to the activity level to which the child is accustomed. With Kathy, (2½ years old), for instance, who spends her time seemingly contented at endlessly scratching at the wall, it would be totally inappropriate to approach her with: let's have a wrestling match, Kathy! Observe how the therapist (Dr. Carlson) invades her world.

Kathy is at the wall scratching with the fingers of her right hand; there is a sort of sad smile on her face, as if her entire life revolved on maintaining this activity 'til the end of time! The therapist goes to the wall and crouches beside Kathy who ignores her completely. The therapist begins to scratch the wall, attuning her movements to those of the child. Little by little the therapist's hand moves toward Kathy's and by and by, as if by accident, the fingers touch. Kathy shows no sign of contact and the therapist returns to her original scratching activity. The cycle of scratching and finger touching is repeated over and over until Kathy, obviously intrigued by what is happening, pulls her hand away and quickly puts it back, *as if she wanted to see what would happen.* What happens is that the therapist persistently continues to mingle in Kathy's fingers until it is Kathy herself who finds delight in placing her hand so as to insure that she will be touched by the therapist's fingers. Thus begins the game of finger touching (the child is not scratching anymore!) where the therapist responds to Kathy's initiative with progressively more and more variation in the play situation, sometimes touching Kathy's fingers quickly and then removing her hand, sometimes pretending, in a teasing way, to approach Kathy's fingers but not doing so. Kathy becomes excited and involved in the game; she is now having fun and the first step in learning how to play has been taken.

With Sammy, (5 years old) the beginnings of Theraplay had to be quite different. Sammy was a hyperactive tornado. Let loose in a room he would run from one place to the other, seemingly intent on creating as much distance as possible from any possible human interaction and most determinedly dedicated to destroying anything he could put his hands on. Unlike Kathy who was the quiet, unobtrusive little girl in the family, Sammy represented for his parents a monstrous terror. In the therapy room Sammy was no different, except that he had very few objects available to destroy; if he had to attack something it would have to be the therapist and this was improbable, since Sammy chose to ignore him. How does one begin to have fun with a hurricane? Sammy had to be stopped long enough to be able to somehow acknowledge that someone else was there. The therapist began by placing himself in various positions on the floor of the room as a physical obstacle in the path of this rampaging child. Thus, Sammy had to sidestep, go around, or jump over the therapist. This maneuver eventually had the effect of slowing Sammy down sufficiently for the therapist to reach out and grab the child's hand or arm. This was done very quickly and just as quickly the therapist would release the child, the idea being to convey to the child that his "freedom and autonomy" were not in danger; no one would enslave him! Sammy tried various ways, at first, to avoid the therapist (at least he was aware of him!), at one point, even stopping altogether his hyperactivity; but as soon as the therapist got off the floor the race was on again! By this time the therapist knew that Sammy was "with him"; every time Sammy flew by, the therapist would lunge, hold him a second, and let him go. Eventually, Sammy expected the move and imperceptibly slowed down, *in order to be caught.* If, perchance, the therapist, out of breath, would neglect his part of the adventure, Sammy would come to a stop and look as if to say: "Well, what's happening to you?" And so it went for many of the early Theraplay sessions with Sammy, until he, himself, would come spontaneously to the therapist, to be held and to sit on his lap for a few minutes!

Theraplay begins slowly in a "fitting" and appropriate way, tailored to the child's level of activity. Theraplay is a patient and persistent maneuver of high affective impact; it has to be fun for the therapist and, eventually, for the child. Once this first phase is accomplished, that is, once the child and the therapist understand and accept each other in this playful, no holds barred, form of human interaction, the way is open for the child to discover, investigate, and respond to, many new forms of situations, circumstances, and events in the therapy encounter. Furthermore, because everything that happens here is imbued with fun and pleasure, it can easily be generalized to any other place where the same kind of fun and pleasure is available.

What this means is that in Theraplay the child begins to learn, and, thus, his world enlarges and his development as a human being goes forward. As the child learns how to play, the therapist can introduce, as part of the play situation, any number of problem-solving activities which are part of his getting acquainted with his world. If, for instance, the child finds excitement and fun at running after the therapist, this could become an occasion to teach him how to climb, how to swing, how to open or close a door, etc., etc. (Picture, if you will, Sammy running after his therapist. If at some point, the therapist chooses to make it part of the game of running that Sammy will have to climb the junglegym to reach the therapist, the latter will use the excitement of the game to introduce this variation. The same would be true, to get Sammy to climb on a chair, and then on a table, and then jump into the arms of the therapist.) What is at issue here is that play—with its tension and anxiety-reducing quality, and with all its characteristics of initiative, imagination, surprise, and novelty—offers the richest possible soil on which learning can grow. Especially for the autistic child whose initiative is limited to avoiding any growth-producing human contacts and whose staunch resistance to change incarcerates him indefinitely in the prison of his self-stimulating autistic rituals and stereotypes.

There is more however to learning than the development of those skills necessary to master and cope with one's environment. Human development through learning involves also the awareness of one's bodily self, the controls one can exercise over one's impulses, the intentionality one can give to one's actions to make them goal-oriented and successful. In this aspect of learning, theraplay also plays a crucial role for the autistic child. Play allows for so many forms and varieties of physical contacts through which any child can become aware of his bodily boundaries, of his separation and differentiation from others in his environment. and of his physical and spatial identity. In the excitement and gratification of play, the child recognizes quickly the presence of that other human being without whom life has no zest or enchantment. With the recognition of this presence and of its exciting impact on him, the child learns to define himself; he is somebody different than the other and yet together with the other.

As the child defines himself in the many and varied experiences which are part of his identity, he becomes also aware of the controls he can exercise over his actions. It does not take very long for the autistic child who has discovered the thrill and delight of playing with his therapist or with his parents, to initiate himself new and unusual forms of play, through teasing, through hiding, through doing the opposite of what is expected, or through simply being mischievous. The child experiments with himself and takes risks, in the absolute certainty that it is all "in fun," and that he need have no fear of being destroyed in the process.

There exists also a most significant relation of playful activities, in the autistic child, to the development of language and speech functions. The delays in language and speech which characterize the development of the autistic child cannot be clearly attributed to defects in cognitive functions; rather, if our understanding of the nature of the autistic infant's behaviors has validity, the intellectual requirements of speech and language are less important in his developmental delays than are the affective foundations of meaningful human experiences. It is our view that the autistic child does not speak because he has nothing to say; furthermore, he has nothing to say because he does not possess language, i.e., the internal images and representations of objects; and lastly, that the development of a symbolic function through which such images and representations are possible, is closely linked to experiences of substitution, pretend, and make-believe which are available to the child through play. (For a more elaborate discussion of this point see: Play, symbolism and language development in the autistic child. In: *Childhood Autism: A Symposium* by Rutter and Schopler, eds., in press).

From very early infancy, learning to play appears to be for any child, learning to substitute one thing for another, to recognize signs of an expected or impending event, to respond to signals directing this or that form of activity, to make-believe, to pretend, and, generally, to act as if one thing can be changed into another thing with all the license and enchantment of a fairy tale (see Bettelheim, 1976). It is on the basis of such accumulated experiences that the human symbolic function progressively develops, through which an internal representation of objects is possible. Play is not only imitation which is a form of accommodation to external events; play quickly becomes through excitement and pleasure, an internal, personal, rearrangement of the elements of the playful situation, and this constitutes, for the child, an assimilation of this situation to his own needs, desires, and wishes. Symbols, "ludic symbols" as Piaget calls them (Piaget, 1951) are essential to the formation and activity of the symbolic function.

The case of Christopher will illustrate this point, it will also provide a more detailed view of the process of Theraplay.

Christopher was nearly 4 years old when he was first brought to me. A slender, healthy looking little fellow, with light brown hair and blue eyes. He presented the central characteristics of early infantile autism as described by Kanner (1943) and reported here by Rutter (1971). The diagnosis had been established by a number of child psychiatrists, pediatricians, and psychologists during the preceding years when his parents had relentlessly been seeking help for him. Christopher was an affectively isolated child, indifferent to people, lacking any communicative speech, prone to distress and tantrums whenever changes were introduced in his routines, and endlessly absorbing himself in rolling, juggling, bouncing balls which he had an uncanny knack of discovering or which he made himself with paper, socks, or any other pliable and soft materials. Neurologically, no findings of any importance had been determined to account for his behaviors, and his medical history was reportedly negative.

Theraplay was consistently used with Christopher during the years of his treatment with me. Christopher—like any other autistic child—caught on rather quickly to the approach. When he came to his first therapy session he brought with him a red ball and ignored completely his parents and the therapist as he isolated himself in the corner of the room, spinning, rolling, juggling his little red ball on the floor or between his hands. I sat beside him on the floor and at short intervals would reach out and take the ball and hold it for a few seconds, and immediately give it back to Christopher before he had time to become upset. After 30 minutes of such intrusion, Christopher appeared reassured that I was not going to take his toy from him. The next move was for myself to keep the ball a little longer so that Christopher, slightly puzzled and surprised, would have to turn to me or reach out for the ball; then, he would again, immediately get it, either by my putting it in his hand or rolling it to him. By the end of the session, Christopher knew that I was there and that he and his ball were safe.

In the early subsequent sessions the time lapse between my taking Christopher's ball and my giving it back to him increased steadily; the variety of playful maneuvers intended to stimulate interaction between Christopher and myself enlarged also considerably. Eventually Chris was off the floor, out of his corner and laughingly running after me in the room to retrieve his ball. At that point, a slight shift in strategy was introduced: instead of taking the ball away from the child I would wait. Christopher himself gave me the ball to run away with. Obviously Christopher had found it more fun to play with me and the ball than to isolate himself with it.

We were now friends and playmates. Whatever I wanted to do in the room, Christopher was ready to do it with me (the happy expression: "he was game to do it," would be most appropriate here!). Playing with the ball became less and less central to our interactions, but it was never completely removed from our games. For instance, if we both sat on the floor to work on putting a puzzle together, Chris had to have the ball in front of him, between his legs. Then the ball game still remained available, but he played less and less with the ball. He played at stacking up elastic doughnuts on a spindle and at looking at me through each doughnut before placing it on the spindle. He played at jumping off the desk into my arms or at balancing himself on his stomach on the sole of my shoes. He had fun bouncing up and down on the couch and landing on my back on the floor. He learned to discriminate colors and shapes while putting puzzles together and laughing out loud if I happened, on purpose to give him a wrong piece of the puzzle. During these sessions, the ball sat on the file cabinet, available, but for the most part, untouched.

Thus, Christopher played and learned. He became a happy child, looking forward to his visits with me twice each week. After 6 months, we were definitely good friends. Though no special effort was made at teaching him anything specific it was amazing how quickly he became interested in learning things, fun things like hide-and-go-seek behind the desk, jumping on my back when I pretended to be a horse, demanding more funny sounds when I growled like a lion or barked like a dog. Childish games, all, but reassuring and exciting to Christopher. One day, when he was sitting and rocking on the couch, I began singing the nursery rhyme: "Sing a song of six pense a pocket full of rye" to the exact pace and rhythm of his rocking. Little by little I increased the tempo of the song and Christopher, caught in this singing happiness, also increased his rocking; then, I would slow down, and he would slow down too. Christopher demanded that this be repeated over and over and, later on, whenever we were tired of more exhausting activities, we would always go back to our singing and rocking game to rest.

It was also on the couch that Christopher said his first word. We were putting together a Playschool puzzle of a monkey eating a banana. Christopher had no trouble putting the puzzle together; but the real game included singing the monkey song, sharing the banana with the monkey, and generally dramatizing the entire adventure of the monkey. The song: Monkey eats the banana was a real hit with Chris; he would work fast while I sang. Then I'd pretend to have a piece of the banana, put it to my mouth and eat it; Chris was encouraged to do the same. After that, came my giving a piece of make-believe banana to Chris, and his placing another piece in my mouth. We'd break down the puzzle and re-do it many times, with any number of funny variations in the singing, the sharing, the eating. And it was when I hesitated once in giving him his piece of banana, that Christopher laughingly shouted: "Banana!" This was definitely an instance of "organic vocabulary," as the Teacher used to call it. The game did not stop, yet whenever I acted as if I had forgotten my part, Christopher was right there to remind me of it by shouting: "banana!"

Christopher's vocabulary increased rapidly in subsequent sessions: one word sentences, then two words together, then short sentences. His parents at home found a wide variety of opportunities to enlarge his vocabulary, always in the context of a fun or pleasant situation. His articulation was not perfect and, frequently, in trying to speak, only the first and last word of his sentence came out understandable. To correct this defect, I learned that if I sang the sentence to him, he could repeat it much more intelligibly.

Today Christopher attends a special education classroom in a public school. He has no difficulty learning there, but the fun situation is considerably reduced. What he enjoys most are the songs the children sing. Otherwise he remains his independent self, having little to do with the other children. In contrast, he plays well at home with his brother and sister, both younger than he is, and he teases his mother and father with a considerable amount of mischief.

This last note concerning Christopher's parents and family underlines a final point which should be made on the value of Theraplay in working with autistic children, a point which was briefly stated earlier. Unlike many changes shaped and effected through behavior modification techniques, the learning which takes place through Theraplay generalize easily from one situation to the other. As long as a playful situation exists, which is exciting and arousing to the autistic child, the activities and behaviors learned in such circumstances, will be sought and repeated. When Kathy learns that it is fun to walk by placing her feet on the therapist's shoes, she has no hesitation in doing the same at home with her mother. When Sammy learns the delight of making a square on the blackboard to the accompaniment of "Swish, -Bing-Bang-Boom!" he has no trouble doing the same thing at home for his father, and more, like triangles, diamonds, etc. Thus to help parents "manage" their autistic child becomes not so much a matter of teaching them how to reinforce good behaviors through rewards or extinguish unacceptable behaviors through "time out," but more excitingly a matter of teaching them how to play and have fun with their child. Which makes the child truly part of the family. Which is ultimately the design and objective of Theraplay.

REFERENCES

Bender, L. (1967). Childhood schizophrenia: a review. *Journal of Hillside Hospital* 16:10–22.
Bettelheim, B. (1967). *The Empty Fortress.* N.Y.: Free Press.
—— (1976). *The Uses of Enchantment.* N.Y.: Alfred A. Knopf.
Des Lauriers, A. M. (1962). The Experience of Reality in Childhood Schizophrenia. New York: International Universities Press, Inc.
Des Lauriers, A., and Carlson, C. F. (1969). *Your Child Is Asleep: Early Infantile Autism.* Homewood, Illinois: The Dorsey Press.
Eisenberg, L. (1968). Psychotic disorders in childhood. In R. E. Cooke, ed., *The Biologic Basis of Pediatric Practice.* N.Y.: McGraw-Hill, Inc.
——, and Kanner, L. (1956). Early infantile autism. *American Journal of Orthopsychiatry* 26:1943–1955.
Jernberg, A. (1976). Theraplay. In Chas. E. Schaefer, ed., *Therapeutic Use of Child's Play.* N.Y.: Jason Aronson.
Kanner, L. (1943). Autistic disturbances of affective contact. *The Nervous Child* 2:217–250.
—— (1965). Infantile autism and the schizophrenias. *Behavioral Science* 10:412–420.
——, and Lesser, L. I. (1958). Early infantile autism. *Pediatric Clinics of North America* 5:711–730.

Murphy, Lois. (1972). Infant's play and cognitive development. In M. Piers, ed., *Play and Development*. N.Y.: Norton.

Piaget, J. (1951). *Play, Dreams, and Imitation in Childhood*. N.Y.: Norton.

Menolascino, F. J. (1970). Infantile autism: descriptive and diagnostic relationships to mental retardation. In F. J. Menolascino, ed., *Psychiatric Approaches to Mental Retardation*. N.Y.: Basic Books.

Rimland, B. (1964) *Infantile Autism*. New York: Appleton-Century-Crofts.

Routtenberg, A. (1968). The two arousal hypothesis: reticular formation and limbic system. *Psychological Review* 75:

Rutter, M. (1971). The description and classification of infantile autism. In D. W. Churchill, G. D. Alpern, and M. K. DeMyer, eds., *Infantile Autism: Proceedings of the Indiana University Colloquium*. Springfield: Thomas.

Schaefer, C., ed. (1976). *Therapeutic Use of Child's Play*. N.Y.: Jason Aronson.

Spitz, R. A. (1945). Hospitalism: an inquiry into the genesis of psychiatric conditions in early childhood. *The Psychoanalytic Study of Childhood* 1:

Tredgold, A. F. & Soddy, K. (1970). *Mental Retardation*. 11th Ed. Baltimore: Williams and Wilkins.

Chapter Twelve

Teaching Self-Help Skills to Retarded Children

J. WALTER JACOBS
J. S. Tarwater Development Center
Wetumpka, Alabama
and MARK H. LEWIS
George Peabody College
Nashville, Tennessee

INTRODUCTION

The first objective of this chapter will be to provide a critical review of the existing literature on teaching self-help skills to retarded children. It will focus on four general skill areas: toileting, feeding, dressing, and grooming. Skill training with the retarded client is largely based on the application of operant techniques (Skinner, 1938, 1953) which have come to be popularly known as behavior modification. This chapter will not attempt to review the broader application of operant technology to the retarded population, this task already having been accomplished by several authors (e.g., J. Gardner, 1969; Nawas and Braun, 1970a,b,c; W.

273

Gardner, 1971). Kiernan (1975) has reviewed the research in this area with exemplary scholarship.

It is basically the assertion of this chapter that operant technology has revolutionalized the habilitation of the more severely and profoundly retarded persons. While behavior modifiers may have at times been too zealous in stating the efficacy of their procedures, the fact remains that in the last decade there has been witnessed a surge of emphasis on the habilitation of the retarded person directly stemming from the application of operant technology. Cynics have observed that the training of retarded persons has a very long history. Students of mental retardation recognize, for example, that the methods of Itard (1932) in his attempt to teach a feral boy discovered in the woods of Aveyron bear some striking similarity to modern operant techniques. One might question that anything new or revolutionary can be discerned in operant technology. Further, one may argue that our society has just now evolved to the point where habilitation of the retarded has become a social concern. Thus, the increased emphasis on habilitation derives from a heightened social emphasis, not from some newly discovered technology.

The operant model is grounded in the empirical laws governing behavior. Early students of behavior no doubt had some understanding of these laws and exploited this knowledge in much the same way that preMendelian students of animal husbandry understood and used knowledge about the transmission of genetics traits. The Mendelian laws of genetics provided a conceptual framework for understanding the transmission of genetic traits. The discovery and formalization into theory of the laws governing genetic transmission profoundly influenced the practice of animal husbandry as well as all of biology. By the same token, the power of behavior modification is derived from the empirical grounding and conceptual clarity of the operant model.

While it seems indisputable that society now places greater emphasis on habilitation, can it be said that this new social concern for the retarded was a necessary precursor to progress in habilitative techniques? This would not seem to be a plausible assertion considering that the legal precedent for the right to habilitation (Wyatt vs. Stickney, Note 1) came after nearly a decade of research on the use of operant techniques with the retarded. Habilitation became a right of the retarded only after research efforts demonstrated that habilitation was feasible. An objective assessment of the recent history of mental retardation indicates that operant technology has, indeed, revolutionalized the care and habilitation of the retarded client and influenced legal practice.

Given the demonstrated effectiveness of operant techniques for teaching a variety of adaptive behaviors, including self-help skills, it becomes the task of the professional to structure these techniques into broad habilitative programs. The latter portion of this chapter will be devoted to the development of such a service delivery system. It has been the experience of the authors that the approach having greatest utility is one that ties behavioral programming to behavioral assessment. The advantages are numerous. An initial assessment of adaptive behavior allows administrative and training staff to precisely identify behavioral deficits to be remediated. If programs for skill training are developed for each item of the adaptive behavior assessment tool, then transfer to habilitative programming is direct and simple. A child with a specific behavioral deficit is trained using a previously validated program for the teaching of that skill. The program offers to the paraprofessional, who is typically charged with the training task, a very precise, step-by-step guide for teaching the skill. Progress of habilitative programs is easily monitored within such an approach and accountability is thus built into the program. Data from assessments of adaptive functioning are easily stored in a computer memory bank. As habilitation progresses, this information may be updated. Computer storage allows for central monitoring of a number of diverse programs and client populations. The latter portion of this chapter will explore the major aspects of this approach: assessment of adaptive behavior, habilitation planning, development of self-help skill programs, and staff training.

PART I: TEACHING SELF-HELP SKILLS TO THE RETARDED: A REVIEW

Toilet Training

One of the more offensive behaviors encountered in the retarded population is incontinence. Consequently, toilet training usually receives first priority in habilitative programming. Eyman, Tarjan, and Cassidy (1970) reported that in a state hospital over a 2-year admission period, 41% of the 620 admissions were not toilet trained and another 16% were only partially trained (e.g., would void in a toilet if placed there at the appropriately scheduled time). Among the retarded population with IQ's of less than 30, fully 64% were incontinent and 18% were only partially trained. Care of the incontinent retarded individual is a time consuming and degrading task. As a consequence, those persons charged with their care and habilitation tend to occupy their working time with nonpatient related chores. Staff attention is primarily elicited by severely disruptive behavior, self-abusive behavior, or soiling. Thus, much of the normalizing influence of positive social interaction is lost. Finally, indiscriminate urination and defecation throughout the ward area constitutes a significant health hazard as the source of numerous enteric pathogens.

Ellis (1963) presented operant conditioning as the theoretically appropriate conceptual model for developing a toilet training program. The eliminatory response (Re) is viewed as an operant which is negatively reinforced by the reduction of anal tension, the drive stimulus (Sd). Toilet training involves establishing as a discriminative stimulus pattern certain behaviors (e.g., lowered pants, seated on the toilet) and physical stimuli (e.g., bathroom). Presumably the operant would then only be emitted in the presence of these stimuli. Toward this end, Ellis suggested recording the time of occurrence of defecation for each resident. (Residents should be at least 12 years of age.) The attendant then is advised to place the resident on the toilet for the period of time during which elimination normally occurs. When the resident successfully voids in the toilet, he is to be immediately rewarded with edibles and praise. As habit training progresses, the support of the attendant in guiding the resident to the toilet and undressing the resident is gradually removed. Accidents are to be ignored for a period of 10 to 15 minutes so as not to provide reinforcement. While this might be mildly aversive, the primary focus of the Ellis approach is on positive contingencies. Control of defecation is the primary objective. Since defecation and urination are correlated in time, it was felt that through the process of generalization, urination would come under stimulus control.

Dayan (1964) implemented a toilet training program based on the Ellis model. Incontinent retardates were placed on the toilet every 2 hours and rewarded with edibles for voiding in the toilet. Increased defecation in the toilet was evidenced by a decrease in the number of diapers used over the training period. No precise data is reported on frequency of bowel accidents, nor is there indication that self initiated toileting was achieved. Baumeister and Klosowski (1965) attempted to train a group of severely retarded residents following closely guidelines set forth in the Ellis model. The eleven subjects selected for inclusion in the program were observed for 30 days during which the time of occurrence of urination and defecation was recorded. These data yielded individual charts indicating the time at which the resident normally had a bowel movement. Initially in training, the attendants were instructed to place the resident on the toilet at that time when voiding had typically occurred in the past. Later, however, the attendants proved better able to predict impending bowel movement from cues provided in the resident's behavior. Steady progress was observed in training. For example, by the 20th day, 62.5% of the defecation and 57.8% of the urination occurred in the toilet. However, on the 49th day of training it was decided to allow the residents to go to the playground for a period of time each day and a dramatic regression in toileting habits was noted. The toileting behavior apparently failed to generalize to the changed environmental conditions.

Hundziak, Maurer, and Watson (1965) conducted a more carefully controlled test of the Ellis model. Severely retarded boys were randomly assigned to one of three groups: (1) an operant conditioning group, (2) a conventional toilet training group, or (3) a control group. Subjects in the operant and conventional groups were placed on the toilet every two hours or when their behavior suggested to the attendant the need to eliminate. The subjects in the operant group were rewarded with candy from a rather elaborate piece of apparatus situated next to the toilet. The conventional group received praise for successful elimination in the toilet and scolding for toileting accidents. The control group was in no systematic toilet training program. While the operant group showed a higher frequency of voiding in the toilet, the rate of soiling and wetting in the cottage area was not appreciably affected. This was felt to be attributable to the failure to bring toileting cues under control of the physiological cues of bladder and bowel tensions. The authors suggest that the problem might be remedied by installing temporary toilets in the classroom then gradually removing these to the restroom area as training progresses. It is perhaps noteworthy to observe that both Baumeister and Klosowski (1965) and Hundziak *et al.* (1965) encountered disruptive, hyperactive behavior when the toilet training program was initiated. However, this difficulty was short-lived.

Two studies (Bensberg *et al.*, 1965; Kimbrell, Luckey, Barbuto, and Love, 1967) are conspicuous both in the high degree of success reported in toilet training the severely retarded and in the absence of any precise description of how this was accomplished. Both allude to the Ellis model and "behavioral shaping" techniques, but neither describe a procedure that could be replicated.

Previously discussed studies on toilet training have almost exclusively focused on positive reinforcement for appropriate toileting behavior. Giles and Wolf (1966) combined the use of positive reinforcers (e.g., food, drink, hugs) for appropriate elimination with the use of aversive contingencies (e.g., physical restraint) for inappropriate behavior. Five severely retarded incontinent males were trained to self-initiate toileting under these contingencies. The type of positive reinforcement and punishment varied from subject to subject depending on what proved most effective. Aversive contingencies were employed only after positive reinforcement alone prove ineffective. Self-initiated toileting was accomplished by confining the subject to the toilet area and shaping approach to and eventually use of the toilet.

Early studies reporting attempts to toilet train low functioning retarded persons are weak on methodological grounds. Appropriate control groups are often absent or inadequate. Success in toilet training has been defined in various ways and, indeed, some studies simply report that procedures were effective. As Gardner (1971) points out, it is necessary to specify precisely the incidence of urination and defecation and the condition under which it occurred. Successes were generally restricted to habit training with little evidence of self-initiated toileting behavior. Several studies (e.g., Baumeister and Klosowski, 1965; Hundziak et al., 1965) report a failure of toileting habits to generalize when environmental changes occurred. As noted by Rentfrow and Rentfrow (1969), follow-up studies were not provided in these studies so enduring effects cannot be assessed. On the more positive side, Giles and Wolf (1966) pointed to a possible solution of the generalization problem by gradually giving access to other areas while maintaining toileting behavior. The addition of punitive measures in their program offered promise of facilitating acquisition of appropriate toileting habits. There remained, however, the problem of how to immediately detect accidents so that contingencies could be used most effectively. Two more recent studies addressed these problems.

Van Wagenen, Meyerson, Kerr, and Mahoney (1969) described a procedure that was effective in establishing self-initiated toileting in nine incontinent retarded children. Aware of the difficulties of backward chaining with toileting behavior, these investigators developed what is described as a forward moving procedure. Crucial to this procedure is an instrument which signals the onset of urination with a loud (90 db) alarm. The device was originally described by Van Wagenen and Murdock (1966); however, several similar sensing and signalling devices are now available commercially.[1,2] While wearing the alarms, the children were allowed to play in a room adjacent to the toileting area. At the alarm signalling urination, the trainer shouts "Stop!" and moves rapidly to the child. The effect is to elicit a startle reflex with the cessation of urination. The trainer grasps the resident by the hand, moves the child quickly to the toilet area, and positions the child appropriately for urination. At this point the child is gently coaxed to reinitiate urination. After a number

---

[1]Mark 2 toilet trainer. Applied Psychology Associates, Box 985, Tempe, Arizona 85281.

[2]Lehigh Valley Electronics Incorporated, Box 125, Fogelsville, Pennsylvania 18051.

of such trials the child begins independently to move to the toilet preliminary to voiding. The training device can now be removed and the child taught to lower his pants. The frequency of urination is increased by encouraging the children to consume large quantities of water, thus allowing as many as 10 training trials in a $3^{1}/_{2}$ hour session. All of the children reached the criterion of autonomous toileting. Follow-up data revealed no significant regression.

In what is essentially an extension, or perhaps culmination of several earlier studies (e.g., Hundziak *et al.*, 1965; Giles and Wolf, 1966; Van Wagenen *et al.*, 1969) Azrin and Foxx (1971) present a fairly complex program which remediates several weaknesses of earlier programs. These authors report successfully toilet training nine severely and profoundly retarded males ranging in age from 20 to 62 years. While in the program, the resident wore a cotton brief containing a moisture sensing device which signalled urination or defecation. This apparatus was described by Azrin, Bugle, and O'Brien (1971) and is commercially available.[3,4] For three days prior to training, the resident was checked each hour for 8 hours per day to determine if urination or defecation had occurred during the previous hour. During training the resident was seated in a chair next to the toilet. Urination was primed by offering liquids every half hour. Residents were given edibles every 5 minutes while they remained dry. Every 30 minutes the residents were placed on the toilet, and in the process undressing and dressing were shaped. Residents were required to sit on the toilet for up to 20 minutes, or until they eliminated. The toilet bowl contained a sensing device which signaled urination or defecation.[5] Successful elimination was followed by edibles and social reinforcers. Several residents were trained simultaneously in order to maximize modeling.

Toileting accidents were signalled by an alarm in the training pants. At this signal the incontinent resident was bodily shaken and scolded. He was required to walk to the laundry room and take out fresh pants, undress himself, shower himself, and dress himself again. The resident is then required to mop or clean the soiled area and wash his soiled clothing. Finally, the chair is removed. Liquids, edibles, and social reinforcement are withheld for 1 hour. Incontinence was quickly reduced by about 90% and within a maintenance program to near zero. Basically, the maintenance program consisted of ward personnel monitoring for incontinence six times during the day and contingent on accident

---

[3]"Pants alert," Lehigh Valley Electronics, Box 125, Fogelsville, Pennsylvania 18051.

[4]"Toilet tutor," Bio-dyne Corporation, 154 East Erie, Chicago, Illinois 60611.

[5]This apparatus is also available from Lehigh Valley Electronics.

detection requiring the resident to go through the same procedure that was employed during initial training sessions. During the initial training sessions toilet approach was prompted. These prompts were gradually faded and upon the occasion of self-initiated approach to the toilet all social prompts ceased.

The entire toilet training procedure has been detailed by Foxx and Azrin (1973) in a book which also includes "trouble shooting" tips. For example, blue litmus paper taped to cotton briefs may serve as an inexpensive and effective substitute for the electronic training pants. At this juncture the Azrin and Foxx program is the most rapid, effective and enduring procedure that has been developed.

Self-Feeding

Self-feeding and refinements of eating skills and habits constitute a significant step toward "normalization" for the retarded child. Self-feeding with a spoon is a skill that can be taught with relative ease. The shaping procedure is simple, and the food serves as immediate reinforcement on a continuous schedule. Spradlin (Note 2) developed a procedure based on response building (c.f., Lindsley, 1964) and the prepotency principle (Premack, 1959). The steps of the procedure are as follows: (1) A spoon is placed in the child's hand and the child is assisted in holding and filling the spoon. (2) The trainer assists the child in moving the food-filled spoon to the child's mouth. (3) The child is required to make the final movement of placing the food into his mouth. (4) the assistance provided the child is gradually reduced requiring the child to complete independently successively greater portions of the response.

Bensberg and Slominski (1965) described a procedure that initially stresses the establishment of a hand-to-mouth motion. Fingers of the child are coated with a sweet substance (e.g., syrup) and then the child's hand is guided to the mouth. Once the hand-to-mouth movement is established, training in self-feeding with a spoon begins. The spoon is coated with syrup in order to establish a spoon-to-mouth movement. Food is then placed on the spoon and guided to the child's mouth. Reversion to putting hands in the food is punished with a brief withdrawal of the food tray. The disadvantage of the Bensberg and Slominski procedure is that it contains two nonessential steps (i.e., teaching hand-to-mouth and spoon-to-mouth movements). There is no evident need to establish these as prerequisite behaviors.

Whitney and Barnard (1966) described a shaping procedure used with a 14-year-old retarded female who was unable to feed herself. The client was reinforced initially for looking at a spoon placed on the table before her. She then was required successively to reach for and finally grasp the spoon in order to obtain reinforcement. Details of the procedure are incomplete and there is no clear description of the transition from grasping the spoon to self-feeding with the spoon. The authors described a forward chaining procedure in which a response is shaped and continues to be reinforced as long as it is the terminal behavior in the chain. When the next behavior in the chain is added, reinforcement of the first behavior ceases. Acquisition of the second behavior depends on the probability of an approximation of such a response occurring naturally. If the probability of such occurrence is low, extinction of the first response may occur often with a regression in behavior. Given a low probability of occurrence for the second behavior, the trainer may facilitate acquisition by prompting the client. A forward chaining procedure is far more laborious and subject to much greater risk of extinction and behavioral regression than the prompting and fading procedure described by Spradlin. Prompting and fading is essentially a backward chaining procedure. The apparent superiority of the backward chaining procedure derives from the fact that the subject first learns the terminal behavior in the chain which is reinforced, then learns successive behaviors in the chain which lead to the reinforced behavior. Most investigators (e.g., Berkowitz *et al.*, 1971; Gorton and Hollis, 1965; Zeiler and Jewey, 1968) have opted for the backward chaining procedure. This basic approach can be extended to other eating skills (e.g., drinking from a cup, using a fork, carrying a tray).

Groves and Carroccio (1971) reported a successful program for teaching self-feeding behavior on a ward wide basis to a group of severely and profoundly retarded adults. These residents apparently had spoon-to-mouth skills within their behavioral repertoires but ate most foods with their hands. In initial sessions, each trainer worked with one resident at a time. Trays were removed for ten seconds contingent on each hand-to-food response. Verbal prompts were given to use the spoon. The tray was terminated if a maximum permissible number of hand-to-food responses was exceeded. Under these contingencies, spoon-to-food behaviors (i.e., appropriate eating) increased markedly with a corresponding decrease in appropriate hand-to-food responses and food stealing. In turn, trainers were able to supervise larger numbers of residents as behaviors improved.

Only slightly less repulsive than incontinence are the eating habits of the untrained profoundly and severely retarded person (e.g., Edwards and

Lilly, 1966). Refinement of eating skills and development of more aesthetically pleasing table manners does much to alter the negative valence of retarded behavior. A number of studies (i.e., Barton *et al.*, 1970; Edwards and Lilly, 1966; Fielding, 1972; Grabrowski and Thompson, 1972; Gorton and Hollis, 1965; Henrickson and Doughty, 1967; Martin *et al.*, 1971b) demonstrate that undesirable eating habits and mealtime behavior can be altered by making access to food contingent upon appropriate behavior.

One of the most commonly encountered problems is the tendency of retarded individuals to eat very rapidly. Within the confines of the institution this is an adaptive behavior. The resident that finishes his meal rapidly is less likely to lose his food to other residents, and if not satiated he can then steal for himself. Blackwood (Note 3) successfully slowed the rate of eating by removing the food tray for a brief period of time when the resident ate too rapidly. The procedure involves differential reinforcement for a low rate of responding (drl schedule) combined with time out. Other undesirable eating habits or mealtime behaviors such as eating with hands, food grabbing, hitting others, or throwing food are also observed to rapidly decrease under various time out contingencies. Edwards and Lilly (1966) and Fielding (1972) immediately terminated the meal for residents who grabbed food and removed them from the dining area. These authors report rapid declines in food grabbing. Fielding, however, reported one particularly resistent case of a male who grabbed only after he had finished his meal. The behavior was substantially reduced when the resident's meals were served in several smaller portions, and these portions were withheld when the resident grabbed food. Successful similar procedures have been reported: (1) removal of the food tray temporarily (Groves and Carroccio, 1971); (2) momentary holding down of the resident's arms (Henrickson and Doughty, 1967); (3) temporary movement of the resident's chair from the dining table (Martin *et al.*, 1971b). All studies reported paired punishment with a verbal cue, thus bringing the behavior under verbal control.

Martin *et al.* (1971) also compared the differential effects of social approval for appropriate eating and time out for inappropriate eating habits. Social approval had no effect on the rate of inappropriate eating in a sample of profoundly and severely retarded adolescents.

Two studies have demonstrated experimental control of undesirable eating habits within applied analysis of behavior designs: Lent (Note 4) employing a reversal technique and Barton, Garcia, Guess, and Baer (1970) using a multiple baseline design and applying contingencies sequentially to several undesirable behaviors.

Dressing and Undressing

Over the last decade numerous operant based programs have been developed for teaching various dressing and undressing skills. Breland (1965) in Bensberg's handbook "Teaching the Mentally Retarded" describes procedures for teaching the retarded person to come to the technician, pay attention, sit down, stay there, dress and undress. Several other studies (i.e., Bensbert et al., 1965; Gorton and Hollis, 1965; Martin et al., 1971a; Minge and Ball, 1967) report similar programs and successful training with such programs.

Basically, the procedure involves breaking each skill into its most elemental components. Individual components are then developed by initially guiding the response with physical prompts. These physical prompts are gradually faded, requiring the subject to complete more of the behavioral sequence each trial. Completion of a behavioral sequence is typically rewarded with an edible and social reinforcement. With fading of the physical prompt, control is transferred to verbal or visual cues. The individual component behaviors are chained together to reconstitute the complete task. Typically the chaining progresses in a backward direction with the terminal behavior being mastered first. Programs for teaching a variety of dressing and undressing skills have been described in the literature (e.g., Martin et al., 1971a). Such programs are also commercially available. These programs will be discussed later in the chapter.

Azrin, Schaeffer, and Wesolowski (1976) have recently described a method for teaching dressing skills that is a radical departure from traditional approaches. Noting that the acquisition of dressing skills is a very slow process among the profoundly and severely retarded, these researchers first suggest intensification of the training process. Profoundly retarded adults were involved 4 to 6 hours per day in training. A forward chaining procedure was used involving the entire dressing or undressing procedure. Manual guidance, continuous instruction and near continuous reinforcement were used. By the end of the 4th day of training, all 20 clients had reached criterion. Such rapid acquisition of dressing skills indicates a dramatic improvement in training technology which would render obsolete programs based on backward chaining. A component analysis to clarify the differential effectiveness of this approach over more traditional ones is now called for. Of particular interest would be a comparison of backward chaining and forward chaining procedures where intensity of training was controlled.

Self-Grooming

The natural extension from the development of toileting, eating, and dressing skills would seem to be to the development of self-grooming skills. Yet there is a paucity of data concerning the development of such skills. Girardeau and Spradlin (1964) used a token economy to strengthen and maintain a broad range of behaviors on a ward with retarded females. It is not clear to what extent the behaviors had to be shaped. For the most part, these skills seem to already have been in the behavioral repertoires of the residents and were strengthened within the incentive system. Grooming behaviors developed included tooth brushing; showering; washing, combing, and setting hair; trimming and filing nails; and the proper use of sanitary napkins. A similar study by Wehman (1974) reported successful maintainance of oral hygiene in a group of retarded adult women through the use of a token system.

Two studies (Bensberg *et al.*, 1965; Hollis and Gorton, 1967) reported teaching grooming skills to profoundly and severely retarded persons. However, these studies fail to reveal specific procedures used. A study by Treffry, Martin, Samuels, and Watson (1970) detailed a forward training procedure using prompting and fading to teach face washing to a group of severely retarded girls. While relatively few studies have reported on programs for teaching grooming skills, many such programs are presently in use. Several such programs have been extensively field tested and are commercially available. These will be described later in this chapter.

PART II: SELF-HELP SKILLS TRAINING: SOME PROACTIVE CONSIDERATIONS FOR PLANNING

Perhaps the most important task facing providers of human services involves the transformation of a substantive body of knowledge such as that previously discussed into the actual delivery of the service to the individual client. Such a process obviously involves a great deal of organizing and planning and it will be the purpose of this section of the chapter to propose a model for how one might organize for such service delivery. It should be underscored that no attempt will be made here to discourse on the "how to" of training since this has been the purpose of other writings to which we would invite the reader's attention (e.g., Watson 1972; Nawas and Braun, 1970a,b,c). More importantly, however, it has been our experience that systematic planning is the key element in delivering effective services. The rather powerful instructional technology that is available to us is rendered useless unless it is employed within a well managed, well organized system, carefully planned to provide quality service. While this may seem perfectly obvious to the reader, it has been our experience that in human services this has been an oft-quoted but seldom practiced tenet. Planning, if indeed such a function is formalized by the agency or organization, is often reactive in orientation. That is, it is problem or crisis oriented and is typically done only when staff are faced with situations such as dangerous maladaptive behaviors, dissatisfied consumers, possible litigation, administrative edict, documented deficiencies in standards, or other situations warranting administrative intervention. Service planning should, of course, be proactive, and, according to our bias, should be conducted by a service planner whose managerial style is participatory in nature and who, along with his staff, is committed to the principle of normalization (Wolfensberger, 1972).

In order to more effectively communicate what we feel might be some components or steps of a proactive planning process, use will be made of a flow diagram or flow chart. This will, hopefully, provide the reader with a clearer picture of the sequence of steps in the planning process and provide a quick referent for the accompanying discussion. Figure 1, then, represents what, at least in our experience, constitutes the important components of the planning process.

Client Assessment

The first task in service planning is to determine, in a rather precise fashion, the characteristics and the needs of the people to be served. One of the defining characteristics of individuals with mental retardation is that they are deficit in adaptive functioning, that is to say that they have not acquired behaviors generally expected of persons of the same chronological age, culture and environment (Grossman, 1973). Given this defining parameter, it follows that the assessment of the client should focus on the assessment of adaptive behavior, for our purposes, those adaptive behaviors relating to self-care. As straightforward as this may appear, it might be pointed out that it has only been since 1959 that assessment of the retarded individual has typically been based on anything more than assessment of intellectual functioning. The intelligence test score was the common form of assessment and it was thought that the person's mental age (MA) could serve as an indicator of level of functioning and any expectations that might reasonably be held for such

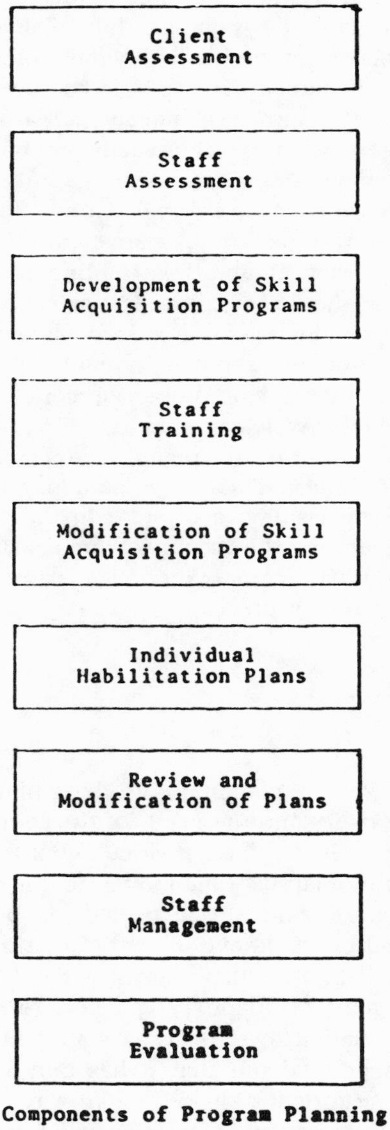

```
┌─────────────────────────┐
│         Client          │
│       Assessment        │
└─────────────────────────┘

┌─────────────────────────┐
│         Staff           │
│       Assessment        │
└─────────────────────────┘

┌─────────────────────────┐
│   Development of Skill   │
│   Acquisition Programs   │
└─────────────────────────┘

┌─────────────────────────┐
│         Staff           │
│       Training          │
└─────────────────────────┘

┌─────────────────────────┐
│   Modification of Skill  │
│   Acquisition Programs   │
└─────────────────────────┘

┌─────────────────────────┐
│       Individual         │
│   Habilitation Plans     │
└─────────────────────────┘

┌─────────────────────────┐
│       Review and         │
│   Modification of Plans  │
└─────────────────────────┘

┌─────────────────────────┐
│         Staff           │
│       Management        │
└─────────────────────────┘

┌─────────────────────────┐
│        Program          │
│       Evaluation        │
└─────────────────────────┘
```

Components of Program Planning

Fig. 1. Components of Program Planning.

an individual. While IQ scores do correlate with behavioral age (Ross and Boroskin, 1972) and social quotient (Adams, 1973), even for samples taken within the profound range of retardation, the information garnered from IQ tests has little utility in habilitative programming. Indeed, the MA concept and the prognosis implied may actually be counterproductive suggesting that the retarded person is capable of much less than is actually the case. Attempts to develop habilitative programs from traditional psychometric data have not been directed toward fostering adaptive behavior skills.

The systematic assessment of adaptive behavior, however, has only recently become possible with the development of adaptive inventories or scales. Such inventories generally present a profile of the individual client which depicts, for differing skill areas, relative competencies and deficits. For example, the American Association on Mental Deficiency's (AAMD) Adaptive Behavior Scale (ABS) (Nihira, Foster, Shellhass, and Leland, 1969) generates a profile of which behaviors the individual has acquired within 66 different skill areas. The ABS is organized around 10 categories of skills or "domains" that include independent functioning, physical development, economic activity, language development, vocational activity and so on. These ten domains are further broken down into 24 "sub-domains" (e.g., toilet use, eating skills, with sub-domains being even further partitioned into 66 "items" or skill areas (e.g., self care at toilet, use of table utensils, etc.). Each item is then further refined to include specific behaviors engaged in by the student (e.g., flushes toilet after use, feeds self with fingers or must be fed, washes hands with soap, etc.).

In addition to the ABS there are a number of other such scales or inventories available to service providers. Some of these include the Vineland Social Maturity Scale (Doll, 1953), the Balthazar Scales of Adaptive Behavior (Balthazar, 1971), the Camelot Behavioral Checklist (Foster, 1974), the Behavioral Characteristics Progression (Vort Corp., 1973), the Self-Help Skill Assessment Checklist (Watson, 1972), and a number of unpublished scales that are used regionally or locally such as the Fairview Self-Help Scale (Ross, Note 5). When evaluating these scales for use in a service system, a number of considerations should be kept in mind. The behaviors or skill areas that are addressed by the inventory should be broken down into relatively small steps or learning objectives, and should be arranged in a developmental or easy to complex sequence (Crosby, 1976). Further, as it is the direct service staff or relatives of the client who will generally be in the best position to provide the information necessary to complete the inventory, the scale should be relatively easy to administer and should avoid the professional argot of the psychologist or educator. Other more rigorous criteria that a potential user might wish to apply relate to the published research available on the scale. For example, particular attention should be paid to whether or not validity and reliability studies have been conducted and what those data suggest. Also, the standardization process should be investigated with some examination of the parameters of the population on which the scale was normed. For example, the AAMD's ABS was standardized on an institutional population and therefore may not constitute the most useful scale when providing services to mildly retarded community clients. Additionally, examination of background information available on the scale will generally suggest the purpose behind the development of the inventory. Clearly, an inventory designed for prescriptive planning would differ from one established to provide an overall score or quotient to be used primarily for diagnostic purposes. Again, it should be stressed that the range of behaviors covered in the scale should be carefully scrutinized along with the level of training or experience necessary on the part of the staff to effectively use the instrument.

A further criterion involves the potential for computerization of the inventory. If there is a fairly large number of clients in the service delivery system, it would be extremely facilitative to computerize the assessment information. Storage and retrieval capabilities will become most useful when the data generated by the inventory are being used for prescriptive planning, grouping, evaluation of programming, and recording client progress or skill gains.

In order to ensure that the assessment information is accurate and therefore provides a valid baseline from which to measure the efficacy of programming, two additional considerations are suggested. First, the inventory selected should lend itself to standardized assessment procedures. That is, the assessment of the skill repertoires of the clients should be carried out in a consistent fashion under the same stimulus conditions for each client. This is particularly important if task materials or objects are used. If the inventory does not provide for standardized administration procedures and materials, the agency or facility should develop such guidelines. Second, at least two independent, trained evaluators should assess each skill or behavior, and their evaluations or observations should achieve some pre-specified criterion for acceptable interrater reliability. Such a procedure provides staff with an internally consistent data base, ensures accurate decisions regarding necessary programming, and provides for accurate evaluation of staff efforts.

In addition to meeting the need for specifying precisely what behaviors are and are not in the repertoires of the handicapped students, other kinds of assessments will be necessary. Such additional assessments will be carried out by professional staff and should provide supplemental information to the adaptive behavior assessment and should be geared toward providing data necessary to setting individualized learning objectives and/or recommendations for training. It is these authors' bias that the major purpose of these professional assessments should NOT be diagnosis or classification but rather they should be prescriptive in nature for, as Baroff (1974) suggests, the purpose of assessment is to identify those learning objectives that are developmentally appropriate to the individual child. Professional assessments that may be necessary to conduct will include a physician's assessment, dietary and social work assessment, a dental evaluation, an evaluation by a physical therapist and optometric and audiological evaluations. While clearly not all these evaluations may be necessary for each and every student, careful consideration should be given to what behavioral or physical charac-teristics of the individual might influence the process of training. It would be necessary, for example, to utilize different training techniques if a client were visually or auditorally impaired. Here a training technology similar to the one developed by Gold (Note 6) would be appropriate. Knowledge of the locations in which clients engage in self-care behaviors and any accompanying family or personal routines used in self-care constitutes important information when individualizing training and such information might well be made available in a social work assessment. Inspecting of the client's living environment and interviewing parents, guardians, or direct care staff provide a wealth of useful data. Certainly, if training were to be done in self-feeding or if foods and/or liquids were to be used as potential reinforcers, a dietary assessment would be helpful. If training involved gross and fine motor coordination as prerequisites or if physical prompts were necessary as training aids, the input of a physician or physical therapist would be extremely important, particularly if there is any kind of physical involvement as is often the case with many profoundly handicapped individuals. The important point to make though, is that mental retardation is a generalized condition requiring, for its effective amelioration, the services of a variety of professional disciplines. The input of all relevant disciplines should be weighed and integrated before actual training is initiated.

Assessment of Staff

The next consideration to which one might direct his attention is perhaps the most neglected, least researched area in service planning, yet one that looms critical when organizing for service delivery. This is the area of *Staff* assessment. Presumably, relative neglect of this issue has been due to such factors as potential political repercussions, anxiety and defensiveness on the part of staff to be evaluated, lack of technological or methodological advances in this area, apprehension on the part of managers as to potential liability, and difficulties with state civil service systems. The above notwithstanding, however, just as the human service planner must be aware of the characteristics, competencies, and weaknesses of the client population, so too must he assess his staff on these parameters.

Perhaps one of the more important kinds of information to be gathered about staff would be the assessment of their attitudes toward handicapped persons, particularly attitudes concerning their potential for habilitation, improvement or eventual productivity. Someone, for example, who believes that a profoundly retarded individual will never learn to care for himself is unlikely to devote a great deal of time, energy and effort toward actualizing such a goal. The attitudes of the staff toward the client population, then, might be an indicator of the frequency of quality of services provided. For example, data indicate that more severely retarded individuals are perceived less favorably than mildly retarded persons (Jones, 1974) and that retarded adults seem to be less favorably looked upon than developmentally delayed children (Gottlieb and Siperstein, 1976). This suggests that providing quality services at an optimal frequency to older, more severely handicapped people would become a more difficult task than might be anticipated.

The actual assessment of attitudes should probably be accomplished with all employees, as there are some data to suggest significant attitudinal differences between grades of staff (e.g., Overbeck, 1971). Additionally, the attitude assessment should, if possible, make use of a standardized rating scale or questionnaire (e.g., Bensberg and Barnett, 1966). This will provide normative data and allow for later evaluation of attitude change interventions, correlations with such factors as job performance, age, sex, etc., and other kinds of useful data.

Obviously, an assessment of the current skill levels of the staff would be indispensable. In the area of self-help skills training this might best be done as a two part assessment. The first evaluation should concern itself with basic knowledge of the principles of instructional technology. A simple paper and pencil test or oral interview would probably suffice here. It is perhaps true that such a verbal repertoire may not be absolutely necessary for one to be a proficient trainer; however, knowledge of behavioral principles has been demonstrated to correlate rather highly with skills in applying these principles (Gardner, 1972). Additionally, it would seem that a common language or information base would greatly facilitate communication and any later in-service training.

Once staff's familiarity with training principles has been assessed, an evaluation should be conducted of employee proficiency in an actual client training situation. Again, such a baseline should be carried out using an objective, standardized assessment instrument. Here, we would suggest the use of the Training Proficiency Scale (TPS) developed by Gardner, Brust, and Watson (1970). This is a 44 item scale that assesses on both quantitative and qualitative parameters the proficiency with which a trainer conducts a self-help skill acquisition program. Such a sample of staff behavior should provide a valid profile of their current skill levels and suggest areas for staff development. An evaluation such as the one suggested above only provides information on staff behavior within the context of a structured training situation, however. Observation of direct service staff as they interact with clients outside formalized training sessions will also be valuable, if not requisite, information. Dependent variables of interest might include whether staff were encouraging clients to perform previously learned skills, whether staff were performing self-care tasks for the student rather than creating learning opportunities, and whether staff were utilizing procedures to ensure the maintenance of learned skills. How much of the total staff time was being invested in training relative to other activities might also be a meaningful question. Inquiries such as these can, of course, be answered in a variety of ways, and it is a relatively easy task to design a behavioral observation system geared toward responding to the specific information requirements of the service planner. However, such instruments as the Behavioral Observation System (BOS) (Hormatz, 1973) or the Attendant Behavior Checklist (ABCL) (Gardner and Giampa, 1971) are available and might well prove appropriate for use in a number of agency or service situations.

Perhaps the most sensitive area of assessment involves measuring the general aptitude, achievement levels and personality traits of people charged with providing services. This latter form of assessment has typically been used in an attempt to identify any significant personality correlates of job performance and/or client behavior change (Gardner, 1972). Because of the equivocal nature of the findings regarding such personality correlates and the fact that most service planners are not in a position to select all or even most of their staff, such an assessment seems less than desirable.

It has been our experience, however, that indication of a staff member's previous education or training is often insufficient and perhaps misleading information. Often, this may result in the service planner assuming certain skill levels or prerequisite behaviors. Further, many service planners do not generally take achievement level into account when communicating with staff, requiring certain performance criteria for which prerequisite behaviors may be lacking, selecting and/or presenting in-service education material and so forth. For these reasons, achievement testing, particularly in the area of reading, may be desirable. If reading achievement data were available, it would be possible for the service planner to subject in-service education materials, written communications, and even skill acquisition programs to a readability analysis (Fry, 1968). Appropriate revisions could then be made in these materials such that resulting reading grade-levels would correspond to the tested grade levels of its consumers. Additionally, material that is easier to read tends to be more interesting for the reader (Kendall, Finch and Gillen, 1976).

A rather careful analysis of staff, then, may suggest a number of areas for consideration by the service planner resulting in fewer staff management problems, increases in job satisfaction and productivity and better client services.

Self-Help Skill Acquisition Programs

Once the need for self-help skill training has been established, it will be necessary to produce and/or develop self-help skill acquisition programs. These are carefully structured instructional sequences that outline in a step-by-step fashion the approach to be used by the trainer. These skill acquisition programs generally consist of a sequential breakdown of the task to be taught plus a description of the training techniques to be used. The former component should be the result of a very careful task analysis that generates a sequentially ordered series of steps carefully describing each behavior that goes into successful completion of the task. These steps should be sequenced so as to make maximal use of available cues or antecedent stimuli. That is, each step should provide the learner with the most salient cue possible as to what behavior should occur next. Once the task has been broken down into teachable components, consideration can be given to what techniques or procedures or instructional paradigms will result in the effective, efficient learning. This would include such decisions as whether to use forward or backward chaining, the selection of potential reinforcers, the selection of instructional materials, etc.

It will be necessary to provide or develop at least one such program for every skill deficit that has been pinpointed in the client population. These should be organized around the behavioral objectives of the assessment instrument or inventory and catalogued for easy matching. Crosby (1976) provides an excellent example of this last point:

> On the AAMD's ABS for self-dressing, for example, an individual may put on socks correctly, without assistance, but may not perform at the next step on the scale, putting on coat or dress without assistance. Observation would then be necessary to determine what skills involved in putting on a coat or dress the individual lacks, and a training program would have to be designed to teach those skills (p. 5).

Such instructional programs may be written by agency staff or may be procured if commercially or otherwise available (e.g., Anderson, Hodson, and Jones, 1975). When available, these so-called "canned" programs would be recommended for a number of reasons. First, this will save valuable staff time otherwise given over to conducting task analyses, sequencing training steps, etc. Second, "canned" programs in a number of cases, will have been field-tested and standardized thereby increasing the probability that clients will reach criterion performance. Additionally, this will save the agency from having to field-test and evaluate the programs written by its staff.

Clearly, there are drawbacks associated with using packaged programs, however. First, many such programs do not report the characteristics of the client population on which they were developed (if, indeed, such standardization took place). This may result in a task analysis that is not sufficiently refined for other client populations. Furthermore, these programs may rely on a standard instructional strategy (e.g., backward chaining) or standard procedures and techniques that may not be either optimally effective or efficient for other clients. These programs, if they are to be maximally effective, should be standardized on a population of trainers and clients to determine what level of staff expertise is needed to carry them out and to determine their efficacy over specific functional levels of the retarded population. For example, a specific instructional program may be effective when implemented with a population of profoundly retarded residents. A good illustration of this point can be seen in a recently published toothbrushing program (Horner and Keilitz, 1975) sugggested for use with moderate to mildly retarded persons and seemingly not appropriate for severely to profoundly handicapped individuals.

If canned programs are to be used, perhaps the best resource as to program availability is Tucker's *Skill Acquisition Program Bibliography* (1974). This bibliography has catalogued 1700 available programs organized around the 399 behavioral objectives of the Camelot Behavioral

Checklist (Foster, 1974). These programs are assigned a 1-, 2-, 3- or 4-star rating based on the stage of development and validation of each program. Criteria included in this rating are plausibility of the task analysis and teaching strategy, the extent to which each was field-tested and the commercial availability of the program.

Some of these catalogued programs that are specifically designed to ameliorate self-help skill deficiencies include Project MORE's *Daily Living Skills Programs.* These programs, designed for a trainable mentally retarded (TMR) population, include noseblowing, toothbrushing, handwashing, etc. They have been carefully field-tested, are commercially available, and generally are recommended for use with a moderately to mildly retarded population. Watson (1972) is another valuable resource and contains most of the basic self-help skills. These appear to be effective with a lower range of functioning client and, in fact, have been field tested at a state residential facility. Another important, general resource is Anderson, Hodson, and Jones (1975). This is an excellent collection of programs and includes all the basic self-help skills as well as a number of other developmental areas.

If training is to be carried out by parents, a recent series by Baker, Brightman, Heifetz, and Murphy (1976) would be most useful. This series is broken down into early, intermediate, and advanced self-help skills and has been extensively field-tested with parents of developmentally disabled children.

Finally, two others resources that deal with a specific self-help skill deficit include Foxx and Azrin (1973) (toilet-training) and Henderson and McDonald (1975) (dressing and undressing). The Foxx and Azrin program is somewhat complex but clearly the most effective and efficient program available for toilet-training retarded children.

It is recommended that a program file be established that is catalogued according to the behavioral objectives as stated in the adaptive behavior inventory. When any one of the objectives appears in the clients individual treatment plan, then staff need simply obtain the corresponding catalogued program and implement training.

Staff Development and Training

Regardless of how well planned or organized a human service system happens to be, effective delivery of treatment depends, to a greater or lesser extent, on the competencies of the individual provider. Just as the expertise of individuals may be neutralized by an ill-managed system, so too, can the impact of a carefully planned system be reduced by individual incompetence. Staff development and training, then, becomes an issue of some consequence and a most important part of total service delivery, albeit an often neglected one. Such neglect is suggested by a review of the recent literature which yielded only about four studies that attempted to present an adequate description of the initial staff training process (Watson *et al.*, 1971; Gardner, 1972; Martin, 1972; Gladstone and Sherman, 1975). The majority of studies examined reported attempts at increasing the occurrence of what are assumed to be previously learned skills (e.g., Bricker *et al.*, 1972).

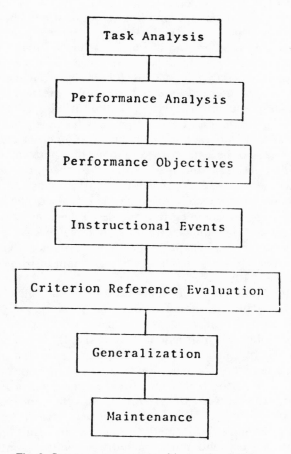

Fig. 2. Sequence components of instructional system.

Designing an effective instructional system requires of the service planner a number of activities sequenced in a manner similar to that depicted in Fig. 2. If one is to speak of the acquisition of competencies, careful consideration must be given to the desired state of knowledge and/or skill to be attained by the learner. More simply, an attempt must be made to address the question of what should the competent trainer be able to do. In order to satisfactorily answer such a question, a task analysis similar to that suggested by Gold (Note 6) must be carried out. What must remain central to any such analysis is the identification of those trainer behaviors which result in the attainment of new skills or competencies on the part of the client. Moreover, once these behaviors are identified they must be sequenced in a fashion that makes maximal use of potential cues or antecedents for subsequent behaviors and such that the response chain to be emitted by the trainer is as efficient as possible. Such identification and sequencing may result from a careful study of staff who are clearly skilled in teaching clients new behaviors and/or by using training manuals or other resources which may be available. Although such aids are indispensable, the task analysis will necessarily undergo numerous revisions based on the feedback provided by trainees as they function in client training situations.

Once the composite of the "competent" trainer has been pieced together, it will be necessary to examine the performance of the individual staff relative to the profile of the competent trainer. Such a comparison will serve to identify individual learner needs and will provide a kind of baseline from which to evaluate the efficacy of the instructional intervention. Further, examining in some detail what staff do and fail to do will generate useful modifications in the task analysis. As mentioned in a previous section of this chapter, such a performance analysis should probably be generated via a standardized assessment instrument or rating scale such as the T.P.S.

Examination of the existing skill repertoire of staff members relative to the competency analysis should result in the generation of performance or learner objectives, that is, clear statements of what the learner will be able to do following instruction (Mager, 1962). These performance objectives should be categorized into small units, each concerned with a subset of skills necessary for over-all goal attainment. For example, there might be a set of performance objectives, each of which is related to reinforcement skills, a second set concerned with appropriate use of prompting and fading techniques and so forth. Such a partitioning is based on the rationale that small learning units result in a greater probability of mastery and more immediate reinforcement of correct learner behavior.

The selection and development of learning experiences and accompanying educational materials is now warranted. These should be designed or selected around each performance objective and should have effective, efficient attainment of that objective as their sole purpose. Extraneous content included as enrichment material or because it's something "they just ought to know" is most undesirable. Again, when selecting the content of the in-service program, the rapid, effective acquisition of the specified performance objectives should be the primary concern.

At this point, we would like to make a number of additional recommendations concerning the development of an in-service training program. First, it should be formatted to allow for individualized instruction and thereby for active rather than passive learning. Active, individual involvement with learning materials results in the learner assuming that major responsibility for his or her development. Additionally, this allows for considerably more latitude in scheduling staff to be involved in such learning, and following the initial development of the in-service training program, results in a considerable saving in instructor time.

To the extent possible the in-service training program should make use of multimedia training packages. Presenting material through different media generally seems to result in more effective learning and a more enjoyable experience for the trainee. Perhaps more important than use of different media, the auto-instructional packages should be self-paced (Keller, 1968). That is, the rate of learning should be controlled by the student rather than by the instructor. Such a shift from the traditional locus of control is recommended due to the inevitable variability in acquisition rates generated by a heterogeneous trainee population. Perhaps the most desirable feature of self-paced instruction is that it allows for the establishment of a mastery criterion or adoption of a "forced excellence" paradigm (Lea and Lockhart, 1975). That is, it allows the instructor to establish a high performance standard (e.g., 90%) for all trainees and allows for students failing to meet such a criterion to remediate or recycle through that unit or training package. Under such a model, advancement to the next unit or training package should be contingent on attainment of mastery criterion.

It has been our experience that beyond dividing the in-service program into units or training packages, it has been advantageous to partition each unit into two segments. Part 1 of the unit should concern itself with basic information or knowledge of habilitation training (e.g., reinforcement must immediately follow a correct response), while Part 2 should attempt to bring about the application of the newly learned principles covered in that unit (e.g., the immediate reinforcement of a correct response in an actual client training situation). This kind of division is helpful in that the learner is acquiring concrete training skills as well as information as he progresses through the instruction. Thus, generalization from basic information to the application of this knowledge is being programmed from the beginning. All too often, staff receive some form of in-service training and are then expected to transfer that information to the client training situation. Predictably, little transfer takes place. Subdividing the units increases the probability of mastery, rapid acquisition, and more immediate reinforcement for correct learner behavior.

Auto-instructional, self-paced systems generally require the use of proctors or tutors (Keller, 1968). Each trainee should be assigned to a proctor with each proctor being responsible for monitoring progress through the in-service program and tutoring the trainee if any difficulty is experienced or any questions arise. Within the suggested unit division mentioned above, the proctor would be responsible for checking out instructional materials, serving as a resource person, evaluating the learner's performance, and providing immediate feedback. In Part 2, the proctor would be responsible for modeling appropriate training techniques, providing verbal prompts and feedback, evaluating performance, and providing immediate reinforcement for correct learner behavior.

Evaluation of learner performance should be frequent, objective, and utilize criterion referenced items or procedures. This last consideration suggests that the learner be evaluated solely on the attainment of the specified performance objectives (Mager, 1973). There should be at least one evaluation procedure for each of the stated objectives. For those objectives concerned with attainment of basic information, a unit quiz would probably suffice. If the performance objective reflects a skill to be emitted in a client training situation, then some kind of performance checklist is indicated (e.g., Training Proficiency Scale). This kind of evaluation should be standardized, objective, and allow for computation of interrater reliability coefficients.

Early attempts at applying the principles of operant conditioning to human service settings often resulted in "magic shows." The behavior analyst would enter into the service delivery system, dramatically change some behavior and then remove himself. The predictably rapid return to the status quo often left staff enraged, and needless to say, left the client with little in the way of durable behavior change.

Such a history lesson graphically portrays the need to carefully plan for generalization or transfer of learning and for maintenance of training gains. This lesson loses little of its impact when applied to in-service or staff development. Rather than stopping at initial acquisition, the instructor must plan to engage in some generalization programming in order to ensure that staff can use a variety of skill acquisition programs with different residents and in different training situations.

Additionally, follow-up evaluation of staff will be necessary in order to determine if criterion performance (as defined in the training program) is being maintained over time. If this is not the case, it might be necessary to provide remedial instruction. The optimal maintenance system, however, is one that allows the trainee frequent use of his newly acquired skills concurrent with a dense schedule of reinforcement and feedback from supervisors for engaging in those newly learned behaviors.

Modification of Skill Acquisition Programs

It has been our experience that training staff in habilitative procedures invariably results in a need to revise the recently procedured or developed self-help skill acquisition programs. Most often, such a need arises when inconsistencies are discovered between the in-service training program and the skill acquisition programs. Those charged with the revision of such habilitation programs should target consistency as their key objective. Each program should make use of the techniques, procedures, data keeping format, instructional paradigms (e.g., chaining), etc., employed in the in-service training course. This should yield a body of programs not only consistent with the educational history of the user but internally consistent as well. This, of course, will facilitate generalization of the staff member's newly acquired trainer skills across skill acquisition programs.

Once staff begin to use these programs, revisions will also be dictated by the fact that, for at least some of the clients in the service system, the programs appear inappropriate. This might be particularly true for physically or sensorily impaired individuals. Nonambulatory, blind, deaf, deaf-blind, and cerebral palsied individuals will need programs with revised task analyses and specially tailored training techniques or procedures. Occasionally, prosthetic devices will have to be incorporated into the program.

Finally, revision of such programs will be necessary if they do not appear to result in acquisition of the skill on the part of the client. The conduct of revisions based on evaluative data will be taken up in a later section of this chapter.

Individual Habilitation Planning

Up to this point in the service planning process the considerations have been fairly molar ones: assessment of the client population, assessment and training of service providers, the development and revision of skill acquisition programs. At this juncture the process shifts in scope to address the more molecular issue of planning for the individual student. Such a process has been referred to as "active treatment" or "active habilitation programming" (Accreditation Council, 1971). Such an effort put forth for each individual student in the service system is not only critical to the delivery of quality self-care training services but, in fact, has been mandated by various standards and regulations (Crosby, 1976), accrediting agencies and court decisions (e.g., Wyatt *vs.* Stickney, Note 1).

As defined by the Accreditation Council for Facilities for the Mentally Retarded (AC/FMR), "active habilation programming" involves targeting the specific habilitative needs of the client, establishing goals to meet those needs, devising methods to meet the stated goals, designating specific staff as responsible agents, reviewing client progress, and modifying the goals and/or methods as necessary (Crosby, 1976). To these components of the definition we would add the specification of client strengths, assets, and resources.

From such a service planning effort must emerge an integrated and individually tailored habilitation plan, the result of the efforts of an interdisciplinary team. This last requirement stems from the assumption that mental retardation is not simply a medical, psychological or educational "problem," but rather a generalized condition requiring a variety of services and the expertise of a number of professional disciplines. Further, the service planning group should be interdisciplinary rather than multi-disciplinary in function so that the focus will be on the needs of the *client* rather than foci bound or limited by professional title or training. This perspective is important to retain even when planners limit their scope from the total developmental needs of the handicapped person to self-care training needs only. Questions such as: What should be considered in establishing training priorities? Where and how should training be conducted? Can the family be actively involved in training? What modifications in training procedures are dictated by the client's physical or medical condition(s)?, all need to be asked. Such questions as these are extremely important ones and can be answered only by processing the input of a number of individuals involved with the client. The input of direct service staff is particularly important and often neglected when professionals engage in decision-making.

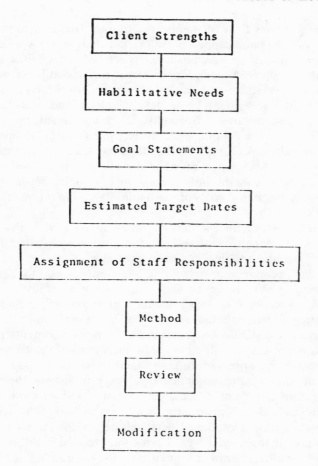

Sequence of tasks necessary for development of an individual student habilitation plan.

Fig. 3.

The above-cited definitional requirements of active programming are of considerable heuristic value in that they provide a kind of task analysis of the development of an individual child's habilitation plan. Figure 3 provides a flow chart of that task analysis indicating the suggested sequence of each activity.

The strengths/assets/resources list developed for the individual is the first task to be completed and should include the client's current self-help skills repertoire plus preferred or high probability activities and other potential reinforcers. This is considered an important aspect of the habilitation plan for a variety of perspectives. First, it is important that those working in the field of mental retardation begin to focus on the competencies of the handicapped person rather than on his weaknesses or deficits. Such a focus on the positive aspects of the client's behavior should result in differential reinforcement of normative behavior rather than attention directed toward "retarded" or deviant behavior. It should also result in the individual being less devalued and less subject to dehumanizing circumstances. Secondly, it should result in a higher probability that staff will build on already existing skills as opposed to attempting to train tasks for which the client has few, if any, prerequisite behaviors. Finally, knowledge of what the client can do and what the client likes to do is valuable information in developing an instructional strategy to meet the stated goals of the habilitation plan (Honts and Scott, 1975).

Much of the strengths list can be taken directly from the recently completed assessment of adaptive behavior, since it will have pinpointed those skills already existing in the repertoire of the client. If the assessment has been computerized, it is a simple task to generate a current self-care skills profile for each client being served.

Information concerning other assets and resources, including preferred activities, other potential reinforcers, interested family, and other available resources, should be found either in the assessments prepared by the various professional disciplines, by interviewing the direct service staff, by direct client observation, or by family communication.

The next step in the sequence involves establishing the self-care training needs of the client. Once again, a completed adaptive behavior rating of the individual will greatly facilitate this task. The completed inventory will provide a profile of what self-help skills the client has not as yet acquired. If these data have been computerized it will be possible to easily and rapidly generate a sequenced self-care training needs list for any child in the service delivery system.

From such a data base, it will then be possible to establish habilitative goals designed to meet the now priority established needs. Such goals or objectives must be behaviorally stated and hence, quantifiable. It should be emphasized that vague or nonquantifiable goals such as "will develop better self-care skills" or "will improve eating skills" or "to dress more neatly" are not acceptable. Goal statements should include a description of the topography of the behavior, the stimulus conditions under which it is to occur and the established criterion for acceptable performance (e.g., percent correct, rate, duration, etc.). It should also be kept in mind that goal statements should reflect "product" or outcomes of training rather than "process." Process statements often involve a description of staff behaviors; goal statements should reflect client behavior only.

Further, in keeping with the developmental model of mental retardation, goals should be prioritized or sequenced. A developmentally sequenced adaptive behavior inventory should ensure this by indicating the next skill in the domain or subdomain to be acquired. Once this determination has been made, the service planner now has a list of client strengths, and individual needs list and prioritized training objectives.

For example, if the service planner were using the Adaptive Behavior Scale and interested in toileting skills he might receive a profile indicating that a client was toilet trained (skills 25–29) and, further, could "lower his pants at the toilet without help" (skill 30) and could "sit on toilet seat without help" (skill 31). The remaining skills under this category (skills 32–35) did not appear on the profile, however, indicating that the client had not as yet acquired the behaviors involved in using toilet tissue (skill 32), flushing the toilet after use (skill 33), putting on clothes without help (skill 34), and washing hands without help (skill 35). As this item involving self-care at the toilet is nicely sequenced, it would be clear to the service planner that the priority training objective might be skill #32 or "uses the toilet tissue appropriately" followed by skills 33, 34, and 35, respectively.

The above is admittedly a rather clear cut example. However, we should caution the reader not to rely too heavily on the adaptive behavior inventory for goal statements. First, it may be necessary to establish much smaller goals than those indicated on the rating scale. For example, a plausible task analysis for using toilet tissue might include anywhere from five to nine steps. Second, either the sequencing of behavior is arbitrary or if the skills within an item are sequenced no attempt is made to sequence sub-domains. For example, the ABS has ordering meals in a restaurant preceding toilet use. Third, the skills are occasionally stated rather nebulously (e.g., uses toilet tissue appropriately) and may have to be restated more clearly or in more behavioral terms. Also, there are a number of factors to be considered in establishing priorities for training and it is not suggested that strict adherence to the sequence of the adaptive behavior inventory is necessary. In fact, if normalization is a guiding principle of the service system then the most important consideration in establishing priorities for training should involve an analysis of what the *individual* client needs to be able to do to successfully function in his particular environment or to gain additional services in his community. However, the adaptive behavior inventory is a heuristically useful tool in determining what training objectives should be addressed and in what order.

Once the objectives have been decided upon, it will be necessary to establish time-guidelines for goal attainment. These guidelines should be reasonable projections for when, given the nature of the goal, available resources, staff expertise, time devoted to training, and so on, the goal will be met. It is well to consider that the more opportunities the staff have for receiving feedback as to goal attainment the higher the probability of maintaining their efforts. Therefore, it is recommended that target dates be set fairly close together. Additionally, the establishment of target dates provides a foundation for a staff accountability system. Information will continue to be generated as to what trainers are meeting target dates for what targeted skills, and using what specific training techniques or procedures.

This assumes, of course, that specific staff members are assigned responsibility for the attainment of specific training objectives. This should be the case. Additionally, assignment of staff responsibilities should include the location of training and the specific times training sessions are to be held. In the acquisition stage of self-help skill development it will be important that the trainer(s), time, and location be consistent. Once the skill is acquired it is then permissible, indeed necessary, to attempt to generalize across trainers, times, and locations.

Determining the instructional approach by which stated training objectives will be reached should, at this point, be a relatively simple task. While it should be stressed that programming, to be effective, must be done on an individual basis, service planners should, to the extent possible, make use of the self-help skill acquisition programs discussed in an earlier section of this chapter. In addition, such considerations as potential reinforcers, length of training session, modifications in the program due to physical or sensory handicaps, etc., should be made on an individual basis and documented in this section of the plan. It is further recommended that in addition to assigning specific staff to be responsible for carrying out the acquisition program, supervisory or professional staff be assigned to monitor the program "agents."

Program Review and Modification

In order to review the clients' progress toward meeting the stated goals and their accompanying time guidelines it will be necessary to establish a review mechanism. One often used vehicle is that of team progress notes. Here, the staff member, on a frequent basis, provides an account of the individual's progress toward the stated goal. Generally there is a minimum criterion established for how frequently staff must engage in such documentation. Progress notes should provide an objective evaluation of the present status of the client and should indicate, in light of that evaluation, what action or actions should result. For example, a progress note might read:

John completed step 30 of the toothbrushing program with no help for five consecutive trials. Tomorrow, training will begin on step 31 of the program.

Progress notes should studiously avoid process kinds of statements and vague generalities. Again, outcome or product statements that are goal-oriented should be the rule.

In addition, or in some cases in lieu of progress notes, trial data for each training session should be available for public inspection. The data for each training session should be available for public inspection. The data tracking system should be a straightforward one and easily used by direct service staff. A rather easily taught system that provides a good deal of useful information might involve indicating for each trial whether the behavior occurred independent of trainer assistance (+), whether verbal help (V) was necessary, a gesture or demonstration (G/D) was used, physical assistance (P) was provided, or the behavior did not occur even after physical prompts were given (−).

In order for the program monitors and service planners to have rapid access to information on client progress, these data should be frequently graphed, preferably daily. Again, the graphs should be simple in format

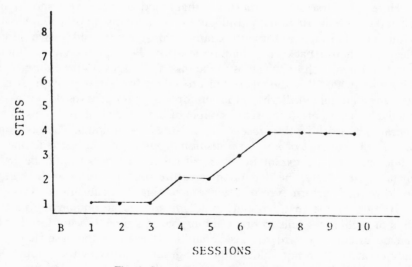

Fig. 4. Sample training session graph.

and depict only the necessary information. A simple but most useful format for graphically depicting data has been suggested by the staff of Project MORE (1974) and is presented in Fig. 4. The trainer simply plots training sessions on the abscissa and the number of steps in the self-help skill acquisition program on the ordinate. Only the steps completed by the client without trainer prompting are graphed. Acquisition of training steps over time is thus depicted.

With the aid of progress notes and trial data for each training session, the monitor or service provider will be able to regularly assess progress toward goal attainment relative to the projected target dates. In larger service delivery systems, it may not be possible to review actual training data or all progress notes. In such a case a procedure involving the random sampling of client records on some sort of variable or intermittent schedule would be useful.

If time to goal attainment consistently exceeds projections, modifications are clearly in order. Perhaps the first area of review would be to examine the trainer's behavior. In this case, the evaluation tool used in the staff development program would provide data as to the proficiency of the trainer. If this evaluation suggests that the trainer has not maintained an acceptable level of competency, it should be a simple task to remediate the specific deficits targeted by the evaluation. If the trainer has maintained the necessary competencies, the skill acquisition program should be scrutinized.

Here, the first set of questions that need to be asked should be directed at the instructional paradigm and accompanying procedures and techniques. Perhaps a forward chaining program would prove more efficacious than a backward chaining strategy. Perhaps the client should be put through each of the steps in the task analysis every time the task is to be taught. Possibly the suggested procedure for fading prompts is not sufficiently graduated. Perhaps the reinforcement procedures do not work effectively. These are just a small sample of the number of questions to be generated concerning the *process* (Gold, Note 6) of training. The revisions made in the conduct of a skill acquisition program should be made one at a time, and to the extent possible, all other variables should be held constant. Obviously, the dependent measure used to assess each change should be the performance of the client or time to acquisition.

If revising the instructional paradigm and its accompanying procedures or techniques fails to bring about goal attainment, attention should then be directed toward the task analysis. It is often the case that task analyses are either not sufficiently fine-grain or are less than optimally sequenced. If it appears that the steps of the skill acquisition program could be further subdivided or sequenced in such a way as to provide more salient cues for the learner, such a revision is indeed warranted.

Other possibilities clearly exist. Overly medicating a client will often result in a lethargic, nonattentive student and training then becomes a most difficult task. There is also the possibility that rather than reinforcing independent behavior, some well-intentioned individual is performing the task for the client. Reinforcer satiation is yet another possibility.

Service planners must be committed to the proposition that if the client is not learning then the situation has not been structured so that he will acquire the targeted skill. Instances of failure to learn should not be explained away by looking inside the client for such constructs, hypothetical or otherwise, as "brain-damage," institutionalization, capacity or defective intelligence. Such an ideology that results in critical examination of the training situation rather than the learner when failure occurs dictates that the service planner will continue to revise and revise and then revise some more until the learner has achieved the stated objectives.

Staff Management

Assigning particular staff members the responsibility of attainment of training goals or the conduct of skill acquisition programs will require that the service planner establish a staff management system designed to ensure accountability and reinforce desirable employee behavior. The present authors' history of trial and error, as well as vicarious learning, has suggested that a major component of an accountability system involves providing staff with clear-cut expectations for what should be accomplished on almost an hour-to-hour basis. Often, if there is the absence of expectation for specifically what staff should do next, little will be accomplished. Careful scheduling of staff times provides needed structure and allows for service providers to be accountable regarding their location, use of time, clients serviced, assigned target goals and so on. Additionally, scheduling results in significantly simplifying the task of the program supervisor.

In most cases self-care training should be allotted probably no more than about 30 to 45 minutes per session. This allows time for the trainer to assemble his materials, provide 15–20 minutes of intensive training, clean up, and graph the session data. For clients requiring self-help skill training, sessions lasting longer than 15–20 minutes are often counterproductive due to such factors as short attention span, fatigue, and reinforcer satiation.

Accountability should involve, beyond all else, accountability to the consumer of the service. Given that, the major dependent variable, if you will, becomes the degree to which clients are achieving the goals established for them in the individual habilitation plan. This, as was mentioned previously, involves reviewing goal attainment relative to the projected time guidelines. Other measurable dependent variables might include the percent of schedules training sessions that were held, trainer competence, and interrater reliability coefficients computed to examine the validity of reported skill gains. Using the skills repertoire of the client as a measure of accountability will be discussed in greater detail in the next section.

Providing an adequate incentive system may be, at least for some service planners, perhaps the most demanding task to be addressed. A review of the relevant research indicates that, although a variety of potential reinforcers have been attempted, feedback and money have been the most frequently used. Pommer and Streedback (1974) used public charts and money to increase the number of tasks completed by attendant staff. Trading stamps have been utilized to (1) maintain attendant performance following in-service in behavior analysis (Hollander and Plutchik, 1972), (2) to increase the work behavior of residents via increasing staff behavior (Hollander et al., 1973), and (3) to shape six classes of attendant behavior considered important in training residents (Bricker et al., 1972).

Feedback has been the most frequently used technique and has been reported successful with such dependent measures as percentage of projects completed (Wallace et al., 1973), frequency of activities initiated for clients (when combined with scheduling) (Quilitch, 1975), and percentage of training sessions conducted (Panyan et al., 1970). Quantitative feedback as to patient improvement brought about improved scores on the Ward Behavior Inventory (Pomerleau et al., 1973) but improvement feedback (versus feedback indicating no patient improvement) was found to have no significant effect on the accuracy with which attendants carried out a token reward and cost procedure (Loeber, 1971).

Monetary reward or the promise of monetary reward has proven very effective in increasing attendant token dispensing and fining (Katz et al., 1972), improvement of patients on Ward Behavior Inventory scores (Pomerleau et al., 1973) and the accuracy with which attendants carried out a therapeutic procedure (Loeber, 1971). Finally, using schedules of monetary reinforcement plus a self-scoring feedback system, Patterson, Griffin, and Panyon (1976) increased the percentage of daily training sessions conducted by institutional attendants.

Recent research plus personal experience indicate that those potential reinforcers considered most powerful by direct service staff most often include money and time-off (Watson, 1972). It is ironic that those potential reinforcers rated as most desirable are often not available for manipulation in human service settings due to a variety of external constraints. An adequate motivational system is considered feasible, however, via the use of a multiple set of incentives. Whereas no single available potential reinforcer may be adequate, a combination of such incentives may well prove effective. It has been suggested earlier that public charts providing highly visible feedback might be an effective strategy. In addition, a reinforcement "menu" might be constructed in order to provide incentives for goal attainment or skill gains, or numbers of training sessions completed. This "menu" might be comprised of such items as the possibility of upgraded job status, TV feedback, selection of preferred days off, and as suggested by Ayllon and Azrin (1968) vacation, holiday, and work-shift preference. Additionally, it might be feasible to create a new within-agency job classification such as "program specialist" or other such distinction. Finally, in situations where an individual employee is eligible to be upgraded it may be possible to make that change in status contingent on client progress, measured trainer competence, or other appropriate dependent measure.

The results of Watson's study (1972) on reinforcer preference by direct service staff (84%, more salary; 71%, more time-off) plus Loeber's (1971) data on feedback as to patient improvement not affecting the accuracy with which a therapeutic procedure was carried out, hold at least one strong implication for service planners: A staff incentive or reinforcement system may, in a variety of settings, be most necessary, and service planners should not assume that client progress will maintain desirable staff behaviors.

Evaluation

Historically, it appears that agencies, whether local, state, or federal have done little to evaluate the effectiveness of human service programs, and with a few exceptions, this also has apparently been true of academic social scientists. This is in sharp contrast to the current trend of legislatively mandated evaluation and accountability. This development has approximately a ten year history and is due, in part, to institution of the Program Planning and Budgeting System (with its focus on the objectives, methods, and outcomes of programs), the accountability movement, consumerism in the public service sector, advances in research methodology, etc., (Evans, 1974). As a result, a preponderance of models and theoretical treatises on the subject of evaluation have appeared (e.g., Grotsky and Proger, 1975; Clements et al., 1975). Although these are of considerable heuristic value, one finds little evidence of empirical evaluation studies in the published literature with such notable exceptions as Colwell, Richards, McCarver, and Ellis (1973). This deficit may well be due to lack of methodological sophistication and/or difficulties in carrying out valid evaluation research.

The purpose of evaluation efforts, to oversimplify the issue, should be to provide empirical evidence of gains made in a program or service. It should not be to generate data on individual client evaluations or to generate lengthy reports documenting number of dollars spent, number of certified staff, or number of children served, although these may be important bits of information. A further refinement on the purpose of evaluation would include the provision of an objective basis for decision-making and the provision of a feedback-loop system that allows for evaluative efforts to result in an on-going improvement of programs and services. It is to discover whether and how well objectives are being fulfilled, to determine the reasons for specific success and failure and to aid in redefining the means to be used for attaining objectives.

Formative or process evaluation and summative or product evaluation constitute the two most general types of evaluation strategies. Formative evaluation refers to judgments concerning whether the service has had proper implementation. During the initial stages of any service this is of utmost importance to the staff. It is a thorough analysis of processes involved in program administration and is constructed so as to provide frequent feedback to staff for decision-making and modification.

Summative evaluation assumes that the service has been properly implemented and is largely concerned with how effectively goals are attained. This *postfacto* judgment is of little utility with new or developing services which should emphasize process. As the optimal implementation is achieved one should then move to incorporate summative evaluation.

Formative Evaluation

In order to ensure effective implementation of the serving planning process, information should be fed back into the system almost continuously, allowing for data-based decision-making and improvement of service components. Such a feedback mechanism should be designed to provide information on all aspects of the service planning process. An excellent vehicle that would allow for just such information gathering is a systems analysis procedure known as Program Evaluation and Review Technique (PERT). PERT defines the activities of the service planning process in specific terms, coordinates the activities in a general, cohesive action plan, estimates the time necessary for each activity and for the entire project, minimizes the estimated time necessary for activities, and communicates in a precise, visual way the necessary activities required to achieve operationalization (Policy Management Systems, 1969). For example, the time required to conduct client assessments or to complete a task analysis or the number of staff and resources required to complete the development of skill acquisition programs within a specified time period would constitute the kind of information specified via PERT charting.

Summative Evaluation

The service planner, now having a viable system to assess the operationalization of the service planning process, can turn his attention to product or outcome evaluation. Such evaluation, when done in human services, demands as its focus changes in human behavior. That is, the service planner is responsible for the direct measurement of changes in client behavior and, further, measured changes relative to some unit of time and/or cost.

Role of Experimental Design

Some evaluators have denied the utility of controlled experimentation in human service evaluation. The claim is made that evaluation efforts cannot (and/or should not) conform to basic research standards. For example, it is contended that in order for comparative designs (control group vs. experimental group) to be valid, treatment and control conditions should be held constant throughout the experiment. The implication here is that new or traditional programs could not be modified in process for then one could not tell what was being evaluated. Further, all children should receive the same amount of the treatment to which they are assigned. It is also held that comparative experimental design conflicts with formative evaluation (the principle that evaluation should facilitate continual improvement of the program) and is useless as a decision-making tool during planning and implementation. Finally, it is felt by some that randomization is not enough to eliminate or control the large number of confounding variables in a human service system and that efforts to increase confidence in the internal validity of the experiment lead to sacrifices in generality (external validity). [With respect to the randomization argument, Glass (1969) has developed the intact-group design in which, while children are randomly assigned, the evaluation matches on other variables such as teachers, times, location, etc. (Worther and Sanders, 1973).]

One should also note that it is considered unethical (and possibly illegal) to withhold, even temporarily, the treatment from any group or to utilize an intervention strategy considered less than optimally effective. In light of this, no-treatment or alternative-treatment controls may be inappropriate for use in human services.

Due to the problems inherent in random assignment, nonrandom or quasi-experimental designs have been developed (Campbell and Stanley, 1966) but these often include a number of possible confounds including the regression artifact which poses a "plausible rival hypothesis" to any obtained outcome. This source of invalidity is particularly salient when dealing with exceptional populations.

Perhaps the most promising class of designs for human services evaluation is the time-series design (Glass *et al.*, 1975). This design avoids many of the above-mentioned arguments against controlled experimentation since each individual or group serves as its own control, thus eliminating the need for a separate comparison group. Here, ongoing observations or measurements are taken at specified intervals, and against such a "baseline," program innovations of changes may be readily assessed via a simultaneous discontinuity in the series of measurements. This design permits longitudinal evaluation as opposed to cross-sectional analyses. It is most important to know not only that an effect is observable at some point in time but whether the effect is immediate or delayed, whether it increases or decreases over time, and whether it is only temporarily or constantly superior to the effects of alternative interventions. Two further advantages, important for evaluation purposes, include its flexibility and utility in analyzing archival data. It has, for example, been used to evaluate situations ranging from the effects of self-monitoring of talk in classrooms (Gottman and McFall, 1973) to SinoIndian relations (Smoker, 1969). It also may be used in unit-repetitive or unit-replicative designs. Here the same unit (child, group, etc.) may be examined over time or replications of a treatment may be examined over time with different but comparable units (e.g., each new client's progress in a toilet training program). The design is also extremely useful in evaluating the effects of intervention by government agencies or other outside sources via a *posthoc* time-series analysis. This is an important part of any summative evaluation effort. Also, because measurement is ongoing, it provides an indispensable aid to formative evaluation.

Demonstrating experimental control also presents no special problems for this design, as a number of modifications of the basic design are available and easily implemented. Some confounds pose potential problems but the many modifications of the basic time-series design should handle them effectively (Glass *et al.*, 1975).

Using such an evaluative tool, the service planner is now in a position to generate specific, quantitative information as to service implementation and outcome. For example, the effects on client progress of implementing an incentive system with staff could be measured. Other examples might include the effects of an in-service training program, the effects of a licensing or accreditation team inspection, or the addition of a new program coordinator.

Measures of Program Effectiveness

Ultimately, the number of self-help skills acquired by the clients in the service system constitutes the primary measure of program efficacy. The adaptive behavior inventories discussed earlier provide excellent instruments for such summative (and formative) evaluation. The inventory would have the current skill level of each client readily available for inspection and provide behavioral, quantifiable objectives. This combination allows the service planner to directly measure skill or behavior gains over time. The inventory or scale should be up-dated each time an adaptive behavior gain is reported. To ensure the validity of the claims, observations should be made by independent raters at different times. Criterion should be prespecified, of course, regarding the number of raters, acceptable reliability coefficients and frequency of observations. Additionally, the service planner should establish some procedure or coding system by which skill gains resulting from enrollment in skill acquisition programs could be distinguished from adaptive behavior gains due to unspecifiable or unmeasurable environmental variables. Such a discrimination results in both an evaluation of the habilitative services offered and the agency's "arrangements for optimal behavioral development" (Brush, Note 7).

Skill losses, if they occur, are also important to document, and must also result in the updating of the adaptive behavior inventory. Just as skills acquired as the result of specific habilitative programs provide useful evaluative data, so do adaptive behavior losses provide valuable information as to the agency's attempt to program the environment for behavioral maintenance (Brush, Note 7).

Updating the adaptive behavior inventories should provide an excellent summary of what has been accomplished with each child, by each trainer, and by the entire service system. Coupled with a time-series analysis it would provide information as to what procedures, training paradigms, skill acquisition programs, managerial interventions, etc., were most effective in bringing about skill acquisition and with what groups of children.

Two perhaps penultimate dependent measures that will profoundly affect the rate of client progress include the existing skill repertoires of the trainers and the extent to which these service providers engage in the habilitative procedures for which they are responsible. If the above premise is valid, it is clearly of some import to evaluate the effects of the in-service training program as well as the effects of a staff management system. Such evaluations can be viewed as both summative and formative.

Evaluating the impact of in-service training on staff behavior is the more straightforward task and such an evaluation may take a variety of forms. In addition to maintaining individual performance data on each employee, the staff trainer would probably, as a minimum, desire some form of pretest, posttest comparisons. A pretest, posttest control group design using an analysis of gain or difference scores could also be easily carried out and would provide the staff trainer with a progress measure of acceptable validity. Random selection of subjects would, of course, be desirable, although a nonequivalent control group design is certainly acceptable and should also serve to generate valid statistical information. Analysis of covariance, using pretest scores as the covariate, is another possible alternative. Use of such experimental designs and statistical analyses would certainly lend more validity to any claims made on behalf of the efficacy of the in-service program.

Evaluating the effects of a staff management system should perhaps be done in a somewhat different fashion. Here, we would argue as was done so eloquently by Webb and his colleagues (1966) for the use of multiple, and where possible, unobtrusive measures. Additionally, these measures are perhaps best examined and interpreted if presented as time-series or "$N=1$" data. The upper limit on potential measures of staff behavior are probably only dictated by the creativity of the service planner, but some that might provide the most meaningful information include number of training sessions conducted, the frequency with which established skills are reinforced, and the percent of staff time spent in training relative to other duties.

It should be mentioned here that increases in such measures might well be due to the impact of the in-service program as opposed to a staff management or incentive system. In such a case, use of a time-series design would allow the service planner to evaluate the separate effects of each of these interventions on the dependent variable(s) in question (i.e., staff behavior).

Cost-Effectiveness

Any evaluation attempt should not be complete without the provision of a comprehensive cost-effectiveness analysis which supplies information as to the cost of achieving service objectives (Levin, 1975). Given the numerous budgetary constraints under which human service workers must function, it is essential that the cost of obtaining any given outcome be minimized, and that the strategy or strategies that maximize desired outcomes, given such fiscal restrictions, be identified. Interventions geared toward minimizing costs while maintaining or increasing effectiveness (i.e., attainment of service objectives) could readily be assessed via the use of a time-series analysis utilizing such archival data as total accounting costs, rate of verifiable skill gains, etc. It will also be important to determine the program's impact (relative to its cost) upon various sub-groups of the client population. For example, conducting a cost-effectiveness analysis may suggest that the number of skill gains registered per unit of cost were inconsequential for children classified as severely multiply handicapped. This may be contrasted with an exceedingly favorable ratio for ambulatory, healthy children.

It should be pointed out, in summary, that evaluations, although it is often neglected and may appear time-consuming and costly, is an integral and essential part of any service planning effort. Service providers must move more vigorously toward becoming accountable for public monies spent, services provided, and above all, for demonstrated increases in the competencies of handicapped individuals.

SUMMARY

Part II of this chapter has attempted to present the components of a data-based habilitation program for teaching self-help skills to retarded children. Its orientation has clearly been one of urging the service provider to assume the role of scientist-practitioner. That is, seeking to establish the service as program planner and program evaluator as well as direct charge agent. Such a role assumption is critical if effective services are to be delivered.

It must be recognized that the actual teaching of a self-care skill is only one of a number of tasks that must be addressed and successfully completed. If effective self-care training is to take place there must be the marriage of behavioral assessments with behavioral programming. Behavioral deficits must be objectively identified in order to develop the necessary skill acquisition programs, train staff in their use, and provide the necessary data base from which to develop individual service plans with training objectives. Additionally, such a marriage ensures accountability by allowing the service provider to use changes in behavioral assessments as a measure of the efficacy of the behavioral programming effort.

REFERENCE NOTES

1. Wyatt vs. Stickney, *et al.* (1972). Civil Action No. 3195-N, District Court of U.S. for Middle District of Alabama, Northern Division, Adequate Habilitation for the Mentally Retarded, February 28.
2. Spradlin, J. E. (1964). The Premack hypothesis and self-feeding by profoundly retarded children: a case report. Working Paper #79, Parsons Research Center, Parsons, Kansas.
3. Blackwood, R. O. (1962). *Operant conditioning as a Method of Training the Mentally Retarded.* Unpublished doctoral dissertation. Department of Psychology, Columbus: Ohio State University.
4. Lent, J. (1967). *Modification of Food Stealing Behavior of an Institutionalized Retarded Subject.* Working Paper #175, Parsons Research Center.
5. Ross, R. T. (1970). *Manual for the Fairview Self-Help Scale.* California: State of California.
6. Gold, M. (1975). *Marc Gold: Workshop on the Training of the Developmentally Disabled.* Atlanta, Georgia, December 3–5.
7. Brush, M. E. (1976). *ABS-System Revision: IV. A Mini-Manual.* Unpublished paper. Regional Developmental Center, Milledgeville, Georgia: Central State Hospital.

REFERENCES

Accreditation Council for Facilities for the Mentally Retarded. (1971). *Standards for Residential Facilities for the Mentally Retarded.* Chicago: Joint Commission on Accreditation of Hospitals (5th printing, 1975).
Adams, J. (1973). Adaptive behavior and measured intelligence in the classification of mental retardation. *American Journal of Mental Deficiency* 78(1):77–81.
Anderson, D. R., Hodson, G. D., and Jones, W. G. (1975). *Instructional Programming for the Handicapped Student.* Springfield, Illinois: Charles C. Thomas.
Ayllon, T., and Azrin, N. (1968). *The Token Economy.* New York: Appleton-Century, Crofts.
Azrin, N. H., and Foxx, R. M. (1971). A rapid method of toilet training the institutionalized retarded. *Journal of Applied Behavior Analysis* 4:89–99.
——, Bugle, C., and O'Brien, F. (1971). Behavioral engineering: two apparatuses for use in toilet training retarded children. *Journal of Applied Behavior Analysis* 4:249–253.

——, Schaeffer, R. M., and Wesolowski, M. D. (1976). A rapid method of teaching profoundly retarded persons to dress by a reinforcement-guidance method. *Mental Retardation* 14(6):29–33.

Baker, B. L., Broughtman, A. J., Heifetz, L. J., and Murphy, D. M. (1976). *Steps to Independence: A Skills Training Series for Children with Special Needs.* Champaign, Illinois: Research Press.

Balthazar, E. (1971). *Balthazar Scales of Adaptive Behavior.* Champaign, Illinois: Research Press.

Baroff, G. (1974). *Mental Retardation: Nature, Causes, and Management.* Washington, D.C.: Hemisphere Publishing Corp.

Barton, E. S., Guess, D., Garcia, E., and Baer, D. M. (1970). Improvement of retardates' mealtime behaviors by timeout procedure using multiple baseline technique. *Journal of Applied Behavior Analysis* 3:71–84.

Baumeister, A., and Klosowski, R. (1965). An attempt to group toilet train severely retarded patients. *Mental Retardation* 3(6):24–26.

BCP Observation Booklet. (1973). Palo Alto, California: VORT Corporation, 1973.

Bensberg, G. J., and Slominski, A. (1965). Helping the retarded learn self-care. In G. J. Bensberg, ed., *Teaching the Mentally Retarded Child.* Atlanta, Georgia: Southern Regional Education Board.

——, and Barnett, C. D. (1966). *Attendant Training in Southern Residential Facilities for the Mentally Retarded.* Atlanta, Georgia: Southern Regional Education Board.

——, Colwell, C. N., and Cassel, R. H. (1965). Teaching the profoundly retarded self-help activities by behavior shaping techniques. *American Journal of Mental Deficiency* 69:674–679.

Berkowitz, S., Sherry, P. J., and Davis, B. A. (1971). Teaching self-feeding skills to profound retardates using reinforcement and fading procedures. *Behavior Therapy* 2:62–67.

Breland, M. (1965). The foundation of teaching by positive reinforcement. In G. J. Bensberg, ed., *Teaching the mentally retarded child.* Atlanta: Southern Regional Educational Board.

Bricker, W. A., Morgan, D. G., and Grabowski, J. G. (1972). Development and maintenance of a behavior modification repertoire of cottage attendants through TV feedback. *Americal Journal of Mental Deficiency* 77:126–128.

Campbell, D. T., and Stanley, J. C. (1966). *Experimental and Quasi-Experimental Designs for Research.* Chicago: Rand McNally & Co.

Clements, J. E., Platt, J., and Simpson, R. (1975). Programming evaluation procedure: a diagnostic and accountability instrument for classroom teachers. *Educational Technology* 15:50–53.

Colwell, C. N., Richards, E., McCarver, R. B., and Ellis, N. R. (1973). Evaluation of self-help habit training of the profoundly retarded. *Mental Retardation* 11(3):14–15.

Crosby, K. C. (1976). Essentials of active programming. *Mental Retardation* 14(2):3–9.

Dayan, M. (1964). Toilet training retarded children in a state residential institution. *Mental Retardation* 2(2):116–117.

Doll, E. A. (1953). *The Measurement of Social Competence.* Minneapolis, Minnesota: Educational Test Bureau.

Edwards, M., and Lilly, R. T. (1966). Operant conditioning: an application to behavioral problems in groups. *Mental Retardation* 4:18–20.

Efron, R. E., and Efron, H. Y. (1967). Measurement of attitudes toward the retarded and an application with educators. *American Journal of Mental Deficiency* 72:100–107.

Ellis, N. R. (1963). Toilet training the severely defective patient: an S-R reinforcement analysis. *American Journal of Mental Deficiency* 68:98–103.

Evans, J. W. (1974). Evaluating education programs—Are we getting anywhere? *Educational Researcher* 3:7–12.

Eyman, R. K., Tarjan, G., and Cassidy, M. (1970). Natural history of acquisition of basic skills by hospitalized retarded patients. *American Journal of Mental Deficiency* 75:120–129.

Fielding, L. (1972). Initial ward-wide behavior modification programs for retarded children. In T. Thomson and J. Grabowski, eds., *Behavior Modification of the Mentally Retarded.* New York: Oxford University Press.

Foster, R. (1974). *Camelot Behavioral Checklist.* Parsons, Kansas: Camelot Behavioral Systems.

Foxx, R. M., and Azrin, N. H. (1973). *Toilet Training the Retarded Child.* Champaign, Illinois: Research Press.

Fry, E. B. (1968). A readability formula that saves time. *Journal of Reading* 11:513–516, 575–578.

Gardner, J. M. (1969). Behavior modification research in mental retardation: search for an adequate paradigm. *American Journal of Mental Deficiency* 73:844–851.

—— (1972). Teaching behavior modification to non-professionals. *Journal of Applied Behavior Analysis* 5:517–522.

——, and Giampa, F. L. (1971). The attendant behavior checklist: Measuring on-the-ward behavior of institutional attendants. *American Journal of Mental Deficiency* 75:617–622.

——, Brust, D. J., and Watson, L. S. (1970). A scale to measure skill in applying behavior modification techniques to the mentally retarded. *American Journal of Mental Deficiency* 74:633–635.

Gardner, W. I. (1971). *Behavior Modification in Mental Retardation.* Chicago: Aldine, Atherton.

Giles, D. K., and Wolf, M. M. (1966). Toilet training institutionalized severe retardates: An application of operant behavior modification techniques. *American Journal of Mental Deficiency* 70:766–780.

Girardeau, F. L., and Spradlin, J. E. (1964). Token rewards in a cottage program. *Mental Retardation* 2(6):345–351.

Gladstone, B. W., and Sherman, J. A. (1975). Developing generalized behavior-modification skills in high school students working with retarded children. *Journal of Applied Behavior Analysis* 8(2):169–180.

Glass (1969) cited by Worther and Sanders (1973).

Glass, G. V., Willson, B. L., and Gottman, J. M. (1975). *Design and Analyses of Time-Series Experiments.* Boulder, Colorado: Colorado Association University Press.

Gorton, C. E., and Hollis, J. H. (1965). Redesigning a cottage unit for better programming and research for the severely retarded. *Mental Retardation* 3(3)16–21.

Gottlieb, J., and Siperstein, G. N. (1976). Attitudes toward mentally retarded persons: effects of attitude referent specificity. American Journal of Mental Deficiency 80(4):276–381.

Gottman, J. M., and McFall, R. M. (1973). Self-monitoring effects in a program for potential high school dropouts: a time-series analysis. *Journal of Consulting and Clinical Psychology* 39:273–281.

Grabowski, J., and Thompson, T. (1972). A behavior modification program for behaviorally retarded institutionalized males. In T. Thompson and J. Grabowski, eds., *Behavior Modification of the Mentally Retarded.* New York: Oxford University Press.

Grossman, H. J., ed. (1973). Manual on terminology and classification in mental retardation. Baltimore, Maryland: Garamond/Pridemark.

Grotsky, J. N., and Proger, B. B. (1975). Third party evaluation of programs run from the state level: two field-tested models. *Educational Technology* 15:44–49.

Groves, I. D., and Carraccio, D. F. (1971). A self-feeding program for the severely and profoundly retarded. *Mental Retardation* 9(3):10–12.

Gunzburg, H. C. (1975). *Progress Assessment Chart of Social and Personal Development*, Form 1 (12th ed.). Bristol, Indiana: U.S.A. Distribution Center.

Henderson, S., and McDonald, M. (1975). *Step-by-Step Dressing*. Bellevue, Washington: Edmark Associates.

Henrickson, K., and Doughty, R. (1967). Decelerating undesired mealtime behavior in a group of profoundly retarded boys. *American Journal of Mental Deficiency* 72:40–44.

Hollander, M. A., and Plutchik, R. (1972). A reinforcement program for psychiatric attendants. *Journal of Behavior Therapy and Experimental Psychiatry* 3:297–300.

Hollander, N. A., Plutchik, R., and Horner, E. (1973). Interaction of Patient and Attendant Reinforcement Programs: The "Piggy-Back" Effect. *Journal of Consulting and Clinical Psychology* 41:43–47.

Hollis, J. H. and Gorton, C. E. (1967). Training severely and profoundly developmentally retarded children. *Mental Retardation* 5(4):20–24.

Honts, P. S., and Scott, R. A. (1975). *Goal Planning with Developmentally Disabled Persons*. Hershey, Pennsylvania: The Pennsylvania State University.

Horner, R. D., and Keilitz, I. (1975). Training mentally retarded adolescents to brush their teeth. *Journal of Applied Behavior Analysis* 8(3):301–310.

Hundziak, M., Maurer, R. A., and Watson, L. S. (1965). Operant Conditioning in toilet training of severely mentally retarded boys. *American Journal of Mental Deficiency* 70:120–124.

Itard, J. M. B. (1932). *The Wild Boy of Aveyron*. Trans. by G. and M. Humphrey. New York: Appleton-Century-Crofts.

Jones, R. L. (1974). The hierarchical structure of attitudes toward the exceptional. *Exceptional Children* 40:430–435.

Katz, R. C., Johnson, C. A., and Gelfand, S. (1972). Modifying the dispensing of reinforcers: some implications for behavior modification with hospitalized patients. *Behavior Therapy* 3:574–588.

Keller, F. S. (1968). "Goodbye teacher . . ." *Journal of Applied Behavior Analysis* 1:79–89.

Kendall, P. C., Finch, A. J., and Gillen, B. (1976). Readability and human interest scores as objective aides in behavior therapy text selection. *Behavior Therapy* 7:535–538.

Kiernan, C. C. (1975). Behavior modification. In A. M. Clarke and A. D. D. Clarke, eds., *Mental Deficiency*. New York: The Free Press.

Lea, C. R., and Lockhart, K. A. (1975). Behavior analyses of forced excellence and grade choice criteria. In J. M. Johnston, ed., *Behavior Research and Technology in Higher Education*. Springfield, Illinois: Charles C. Thomas.

Levin, A. M. (1975). Cost-effectiveness analysis in evaluation research. In M. Buttentag and E. L. Struening, eds., *Handbook of Evaluation Research*, Vol. 2. Beverly Hills, California: Sage Publications.

Lindsley, O. R. (1964). Direct measurement and prosthesis of retarded behavior. *Journal of Education* 147:62–81.

Loeber, R. (1971). Engineering the behavioral engineer. *Journal of Applied Behavior Analysis* 4:321–326.

Mager, R. F. (1962). *Preparing Instructional Objectives*. Belmont, California: Fearon Publishers.

—— (1973). *Measuring Instructional Intent*. Belmont, California: Fearon Publishers.

Martin, G. L. (1972). Teaching operant technology to psychiatric nurses, aides, and attendants. In F. W. Clark, D. R. Evans, and L. A. Hamerlynck, eds., *Implementing Behavioral Programs for Schools and Clinics*, pp. 63–87. Champaign, Illinois: Research Press.

——, Kehoe, B., Bird, E., Jensen, V., and Dorbeyshire, M. (1971a). Operant conditioning in dressing behavior of severely retarded girls. *Mental Retardation* 9(3):27–31.

——, McDonald, S., and Omichinski, M. (1971b). An operant analysis of response interaction during meals with severely retarded girls. *American Journal of Mental Deficiency* 76:68–75.

Minge, M. R., and Ball, T. S. (1967). Teaching of self-help skills to profoundly retarded patients. *American Journal of Mental Deficiency* 71:864–868.

Nawas, M. M., and Braun, S. H. (1970a). The use of operant techniques for modifying the behavior of the severely and profoundly retarded, Part I: Introduction and initial phase. *Mental Retardation* 8:2–6.

—— and Braun, S. H. (1970b). The use of operant techniques for modifying the behavior of the severely and profoundly retarded, Part II: The techniques. *Mental Retardation* 8(3):18–24.

—— and Braun, S. H. (1970c). An overview of behavior modification with the severely and profoundly retarded, Part III: Maintenance of change and epilogue. *Mental Retardation* 8:4–11.

Nihira, K., Foster, R., Shellhaas, M., and Leland, H. (1969). *AAMD Adaptive Behavior Scales*. Washington, D.C.: American Association on Mental Deficiency.

Overbeck, D. (1971). Attitude sampling of institutional charge attendant personnel: cues for intervention. *Mental Retardation* 9:8–9.

Panyan, M., Boozer, H., and Morris, M. (1970). Feedback to attendants as a reinforcer for applying operant techniques. *Journal of Applied Behavior Analysis* 3:1–4.

Patterson, R., Cooke, C., and Lieberman, R. P. (1972). Reinforcing the reinforcers: a method of supplying feedback to nursing personnel. *Behavior Therapy* 3:444–446.

Policy Management Systems, Inc. (1969). *PERT for CAA Planning: A Programmed Course of Instruction in PERT*, Vols. I and II. Office of Economic Opportunity Training Manual 6321–1.

Pomerleau, O. F., Bobrove, P. H., and Smith, R. H. (1973). Rewarding psychiatric aides for the improvement of assigned patients. *Journal of Applied Behavior Analysis* 6:383–390.

Pommer, D. A., and Streedbeck, D. (1974). Motivating staff performance in an operant learning program for children. *Journal of Applied Behavior Analysis* 7:217–221.

Premack, D. S. (1959). Toward empirical behavior laws: I. Positive reinforcement. *Psychological Review* 66:219–233.

Project MORE (1974). *How to do MORE: A Manual of Basic Teaching Strategy*. Nashville, Tennessee: Project MORE.

Quilitch, H. R. (1975). A comparison of three staff management procedures. *Journal of Applied Behavior Analysis* 8:59–66.

Rentfrow, R. K., and Rentfrow, R. K. (1969). Studies related to toilet training of the mentally retarded. *American Journal of Occupational Therapy* 23:425–430.

Ross, R. T., and Boroskis, A. (1972). Are IQ's below 30 meaningful? *Mental Retardation* 10(4):24.

Skinner, B. F. (1938). *The Behavior of Organisms*. New York: Appleton-Century-Crofts.

—— (1953). *Science and Human Behavior*. New York: MacMillan.

Smoker, P. (1969). A time-series analysis of Sino-Indian relations *Journal of Conflict Resolution* 13:172–191.

Treffry, D., Martin, G., Samuels, J., and Watson, C. (1970). Operant conditioning of grooming behavior of severely retarded girls. *Mental Retardation* 8:30–34.

Tucker, D. J. (1974). *Skill Acquisition Program Bibliography.* Parsons, Kansas: Camelot Behavioral Systems.

Van Wagenen, R. K., and Murdock, E. E. (1966). A transistorized signal-package for toilet training of infants. *Journal of Experimental Child Psychology* 3:312–314.

——, Meyerson, L., Kerr, N. J., and Mahoney, K. (1969). Field trials of a new procedure for toilet training. *Journal of Experimental Child Psychology* 8:147–159.

Vort Corp. (1973). *Behavior Characteristics Progression*: Palo Alto. Calif.

Wallace, C. J., Davis, J. R., Liberman, R. P., and Baker, V. (1973). Modeling and staff behavior. *Journal of Consulting and Clinical Psychology* 41:422–425.

Watson, L. S. (1967). Application of operant conditioning techniques to institutionalized severely and profoundly retarded children. *Mental Retardation Abstracts* 4(1):1–18.

—— (1972). *How to Use Behavior Modification with Mentally Retarded and Autistic Children: Programs for Administrators, Teachers, Parents, and Nurses.* Libertyville, Illinois: Behavior Modification Technology, Inc.

——, Gardner, J. M., and Sanders, C. (1971). Shaping and maintaining behavior modification skills in staff members in an MR institution: Columbus State Institute behavior modification program. *Mental Retardation* 9:39–42.

Webb, E. J., Campbell, D. T., Schwartz, R. D., and Sechrest, L. (1966). *Unobtrusive Measures: Non-Reactive Research in the Social Sciences.* Chicago: Rand McNally Corp.

Wehman, P. (1974). Maintaining oral hygiene skills. *Mental Retardation* 12(4):20.

Whitney, L. R., and Bernard, K. E. (1966). Implications of operant learning theory for nursing care of the retarded child. *Mental Retardation* 4:26–29.

Wolfensberger, W. (1972). *The Principle of Normalization in Human Services.* Toronto, Canada: National Institute on Mental Retardation.

Worther, B. R., and Sanders, J. R. (1973). *Educational Evaluation: Theory and Practice.* Worthington, Ohio: C. A. Jones Publishing Co.

Zeiler, M. D., and Jeruly, S. S. (1968). Development of behavior: self-feeding. *Journal of Consulting and Clinical Psychology* 32:164–168.

Chapter Thirteen

Problems of Behavioral Interventions with Delinquents in an Institutional Setting

MICHAEL M. HOLT and TOM R. HOBBS

INTRODUCTION

The purposes of this chapter are threefold: to briefly summarize the philosophical and pragmatic problems confronting practitioners, administrators, and researchers in developing therapeutic programs for delinquent youngsters in institutional settings; to illustrate the application of a behavioral technology to the modification of delinquent behavior in a classroom and cottage setting; and to discuss the ethical issues arising from the implementation of treatment programs for delinquents in closed settings.

Practitioners responsible for the design of therapeutic programs for delinquent youth are faced with a number of philosophical problems. Possibly the most important problem concerns the social and legal system which defines the nature of the relationship between the therapist and client. Early proponents of an independent justice system for juveniles were well-intentioned in their efforts to intervene early in the lives of wayward youth, rehabilitate rather than punish, and shield children from the negative influence of hardened adult criminals. However, not only have the results of the juvenile justice system been disappointing in reducing juvenile crime, the youthful offender has been paradoxically and unwittingly stripped of a number of legal protections usually afforded the adult lawbreaker. His lack of right to bail, to counsel, to confront his accusers, as well as other consequences of the "doubleedged sword" of the juvenile court system have been eloquently summarized by Kittrie (1971). The juvenile offender suffers the vulnerability of fewer legal safeguards in comparison to his adult counterpart. Also, he must labor under the burden of an amorphously defined societal label. Although the adult justice system has been historically very meticulous in defining the boundaries of criminal misconduct, the phrase "juvenile delinquent" may refer to behaviors ranging from being disagreeable to growing up in an unhealthy environment (Kittrie, 1971). Consequently, the label "juvenile delinquent" is likely to be more liberally bestowed due to its definitional ambiguity and resulting "catch-all" status.

Although well-intentioned, judicial labeling of youthful offenders poses additional barriers to effective rehabilitation. The iatrogenic effects of labeling "deviant" individuals have been well-documented (Stuart, 1970). However, the legal diagnosis of "juvenile delinquent" poses especial restraints on the client–therapist relationship. Generally, the delinquent is involuntarily thrust into the "therapeutic" program, carries a societally visible label which has been legally prescribed, and is expected to participate in a treatment program which is unlikely to alter his legal or community identity. As a result, the legal definition of the problem, the youngster's degree of commitment to the therapeutic program, and most importantly, the likely outcome in terms of changing the youngster's legal or community status are all beyond the control of the therapist or program designer. Possibly these difficulties may be partially responsible for our past tendency to focus on questions of technological efficacy while conveniently avoiding the broader social context in which our work is conducted as well as the predetermined pessimistic outcomes for our clients.

In addition to the philosophical dilemmas which confront the program designer, program implementation also faces a number of practical problems. Possibly the most important problem involves the strong peer group influence which characterizes delinquent populations, especially in closed settings. Buehler, Patterson, and Furniss (1966) have demonstrated that deviant behaviors in institutional settings are often reinforced by peers more times than they are punished by staff, and socially conforming behaviors are punished more often by peers than they are reinforced by staff.

In addition, Ross (1968) demonstrated that peer reinforcement of antisocial behavior is often more immediate than contingent social or token reinforcement from staff members. Consequently, the implementation of any therapeutic program will by necessity have to overcome or rearrange the powerful "natural" contingencies operating in an institutionalized delinquent peer group.

The following two studies illustrate the application of a behavioral approach with delinquent youngsters in a large state correctional institution. Study #1 (Holt *et al.*, 1976) illustrates the use of a token economy to modify the various behaviors composing the global category, "appropriate classroom behavior". Study #2 (Hobbs and Holt, 1976) illustrates the use of a token system to modify several behaviors of a large population of delinquents in the cottage setting. Both studies demonstrate the successful application of a behavioral methodology to the difficulties of delinquent youngsters and both studies raise serious ethical questions.

STUDY 1

Method

Subjects

Subjects were 19 adolescent adjudicated delinquent boys committed to the Alabama Boys Industrial School (ABIS). Precommitment court charges ranged from violation of probation to assault with intent to murder. Age ranged from 13 years, 5 months to 16 years, with a mean of 14 years, 8 months. IQ's ranged from 66 to 107 with a mean of 84. Mean grade placement was 7.3 although achievement testing indicated a mean grade equivalent of 4.1. All boys had been described by school personnel as academic and/or behavior problems. Six boys were black.

Setting

ABIS is one of three state training schools providing residential treatment for delinquents. The present study was conducted in an academic program which had been operating under a token economy system for 18 months. A centralized token store (for the weekly purchase of tangible items) had been established, as well as an elaborate system of contingent off-campus privileges, including 4-day passes; methods of token distribution and exchange had been formulated; a banking system was in operation; and the majority of the staff had been trained in behavior modification principals and techniques.

In addition to the token economy, a campus-wide disciplinary system was in effect that enumerated specific consequences for inappropriate behavior. In the academic program, a specific infraction (e.g., refusal to follow instructions) resulted in a hierarchy of pre-determined consequences ranging from time-out in the classroom for the first offense to removal from the classroom for subsequent offenses. The type of consequence depended upon the specific infraction and its frequency of occurrence.

All boys were members of a language arts class which met for 50 minutes on alternate mornings. The class was limited to no more than 11 boys at any one time. The teacher was a 23 year old white male who had been involved in teacher-training sessions and had been using the token economy for 6 months.

Response Definition

The teacher defined "appropriate classroom behavior" in terms of behavioral categories believed to be critical to academic progress and classroom order. The operational definitions were:

1. On-time/in-seat: student should be seated in an appropriate desk by the second bell
2. On-task: student must be either:
   (a) looking at assigned material
   (b) looking at the teacher (during lecture)
   (c) following instructions, i.e., engaged in an activity assigned by the teacher such as special projects, etc.
3. Social interaction: student must either:
   (a) Initiate an appropriate request for instructions, help, material, etc. The request should be obviously and distinctively different from a command, i.e., "Will you please be quiet?" as opposed to "Shut your mouth!."
   (b) Obviously and explicitly ignore an inappropriate behavior on the part of a classmate or group, i.e., student continues with assigned work despite distractions by classroom peers.

(c) Obviously and verbally encourage another classmate or class-
mates to follow classroom instructions, i.e., "You had better
do the work if you want the tokens."

(d) Obviously help another student or students either independently or at the request of the teacher. "Helping" could be
defined as giving instructions to other students, providing
appropriate answers, checking work, etc.

4. Assignment: Assignment is divided into five components which are
judged independently:

(a) The student must have the correct heading on an assigned paper.
A correct heading requires both name and date.

(b) The student must hand in a neat paper. The paper should not be
torn, erasures should be clean, work should not be scratched
through, there should be no doodling.

(c) The student must complete the assigned material. The student
must at least attempt to do the majority of the assigned work.
Accuracy is not considered.

(d) The student must complete the assigned material with 70%
accuracy.

(e) If the student completes the assigned material with 90%
accuracy, he received credit for *both* (d) and (e).

Observational Method

Figure 1 illustrates the Class Behavior Record, the data form used by
the teacher to record response occurrence for each class member.

The teacher checked each behavioral category in the following
manner. On-time/in-seat was checked at the ringing of the second bell,
which was usually considered to indicate tardiness, or beginning of the
class. On-task behavior was checked 6 times on a random 7-minute
variable interval time sampling schedule. A small kitchen timer was
positioned on the teacher's desk and signalled the end of each interval.
The sequence of intervals was changed weekly, resulting in no sequence
being in effect for more than three consecutive class meetings. Social
interaction was measured on an event basis; each time one of the
previously defined social interaction behaviors occurred, one of the blocks
on the data sheet was checked.

For each behavioral category, the percentage of appropriate behavior
was calculated by summing the number of blocks checked for appropriate
behavior, dividing this number by the total number of blocks within the

CLASS BEHAVIOR RECORD

Boy's Name	TOTAL	On Time/In Seat	On Task	On Task	On Task	On Task	On Task	On Task	Social Interaction	Social Interaction	Social Interaction	Assignment	Assignment	Assignment	Assignment	Assignment	BONUS (Specify)	

Fig. 1. Classroom Behavior Record.

category, and multiplying by 100. A global estimate of appropriate classroom behavior was calculated by summing the number of blocks checked for all categories, dividing this number by the total number of blocks on the sheet, and multiplying by 100.

Reliability

During each class period, an observer rated each boy's behavior according to the criteria for each category. The observer judged each boy on each category at approximately the same point in time as the teacher. For task assignment, the teacher judged and recorded each student's paper and the observer then judged the paper independently. Percentages of agreement were calculated in the following manner (number of agreements/number of agreements + disagreements) × 100. An agreement was defined as an identical rating for a given boy on a given category. A percentage of agreement for total classroom behavior was calculated in the same manner, except that agreements and disagreements were tallied across all categories.

Reliability estimates were taken on 36 of the 40 class meetings. Approximately every fourth class period, conferences were held with the teacher and observer and the response definitions for each category were reviewed. Mean percentages of agreement were 98% for on-time/in-seat, 96% for on-task, 89% for social interaction, 96% for assignment, and 95% for total classroom behavior.

Procedure

Tokens. During the initial phase, a boy could earn one token for the satisfactory completion of on-time/in-seat, 6 for on-task, 3 for social interaction, and 5 for assignment, resulting in a possible total of 15 tokens for the class period. At the beginning of this phase, the teacher thoroughly explained each behavioral category and its token value. All boys indicated that they understood the specific requirements of the various categories. Administrative scheduling required the class to meet for two separate and non-consecutive 50-minute periods with this teacher during the morning. Data were collected during the first period only. As the task assignment categories could not be scored by the teacher and observer until the end of class, tokens were not dispensed until the end of the second period. At this time, boys received tokens for both the first and second periods. The teacher issued a paper token equal in size to a dollar bill and containing the following data: the boy's name, teacher's code number, date, and number of tokens earned. This phase continued for 8 class periods.

Reversal₁. During Reversal$_1$ the token system was withdrawn for all behavioral categories during the first period. The teacher stated that the token economy was being studied for experimental purposes and that tokens would no longer be dispensed. The students were verbally encouraged to satisfy the criteria for each behavioral category and continued to earn tokens from this teacher during the second period as well as from teachers in all other academic classes. Withdrawal of tokens during the first period was equivalent to a 14% reduction in daily earning power within the academic department. Reversal$_1$ continued for 6 class meetings.

Reversal₂. During this phase tokens were also withdrawn during the second period. Thus, students did not receive tokens during either the first or second periods. Due to administrative decisions, the two class periods were scheduled to occur consecutively during Reversal$_2$ and the final tokens phase. Data were collected during the first period only. This phase continued for 13 sessions.

Tokens. The token system was reinstated in both periods and the criteria for successful completion of each behavioral category were explained. Tokens were dispensed at the end of the second period. Data were collected during the first period only. This phase consisted of 14 sessions.

Results

The mean percentage of appropriate behavior was 75% during the Tokens phase, 74% during the Reversal₁ phase, 60% during the Reversal₂ phase, and 82% during the final Tokens phase. No substantial change in total appropriate classroom behavior occurred from the Tokens to Reversal₁ phases but a noticeable decrease in the mean level occurred during the Reversal₂ phase. A substantial increase in appropriate behavior occurred during the final Tokens phase which resulted in a level of appropriate behavior somewhat above that observed during the initial Tokens phase.

The mean percentage of on-task behavior was 91% during the Tokens phase, 87% during the Reversal₁ phase, 72% during the Reversal₂ phase and 91% during the final Tokens phase. The mean percentage of assignment behavior was 77% during the Tokens phase, 73% during the Reversal₁ phase, 57% during the Reversal₂ phase, and 74% during the final Tokens phase. The mean levels of each of these behaviors shifted in similar directions with no appreciable change occurring from the Tokens to the Reversal₁ phases, an obvious decrease occurring in the Reversal₂ phase, and a noticeable increase occurring in the last Tokens phase. However, on-task behavior showed an ascending trend during the Reversal₂ phase while assignment behavior showed more variability across all phases.

The mean percentage of on-time/in-seat behavior was 99% during the Tokens phase, 100% during the Reversal₁ phase, 84% during the Reversal₂ phase, and 98% during the final Tokens phase. The mean percentage of appropriate social interaction behavior was 24% during the Tokens phase, 40% during the Reversal₁ phase, 32% during the Reversal₂ phase, and 64% during the final Tokens phase. On-time/in-seat behavior showed no change from the Tokens to Reversal₁ phases, a noticeable decrease during the Reversal₂ phase, and an obvious increase during the final Tokens phase. However, social interaction behavior showed a substantial increase from the Tokens to Reversal₁ phase, followed by a small reduction during the Reversal₂ phase and then an obvious increase during the last Tokens phase.

STUDY 2

The second study was also conducted at ABIS but focused on social recreational, and compliance behaviors in the cottage setting classroom rather than on behaviors targeted in the first study.

Method

Subjects and Setting

Boys reside in five independent cottage units. Recreational activities are conducted and opportunities offered to engage in individual or group counselling. Four of the cottage units, each containing approximately equal numbers of boys, were the setting for the present study. Seventeen staff members, 13 male and four female, were involved in the token economy (mean educational level = 1 year of college, mean age was 40.3 year). The staff-student ratio was 7.35 boys per staff member. One cottage supervisor was primarily responsible for the treatment program in each cottage. A counsellor in each cottage served as a reliability observer. The staff had no behavioral training before the program.

Procedure

Training and program planning. Two behavioral consultants conducted a group training program for the cottage staff. This program consisted of three 4-hour introductory sessions covering basic operant principles and techniques. Hall's (1971) *Managing Behavior Series* (parts 1, 2, and 3) was used as a text. A lecture format, "homework" assignments, and small discussion groups were utilized. The superintendent and assistant superintendent occasionally attended and stressed the importance of the behavioral program. The superintendent praised cottage supervisors who appeared to be putting forth the most effort. Following the group sessions, individualized sessions were held twice weekly in each of the cottages over a 3-month period. The following topics were discussed: the identification and definition of target behaviors, observational techniques, methods of assessing reliability of observations, means of recording and tabulating data, social and token reinforcement, and reinforcement delivery systems. Committees were formed of staff and administrative personnel to identify target behaviors, back-up reinforcers, and to work out logistical problems. While the consultants attempted subtly to guide decision-making, the final responsibility for program planning was clearly placed on the staff. After the initial training and planning phases were completed, follow-up sessions were held weekly to assess operation of the program.

Target Behaviors. Cottage Behaviors before dinner (BD) and after dinner (AD) were selected as target behaviors because the staff was concerned about the low frequency of appropriate social behavior at these times. Some students interacted very little, while others showed high frequencies of disruptive and aggressive behaviors. Also, many students failed to participate in group recreational activities. Line Behavior was selected because staff reported a high frequency of assaultive behavior when students were walking to and from destinations on campus. Students frequently walked in unorganized groups, which made monitoring by the staff difficult.

The specific behaviors were:

1. *Cottage Behavior BD*
   a. Following rules of group games (e.g., football, baseball, basketball).
   b. Completing chores assigned by the cottage supervisor (e.g., sweeping, carrying out garbage, mopping floor, cleaning bathroom).
   c. Following cottage rules (e.g., no smoking during recreational period, staying in the recreation room, not destroying property of self, others, or institution).
   d. Following instructions of cottage supervisor (e.g., familiarizing a new student with game and cottage rules, decreasing noise level of play, sharing games).
   e. Cottage Behavior BD was scored as inappropriate if any assaultive behavior occurred. Examples of assaultive behavior are cursing, loud accusations, threats, hitting, kicking, and shoving.
2. *Cottage Behavior AD*
   a. Interacting with one or more peers 30 to 50% of the time (depending on the cottage) between dinner and bedtime. Interacting was defined as a boy's behavior meeting at least four of the following conditions: maintaining a proximity of three feet or less from a peer(s), talking to a peer(s), looking at a

peer(s), and manipulating game materials in accord with game rules.
   b. Following cottage rules.
   c. Following instructions of the cottage supervisor.
   d. Cottage Behavior AD was scored as inappropriate if any assaultive behavior occurred.
3. *Line Behavior*
   a. Walking to and from destinations on campus in a group.
   b. Walking in a straight line.
   c. Following instructions of cottage supervisor.
   d. Line behavior was scored as inappropriate if any assaultive behavior occurred.

A boy's behavior had to meet each of the criteria in order to be judged appropriate.

Data Collection. The boy's names were listed on a daily behavior chart and the cottage supervisor marked each behavioral category when the boy had met the criteria for appropriate behavior. Thus, both group and individual data were obtained.

The three target behaviors were recorded in the following manner:

1. *Cottage Behavior BD*—the cottage supervisor began observing the boy's behavior when they returned to the cottage from school or vocational assignment and continued observing for approximately 1 hour until the boys prepared to leave for dinner. Then he rated each boy on the daily behavior chart.
2. *Cottage Behavior AD*—the cottage supervisor began observing at the beginning of the recreation period immediately after dinner and when all of the students were in a large recreational room. The cottage supervisor positioned himself so that he could observe all of the students. He continued observing for 2 hours. When the boys began preparing for bed, he rated each boy's behavior on the daily behavior chart.
3. *Line Behavior*—the cottage supervisor began observing the boy's behavior when they formed a line to leave the cottage for dinner. He continued to observe until the boys arrived at the dining hall. After dinner, he observed their behavior as they returned to the cottage. Then he rated each boy on the daily behavior chart.

No other specific structure was imposed on the observational system.

Baseline and token reinforcement. Cottage staff gathered baseline data by observing and tabulating whether each boy met the criteria for each of the categories on a daily behavior chart. The boys were told that the staff was taking records. No further explanation was provided. A multiple-baseline design (Baer *et al.*, 1968) was employed by sequentially introducing the token reinforcement phase across cottages. One of the six cottages on the ABIS campus was eliminated at the outset because of

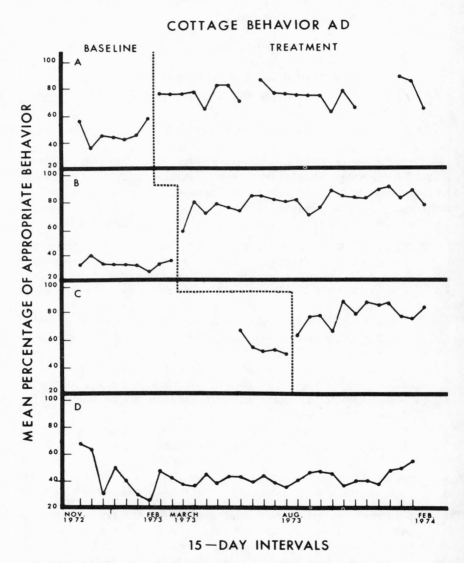

Fig. 2. Effects of Token Reinforcement on Cottage Behavior (Cottage AD).

high staff turnover. A second cottage served as a comparison cottage and continued the baseline phase. This cottage was a temporary residence, where orientation was provided for boys entering ABIS. The following criteria were used to determine the onset of token reinforcement: the

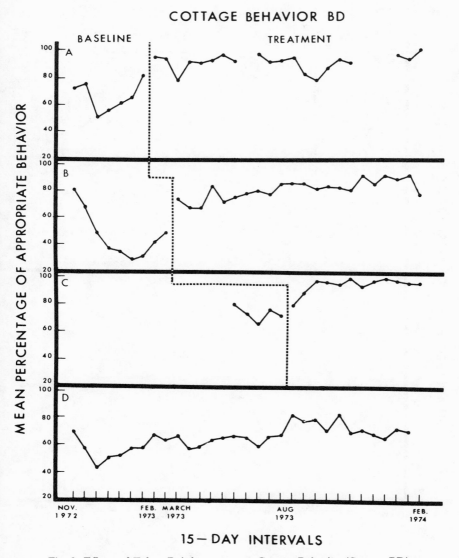

Fig. 3. Effects of Token Reinforcement on Cottage Behavior (Cottage BD).

ongoing, consistent collection of data; observer agreement of 80% or more; enthusiasm and interest of the cottage and administrative staff as subjectively assessed by the authors. Due to practical considerations,

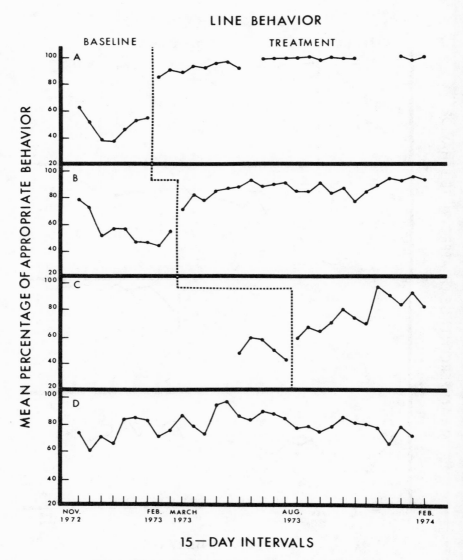

Fig. 4. Effects of Token Reinforcement on Line Behavior.

token reinforcement was implemented for all three target behaviors simultaneously in each cottage.

When token reinforcement began in each cottage, the supervisor discussed the behavioral criteria for each category. Signs were posted listing the criteria. The boys were told the number of posted listing the criteria. The boys were told the number of tokens they could earn in each category. Before bedtime and before the boys left the cottage for school, the cottage supervisor counted the tokens each boy had earned. A printed paper token, equal in size to a dollar bill, was issued to the boy and contained the boy's name, the cottage supervisor's code number, date, and number of tokens earned.

Back-up reinforcers. The boys went to a token economy store weekly and exchanged their tokens for a variety of reinforcers including drinks, candy, trinkets, toys, games, and cigarettes. Tokens could be saved in a bank, which paid interest, for more expensive reinforcers, such as on and off-campus recreational activities and trips to football and basketball games, and to a nearby girl's training school when dances were held. Also, tokens could be used to purchase a 4-day pass home; final release from ABIS was contingent on the cumulative number of tokens earned.

Reliability. Boys in each cottage were independently rated on each target behavior by two staff members (cottage supervisor and cottage counsellor) who completed a daily behavior chart. The cottage counsellor knew the boys well, was familiar with the cottage routine, and was trained in the response-definition and data-collection procedures. Seventy-five reliability checks were made throughout the study (mean of 1.2 checks per week). Reliability estimates were computed in the following manner: (number of agreements/number of agreements + disagreements) × 100. An agreement was defined as both observers simultaneously and independently rating a boy's behavior as appropriate or inappropriate with respect to a given target behavior. The number of agreements refers to the number of boys within a given cottage that were given identical ratings by the observers. The number of agreements plus disagreements refers to the total number of boys observed. The means and ranges of the reliability estimates for the three target behaviors in the four cottages are shown in Table 1.

Calculation of percentages of agreement was conducted by dividing that number of times both observers marked the target response as occurring (agreements) by the number of agreements plus the number of times one observer marked response occurrence and the other did not, and multiplying by 100 (Kazdin, 1975). This reanalysis yielded an average decrease of 4.6 percentage points, compared to the abovementioned reliability estimates.

Table 1. Means and Ranges of Reliability Estimates

Cottage	Line behavior		Cottage behavior BD		Cottage behavior AD	
	Mean (%)	Range (%)	Mean (%)	Range (%)	Mean (%)	Range (%)
A	93	80–100	90	80–100	87	80–100
B	83	60–100	82	70– 97	85	40–100
C	98	93–100	98	90–100	97	91–100
D	73	50–100	72	50–100	75	54–100

Note. Reliability estimates made during staff training, baseline, and token reinforcement phases are included.

Results

Figure 3 illustrates the effects of the token program on Cottage Behavior BD. Data were collected for 14 months for three or four cottages. Due to practical difficulties, data collection for Cottage C was delayed. When introduced, the token system resulted in an increase in mean percentage of appropriate behavior for each cottage, with no noticeable improvement in other cottages.

For Cottage A, appropriate behavior increased from a baseline mean of 66% to a treatment mean of 91.6%; for Cottage B, from a mean of 46.7% to 80.8%; and for Cottage C, from a mean of 73.2% to 94.2%. Cottage D indicated a fairly stable mean percentage of appropriate behavior over time.

Figure 2 illustrates the effects of the token system on Cottage Behavior AD. Increases in the mean percentage of appropriate behavior from baseline to experimental phases were: from 47.3% to 75.9% for Cottage A; from 33.9% to 80.6% for Cottage B; and from 56.4% to 80% for Cottage C. In Cottage D, no token system, performance was stable.

Figure 4 represents the effects of the token economy when applied to Line Behavior. Increases in the mean percentage of appropriate behavior from baseline to experimental phases were: 49.6% to 96.4% for Cottage A; 56.7% to 86.9% for Cottage B; and 51.8% to 78.2% for Cottage C. Cottage D indicated a generally high and stable mean percentage of appropriate behavior across phases.

Although two cottages reflected ascending baseline trends (Cottage A in Figures 2 and 3; Cottage B in Figure 3), generally the mean percentage of appropriate behavior increased after the token system was introduced.

DISCUSSION

The major goal of the two studies was to document the effectiveness of a large scale behavioral treatment program for delinquent adolescents in an applied setting including both classroom and cottage situations. The results of the first study showed that token reinforcement exerted significant influence over the behavior of delinquent youngsters in a classroom setting. This finding is consistent with those of Meichenbaum *et al.* (1968) and Graubard (1969) and can be accepted with considerable confidence due to the frequent reliability estimates utilized and the procedures used to insure consistency of response definitions during the study. On the other hand, when specific classroom behaviors were analyzed, the effects of token reinforcement were rather variable. On-time/in-seat behavior was most clearly influenced by token reinforcement and assignment behavior seemed clearly influenced by reinforcement contingencies but showed more variability. Although on-task behavior showed a somewhat ascending trend during the reversal two phase, it seemed under some reinforcement control. Social interaction behavior, one of the more important target behaviors with the delinquent population, showed substantial variability which seemed unconnected to the behavioral contingencies employed.

The increased effectiveness of token reinforcement control over on-time/in-seat behavior, assignment behavior, and on-task behavior as compared to the control of social behavior may be partially attributed to differences in the effort required for these behaviors. It is likely that the acquisition and control of social behavior was more demanding than that of simpler on-time/in-seat, on-task, and assignment behavior. Also, social behavior could be expected to occur at a low frequency in a delinquent population since deficits in appropriate social behavior are usually associated with delinquency (Kazdin and Bootzin, 1972). Additionally, teachers may have placed more attention on academic behavior, including on-task and assignment than on social behavior since academic behaviors would seem to be more consistent with the superficial objectives of the teaching situation. In retrospect, it would have probably been wiser to institute a shaping procedure of social behavior that reinforced successive approximations of the final target behaviors.

The maintenance of behavior during the reversal one phase was one of the more interesting aspects of the first study. This maintenance can be probably attributed to generalization effects since there were minimal cues differentiating the tokens and Reversal$_1$ phases. For example, during the Reversal$_1$ phase students were continuing to earn tokens for similar behaviors in other classes. Also, while students were told they were no longer receiving token reinforcement in the Reversal₁ phase, they could have easily perceived that they were only earning about half as many tokens during both classes because during the token phase, reinforcement occurred at the end of the second class.

The most important finding of the first study involves the differential effects on social behavior as compared to academic behaviors and the differential effects of component behaviors as compared to global classroom behavior measures. The findings of the first study suggests that more complicated and more powerful contingencies are required to effectively modify social behavior. However, if component behaviors had not been specifically analyzed, this failure to control social behavior would have been overlooked. Thus, the use of global or composite behavior measures may mask crucial outcomes of behavioral programs.

The second study demonstrated the effects of a token economy system on the behavior of delinquent youngsters in cottage settings. In each of the cottages and with each target behavior, the initiation of token reinforcement was followed by an increased frequency of appropriate behavior. In several instances, for example in cottage A and B for cottage behavior BD, an ascending baseline trend was demonstrated. While it would have been preferable to delay introduction of reinforcement until baseline data had stabilized, it was evident that continued delay of the initiation of reinforcement would have resulted in a corresponding decrease in commitment and interest on the part of the cottage staff. Despite the somewhat equivocal effects in several instances due to compromise of issues involving the experimental control of behaviors in applied settings, the token reinforcement system generally demonstrated substantial control over behaviors in cottage settings.

Table 2 indicates the cost of the token system to the institution above regular cost for general operations. The institutions monthly financial expenditure for the token economy program averaged 7 dollars and 85 cents per boy per month. The program was developed and supervised by two behavioral consultants who were employees of the Jefferson County Department of Health. These consultants were provided free of charge to the institution in return for administrative cooperation and support for the behavioral program. Actual staff time of the staff members of the institution required to develop and maintain the program averaged three hours per cottage per week. The degree of the behavioral consultants' professional supervision averaged 8 hours per week for the total cottage program. An additional average of approximately 5 hours per week was spent in the classroom setting.

Beyond reporting initial behavior changes, few studies have gener-ated data reflecting behavior change across different settings and the

Table 2. Program Costs to ABIS

Item	Amount
Staff salaries	$9339.00
Token store and capital outlay	1517.04
Printing, paper, and supplies	504.00
Miscellaneous	420.00
Total	11780.04
Per boy per year	94.24
Per boy per month	7.85

long-term effectiveness of behavior change program, especially with institutionalized delinquent populations. Data from these two studies reflects successful behavior change across two settings and the maintenance of initial behavior change for periods ranging from 7 to 12 months, depending on the cottage. However, no data are available regarding maintenance of behavior change following release from the program. The generalization of program effects from a treatment to a nontreatment setting remains a critical question.

Anecdotal data indicated a gradual deterioration of the token economy in both the classroom and cottage settings following the termination of the formal research program. The behavioral consultants had established an agreement with the administration to terminate their primary responsibility for the program. As the primary responsibility for maintaining the token economy system gradually shifted from the consultants to the institution a variety of problems became increasingly serious. While these problems were more clearly evident following the formal research program, in retrospect it was clear that they had been present since the beginning of the program. These difficulties, while all connected, can be divided into two categories for the convenience of discussion. First, there are those problems which tended to limit the success of the token economy program. Second, there were ethical issues that question whether the token economy system should have existed at all, and whether, in fact, it addressed problems of the client population.

PROBLEMS LIMITING PROGRAM EFFECTIVENESS

Problems that restricted success of the token economy program were very similar to those described in a very good discussion by Repucci and Saunders (1974), based on their work in a similar setting. Repucci and

Saunders described eight problems that they encountered in developing a token economy program in an institution for delinquent boys. It is their conviction that these problems are generally encountered in developing behavioral problems in the natural setting. The difficulties they discussed included: institutional constraints, external pressure, terminology, two populations, limited resources, perceived flexibility, and compromise. While the authors experienced all of these problems, for the purpose of brevity this discussion will be limited to the three most serious difficulties.

The three problems that pose the most significant difficulty for the authors, and the problems likely to pose the most difficulty generally, include the problem of institutional constraint, external pressure, and compromise. A brief illustration of each of these problems will be provided. The problem of institutional constraints was most clearly seen in two areas. First, the administrative structure by which the institution was organized did not facilitate the development, implementation, or maintenance of an effective treatment program. More specifically, there were limited opportunities for staff to communicate about objectives, treatment methods, and the evaluation of individual youngsters or overall programs. Second, the administration established the properties for the institution which were in many cases somewhat independent of either a behavioral orientation or, strictly speaking, a treatment orientation. In many instances the priorities seem to flow from political decisions designed to enhance the survival of the administration without direct concern as to treatment issues. Unfortunately, the institution was structured in such a way that there was minimal communication between administrative and treatment personnel. Thus, a variety of specific problems emerged from the structure of the institution which was not open to change.

The second problem to be discussed involves external pressure applied to the treatment program or to the institution. During the formal research project, and especially in the period following the research project, strong competition emerged centering on the control of the institution. The competing bodies were the administrative section of the institution and a state wide organization that was working toward the eventual control of the entire youth services system. An extensive power struggle emerged between the administration and this state organization that seemed to have very little to do with treatment issues. As a result, the administration tended to ignore or focus only passively on the behavioral treatment program. Within the institution itself there seemed to be competition for control between the administrative component and the treatment component of the staff. These power struggles consume considerable time and energy and frequently diverted attention away from issues involving the outcome of treatment programs. Unfortunately, these power struggles were largely beyond the influence of the behavioral consultants or specific members of the treatment staff.

The third problem involves the question of compromise. Behavioral practitioners establishing treatment programs in natural settings must inevitably compromise behavioral principles in order to accommodate themselves to the setting in which they work. The primary dilemma is, how far can a practitioner go in compromising behavioral principles and still establish an effective treatment program. There were a variety of examples of this problem during the development and maintenance of the token economy program. One example involves the time of initiation of token reinforcement in the cottage setting. Ideally, token reinforcement would not begin until a stable or descending baseline function was demonstrated. However, it was clear that in several cottages the morale, interest, and investment of the staff would have deteriorated substantially if the onset of reinforcement was delayed. Due to these considerations, token reinforcement was initiated at times in spite of ascending baseline trends. Other examples of compromise involve the type of reinforcers available to youngsters and the frequency of access to those reinforcers. The position of the institution was to make a rather limited number of reinforcers available to the youngsters and to limit their access to these to the point that the potency of the reinforcers would have been probably minimal. Once again, negotiating a compromise regarding the number of items and the frequency of accessibility resulted in reinforcement procedures that were less than optimally desirable. A final example concerns both the cottage and classroom settings. The institution tended to place a much lower priority on procedures employed to obtain behavioral data than did the behavioral consultant. Generally, the staff of the institution wished for behavioral measures that were so global and vague as to make them unreliable and meaningless. Thus, the final target behaviors, and the procedures utilized to measure them, were not always as specific as they might ideally have been. For example, the behavioral definition of appropriate social behavior in the classroom setting was probably overly ambitious and may have been the crucial factor in the failure to demonstrate reinforcement of that behavior. In the cottage setting, it would have been desirable to specify more target behaviors than were realistically possible based on the number of staff and the amount of staff time available. In summary, behavioral principles must be frequently compromised as behavioral programs are initiated and maintained. Unfortunately, these compromises may significantly limit the effectiveness of the final program.

In the past, the literature regarding the application of behavioral principles to natural settings has focused almost exclusively on specific technical issues involved, the characteristics of the subject population, characteristics of the limited and immediate environment in which the study took place, the method used by the investigator and the outcome. Thus focus is obviously inherited from the approach used in experimental settings. As Repucci and Saunders (1974) have suggested, probably the most serious deficit in the literature concerns an ignorance of differences between experimental and natural settings. If behavioral practitioners are to initiate and maintain successful behavior change programs it would appear reasonable for them to more seriously consider those factors and variables in natural settings over which they have limited or no control as well as the particular technical methods and variables they manipulate. Attention needs to be given to the entire social system in which the particular behavioral study or program is embedded. Some important questions in considering the relationship of the general environmental setting in which a particular study or program is embedded include: How rigidly structured is the environment in which the program or study is to be initiated and maintained? To whom is the behavioral practitioner accountable and what are the explicit and implicit expectancies of this agent? How much control does the practitioner have over the general environmental settings, and in particular, the staff involved in the behavioral program? What are factors that are likely to limit the programs' success that the practitioner cannot control (e.g., staff–client ratio, staff salary, the advancement of particular staff members, funding sources, budget, institutional priorities)? How will the outcome of the study or behavioral treatment program be used? While these questions may be of little interest to the behavioral experimenter in the laboratory, the answers to these questions may be of equal importance to the technical expertise of the behavioral practitioner in natural settings. The failure to clearly differentiate issues relevant to successful outcomes in natural settings as opposed to the laboratory setting may contribute to the paucity of successful long term community supported behavioral treatment programs, especially for institutionalized delinquent populations. It is the authors' experience that ignoring the above mentioned questions is likely to lead to a rather weak behavioral treatment program with an abbreviated life span.

ETHICAL ISSUES

During the past 2 years, ethical, moral, and legal problems associated with the use of behavioral procedures in institutions have received increasing attention (Repucci and Saunders, 1974; Saunders, Note 1;

Wexler, 1973). Ethical issues take on added importance in institutions in which individuals are involuntarily held, such as the institution in which the two studies described in this chapter took place. The most crucial ethical issue emerging from the ABIS program involved the definition of the real client population of the behavioral consultants. After working in the institutional setting for some time, it became clear that there were a variety of potential clients groups including the stated client population, delinquent youngsters, as well as the staff of the institution, the administrative staff, the entire institution, the court system, and other governmental agencies providing funding for the institution. Unfortunately, the various interests of all of these groups are not always consistent and compatible. For example, there were instances where there seemed to be a clear conflict between the needs of the institution and the needs of the delinquent youngsters. The inclusion of Line Behavior as a target behavior in the cottage setting provides an illustration of such a conflict. In order to keep track of the youngsters and make sure that all the boys in each cottage were present and accounted for, it was desirable for the boys to march in a straight line from one destination to another on campus. However, it is extremely doubtful that acquiring such a behavior was in the interest of developing more appropriate and successful behaviors for individual boys. The institution chose a variety of target behaviors and treatment procedures in order to maximize convenience for the institution rather than because those behaviors and procedures might contribute to the student's successful community adjustment.

A second ethical issue involves the infringement of behavioral programs in institutions on the rights of delinquents. Behavioral problems have been shown to shape and maintain desirable behaviors while the delinquent is in the institution; however, there is very limited evidence indicating generalization of behavior change to noninstitutional settings. Since the delinquent is institutionalized because of undesirable behavior in the home or community, and not because of misbehavior in institutions, behavioral programs may be largely irrelevant to the problems of the delinquent. In fact, it can be argued that behavioral programs exist primarily to control the delinquent in the institution and not to provide him with behaviors that will enable him to succeed in his home and community. If the primary purpose of behavioral programs is to control rather than treat the delinquent, then it is important to question the degree to which this control may infringe upon the legal rights of the delinquent. The delinquent should probably be provided legal rights similar to those of involuntarily committed mental patients (Wyatt vs. Stickney, 1972) including privacy, space, reasonable freedom and lack of restraint, food, clothing, and recreation. Thus, when the practitioner establishes a behavioral program, he must carefully wiegh the degree to which the program benefits the delinquent against the degree to which it may infringe on the delinquent rights and only provide control while he is institutionalized.

Due to the lack of consideration of practical and ethical problems arising from behavioral programs in natural settings, it is difficult for behavioral practitioners to precisely identify their role relative to institutionalized populations, treatment staff, administrators, and the juvenile justice system. A more accurate definition of this role will probably emerge only if behavioral practitioners more squarely face the social and historical context in which they work. The excellent discussion of Kittrie (1971) provides one view of that context.

REFERENCE NOTES

1. Saunders, A. G. (1974). *Behavior Therapy in Prisons: Walden II or Clockwork Orange?* Paper prepared for the *8th Annual Convention of the Association for Advancement of Behavior Therapy*, Chicago, November.
2. Wyatt vs. Stickney, *et al.* (1972). Civil Action No. 3195-N, District Court of U.S. for Middle District of Alabama, Northern Division, Adequate Habilitation for the Mentally Retarded, February 28.

REFERENCES

Baer, D. M., Wolf, M. M., and Risley, T. R. (1968). Some current dimensions of applied behavior analysis. *Journal of Applied Behavior Analysis* 1:91–97.

Buehler, R. E., Patterson, G. R., and Furniss, J. M. (1966). The reinforcement of behavior in institutional settings. *Behavior Research and Therapy* 4:157–167.

Graubard, P. S. (1969). Utilizing the group in teaching disturbed delinquents to learn. *Exceptional Children* 35:267–272.

Hall, R. V. (1971). *Managing Behavior*, Parts 1, 2, and 3. Lawrence, Kansas: H & H Enterprises.

Hobbs, T. R., and Holt, M. M. (1976). The effects of token reinforcement on the behavior of delinquents in cottage settings. *Journal of Applied Behavior Analysis* 9:189–198.

Holt, M. M., Hobbs, T. R., and Hankins, R. (1976). The effects of token reinforcement of delinquents' classroom behavior. *Psychology in the Schools.* 13(3):341–347.

Kazdin, A. (1975). *Behavior Modification in Applied Settings.* Homewood, Ill. Dorsey Press.

——, and Bootzin, R. (1972). The token economy: an evaluative review. *Journal of Applied Behavior Analysis* 5:343–372.

Kittrie, N. N. (1971). *The right to be different.* Baltimore: Penguin.

Meichenbaum, D. H., Bowers, K., and Ross, R. R. (1968). Modification of classroom behavior of institutionalized female adolescent offenders. *Behavior Research and Therapy* 6:649–660.

Repucci, N. D., and Saunders, J. T. (1974). Social psychology of behavior modification: problems of implementation in natural settings. *American Psychologist* 29:649–660.

Ross, R. R. (1968). *Application of Operant Conditioning Modification of Institutionalized Adolescent Offenders*. Unpublished progress report, University of Waterloo.

Stuart, R. B. (1970). *Trick of Treatment: How and When Psychotherapy Fails*. Champaign, Ill.: Research Press.

Wexler, D. B. (1973). Token and taboo: behavior modification, token economies, and the law. *California Law Review* 61:81–109.

Chapter Fourteen

Drugs Administered to Children: Benefits and Problems

JOHN A. ROSECRANS, MARY JEANNE
KALMAN, and WILLIAM T. CHANCE

INTRODUCTION

The scope of this book, thus far, has been to describe the use of psychological techniques to effect change in the behavioral problems of children. The possibility of using chemical agents in such endeavors has been a controversial issue creating much debate. The remarkable success in curing infectuous diseases with antibiotics, the control of reproductive function with oral contraceptive drugs, as well as the ability to maintain epileptics convulsion free suggests that we should be able to find the "magic bullet" to cure behavioral problems as well. Such reasoning has extended into all mental problems. In the area of drug abuse, researchers have the preoccupation of attempting to find the drug which will save us from heroin dependence, e.g., methadone. In fact, heroin was originally created as a safe alternative to opium. So overwhelming is this attitude that even the flower children of the 50's and 60's used psychodelics (hallucinogens, i.e., LSD, mescaline) to enhance the perception of reality and to enable them to better enjoy nature and friends. The senses of these individuals were so flooded with technology, television, computers, etc. that they felt they had to find some way of creating reality in a technical world. In fact, the motto of that era was "better living through chemistry."

The American dream has dictated that each of us be happy and free. The pursuit of happiness can be assisted with chemical agents. As pointed out in a fascinating treatise by Lennard *et al.* (1971), all we need to do is to declare any human problem a medical problem and then we can use a drug to cure it. Thus, if we have anxiety, an overactive child, trouble with a mother-in-law, etc., all we need to do is ingest, spray on, or rub on some chemical or collection of chemicals. Drugs have become the panacea of our society.

Please forgive the facetiousness of these opening remarks. The point we would like to make is that we have been too easily led to believe that we can cure all diseases with drugs. As suggested by Lennard *et al.* (1971), the solution to any social or emotional problem is too easy when you have drugs. One of the inherent difficulties in ascertaining the role of drugs in treatment is the simplicity of using them. The school principal may believe that he will have an orderly, quiet school if stimulants are used to treat hyperactive children. Similarily, a warden of a state prison can see relief if chlorpromazine (an antipsychotic) is part of the prisoners' daily diet. Analogously, a city councilman can see a reduction of health and welfare spending when chlordiazepoxide (Librium®) or diazepam (Valium®) are given to the elderly at a public retirement facility. The solutions are so simple: the behavioral control of people with drugs is too easy.

Documentations of these above examples of drug misuse can be made over and over again. Even the Central Intelligence Agency and the United States Military have given thought to the possibilities of the use of drugs in the control of behavior of its enemies. Parents who can't understand the behavior of their child are relieved when the pediatrician tells them that their child is hyperactive. He can merely say that we can control this disease with a CNS stimulant. This procedure serves several functions (Lennard *et al.*, 1971). First, the physician has served his role as curer of the sick, even though he may not be sure of the outcome or even whether or not there is an illness. Second, and most important, the use of the drug (in this case the stimulant drug) serves the purpose of relieving the parent from responsibility for the problem. Obviously, their child is sick with minimal brain dysfunction (MBD) but can be cured by the use of CNS stimulants. Thus, they had no part in the cause and need do little thereafter, since the drug will do the job.

Our purpose in this chapter is not to criticize parents, physicians, or anyone. We would like to illustrate the problems associated with the use of drugs in the treatment of behavioral disorders. The use of drugs in any psychological situation is complicated, and this is especially true with children. The difficulty is that drugs can provide us with a fast and economical method of dealing with a behavioral problem. We contend that these latter factors tend to blind us from a more intensive investigation of the problems at hand. At this point, it seems that environmental, sociological, and psychological contingencies may be at the root of many of the behavioral problems of children, especially in hyperactivity (Whalen and Haenker, 1976). The thought that a chemical agent can reverse all the psychological events leading to inappropriate behavior is too simplistic.

What we would like to do in this chapter is the following: (1) present a survey of prescribing habits of the pediatrician as an indicator of psychoactive drugs currently prescribed for children; (2) discuss the use of psychoactive drugs in behavioral disorders such as hyperactivity; (3) present a neurophysiological-neurochemical model of behavioral disorders in children; and (4) discuss the long range consequences of drug taking in children.

DRUGS PRESCRIBED BY PEDIATRICIANS

Rather than present a cookbook approach of psychoactive drugs given to children (there are many texts that can provide such information) we felt that it would be more enlightening to provide information concerning the prescribing habits of pediatricians. The results of such a study are provided in Table 1. This investigation ulilized the prescription records ($N = 19,860$) of a selected group of pharmacies in the Richmond area. While the study is not as scientific as we would have preferred, the data provides us with a point to begin our discussion of drugs used with children.

Analgesics and Antitussives

A survey such as this can provide us with many interesting facts. Of all psychoactive drugs prescribed, it was estimated that about 20% were given for behavioral disorders. The drugs most often prescribed were in the analgesic class; about 32%. It is interesting to note that this figure is quite similar to the percent of analgesics prescribed to adults. However, in the analgesic class codeine was most often given to children (22%) while propoxyphene (Darvon®) accounted for most of the analgesics given to adults (13%). The therapeutic indications for these drugs are for pain relief, and in some cases to relieve coughing due to colds. As one would also suspect, paragoric (a preparation containing 10% opium) accounted for 6% of the analgesic drugs given to children, while little was prescribed for the adult population. This drug is usually given to infants to relieve teething pain or to reduce diarrhea due to infections such as the flu. Drugs used as antitussives (relieve coughing) were also presented, since children receive this type of preparation more often than adults. This fact was supported in our survey with drug mixtures such as codeine and promethazine (Phenergan® with codeine) comprising the total percent prescribed. In comparison, the overall frequency of prescribing this drug for all patients was only 1.6%.

Barbiturates

The barbiturates ranked second in total number of Rx's given to children. This observation was quite interesting since it was twice what the overall population received (8.6%). Pentobarbital (Nembutal®) and phenobarbital (Luminal®) were prescribed most often. As recommended by the PDR (Physicians's Desk Reference), these drugs can be used as day-time sedatives in children. However, the barbiturates are also indicated as anticonvulsants and are sometimes used to induce sleep in infants and young children who stay awake because of physiological problems caused by infections etc. It is difficult to assess what these drugs were used for, but we are sure that some of these prescriptions were used to produce sedation in anxiety situations. Since prescriptions written by neurologists were not evaluated, we are not sure of the amounts of barbiturates given as anticonvulsants, if any.

Antianxiety Drugs

Antianxiety drugs ranked fourth, with diazepam (Valium®) being given most often (5.6%) and hydroxyzine (Atarax®) accounting for 3.2% of these prescriptions in children. Interestingly, valium constituted 19.7%

of the total psychoactive prescriptions written, which suggests that adults are given this drug much more often than children. Another interesting comparison involves the drug flurazepam (Dalmane®), a drug used to induce sleep in insomniacs. While the overall prescription rate for flurazepam was 5.6%, the prescription rate in children was only 0.7%.

Stimulants

Central nervous system (CNS) stimulants accounted for 8.6% of the psychoactive drugs prescribed for children. Methylphenidate (Ritalin®) was given 6.5% of the time. The indications of this drug are in the treatment of hyperactivity. Prescriptions usually given for weight reduction accounted for only one or two prescriptions of the total given to children.

Antipsychotic and Antidepressant Drugs

The survey indicates that antipsychotic drugs constituted 5.0% of the prescriptions written for children. This figure is similar to the overall percent given to the population. However, the major drug prescribed for children was chlorpromazine (Thorzaine®). This drug is a powerful antiemetic (prevents vomiting) and is often administered via a suppository for this purpose in infants and children suffering from severe vomiting due to colic or infections. Chlorpromazine has also been indicated in hyperactivity. Only six prescriptions for antidepressants were written for children. The indications of this drug class are in psychological depression, although antidepressants are sometimes given to prevent bed · wetting. However, these drugs have high toxicity levels in children.

The above survey provides us with an excellent view of the psychoactive drugs prescribed for children. The total number of psychoactive drugs given children represented 3.4% of all prescriptions written. The study is in line with other surveys (Blackwell, 1973; Parry et al., 1973) suggesting that these findings may be generalized to other populations. The reader should remember that these drugs were prescribed through pharmacies. Therefore, this survey does not provide us with any information concerning institutional drug use. Information from the latter source is extremely difficult to obtain.

DRUGS USED IN SPECIFIC BEHAVIORAL DISORDERS

As indicated in the prescription survey, a relatively small percentage (10–20%) of drugs was given for behavioral disorders. Most of the medications appeared to be prescribed for the symptomatic relief of physical problems. It appears, however, that some drugs were prescribed to children for anxiety. In addition, 58 prescriptions were written for CNS stimulants mainly for methylphenidate (Ritalin®). At this point in time, CNS stimulants remain as the primary treatment for hyperactivity. Drugs such as imipramine (Tofranil®) and chlorpromazine (Thorazine®) have also been utilized with some success. It should be reiterated that our discussion to this point has not involved the institutional use of psychoactive drugs. Drugs such as diazepam and chlorpromazine have been utilized in the symptomatic relief of problems associated with a variety of behavioral problems in children where the subject's activity must be reduced. However, psychoactive drug administration does not generally serve a primary curative function in these situations.

HYPERACTIVITY AND STIMULANT USE

The treatment of hyperactivity in children is the most controversial area in pediatric pharmacology. Many articles have been written on the subject, and we will discuss only those which are pertinent to this chapter. The syndrome of hyperactivity can encompass almost any abnormal behavior in children. This syndrome has now taken on the name "minimal brain dysfunction" (MBD). Grinspoon and Hedblom (1975) have suggested that MBD is "man made" rather than a real "disease." Within the public health model a disease has an etiology, symptoms and a cure. The etiological aspect will be discussed separately. At this point, we will attempt to present a description of the syndrome and how it is treated chemically. The most comprehensive analysis of MBD has been written by S. D. Clements (1969):

> The term "minimal dysfunction syndrome" refers . . . to children of near average, average or above average general intelligence with certain learning or behavioral disabilities ranging from mild to severe, which are associated with deviations of function of the central nervous system. These deviations may manifest themselves by various combinations of impairment in perception, conceptualization, language, memory, and control of attention, impulse or motor function.

Similar symptoms may or may not complicate the problems of children with cerebral palsy, epilepsy, mental retardation, blindness, or deafness.

The aberrations may arise from genetic variations, biochemical irregularities, perinatal brain insults, or other illness or injuries sustained during the years which are critical for the development and maturation of the central nervous system, or from unknown causes.

As we can immediately observe, the symptoms are rather broad and undefined. From a conference conducted by the Office of Child Development, HEW (Freedman, 1971) it was estimated that 3 out of 100 school children are hyperactive. More males than females are affected, which is also observed for other behavioral problems such as child delinquency. The panel also reiterated the fact that diagnosis was difficult, and the causes of MBD are quite unknown and could be related to many behavioral or neurological problems as the result of changes in the physical or mental milieu. In addition, these problems could also be related to either pre- or postnatal factors.

In relation to treatment, the panel stated that stimulants can be beneficial in about one-half to two-thirds of the subjects in which *trial drug* use is warranted. The panel also stated that the goal of medication should be as follows: "In such cases (where drugs are used) the aim is not to 'solve problems with drugs' but to put the severely handicapped child in a position to interact with his environment to the extent that his conditions permit." Thus, what the panel has said is that MBD is a behavioral problem which is difficult to diagnose and that medications should not be the single treatment. This panel (Freedman, 1971) also made one point important to all of us involved in the treatment of behavioral disorders of children. They pointed out that while children constitute more than half the population they receive a disproportionately low share of skilled research attention. Thus, we need more emphasis in all areas of mental health research, which attempt to study the causes and treatment of the hyperactive syndrome.

Unfortunately, most of our research attention has been directed towards the pharmacological approach to the problem. One can find almost any result in terms of therapeutic outcome from 10% to 100% success. An excellent review of studies involving drug treatment of hyperactiveness was written by Werry (1976). He concludes that *d*-amphetamine and methylphenidate are the most effective in controlling hyperactivity. The antipsychotic drugs are useful in some situations but their severe side effects involving the autonomic nervous system and extrapyramidal system limit their usefulness. Antidepressant drugs such as imipramine (Tofranil®) appear beneficial when used carefully but they are still in an experimental stage. The antianxiety drugs have not been widely used but do warrant further investigation. In addition, drugs such as caffeine and magnesium pemoline (Cylert®), which are mild stimulants, have also been studied (Conners *et al.*, 1972; Huestis *et al.*, Smeltzer, 1975). Only pemoline was observed to have any beneficial effects in these well controlled studies. Conners *et al.* (1972) concluded that pemoline may be a suitable alternative to the use of stimulants in the treatment of hyperkinesis. The initial work with caffeine did indicate a positive outcome, but as pointed out by Huestis *et al.* (1975) they used a caffeine powder preparation while earlier investigators (Schnackenberg, 1973) used coffee. An interesting observation by Schecheter (personal communication) suggests that doses of caffeine in combination with *d*-amphetamine will lower the behaviorally effective dose of the latter drug in rats. Thus, in terms of additional drug investigations one might study combinations of other drugs as well as the combined effect of caffeine and *d*-amphetamine in children. Such an approach might be beneficial, especially in lowering potential side effects of drugs such as *d*-amphetamine (cardiovascular side effects primarily).

While most of the clinical pharmacological research has involved attempts to discern which drugs would be effective in the control of acute hyperactivity, few studies have been conducted concerning the long term therapeutic outcome of drug therapies. If 200,000 children are diagnosed as hyperkinetic annually (Freedman, 1971) and half received medication over the last 20 years, then hundreds of thousands of children may in fact, have been given some form of drug for this apparent disease at some time in their lives. This fact is hard to digest, especially since very few follow-up studies have been reported. As pointed out by Whalen and Haenker (1976), only 174 children have been followed up from 2–5 years after an initial diagnosis of hyperactivity. Mendelson, Johnson, and Stewart (1971) found that the use of *d*-amphetamine or methylphenidate was uneffective in half of these children post drug use. Fifty percent of these children exhibited as many symptoms of restlessness, distractibility, impulsiveness, excitability and aggressiveness as before treatment, even though this behavior was measured 2–5 years after the cessation of stimulant treatment. Thus, the prognosis in treating hyperactivity is not as good as we are led to believe. These drugs appear to be producing symptomatic relief of the behavior at best. No permanent behavioral changes were observed in these follow-up studies in at least half of the population examined.

There have been some attempts to study the physiological correlates of the syndrome as well. Satterfield and his coworkers (Satterfield *et al.*, 1972; Satterfield *et al.*, 1974) conducted a series of investigations with hyperactive children to evaluate various pre- and post-drug physiological measures such as EEG, mean skin conductance, and auditory-evoked responses in control subjects' poor stimulant responders, and the best responders to stimulant drugs. These workers suggested that hyperactive children with a lower arousal level than controls responded better to stimulant drugs than those subjects with a higher arousal level. In addition, they also speculated that the high arousal group came from pathological families and that these children would become antisocial in later life. This latter comment is especially enlightening since Mendelson et al. (1971) observed half of their subjects to remain hyperactive post stimulant use. One wonders if both workers were discussing similar populations. Speculating a little further, one wonders whether the poor responding group might have responded better to a drug such as chlorpromazine which would tend to reduce high arousal levels. Furthermore, if such children (poor responder group) were from a psychopathological environment and were consequently depressed by it, one would expect a drug such as imipramine (an antidepressant) to be quite useful. Cantwell (1972) attempted to evaluate psychiatric illness in the families of hyperactive children and observed an increase in the prevalence rates for alcoholism, sociopathy and hysteria in the parents of hyperactive children.

The thrust of these studies suggests that there are at least two categories of hyperactivity when evaluated via a rigorous set of psychophysiological measures. One group appears to represent children who have a low arousal level suggesting a sensory deficit, while a second group appears to exhibit abnormal behavior because of environmental conditions. Thus, some drug specificity could be employed and the correct drug selected. However, the problem of long term effects still haunts us, and one can't be sure that the administration of a drug to increase arousal level (stimulants), decrease arousal level (chlorpromazine) or reduce depression (imipramine) will be beneficial. It appears that to ensure a long term positive outcome one needs to also apply behavioral technologies to produce a meaningful change. Drug therapies may be useful in some situations, but we should be directing more attention toward understanding hyperkinesis which would lead to better alternatives for the child, parent, and that principal who deserves a quiet school.

Behavioral Mechanisms of CNS Stimulants

The ability of both d-amphetamine and methylphenidate to reverse hyperactivity in children has been termed a "paradoxical" effect (Bradley, 1937) because these drugs are usually thought to elicit a stimulation of behavior in human subjects. Studies, since the initial observations of Bradley, have failed to support this concept (Grinspoon and Hedblom, 1975). Most investigators who have measured activity changes in children find that stimulants produce either little effect or a stimulation of behavior. These drugs have been suggested to act by redirecting or redistributing behaviors such that the child gives the appearance of slowing down. Thus, a child may be just as active following stimulant administration, only the behavior is now more constructive than before (Cole, 1969).

To obtain some insights to the behavioral changes involved, one should consider all the behaviors emitted by the child and determine stimuli and events that lead to them. As described before, some of the behaviors observed in hyperactive children could be a symptom of depression (Cantwell, 1972) or other psychological problems resulting from abnormal parental behavior. Thus, drugs such as methylphenidate or even pemoline might be expected to improve such behaviors if depression was concommitant with the hyperactivity. In support of this hypothesis, Rickels et al. (1970) showed that both of these drugs effected an improvement in depressed adults.

Another aspect of evaluating these behaviors was provided by Satterfield et al. (1974) who suggested that some hyperactive children may have in common a low arousal system. Again, if this can explain one portion of the problem, then one would expect an increase of arousal following stimulant medication, since these drugs appear to produce some of their arousal effects by directly stimulating the reticular activating system (Ray, 1975). Similar mechanisms may operate to initiate and maintain cigarette smoking in teenagers. This is important to the present discussion because many investigators have attempted to provide a link between the actions of nicotine and the stimulants. Much research (Rosecrans and Chance, 1977) has shown that nicotine will increase the activity level of low arousal animals which may be analagous to the young person who uses tobacco. Thus, individuals with a low arousal level may be more susceptible to smoking as a means of increasing a sluggish CNS. At this point, it would be interesting to study smoking vs. non-smoking in teenagers using the same approaches as Satterfield. Such a mechanism has also been suggested by Dunn (1976) to explain adult smoking behavior.

The last hypothesis to be discussed concerns some observations made by Petrie (1967) and Buchsbaum (1977). The theoretical framework stems from research of Petrie who used kinesthetic approaches to the more recent work of Buchsbaum using visual evoked responses (VER). The studies of these researchers suggest that individuals handle sensory input differently. The postulates are: (1) In some individuals the cortical response to sensory input tends to increase in magnitude with repetitive presentations and such individuals are defined as *augmentors*; Buchsbaum has shown that the VER increases in magnitude with increasing stimulus intensity; and (2) at the other end of the continuum, some individuals tend to handle sensory input in the opposite manner: VER activity declines rapidly or remains the same following an increase of stimulus intensity and these individuals are termed *reducers*. Since most of us are not augmentors or reducers at all times, we can handle stimulus fluctuations with relative ease. However, how does an extreme *reducer* or *augmentor* handle environmental sensory input? In the extreme reducer, sensory input falls off very rapidly, while in the extreme augmentor this input is constantly amplifying and building up.

The augmentor–reducer model is appropriate to an understanding of hyperactivity. However, the applications of such a model to the understanding of human behavior is quite difficult. Buchsbaum and Wender (1973) suggest that hyperactive children are augmentors and stimulant drugs tend to bring them down to the reducer portion of the continuum. However, other researchers (Hall *et al.*, 1976) have been unable to replicate these findings. Hall *et al.* (1976), on the other hand, suggest that VER factors other than the augmentor–reducer model may be involved in the hyperactive syndrome.

Isaac and his co-workers have postulated that amphetamine and methylphenidate decrease the arousing capabilities of environmental sensory stimuli (Alexander and Isaac, 1965; Kallman and Isaac, 1975; Troelstrup and Isaac, 1969). Kallman and Isaac (1975) suggest that the stimulants decrease gross locomotor activity but increase attentive behaviors in the hyperactive child.

While Buchsbaum's data suggest that hyperactive children are augmentors, the opposite may be true, that is hyperactivity may reflect a reducer function. Support for this latter contention appeared first in the studies of Satterfield *et al.* (1972, 1974) and more recently from the work of Prichep *et al.* (1976). In both studies VER activity was indicative of low arousal in a sample of hyperactive children. In addition, both research groups indicate that stimulants tend to increase arousal levels more towards the control arousal level. What is proposed is that the hypoarousal observed is related to the reduction of sensory input. In addition, it is postulated that such children are sensory seekers and their hyperactive behavior reflects an attempt to increase arousal levels. An analogous model has been suggested by Petrie (1967). She suggests that juvenile delinquency is a function of an individual attempting to seek sensory stimulation because of the too-rapid reduction of sensory input. Likewise, we propose that stimulant medication satisfies the sensory seeking behavior, and because of this, the child can function better in other tasks. Our current working model is that many behavioral problems in children are a function of the reducer–augmentor type of an individual. Thus, the goal of behavioral or chemical intervention would be to reduce the extremes of augmentation or reduction.

Biochemical Mechanisms of CNS Stimulants

Before we can adequately discuss the neurochemical basis of these drugs, the neuroanatomical arrangement of the neuron systems believed to be involved in behavioral problems such as hyperactivity or psychoses should be discussed. This area of research has developed only within the last 20 years, and information has been acquired, both in experimental and clinical terms. Many of the drugs used to manage behavior appear to work by the subtle alteration of these neurochemical systems. Three biogenic amine systems appear to be most involved. These systems are primarily ascending and project from areas within the brain stem to many rostral structures (McGeer, 1971). The systems include the following:

(1) Dopamine (DA) containing neurons project from the substantia nigra to the caudate nucleus and midbrain to the nucleus accumbens and tuberculum olfactorium.

(2) Norepinephrine (NE) containing neurons project from the locus coereleus and reticular formation to the neocortex, hypothalamus, and limic forebrain.

(3) Serotonin (5-HT; 5-hydroxytryptamine) containing neurons project from the raphe nuclei to the hypothalamus, limbic forebrain, caudate nucleus, and neocortex. The 5-HT system consists of several neuron populations which include the dorsal raphe, medial raphe, and the raphe magnus.

All of these systems have nerve cell bodies located in the brain stem which project long axons to the areas described. There are some descending systems, especially the raphe magnus, which appear to be intimately involved with pain perception. These systems are in a unique balance within and between each other (McGeer, 1971).

The major role of these pathways appears to involve control of sensory input and emotional behavior. The DA system also seems to play an important function in motor control, with destruction of this system resulting in Parkinson's disease. Because of the delicate balance between these systems, which can evoke inhibitory (5HT) or excitatory (NE) neuronal effects, the slightest intervention with drugs or stressful events can greatly magnify or reduce the behavioral responses of a subject to the environment.

In relation to our task here, it seems that many of these systems are still in the developmental stage in children. Thus, any extreme environmental change could alter neuronal function and produce aberrant behaviors. Such thinking has also been considered in the development of psychosis. Thus, environment, life stress or even genetic factors can play a role in altering such a delicate neurochemical balance which could lead to psychoses or other abnormal behaviors (Buchsbaum *et al.*, 1973; Goodwin and Post, 1975; Redmond *et al.*, 1975).

Both *d*-amphetamine and methylphenidate produce pronounced effects in which the DA and NE systems appear to be involved (Groves and Rebec, 1976). These drugs produce most of their effects by releasing neuronal stores of NE and DA. In animals and man the behavioral effects resulting from these chemical changes may range from a minor facilitation of arousal levels to stereotype, hallucinations, and psychoses (paranoia). These effects are dose related, but whether NE and DA are involved in all or some of these effects remains to be a much debated issue. However, more recent data suggest that 5-HT may be involved as well (Brase and Loh, 1975).

Because these stimulants appear to induce their behavioral effects via one or more of these neurochemical systems, it has been assumed that hyperactivity is a function of some neurochemical imbalance. Furthermore, it is suggested that stimulant medication, in correcting hyperactivity, is acting by returning such balances to within normal limits (Wender, 1974; Brase and Loh, 1975). The causes of this imbalance can be envisioned to be due to genetic effects, alterations in environmental mileu, or even to artificial food flavors or colors (Feingold, 1975). One can easily see how such neurochemical alterations could occur via either chemical or stress (possibly via steroid release) induction. Rates of biosynthesis, release or metabolism of such neurotransmitters are also in a delicate balance contingent upon the chemical mileu, especially during the developmental period encompassing the hyperactive syndrome (3–12 years of age). Thus, a subtle change could produce an alteration in perception or sensory input. In addition, some investigators contend that these neurochemical systems do not mature as rapidly in those subjects who develop the hyperactive syndrome (Snyder, 1973). In the latter case, it is suggested that stimulants serve the purpose of priming these neurochemical systems until they can mature naturally. Thus, the hypothesis suggested by these investigators is that hyperactivity is a function of some neurochemical imbalance and that stimulant medications tend to normalize these events. This hypothesis can be fitted in quite well with the augmentor–reducer model which may be a reflection of such a chemical imbalance. However, besides chemical intervention, it is our contention that these chemical imbalances can be made normalized by behavioral intervention by positive reinforcement and biofeedback procedures.

The neurochemical basis of hyperactivity and the mechanism of action of the stimulants on this behavior provide a very logical and believable picture. However, one difficulty with this hypothesis does exist. If hyperactivity is a reflection of a slowly developing neurochemical system or some imbalance then one would expect a more positive outcome in follow-up studies (Mendelson et al., 1971). However, one should not completely rule out such chemical hypotheses. An intense research effort should be currently initiated which would evaluate all the previously mentioned physiological and neurochemical parameters in a systematic, well controlled series of studies. In addition, studies attempting to evaluate similar parameters in adults who received stimulant drugs for hyperactivity in childhood must also be undertaken. Little more can be said until such research measures are completed.

SEDATIVES AND HYPNOTICS

The sedative and hypnotic drugs include both barbiturates (Nembutal®, Luminal® etc.) and nonbarbiturate compounds (Chloral hydrate® etc.). Although the barbiturates are similar in chemical structure, the nonbarbiturates vary considerably in chemical structure but share common behavioral and physiological effects. Many compounds produce both sedative and hypnotic effects but relatively few are useful as therapeutic agents, due to the accompanying undesirable side effects (Maynert, 1971).

As the nomer "sedative and hypnotics" suggests these drugs produce both reduced activity and somnolence. Decreased activity and responsivity are not characteristics peculiar to the sedative. Both the antianxiety (minor tranquilizers) and antipsychotic (major tranquilizers) drugs also produce sedation but these were not available clinically until about 40 years after the availability of the traditional "sedative and hypnotics." The behavioral changes subsequent to administration of the sedatives and hypnotics are dose dependent; i.e., high doses produce sleep while doses approximately one-quarter to one-third of those producing sleep produce sedation. Low dose effects of the barbiturates are more variable in individual children, sometimes producing excitation and agitation rather than sedation.

Adjunctive to the decreased activity produced by these compounds, a decrease in general neural functioning is frequently observed rather than solely a decrease in motor behavior. Measures of specific mental tasks such as reaction time, discrimination, and judgmental tasks, show decreased proficiency when sedatives are given (Goldstein *et al.*, 1960; Loomis and West, 1958). Reports of deficits in acquiring new tasks and IQ have not been obtained (Wopner *et al.*, 1962).

Some of the compounds, specifically the barbiturates, are employed as anticonvulsants in the treatment of epilepsy. Since epilepsy is primarily a neurological disorder rather than a psychological or behavioral disorder, use of the sedatives and hypnotics as anticonvulsants will not be included in this discussion. The barbiturates do stabilize abnormal EEG patterns and raise thresholds for precipitated seizures.

The sedatives and hypnotics are indicated in the therapeutic treatment of sleep disorders, to produce basal anesthesia, as a treatment for epilepsy and in psychological disorders where daytime sedation is warranted. Most frequently the use of these compounds as sedatives is symptomatic rather than an attempt to alter all the undesirable behaviors characteristic of a specific psychological disorder. Fish (1960) has suggested that some specificity be employed in the prescription of sedatives. She recommends that sedatives should not be used with retarded children, especially retarded autistics. Success of drug treatment is relatively good with schizophrenic children with normal intellectual ability or with organic childhood disorders characterized by hyperactivity. The lack of success with retarded children is typically characterized by too much dulling of intellectual abilities and over sedation.

Hypnotic doses produce alterations in sleep patterns. These alterations are produced in two ways. The time to onset of sleep is reduced, while the duration of sleep time is increased. Grogginess and "hangover" are frequently reported the morning after the administration of hypnotics and decrements in performance have been observed for 10–22 hours later (McKenzie and Elliott, 1965). This undesirable side effect may preclude the use of hypnotics with school children.

Initially the barbiturates reduce time spent in REM sleep. As habituation to barbiturate administration occurs, however, sleep patterns return to normal (Kay *et al.*, 1972). When medication is discontinued the disrupted sleep pattern reappears and may persist for 1–1½ months after discontinuing the drug (Oswald and Priest, 1965). Thus, if sleep medication is given for a few nights for sleeping problems and then stopped, the subsequent effect on the EEG and stages of sleep encourages continued medication.

Two distinct types of sleep disorders have been treated with hypnotics. One type is disorders of sleep onset and the other type includes disorders of duration and depth of sleep. Decreases in the frequencies of night terror episodes and somnambulism have been maintained by the administration of the hypnotics at bedtime. Some specificity in the selection of hypnotics for treating sleep disorders is recommended, since wide variations in time to onset and duration of action have been observed between the specific compounds available (Maynert, 1971).

Long term therapeutic outcome is dramatically affected by the development of habituation to the sedation produced subsequent to repeated drug administration. Typically, this effect results in increased dosage which can lead to hazardous effects since no alteration in the lethal dose is observed, although habituation to the sedative effects does develop. Long term use leads to dependence similar to the dependence observed with alcohol therefore gradual dose reduction is necessary to prevent withdrawal symptoms. The physical effects of long term use are extremely serious. Thus, chronic administration should be reserved for serious disorders where medical supervision is routine. Campbell and Small (1976), in their review of psychotropic drug use in children, conclude that the barbiturates should not be used with children except as an anticonvulsant since other drugs are available with equivalent sedative properties. This is a most interesting conclusion in the context of our survey results indicating that the barbiturates rank second in frequency of psychoactive drugs prescribed for children by pediatricians and that the barbiturates were given twice as often to children as to adults.

The barbiturates produce a generalized depression of cellular activity but the biochemical mechanism which produces this depression is unclear. Both interference with ion transport and cellular energy mechanisms have been postulated as modes of cellular disruption produced by the sedative-hypnotic drugs. The major action of the sedative-hypnotics is to block postsynaptic transmission (Maynert, 1971).

When given in clinically therapeutic doses the sedative-hypnotic drugs show the greatest effect on central rather than peripheral tissue. Attempts to localize the action of the barbiturates to a specific neuroanatomical structure have been numerous (Killam, 1962; Rosner and Clark, 1973). The reticular activating system has been investigated most extensively as a possible site for barbiturate action. The threshold for reticular formation activation in response to sensory stimulation and direct electrical stimulation is reduced by the barbiturates; suggesting a general depression the cellular level of the reticular formation (Killam, 1962). Other observations following barbiturate administration indicate the drug effects are not specific to the reticular formation. The hippocampal component of the EEG arousal response disappears with drug administration. Also, partial damage to the septal area lowers the dose of barbiturates effective in producing sedation (Roth and Harvey, 1968). Thus, these structures both appear to be involved in the behavioral effects of the sedative hypnotics.

ANTIANXIETY DRUGS

This group of drugs includes meprobamate (Miltown®, Equanil®), chlordiazepoxide (Librium®), diazepam (Valium®), oxazepam (Serax®) and hydrozine HCl (Atarax®, Vistaril®). According to Blackwell's survey in 1973 one half of all psychotropic drug use in adults can be attributed to prescriptions for chlordiazepoxide and diazepam alone. Additionally, Blackwell observed that diazepam had the largest growth in popularity of all the psychotropic compounds on the market. These figures are quite alarming since they suggest that our society is becoming more and more amenable to treating relatively minor psychological problems by drug intervention. Manheimer et al. (1973) examined social attitudes about drug treatment of relatively minor psychological problems. The general public condoned the treatment of anxiety with drugs more than any of the other minor psychological problems. Although these are adult statistics, the treatment of children with antianxiety drugs is controlled by adults and obviously adult attitudes influence current as well as future treatment of children with these agents. Our survey suggests that use of the antianxiety drugs in children is not currently as popular as the antianxiety drugs appear to be with adults but diazepam was the most popular of the antianxiety drugs in treating childhood problems.

According to the PDR, indications for the use of the antianxiety drugs are states of tension and anxiety due to stress and to produce general muscle relaxation. The efficacy of the antianxiety drugs in treating anxiety symptoms has been extensively examined. Wheatley (1972), in a review of alterations in anxiety responses following all types of treatments, reported that about 75% of the patients evaluated showed improvement. Leedy (1970) reported some improvement in neurotic symptoms in 100% of his patients treated with antianxiety drugs. This improvement measure should be evaluated within the context that 50% of patients with anxiety complaints show improvement on placebo medication (Wheatley, 1972). A high rate of improvement in neurotics on placebo medication has been observed by others and may be related to this particular psychological problem since a number of nonspecific factors such as sex, social and economic status, chronicity and previous drug experience are all correlated with drug efficacy (Rickels et al., 1966; Rickels, 1968).

Several investigators have suggested that efficacy of treatment with the antianxiety drugs can be enhanced by discriminative specificity when prescribing these agents. Chlordiazepoxide has been observed to be relatively useful in treating pediatric anxiety and in treating depressed, inhibited children (Fish, 1968). While chlordiazepoxide may be superior to placebo in treating hyperactive children, the stimulants are the drugs of choice for hyperkinesis (Zrull et al., 1963). Children who have anxiety symptoms secondary to brain damage, epilepsy or an abnormal EEG, also show poor response to treatment with antianxiety drugs.

Recent literature has suggested diazepam as a treatment for facial tics (Frederiks, 1970) and in treating several types of sleep disorders (Glick et al., 1971; Fisher et al., 1973). The sleep disorders of nocturnal enuresis, somnambulism, nightmares, and night terrors which occur predominately during stage 3–4 sleep (Broughton, 1968) respond successfully to diazepam treatment. Currently, the mechanism of diazepam action in these disorders is unclear, although changes in the sleeping EEG of diazepam medicated children has been documented (Fisher et al., 1973).

Usefulness of sedative doses of diazepam for dental procedures in the apprehensive or retarded child has received recent research attention (Healy and Hamilton, 1971; Chambiras, 1972; Healy et al., 1970; Baird and Flowerdew, 1970). Diazepam appears to be relatively safe and effective in producing sedation for dental procedures under these circumstances.

Increased stimulation and excitation is the most frequently observed undesirable effect of the antianxiety drugs. This adverse behavioral reaction has been observed in some children with neurological abnormalities (Kraft et al., 1965). Several investigators have reported increased aggression and hostility following administration of the antianxiety drugs in children with poor impulse control and a high frequency of aggressive behaviors prior to drug treatment (Gardos et al., 1968; Irwin, 1974). Other researchers (Rickels and Downing, 1974) have been unable to replicate this observation. Additionally, undesirable effects have been observed with children who have psychotic or borderline psychotic symptoms. Following treatment with antianxiety drugs these children may show an increase in psychotic symptoms (Fish, 1968). In general, these drugs are most useful in treating anxiety that results from environmental stress rather than anxiety states that may be concomitant with neurological problems or anxiety symptoms that are adjunctive to psychotic or aggressive behaviors. Tolerance and physical dependence are the most serious effects subsequent to long term medication with the antianxiety drugs. Withdrawal symptoms are not observed if the dosage remains low (Byck, 1975). Growth inhibition with long term administration, as serious consideration with maintenance drug use in children, has not been observed in animal investigations (Zbinden et al., 1961).

Success with behavioral treatments for anxiety is considerably better than with other psychological problems. Thus, behavioral intervention would be initially recommended in treating neurotic children. If unsuccessful, placebo medication has a success rate of 50% in neurotics and should be tried before longterm medication of children with antianxiety drugs is initiated.

Although many of the characteristics of anxiety are associated with the peripheral autonomic nervous system, the action of clinical doses of antianxiety compounds is predominately a central action rather than a peripheral one. Behavioral data indicate that the antianxiety drugs reduce aggressive behavior (Randall et al., 1961), reduce septal irritability (Schallek et al., 1962, 1964) and reduce ulceration in stressed animals (Haot et al., 1964). Many of the behavioral effects induced by the antianxiety drugs are similar to the behavioral effects of the sedative-hypnotics.

The diminution of anxiety responses to stress by the antianxiety drugs seems to occur by a blockade of arousal responses to stressful stimuli. Like the barbiturates, the antianxiety drugs block EEG arousal from electrical stimulation of the reticular formation (Domino, 1971). Furthermore, combined administration of other CNS depressants and antianxiety drugs produces an additive depressant effect suggesting that these drugs may have similar actions. Reports of lessened effects of the antianxiety drugs in smokers is indicative that nicotine may counteract the antianxiety drug effects.

In addition to the proposed disruption of arousal response via the reticular formation, the antianxiety drugs drastically alter ongoing activity in the limbic system. These drugs decrease electrical activity in the septal area, the amygdala, and hippocampus (Domino, 1971). The relaying of information between these structures is also disrupted because electrical responses of the hippocampus following direct amygdala stimulation is reduced when antianxiety drugs are administered (Morillo et al., 1962). Autonomic responses, which typically occur following hypothalamic stimulation, are also abolished in the drugged state. Therefore, the decrease in autonomic activity which is associated with high anxiety situations is decreased by action of the antianxiety drugs on the limbic system rather than a peripheral action.

The marked muscle relaxant properties of these drugs is also attributed to central drug effects. Administration of the antianxiety drugs produces a reduction of polysynaptic reflexes which is exacerbated in decerebrate cats (Ngai *et al.*, 1966) suggesting that these agents are altering supraspinal control mechanisms.

ANTIPSYCHOTICS

The antipsychotic drugs are used to reduce psychotic symptoms. Typically, children are diagnosed as psychotic if they have impaired mental functioning, characterized by hallucinations, delusions or distorted perception. Other psychotic symptoms include distortion of reality and defects in language and memory (Ullman and Krasner, 1969). Since children with psychotic symptoms are unable to function and interact in a normal environment, many of them are hospitalized or placed in an institutional facility.

The most common antipsychotic drugs are chlorpromazine (Thorazine®), reserpine (Serpisil®), haloperidol (Haldol®) and trifluperidol (Stelazine®). The effectiveness of these drugs in treating adult psychotic symptoms is relatively well accepted. However, well controlled investigations of the influence of antipsychotic drugs in treating childhood psychotic symptoms are sparse. Clinical observations suggest that the antipsychotic drugs are effective with psychotic, agitated mentally retarded, and brain damaged children. Fish and Shapiro (1964, 1965) reported that 80% of the children treated with antipsychotic drugs showed a reduction in psychotic behaviors. Fish (1960) has also observed that some prepuberty children diagnosed as schizophrenic may also exhibit excessive sedation and interference with learning and normal functioning. These problems seem to be especially evident when the children are medicated with chlorpromazine. Some specificity of drug selection for treating behavioral symptoms is suggested by the literature currently available. Children who are hypoactive and/or apathetic may become sedated when given chlorpromazine. Since trifluperidol has some stimulant properties, this drug is recommended as the drug of choice for hypoactive or autistic children (Fish, 1970; Fish *et al.*, 1969). Several authors have reported that although there is a change in some psychotic symptoms with antipsychotic drug medication, aggressive and assaultive behaviors are not altered (Werry *et al.*, 1966; Faretra *et al.*, 1970). Other reports have failed to support these findings (Serrano and Forbis, 1973).

Werry *et al.* (1966) have observed improvement in hyperactive children following the administration of antipsychotic drugs. Effectiveness of antipsychotic drugs in altering hyperkinesis was unrelated to a diagnosis of brain damage.

The behavioral effects of the antipsychotic drugs are different for the psychotic and nonpsychotic patient population (Byck, 1975). When administered to psychotics, these drugs reduce the psychotic symptoms and the individuals appear more normal. In contrast, normal individuals maintained on antipsychotic medication exhibit bizarre, abnormal behavior. Thus, these drugs do not produce the same effects in all populations.

Generally, the antipsychotic drugs produce a reduction in psychotic behaviors as well as sedation or what has been referred to as the "neuroleptic syndrome" characterized by psychomotor slowing, emotional quieting, and affective indifference (Delay and Deniker, 1952). Although tolerance to the sedative qualities of the antipsychotics occurs relatively rapidly, no tolerance has been observed to the antipsychotic properties of these drugs.

The most serious side effects of these drugs are the extrapyramidal syndromes (Parkinson syndrome, akathesia, acute dystonic reaction, and tardive dyskinesia), which may accompany antipsychotic drug medication. In addition, chlorpromazine treatment may increase the probability of epileptic problems in children (Byck, 1975).

A plethora of research has been directed towards understanding the physiological correlates of psychotic behaviors. One approach has been to examine the neurological tissue of deceased individuals diagnosed as psychotic. The Scheibels (1962) have implicated the brain stem reticular formation as the most likely candidate for involvement in hallucinations. Bradley, searching for the drug site of action (1972), has reported that chlorpromazine effectively blocks the afferent collateral input at the level of the brain stem reticular formation. Additional support for the involvement of this system comes from behavioral reports that selective attention is disrupted in psychotics (McGhie, 1972), further implicating involvement of the reticular formation or sensory control mechanisms in these disorders (Weinberger, 1971). Fisman (1975) has recently published a report on postmortem examination of neurological tissue from 34 mental hospital patients. A positive correlation between post hallucinatory complaints and midbrain damage was observed, further supporting the implication of the reticular formation dysfunction in psychotic disorders.

Another approach to elucidate how the antipsychotic drugs alter psychotic behaviors has been directed toward comparisons with amphetamine psychosis. Amphetamine psychosis was first described in

1938 (Young and Scoville, 1938) and the behaviors subsequent to amphetamine usage (amphetamine psychosis) are similar to psychotic behaviors. Symptoms for both schizophrenia and amphetamine psychosis include hallucinations, delusions, affectual flattening, thought disorders, and frequently withdrawn, depressed characteristics.

Biochemical observations have implicated the disruption of both dopamine and norepinephrine neurochemical systems in the action of amphetamine (Creese and Iversen, 1973). In addition, haloperidol, an antipsychotic drug, also antagonizes amphetamine-induced symptoms (Angrist *et al.*, 1974), supposedly by its relatively specific antidopaminergic properties. These data tend to support the view that psychosis or at least many of the symptoms related to psychoses may result from the over active dopamine system; therefore, the antipsychotic drugs may reduce psychosis by blocking dopaminergic activity (Siomopoulus, 1975; Angrist *et al.*, 1974).

These are not the only approaches that have been applied to determine psychotic functioning and how administration of the antipsychotic drugs act to alter the psychotic behavior. The ideas presented are indicative of the types of approaches which are currently popular. Hopefully, continued endeavors will further elucidate the actions of the antipsychotic compounds.

THE LONG TERM CONSEQUENCES OF GIVING DRUGS TO CHILDREN

The major consequence of giving drugs to children is that they may have no effect other than to reduce the symptoms of a specific symptom of a behavioral problem. Thus, the problem may reappear once the drug is no longer administered. This difficulty is not an unusual problem since it is the case with most psychoactive drugs given to humans. However, besides giving one a false sense of security, there are some other dangers. First, and most prominent, what does giving a child a drug do to individual behavioral development? Thus, one wonders what the effects of giving a drug, such as an antianxiety or a CNS stimulant will have on psychological development. A certain degree of anxiety and experience with stress situations is necessary for proper development (Seligman, 1975), and drugs (especially drugs such as Valium®) may interfere with this process. In addition, what is giving a drug saying to the child? It seems to us that a child may tend to feel unable to cope or solve the problem, especially since he is given little opportunity to exert control;

instead he is given a drug. Finally, what happens when this child becomes an adult? The suggestion is that such individuals may more readily resort to chemical solutions to human problems than those individuals not exposed. As reported by Blum and his associates (1965), adult drug use was somewhat proportional to how many drugs their parents used, and to the degree of importance attributed to sickness in childhood. Thus, the greater the rewards for being sick (staying home from school or getting attention) or the greater the number of the drugs in the medicine cabinet, the higher the probability that such individuals will use psychoactive agents as adults. One wonders if we are creating a new generation of individuals who rely on drugs as primary problem solving devices.

Another liability in long term drug use with children involves the transfer of material learned under drug influence to nondrug situations. This becomes a serious problem when both drug and psychological treatment techniques are combined. A large body of data exists demonstrating that learning is state dependent, i.e., occurs only under similar organism conditions as occurred during conditioning (Overton, 1971). Thus, behavioral techniques may not be as effacious when applied to a child who is on drug maintenance as when applied to a drug free child. Additionally, some concern should be expressed for the school performance of children with relatively minor problems but maintained on longterm drug treatment.

As stated in our introduction, drugs are too easy to use as the benefits are enormous. Before we go any further however, we should begin designing and carrying out some long range research projects to determine what the long term effects of these drugs are in terms of the individual and society. In addition, we need to develop more insight into the causes of these behavioral disorders and begin to develop the behavioral strategies necessary to assist children to be able to cope without chemical assistance, or at least minimal assistance.

SOME FINAL COMMENTS: SO, WHAT IS THE ROLE OF DRUG USE IN CHILDHOOD BEHAVIORAL DISORDERS?

This chapter has generally presented a cautious to negative view of drugs used in treating behavioral problems in children. However, there are undoubtedly situations in which drug use is warranted, especially when used in conjunction with a total behavioral program involving all the principles of the child, the school psychologist, the parent, and the physician. This is the case at mental health centers which can provide a

Table 1. Drugs Most Prescribed by Pediatricians by Drug Class[a]

Drug Class	Pediatricians (N = 678)	Overall
Analgesics	32.6 (228)	30.3
Barbiturates	20.5 (139)	8.9
Expectorants and Antitussives	17.0 (115)	1.6
Antianxieties	8.8 (60)	33.5
Stimulants	8.6 (58)	3.7
Antipsychotics	5.0 (34)	4.7
Antidepressants	0.1 (6)	7.0
Other	7.4 (38)	8.9

[a]These data represent the distribution of psychoactive drugs prescribed by pediatricians in a survey involving the records of selected pharmacy's N = 19,860; the percent of psychoactive prescriptions by pediatricians was equal to 3.4% of the total. Values in parentheses represents the number of prescriptions written. Specialities for prescriptions were determined from public sources. This information was provided by Dr. E. Gullick, L. King, D. Mott (NIDA-1H 81DA 01 46801).

complete treatment program. However, as pointed out by Solomons (1973), most of the psychopharmacological drugs given to children are prescribed by pediatricians (Table 1) who exert little control over the child, and do not follow up the results of the medication. Thus, once a proper diagnosis of the child's behavior and the total family contribution to problems are evaluated (Satterfield et al., 1972), then the clinician is in the position of administering a psychoactive drug; the intent being to bring the behavior under control so that psychological methodologies can be utilized. But, along with this, the treatment plan must include parent and teacher education as one begins to reshape the previous inappropriate behavior.

In relation to the first question, diagnosis, the issues are enormous. As pointed out by Sprague (1973) there are many problems associated with attempting to classify every child that has a behavioral problem. First, the lack of a clear criteria for diagnosing behavioral disorders, such as hyperactivity, sometimes prevents the development of a successful treatment plan, especially at the community level. Second, the diagnosis may be irrelevant to the task of enabling a child to read; the work is hard. Third, as mentioned before, the diagnosis is sometimes not directly related to the program of treatment best suited to the child. Finally, the labeling of a child into a specific category may; (1) stigmatize the child, and (2) reduce the professional expectations of the child's ability to cope with the problem such that the child is not given the opportunities for behavioral change. The latter point is extremely relevant as Sprague (1973) has shown he could train mentally retarded subjects to complete tasks not expected by the rehabilitation staff.

In relation to treatment, Novack (1971) points out that teachers are not able to cope with children with behavioral problems because they are not given enough information about the behaviors and drugs given to children. In addition, they do not have the training in behavioral control techniques. As Novack points out in his short article, much success has been observed in using behavioral techniques in the control of the hyperactivity syndrome. However, such treatment regimens are time consuming, require well trained professionals, and are costly. At this point in time, as a society, we have not yet developed the will to expend the time and resources to accommodate such rational approaches. The drug solution is too easy; after all, relief is just a swallow away.

REFERENCES

Alexander, M. and Isaac, W. (1965). Effect of illumination and d-amphetamine on the activity of the rhesus macaque. *Psychological Reports* 16:311–315.

Angrist, B., Sathananthan, G., Wilk, S., and Gershon, S. (1974). Amphetamine psychosis: behavioral and biochemical aspects. *Journal of Psychiatric Research* 11:13–23.

Baird, E., and Flowerdew, G. (1970). Intravenous diazepam in conservative dentistry. *British Dental Journal* 129:11–14.

Blackwell, B. (1973). Psychotropic drugs in use today: The role of diazepam in medical practice. *Journal of the American Medical Association* 225:1637–1643.

Blum, R. & Associates. (1970). *Drugs I: Society and Drugs.* San Francisco: Jossey-Bass.

Bradley, C. (1937). The behavior of children receiving benzedrine. *American Journal of Psychiatry* 94:572–585.

Bradley, P. (1972). The action of drugs on single neurons in the brain. In B. Bradley and R. Brimblecombe, eds., *Progress in Brain Research, Vol. 36.* Amsterdam: Elsevier Publishing Company.

Brase, D. A. and Loh, H. H. (1975). Possible role of 5-Hydroxytryptamine in minimal brain dysfunction. *Life Sciences* 16:1005–1016.

Broughton, R. (1968). Sleep disorders: disorders of arousal? *Science* 159:1070–1078.

Buchsbaum, M. (1977). Average evoked response augmenting/reducing in Schizophrenia and affective disorders. In D. Freedman, ed., *The Biology of the Major Psychoses: A Comparative Analysis.* New York: Raven Press.

———, and Wender, P. (1973). Average evoked responses in normal and minimally brain dysfunctioned children treated with amphetamine: a preliminary report. *Archives of General Psychiatry* 29:764–770.

———, Landau, S., Murphy, D., and Goodwin, F. (1973). Average evoked response in bipolar and unipolar affective disorders: relationship to sex, age of onset, and monoamine oxidase. *Biological Psychiatry* 7(3):199–212.

Byck, R. (1975). Drugs and the treatment of psychiatric disorders. In L. Goodman and A. Gilman, eds., *The Pharmacological Basis of Therapeutics* (5th Edition). London: The Macmillan Company.

Campbell, M., and Small, A. (1976). The use of psychotherapeutic drugs in pediatrics. In L. Simpson, ed., *Drug Treatment of Mental Disorders*. New York: Raven Press.

——, Fish, B., Shapiro, T., and Floyd, A., Jr. (1972). Acute responses of schizophrenic children to a sedative and "stimulating" neuroleptic: a pharmacologic yardstick. *Current Therapeutic Research* 14:759–766.

Cantwell, Dennis P. (1972). Psychiatric illness in the families of hyperactive children. *Archives of General Psychiatry* 27:414–417.

Chambiras, P. (1972). Sedation in dentistry: intravenous diazepam. *Australian Dental Journal* February: 17–23.

Clements, S. D. (1966). Task force I: minimal brain dysfunction in children. Institute of Neurological Diseases and Blindness, Monograph no. 3, Department of Health, Education and Welfare, Washington, D.C.

Cole, J. (1969). The amphetamines in child psychiatry: a review. *Seminars in Psychiatry* 1(2):174–177.

Conners, C. K., Taylor, E., Meo, S., Kurtz, M. A., and Fournier, M. (1972). Magnesium pemoline and dextroamphetamine: a controlled study in children with minimal brain dysfunction. *Psychopharmacologia* 26:321–336.

Creese, I., and Iversen, S. (1973). Blockage of amphetamine induced motor stimulation and stereotype in the adult rat following neonatal treatment with 6-hydroxydopamine. *Brain Research* 35:369–382.

Delay, J., and Deniker, P. (1952). Trente-huit cas de psychoses traites par la cure prolongee et continue de 4560 RP. Le Congres de Al. et Neurologie de Langue France. In *Compte rendu du congres*. Masson et Cie, Paris.

Domino, E. (1971). Antianxiety drugs. In J. Dipalma, ed., *Drill's Pharmacology in Medicine* (4th edition). New York: McGraw-Hill Book Company.

Dunn, W. (1976). Smoking as a possible inhibitor of arousal. Paper presented at the *1st International Workshop on Behavior and Nicotine*, Zurich, Switzerland.

Faretra, G., Dooher, L., and Dowling, J. (1970). Comparison of haloperidol and fluphenazine in disturbed children. *American Journal of Psychiatry* 126:1670–1673.

Feingold, B. F. (1975). Hyperkinesis and learning disabilities linked to artificial food flavors and colors. *American Journal of Nursing* 75(5):797–803.

Fish, B. (1960). Drug therapy in child psychiatry: pharmacological aspects. *Comparative Psychiatry* 1:212–217.

—— (1968). Drug use in psychiatric disorders of children. *American Journal of Psychiatry* 124:31–36.

—— (1970). Psychopharmacologic response of schizophrenic adults as predictors of responses in young schizophrenic children. *Psychopharmacology Bulletin* 6:12–15.

——, and Shapiro, T. (1964). A descriptive typology of children's psychiatric disorders. II. A behavioral classification. *Psychiatric Research Reports* 18:75–86.

——, and Shapiro, T. (1965). A typology of childrens' psychiatric disorders. I. Its application to a controlled evaluation of treatment. *Journal of the American Academy of Child Psychiatry* 4:32–52.

——, Campbell, M., Shapiro, T., and Floyd, A. Jr. (1969). Comparison of trifluperidol, trifluoperazine, and chlorpromazine in preschool schizophrenic children: The value of less sedative antipsychotic agents. *Current Therapeutic Research* 11:589–595.

Fisher, C., Kahn, E., Edwards, A., and Davis, D. (1973). A psychophysiological study of nightmares and night terror. *Archives of General Psychiatry* 28:252–259.

Fisman, M. (1975). The brain stem in psychosis. *The British Journal of Psychiatry* 126:414–422.

Fredericks, J. (1970). Facial tics in children: The therapeutic effect of low dosage diazepam. *The British Journal of Clinical Practice* 24(1):17–20.

Freedman, D. H. (1971). Report of the conference on the use of stimulant drugs in the treatment of behaviorally disturbed young school children. *Journal of Learning Disabilities* 4(9):523–530.

Glick, B., Schulman, D., and Turecki, S. (1971). Diazepam (Valium) treatment in childhood sleep disorders. *Diseases of the Nervous System* 32:565–566.

Goldstein, A., Searle, B., and Schinke, T. (1960). Effects of secobarbital and of *d*-amphetamine on psychomotor performance of normal subjects. *Journal of Pharmacology and Experimental Therapeutics* 130:55–58.

Goodwin, F. K., and Post, R. M. (1975). Cerebrospinal fluid amine metabolites in affective illness and schizophrenia: Clinical and pharmacological studies. *Psychopharmacology Communications* 1(6):641–653.

Gardos, G., DiMascio, A., Saltzman, C., and Shader, R. (1968). Differential actions of chlordiazepoxide and oxazepam on hostility. *Archives of General Psychiatry* 18:757–760. 18:757–760.

Grinspoon, L., Hedblom, P. (1975). *The Speed Culture*. Boston: Harvard University Press.

Groves, P. M., and Rebec, G. V. (1976). Biochemistry and behavior: some central actions of amphetamine and antipsychotic drugs. *Annual Review of Psychology* 27:91–127.

Hall, R. A., Griffin, R. B., Mayer, D. L., Hopkins, K. H., and Rappart, M. (1976). Evoked potential, stimulus intensity, and drug treatment in hyperkinesis. *Psychophysiology* 13(5):405–418.

Haot, J. Djahanguiri, B., and Richelle, M. (1964). Action protectrice dus chlordiazepoxide sur la ulcere de contrainte chez le rat. *Archives of International Pharmacodynamies* 148:557–559.

Healy, T., Edmondson, H., and Hall, N. (1970). The use of intravenous diazepam during dental surgery in the mentally handicapped patient. *British Dental Journal* 129:22–23.

——, and Hamilton, M. (1971). Intravenous diazepam in the apprehensive child. *British Dental Journal* 130:25–27.

Huestis, R. D., Arnold, L. E., and Smeltzer, D. J. (1975). Caffeine versus methylphenidate and *d*-amphetamine in minimal brain dysfunction: A double-blind comparison. *American Journal of Psychiatry* 132(8):868–870.

Irwin, S. (1974). The uses and relative hazard potential of psychoactive drugs. *Bulletin of the Menninger Clinic* 38:14–48.

Isaac, W., and Troelstrup, R. (1969). Opposite effect of illumination and *d*-amphetamine upon activity in the squirrel monkey (Saimiri) and owl monkey (Aotes). *Psychopharmacologia* 15:260–264.

Kallman, W., and Isaac, W. (1975). The effects of age and illumination on the dose response curves for three stimulants. *Psychopharmacologia* 40:313–318.

Kay, D., Jasinski, D., and Eisenstein, R. (1972). Quantified human sleep after phenobarbital. *Clinical Pharmacology and Therapy* 13:221–231.

Killam, E. K. (1962). Drug action on the brain-stem reticular formation. *Pharmacological Reviews* 14:175–223.

Kraft, I., Ardeli, C., Duffy, J., Hart, J., and Pearce, P. (1965). A clinical study of chlordiazepoxide used in psychiatric disorders of children. *International Journal of Neuropsychiatry* 1:433–437.

Leedy, J. (1970). What we learned from a double blind study of librium. *Medical Times* 98(12):72–79.

Lennard, H., Epstein, L., and Bernstein, A. (1971). *Mystification and Drug Misuse.* New York: Ranson.

Loomis, T., and West, T. (1958). Comparative sedative effects of a barbiturate and some tranquilizer drugs on normal subjects. *Journal of Pharmacology and Experimental Therapeutics* 122:525–531.

Manheimer, D., Davidson, S., Balter, M., Mellinger, G., Cisin, I., and Parry, H. (1973). Popular attitudes and beliefs about tranquilizers. *American Journal of Psychiatry* 130(11):1246–1253.

Maynert, E. (1971). Sedatives and hypnotics I: Non-barbiturates, II; Barbiturates. In J. DiPalma, ed., *Drill's Pharmacology in Medicine* (4th Ed.). New York: McGraw-Hill Book Company.

McGeer, P. L. (1971). The chemistry of mind. *American Scientist* 59:221–229.

McGhie, A. (1972). Attention and perception in schizophrenia. In R. Cancro, ed., *Annual Review of the Schizophrenia Syndrome, Vol. 2.* New York: Bruner-Mazol.

McKenzie, R., and Elliott, L. (1965). Effects of secobarbital and *d*-amphetamine on performance during a simulated air mission. *Aerospace Medicine* 36:774–779.

Mendelson, W., Johnson, N., and Stewart, M. (1971). Hyperactive children as teenagers: a follow-up study. *Journal of Nervous and Mental Disease* 153(4):273–279.

Morillo, A., Revzin, A., and Knauss, T. (1960). Physiological in cats. *Psychopharmacologia* 3:386–394.

Ngai, S., Tseng, D., and Wang, S. (1966). Effect of diazepam and other central nervous system depressants on spinal reflexes in cats. A study of site of action. *Journal of Pharmacology and Experimental Therapeutics* 153:344–351.

Novack, H. S. (1971). An Educator's view of medication and Classroom behavior. *Journal of Learning Disabilities* 4(9):43–44.

Oswald, I., and Priest, R. (1965). Five weeks to escape the sleeping pill habit. *British Medical Journal* 2:1093–1099.

Overton, D. (1971). Discriminative control of behavior by drug states. In T. Thompson and R. Pickens, eds., *Stimulus Properties of Drugs.* New York: Appleton-Century-Crofts.

Parry, H., Balter, M., Mellinger, G., Cisin I., and Manheimer, D. (1973). National patterns of psychotherapeutic drug use. *Archives of General Psychiatry* 28:769–775.

Petrie, A. (1967). *Individuality in Pain and Suffering.* Chicago: University of Chicago Press.

Prichep, L. S., Sutton, S., and Hakern, G. (1976). Evoked potentials in hyperkinetic and normal children under certainty and uncertainty: a placebo and methylphenidate study. *Psychophysiology* 13(5):419–428.

Randall, L., Heise, G., Schallek, W., Bagdon, R., Banziger, R., Baris, A., Moe, R., and Abrams, W. (1961). Pharmacological and Clinical Studies on Valium®—a new psychotherapeutic agent of the benzodiazepine class. *Current Therapeutic Research* 3(9):405–425.

Ray, O. S. (1975). *Drugs, Society and Human Behavior.* St. Louis: C. V. Mosby Company.

Redmond, D. E., Borge, G. F., Buchbaum, M., and Maas, J. W. (1975). Evoked potential studies of brain catecholamine alterations in monkeys. *Journal of Psychiatric Research* 12:97–116.

Rickels, K. (1968). Drug use in outpatient treatment. *American Journal of Psychiatry* 124(8):20–31.

——, and Downing, R. (1974). Chlordiazepoxide and hostility in anxious outpatients. *American Journal of Psychiatry* 131:442–444.

——, Gordon, P., Gousman, D., Weise, C., Pereira-Ogan, J., and Hesbacher, P. (1970). Pemoline and methylphenidate in mildly depressed outpatients. *Clinical Pharmacology and Therapeutics* 11(5):696–710.

——, Lipman, R., and Raab, E. (1966). Previous medication, duration of illness and placebo response. *Journal of Nervous and Mental Disease* 142(6):548–554.

Rosecrans, J., and Chance, W. (1977). Cholinergic and noncholinergic aspects of the discriminative stimulus properties of nicotine. In H. Lal, ed., *Drugs as Discriminative Stimuli*. New York: Raven Press.

Rosner, B., and Clark, D. (1973). Neurophysiologic effects of general anesthetics. II. Sequential regional actions in brain. *Anesthesiology* 39:59–81.

Roth, B., and Harvey, J. (1968). Altered response of cerebral respiration to thiopental and potassium ions *in vitro* after septal lesions. *Journal of Pharmacology and Experimental Therapeutics* 161:155–162.

Satterfield, J., Cantwell, D., Lesser, L., and Podosin, R. (1972). Physiological studies of the hyperkinetic child. *American Journal of Psychiatry* 128(11):1418–1424.

——, Cantwell, D., and Satterfield, B. (1974). Pathophysiology of hyperactive child syndrome. *Archives of General Psychiatry* 31:839, 844.

Schallek, W., Kuehn, A., and Jew, N. (1962). Effects of chlordiazepoxide (Librium) and other psychotropic agents on the limbic system of the brain. *Annuals New York Academy of Science* 96:303–314.

——, Zabrausky, F., and Kuehn, A. (1964). Effects of benzo-diazepines on central nervous system of cat. *Archives of International Pharmacodynamies* 149:467–483.

Scheibel, M., and Scheibel, A. (1962). Hallucinations and the brain stem reticular core. In L. West, ed., *Hallucinations*. New York: Wiley.

Schnackenberg, R. (1973). Caffeine as a substitute for schedule II stimulants in children. *American Journal of Psychiatry* 130:796–798.

Seligman, M. (1975). *Helplessness*. San Francisco: W. H. Freeman and Company.

Serrano, A., and Forbis, O. (1973). Haloperidol for psychiatric disorders in children. *Diseases of the Nervous System* 34:226–231.

Siomopoulos, V. (1975). Amphetamine psychosis: overview and a hypothesis. *Diseases of the Nervous System* 36:336–339.

Solomons, G. (1973). Drug therapy: initiation and follow-up. *Annals New York Academy of Sciences* 205:335–344.

Sprague, R. L. (1973). Minimal brain dysfunction from a behavioral viewpoint. *Annals New York Academy of Sciences* 205:349–361.

Snyder, R. (1973). Amphetamine psychosis: a "model" schizophrenia mediated by catecholamines. *American Journal of Psychiatry* 130:58–61.

Ullmann, L., and Krasner, L. (1969). *A Psychological Approach to Abnormal Behavior* (2nd Edition). Englewood Cliffs: Prentice Hall.

Weinberger, N. (1971). Attentive processes. In J. L. McGaugh, ed., *Psychobiology*. New York: Academic Press.

Wender, Paul H. (1974). Some speculations concerning a possible biochemical basis of minimal brain dysfunction. *Life Sciences* 14:1605–1621.

Werry, J. S. (1976). Medication for hyperkinetic children. *Drugs* 11:81–89.

Werry, J., Weiss, G., Douglas, V., and Martin, J. (1966). Studies on the hyperactive child. III. The effect of chlorpromazine upon behavior and learning ability. *Journal of the American Academy of Child Psychiatry* 5:292–312.

Whalen, C. K., and Haenker, B. (1976). Psychostimulants and children: a review and analysis. *Psychological Bulletin* 83(6):1113–1130.

Wheatley, D. (1972). Evaluation of psychotropic drugs in general practice. *Proceedings of the Royal Society of Medicine* 65:317–326.

Wopner, W., Thurston, D., and Holowach, F. (1962). Phenobarbital: its effect on learning in epileptic children. *Journal of the American Medical Association* 182:937.

Young, D., and Scoville, W. (1938). Paranoid psychosis in narcolepsy and the possible dangers of benzedrine treatment. *Medical Clinic of North America* 22:673.

Zbinden, G., Bagdon, R., Keith, E., Phillips, R. and Randall, L. (1961). Experimental and clinical toxicology of chlordiazepoxide. *Psychophysiology* 13(5):419–428.

Zbinden, G., and Randall, O. (1967). Pharmacology of benzodiazepines: Laboratory and clinical correlation. In S. Garattini and P. Shore, eds., *Advances in Pharmacology Vol. V*. New York: Academic Press.

Zrull, J., Westman, J., Arthur, B., and Bell, W. (1963). A comparison of chlordiazepoxide, *d*-amphetamine, and placebo in the treatment of the hyperkinetic syndrome in children. *American Journal of Psychiatry* 120:590–591.

SUBJECT INDEX

AUTHOR INDEX

383